Media Industry Transactions

Other books by Michael Henry include:

Media Industry Documentation – Butterworths 1998

Current Copyright Law – Butterworths 1998

Entertainment Law Volume 15 Encyclopaedia of Forms and Precedents
Fifth Edition Reissue – Butterworths 1998

Publishing and Multimedia Law – Butterworths 1994

Practical Lending and Security Precedents (Security Over
Intellectual Property Section)
FT Law & Tax 1992

International Agency and Distribution Agreements (UK Section)
Butterworths US 1990

Entertainment Law Volume 15 of the Encyclopaedia of Forms and Precedents
Butterworths 1989

The Film Industry – A Legal and Commercial Analysis
Longman 1986

Jacques the Fatalist (Translation)
Denis Diderot – Penguin Classics 1986

All royalties from this book will be applied by Actionaid toward the relief of poverty
in the developing coutries.

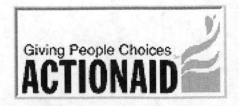

Media Industry Transactions

Michael Henry
Partner, Henry Hepworth, Solicitors

Butterworths
London, Edinburgh, Dublin
1998

United Kingdom	Butterworths, a Division of Reed Elsevier (UK) Ltd, Halsbury House, 35 Chancery Lane, LONDON WC2A 1EL and 4 Hill Street,
	EDINBURGH, EH2 3JZ
Australia	Butterworths, a Division of Reed International Books Australia Pty Ltd, CHATSWOOD, New South Wales
Canada	Butterworths Canada Ltd, MARKHAM, Ontario
Hong Kong	Butterworths Asia (Hong Kong), HONG KONG
India	Butterworths India, NEW DELHI
Ireland	Butterworth (Ireland) Ltd, DUBLIN
Malaysia	Malayan Law Journal Sdn Bhd, KUALA LUMPUR
New Zealand	Butterworths of New Zealand Ltd, WELLINGTON
Singapore	Butterworths Asia, SINGAPORE
South Africa	Butterworths Publishers (Pty) Ltd, DURBAN
USA	Lexis Law Publishing, CHARLOTTESVILLE, Virginia

A CIP Catalogue record for this book is available from the British Library.

ISBN 0-406-04977-7

Printed and bound at the Bath Press

Visit us at our website: http://www.butterworths.co.uk

*To Joseph Grand**

Preface

The objective of this book is to provide a practical guide to commercial practice in media industry transactions. The range of transaction types in the media is very wide—over 50 different types are identified in this book. Prevailing commercial practices vary from sector to sector, and persons moving outside their normal sphere of activities, or coming into the media industry for the first time, may generally find guidance on what to look for in a particular deal very hard to come by.

Some sectors of the media industry are shark-infested, and some of the sharks legally qualified. "Sharp" drafting is not illegal and some documents are drafted with the express intention of obtaining unfair advantage. Although an all-encompassing book, identifying every conceivable possibility, is beyond the capacities of this particular author, the transaction analyses provided should give some help in shark-spotting and identifying sharp provisions.

No book on media industry transactions would be complete without an analysis of their financial provisions, and it is hoped that the explanations provided in Chapter 1 and in Chapter 24 will assist in identifying ways of improving the value of any deal.

When negotiating the terms of any proposed transaction, it is useful to have some grounding in contract law, if only to avoid inadvertently creating a contract. A short practical summary of the law relating to contract and agency has been included in Chapter 54. Non-lawyers may find it useful to read this before referring to any specific transaction analysis.

For the benefit of persons who are unfamiliar with industry jargon, a short glossary is included at the back of this book. Words which are defined in the glossary are identified in the text by an asterisk*.

Finally, it is hoped that at least some reassurance as to the objectivity of the various transaction analyses contained in this book may be had from the fact that the author is a practising lawyer whose clients include companies and individuals active in the music industry, film and television, multi-media, merchandising, product endorsement, publishing and the theatre. Persons seeking to quote this book against the author in any negotiations will be required to pay a quotation fee of suitably punitive proportions!

Michael Henry
Henry Hepworth
5 John Street
London
WC1N 2HH
29 September 1998

Contents

Contents

A: Music Industry Transactions

1 Term Recording Contract

1.1 Description of a Term Recording Contract

The recording contract* is one of the two principal transaction documents in the music industry, the other being the publishing agreement* (examined in Paragraph 2).

The parties to this particular transaction are:

- the recording artist or artists being signed up by a record company (collectively referred to in this Chapter as the "Artists"); and
- the recording company signing the artist (referred to in this Chapter as the "Company").

A recording contract generally provides that the Company has the exclusive rights to the recording services of the Artists, normally both audio and audio-visual (subject to a few exceptions dealt with below), for a period of time which is normally calculated as a term* of years. For this reason, it is frequently referred to as a "term recording contract" in order to distinguish it from a recording contract for a limited number of works, such as a single or a specific album which is examined in Chapter 11.

This Chapter examines the provisions of a term recording contract from the point of view of the Artists or their legal advisors.

1.2 Transaction Analysis

A typical recording contract might be expected to contain the following clauses:

- Engagement (see Paragraph 1.3)
- Options* (see Paragraph 1.4)
- Grant of rights (see Paragraph 1.5)
- Advances* (see Paragraph 1.6)
- Artists' warranties and obligations (see Paragraph 1.7)
- Group provisions (see Paragraph 1.8)
- Recording restrictions and prior recordings (see Paragraph 1.9)

- Royalties* (see Paragraph 1.10)
- Royalty Accounting (see Paragraph 1.11)
- Controlled compositions* (See Paragraph 1.12)
- Credit (see Paragraph 1.13)
- Conduct (see Paragraph 1.14)
- Suspension (see Paragraph 1.15)
- Effect of suspension (see Paragraph 1.16)
- Termination (see Paragraph 1.17)
- Effect of termination (see Paragraph 1.18)
- Boilerplate* (see Paragraph 1.19)

1.3   Engagement

Term

The Company will wish to acquire the recording services of the Artists for a specified term. The precise length of the term will vary according to the circumstances. It is important that a balance be struck between, on the one hand, acknowledging the Company's investment and providing it with a period long enough to earn a fair return on this investment and, on the other hand, avoiding tying the Artists to one company for an excessively long period of time.

Some recording contracts provide for an initial period, which may be between one and three years, and may be extended by the Company exercising a series of options (see Paragraph 1.4). The option periods are normally for one year and it is not unusual for a recording contract to provide for three or four successive options, each giving the Company the right to extend the initial period of the term for a further year. The laws of some countries do not allow agreements for exclusive services to last beyond a maximum number of years. A reasonable balance between the interests of the Company and the Artists may be an initial period of three years followed by three one-year options for the Company to extend.

Some contracts specify simply the minimum product commitment required from the Artists and provide that the term will end six months after the release of the last album that has to be recorded under the contract in order to meet this product commitment.

Exclusivity and Scope of Services

It is normal for a recording contract to provide that the Company has exclusivity in relation to the services of the Artists. This means that the Artists cannot record for other people during the term. It is also normal for record companies to wish to acquire exclusive rights in relation to both audio and audio-visual services of artists.

The precise scope of the services will, in each case, require adjustment to accommodate the needs of the Artists. For example, it may be necessary to specify that the Company's exclusivity does not extend to the services of the

Artists as film actors or actresses. The Artists may also wish to have the right to perform in live events for charitable purposes. The consent of the Company would be required if such events were to be broadcast or recorded.

Performance of Services

A recording contract will normally require the Artists to agree to perform their services to the best of their skill and ability at locations specified by the Company and in full co-operation with persons engaged by the Company.

A key factor from the Artists' point of view is often the identity of the producer the Company wishes to engage to produce the Artists' recordings. In many circumstances, Artists will wish the identity of the producer to be subject to mutual agreement with the Company.

Where the Artists do not perform material they have written, the Company will normally require approval of what they propose to record and may also wish to tell the Artists what the Company wishes them to record. In certain cases (but by no means all), the Artists will require extensive assurance on these essential creative matters. In such cases, the Artists may wish to ensure that they are free to select the producer and material of their choice. If the Company is not prepared to agree to this, the Artists will be reliant on their relationship with their A & R man (or woman). In this event, a key person clause requiring the Company to make available the services of the relevant individual might be advisable. This may not, of course, be acceptable to the Company.

Press and Promotional Activities

Normally the Company will require the Artists to undertake certain press and promotional activities and the contract may provide for these services to be rendered free of charge apart from payment of approved travel and other expenses. This is generally acceptable, provided the number of days is limited, and the obligation is subject to the Artists' prior professional commitments.

The recording contract may also require the Artists to make promo videos and will not provide for separate remuneration for the Artists' services in doing this, unless payment is required pursuant to the terms of any agreement with a talent union (Equity or Musicians Union/American Federation of Musicians). This is also generally acceptable.

Other Provisions

Sometimes a recording contract will contain a provision restricting the Artists' right to change their style or appearance. This type of provision may be acceptable in particular circumstances, but is generally unacceptable.

Occasionally, a recording contract may seek to limit the freedom of the Artists to appoint a new business manager or agent without the written consent of the Company. From the point of view of the Artists, this is undesirable since it limits the Artists' right to obtain free representation.

5

Product Commitment

A recording contract will frequently require the Artists to record a specified number of tracks in each year during the term. The Company will generally want to ensure that it has sufficient tracks to release an album for each contract period, plus one or two singles, and may therefore specify a product commitment of between eight and 14 tracks—a track generally being on average three minutes in length. Normally, the Company will regard the product commitment as being met only if the Artists deliver material which the Company considers to be of acceptable technical and artistic quality. Where established Artists are involved, the delivery criteria may be altered simply to refer to technical quality.

Clearly it is not in the interests of the Artists any more than it is in the interests of the Company for unacceptable material to be released. Difficulties relating to final artistic acceptance of recorded product may be avoided if the Company and the Artists collaborate closely in relation to the selection of material and selection of the producer from the point of view of the Artists (see above).

1.4   Options

Options Generally

It is not uncommon for recording contracts to be for a term which consists of an initial period which the Company may extend by exercising one or more successive options. A recording contract, therefore, may specify that the Company may give the Artists notice of exercise of the first option at the end of the initial period. Exercise of an option normally requires payment of an additional advance (see Paragraph 1.6). If the Company exercises its first option it will normally be entitled to exercise a second option, and so on. The total duration of the term (ie the initial period plus all option periods) should not be excessively long (see Paragraph 1.3).

Product Requirement Extensions

There may be circumstances, however, where the Artists have not delivered the product commitment. In such circumstances, the Company will clearly be unable to determine whether or not it wishes to exercise its option, since it will not have the benefit of being able to consider the product recorded during the previous contract period. Some recording contracts therefore provide that, if the Artists have failed to deliver the product commitment, the time for exercise of the option will be extended until 90 or 180 days following delivery of the masters containing the relevant product commitment.

An extension like this should not operate if the inability of the Artists to deliver the product commitment arises from something that is outside their control. Generally, illness or absence of other members of the group will not be regarded as being outside the control of the Artists. It is also important to avoid creating an open-ended extension. If the Artists never deliver the product commitment, the Company's extension of the term would be for an indefinite period. It is likely that a provision of this type would be found unenforceable in many jurisdictions as being an unreasonable restraint of trade. It is advisable therefore for the Company to limit the period of any extension on account of failure to deliver product requirement to a maximum of 24–36 months.

Option Period Extensions

If the Company fails to exercise its option by the due date, the normal result is that the contract expires. Some contracts contain a provision which states that if the Company fails to exercise its option, the contract will nonetheless continue until the Artists give notice to the Company of its failure, following which the Company will have a further 45 days to exercise the option. Obviously this type of provision should be resisted by Artists. Although clerical oversights occur, no company which is committed to and enthusiastic about an artist is likely to overlook the date for exercise of their option.

1.5 Rights

Copyright in Sound Recordings

It is normal for record companies to acquire a number of specific rights in recording contracts. Usually the rights in sound recordings made by Artists during the term of the contract will automatically belong to the Company. This is because normally the Company makes the arrangements for the sound recordings to be made and is, therefore, automatically the owner of the copyright in the recordings. An acknowledgement in the contract by the Artists that the Company owns all rights in the sound recordings is entirely regular. In those cases where the Artists own the copyright in the sound recordings an assignment or licence to the Company (for the difference between them see Paragraph 53.2) will be required. Obviously in these circumstances, the Artists would wish the amount of the advance payable on signature (see Paragraph 1.6) to cover the cost of making the recordings.

Copyright in Other Works

In addition it is possible that the Artists may, during the course of rendering the services, create certain copyright works. Although copyright does not exist in performances, it is possible that the Artists may create some literary, dramatic, musical or even artistic works during the course of their services and the Company will normally wish to acquire all these rights in order to be able to exploit them. Although rights in songs written by the Artists may be acquired by a record company's associated music publishing company (see Chapter 2), recording contracts frequently contain provisions which assign to the Company the product of all the Artists' services. These provisions need to be adjusted carefully to ensure that they do not conflict with copyright ownership provisions in any publishing agreement entered into by the Artists.

Performers' Rights

The Company will also need to contain a consent on the part of the Artists to their performances being recorded and exploited. This is because the making and/or exploitation of a recording without the consent of all relevant artists is unlawful. The consent will normally authorise exploitation of their performances throughout the world for the full period of copyright and for the full period in which performers' rights exist. The Company may also require confirmation that the sums paid to the Artists constitute equitable remuneration in relation to their performances (see Paragraph 51.6). Provisions of this type are, once again, entirely normal.

Moral Rights Generally

Four moral rights exist under United Kingdom law. Two are of no relevance to recording contracts (the right not to have a work falsely attributed to oneself and the right to privacy for photographs or films commissioned for domestic use) and two could be relevant (the right to be identified and the right to object to derogatory treatment of a work). These rights exist in relation to copyright works other than sound recordings. Since many recording contracts do not involve the creation of copyright literary or musical works (either the Artists do not write material or the ownership of copyright in it is dealt with in a separate publishing agreement—see Paragraph 2), moral rights provisions are often of no concern to the Artists. Moral rights do not subsist in performances.

Normally recording contracts will contain an absolute irrevocable waiver by Artists of their moral rights. This is a standard provision which is normally quite acceptable.

Statutory Rights and Contractual Rights

Since most recording contracts contain provisions under which the Company agrees to accord credit to the Artists, there is generally no difficulty in the Artists waiving their statutory right to be identified in circumstances where they have a contractual right* to be identified. There is little practical difference between the rights. A statutory right created by statute (in this case, the Copyright, Designs and Patents Act 1988) is available to all persons who are eligible under the statute. A contractual right is created by a contract and is available to the parties to the contract. If the contractual position is satisfactory there is no difficulty in the Artists waiving their statutory right.

Derogatory Treatment

So far as concerns their right not to have their works subjected to derogatory treatment, since the Artists will have had significant if not total control of all elements in relation to their performances in the recording, the essential shape is therefore likely to have been largely determined by the Artists working in collaboration with the production of the recordings.

In view of the fact that moral rights do not exist in relation to performances, and many recording contracts do not result in the creation of works in which moral rights subsist, a provision confirming the waiver of the right to object to a derogatory treatment will normally be acceptable to Artists.

Name and Likeness

Most recording contracts contain provisions giving the Company the right to use the Artists' names, likenesses and biography for the purpose of promoting the sale of records. The use of a person's name or likeness without their consent is unlawful in some jurisdictions (excluding the United Kingdom, but including a number of states in the USA, where unauthorised use constitutes a criminal misdemeanour). The Company will therefore need to acquire the Artists' consent. The Artists should ensure that such consent should not extend to any merchandising use, since the right to merchandise material relating to the Artists is of substantial economic importance.

The Artists should also consider whether they require, for merchandising-related reasons, approval of album covers, sleeve notes, designs etc. If the Artists have devised a logo they should ensure it is protected as a trademark. If they intend to use elements of album designs or publicity material created by the Company for merchandising purposes, they should ensure that the contract transfers these rights to them.

Further Assurance

The final provision which is frequently encountered in a grant of rights clause is what lawyers refer to as a "covenant for further assurance". This is an undertaking on the part of the Artists to do any acts and execute any documents which may be necessary in the future to transfer the rights assigned or granted to the Company. Again, this is a regular provision and one that may be accepted by the Artists. Frequently covenants for further assurance are backed up by powers of attorney. Although a power of attorney limited to the specific subject area of the contract is acceptable, a general power of attorney should never be given by Artists—and there is no legitimate business reason for a record company to ask for one (see Paragraph 53.13).

1.6   Advances

All recording contracts should provide for the payment of advances. It is normal for recording contracts to provide that advances are recoupable from royalties—in other words, the record company has the right to suspend payment of a royalty until such time as the total royalties payable equal or exceed the advance.

From the Artists' point of view, it is also customary to seek to have the advances categorised as a "non-returnable recoupable advances". This may be of use in circumstances where, for example, some event beyond the control of the Artists prevented the Artists from recording the product requirement. Ideally, however, situations like this should be dealt with specifically and not allowed to hinge on whether or not the advance is non-returnable in all circumstances.

There may be a number of advances payable during the term of the Agreement. Normally the first advance will be paid partly on signature, partly on commencement of recording of the product requirement for the first year and partly on completion of recording. The amounts and the instalments, and the events linked to the instalments are, of course, entirely negotiable.

Some recording contracts seek to make the cost of recording masters recoverable as an advance from the royalties. This means that the Artists alone are paying the recording costs and this is highly undesirable from their point of view.

Where further advances are payable on the exercise of options (as would be normal) the dates on which these are payable are similar to the dates on which the first advance was payable—and again entirely negotiable.

The Artists may also wish to discuss with the Company the possibility of the Company providing financial support for tours to be undertaken by the Artists. Since tour activity normally increases sales of records, there may be occasions where the Company is prepared to give support. From the Artists' point of view it is preferable not to have the amount of any financial contribution treated as an advance, since this will be recovered from future record royalties. It would be advantageous to the Artists if the Company recovered its contribution from the receipts of the tour that remained after payment of the Artists' share of tour receipts and after (or at the same time) as the tour promoter recovers their investment.

In some cases, the agreement may provide that the Company contributes 50% of agreed video production costs to be recouped from video royalties.

1.7   Artist's Warranties

There are a number of warranties that the Company will normally wish to obtain from the Artists. These include the following matters.

Majority

The Company will normally want assurance that the Artists have attained the age of 18—because contracts with minors are unenforceable in certain circumstances (see paragraph 54.3).

Ability to Contract

The Company will want to know that the Artists are the sole and absolute owners of all rights granted to the Company and that the Artists have the capacity to grant the rights to the Company and are not under any restriction or prohibition which might interfere with the Artists' obligations under the contract.

Copyright Status

The Company will generally want to ensure that copyright subsists in the product of the Artists' services. This is normally determined by the Artists' nationality or residence and is very rarely a problem for anyone living or working in the western world.

No Conflict

The Artists will normally be required to warrant that the Artists have not entered into any arrangement which might conflict with the recording contract. Any recording bars* (see Paragraph 1.9) will therefore need to be disclosed.

Originality etc

The contract will normally contain a warranty that the services of the Artists are not obscene or defamatory and are original to the Artists.

Non-infringement

The contract will normally contain a warranty* that the services of the Artists and the product of their services does not infringe any right of copyright or any other right of any other person.

Right to Use or Adapt

The contract will normally contain a warranty that the Company has the right to use, adapt, change, delete from, add to/rearrange material produced by the Artists to the extent the Company wishes.

Rearrangement

Some contracts contain an acknowledgement on the part of the Artist that, if the Artists rearrange any musical work, the Artists will not be entitled to receive performance royalties from the Performing Right Society Limited (see Paragraph 2.5). This will normally be unacceptable to the Artists.

Return of Property

Some contracts may contain provisions requiring the Artists to return any property of the Company lent to the Artists or in the possession of the Artists at the end of the recording contract.

No Expenditure

Although a recording contract does not normally give Artists the right to make expenditure on behalf of the Company, some contracts contain a specific provision excluding this possibility—presumably in the light of experience.

Unions and Work Permits

Many record contracts contain a warranty that the Artists are members of the appropriate union (Musicians Union or Equity etc) and confirm that the Artists will obtain all necessary work permits required to enable the Company to make use of the Artists' services. If the Artists are engaging in foreign travel at the request of the Company, it may be reasonable for the Artists to shift the burden of obtaining work permits on to the Company.

Non-disclosure

Most recording contracts will contain a confidentiality provision requiring the Artists not to disclose information, except to their professional advisors.

Publicity

Some contracts contain an express restriction on the Artists issuing any publicity relating to records. This type of restriction may be reasonable pre-release. A general restriction on the Artists participating in any interview or any other publicity without the Company's consent is, however, unreasonable.

Morals

The contract may contain a warranty that the Artists will not do anything which would or might prejudice or damage the reputation of the Company. These types of provisions are, however, rare in recording contracts, where notoriety or moral turpitude (as lawyers call it) does not seem to cause difficulties in selling records.

Insurance

Some contracts require a warranty that the Artists are in a state of good health coupled with an undertaking that the Artists will comply with the requirements of the Company's insurers. This type of provision is sensible in circumstances where a record company is (say) intending to provide tour support to Artists, or expend a large amount of money on promotional video material.

Dangerous Pursuits

Some recording contracts contain contractual restrictions excluding the Artists from pursuing dangerous pursuits. In many cases, such an exclusion is inappropriate and provisions of this type should be considered in the light of the relevant circumstances.

Rules and Regulations

The Artists will usually be required to comply with all rules and regulations at any place where the Artists render services. This is reasonable.

Referral of Enquiries

The Company may wish to be kept informed of the Artists' plans for personal appearances, concerts etc. If the Company has exclusive audio-visual rights then television and film appearances and the like will need the consent of the Company (see Paragraph 1.3).

Name

The Artists may be required not to change the Artists' group name or perform under any other name. (See Paragraph 1.8)

Whereabouts and Tax Residency

An obligation to keep the Company informed of the Artists' address telephone number(s) and whereabouts may also be included. This is not unreasonable. An obligation to notify the Company of any change in tax residency is also reasonable, since any change could require the Company to deduct witholding tax from the royalties.

Legal Advice

The Company is normally concerned to see that the Artists have obtained legal advice from a solicitor specialising in this type of agreement. This provision is designed to insulate the Company from claims that the contract is voidable.

Indemnity

Some recording contracts seek to impose indemnity obligations on Artists. These obligations are capable of being unfair and oppressive and should always be resisted for the reasons referred to in Paragraph 53.1.

1.8   Group Provisions

There are a number of aspects relating to group provisions which need careful thought. These provisions are among the most complex in any recording contract and have a fundamental impact on the interrelationship of group members. These provisions should be considered in the light of the matters discussed in Chapter 15.

Joint and Several Liability

It is relatively standard practice for recording contracts to provide that artists are jointly and severally liable. This means that every individual is liable, not only for his or her own default breach, but also for the default/breach of every other member of the group. Consequently one badly behaving member can cause loss to all the other members—although they will probably have the right to recover some of their losses from the misbehaving member. Many record companies insist on all members of a group being jointly and severally liable, in the knowledge that this may have a cohesive effect.

Professional Name

In some cases the business arrangements between members of a group are set out in a partnership agreement. One of the matters normally dealt with in a partnership agreement is the ownership of the group name. It is important for the Company to be able to exploit an Artists' name, even if the individual line-up of the Artists changes subsequently. Normally, therefore, a recording contract will contain an acknowledgement on the part of all the members of the group that if any individual member leaves the group the remaining members will be entitled to the use of the professional name.

The contract will normally also permit the Company to continue to use the professional name following the end of the term for the full period of copyright protection in relation to sound recordings made during the term. Where the name has been registered as a trademark, the Company will normally also require the benefit of a trademark licence.

Leaving Members

Where a member of a group leaves during the term of a recording contract, in some recording contracts, the Company's rights are expressed to continue over

14

the individual leaving member. From that member's point of view, the situation may not be ideal, since if (s)he wishes to team up with another individual who has left another group, the two artists may find themselves in a situation where each is still contractually tied to a different record company.

From the point of view of remaining members there may be difficulties if the leaving artist was the main songwriter. Their departure may effectively prevent the remaining members from delivering the product requirement for each contract period. In situations involving groups with one or two main songwriters, this possibility must be identified before signing a contract, so that the leaving provisions may be adjusted in an appropriate way.

A further area where adjustment will be necessary is that of continued joint and several liability. Where a member has left the group, it is clearly inappropriate for the remaining members to continue to be liable for the leaving person's breaches under his or her ongoing arrangement with the record company and vice versa. Many documents fail to address this point.

Allocation of Income

There may be circumstances which justify one member of the group receiving a greater share of royalty income than the others. If such circumstances exist, the group provisions may provide an appropriate place in the contract for the provision to be inserted. They should certainly state what percentage of the advances and royalties each member receives, unless all royalties are payable to the Artists' manager or agent, to be applied in accordance with the Artists' agreement between themselves (see Chapter 15).

Royalty Apportionment

A further complication arises in apportioning advances which are unrecouped. If, at the time a departing member leaves, there are advances which are unrecouped, it is possible that they may be recouped out of future records made by the remaining members of the band which do not involve the leaving member. When the advances are recouped, record companies start paying royalties, and normally all royalties are cross-collateralised* for the purpose of recouping advances.

This means that if a group have only moderate success with album one, made with the departing member, but album two, made after the member left, proves to be a huge success, royalties from album two will be applied towards recoupment of the advance and possibly recording costs of album one. This will have two effects: first, it will accelerate the leaving member's entitlement to royalties on album one; second, it will reduce the amount of royalties payable to group members on album two since effectively they are being cross-collateralised to pay off the losses on album one.

The accounting provisions in the contract need, therefore, to be amended to reflect this fact, de-cross-collateralising royalties after the Company has recouped and transferred from the departing member's royalty account to the remaining members' royalty account, any income relating to records made after departure which has been applied, to recoup advances (or recording costs) paid before departure.

New Member

A recording contract will also provide that any new member will enter into a written agreement acknowledging that the new member is bound by the terms of the existing recording contract. In practice, it may be necessary for the existing members to sign the same document if all the new members are to assume joint and several liability.

At the time the new member executes the additional documentation, it will be appropriate for the record company to release the leaving member from his or her joint and several liability in relation to future actions of the remaining members and the new member. The leaving member may also be required to confirm that (s)he has no right in or to the professional name.

1.9   Recording Restrictions: Recording Bar and Prior Recordings

Exclusivity

The scope of the Company's exclusivity has already been commented on above (Paragraph 1.3). If the Company consents to the Artists giving a live performance which is recorded, the Company will not normally wish the live recording to count towards the product commitment (see Paragraph 1.3).

Recording Bar

Record companies also wish to protect themselves from Artists re-recording their greatest hits with a competing record company and releasing them immediately after the end of the term. Even if a record company's associated publishing company owns the copyright in songs written by Artists, there may be circumstances where the Artists' new record company would be able to obtain a mechanical licence, giving the new company the right to reproduce songs previously written by the Artists.

Many contracts therefore provide a contractual undertaking from the Artists that they will not re-record any work recorded under the contract until the expiry of 5 full calendar years from the contract end. Such a provision is normally quite acceptable.

Prior Recordings

Record companies generally wish to know what previous unreleased recordings may exist, since the release of these on to the marketplace by another record company may have an effect on sales. The Company may therefore wish to obtain a warranty from the Artists as to the number and identity of any unreleased recordings.

1.10 Royalties

Royalty Clauses Generally

The royalty clause is likely to be the most scrutinised clause in any recording contract. It is also likely to be one of the longest and most complicated, containing numerous "breaks".

A royalty break* is a provision where the Company's royalty obligation is broken down in a particular set of circumstances which justify the reduction of the Royalty Rate or the Royalty Base Price*. Royalty breaks are generally cumulative—that is to say that there are frequently circumstances where more than one break provision will apply and both the Royalty Rate and the Royalty Base Price may be reduced for more than one reason.

There are three basic components of a royalty clause, the Royalty Rate, the Royalty Base Price and the number of units they are multiplied by—or Net Sales*. Each of these are examined below.

Royalty Rate and Royalty Base Price

The Royalty Rate in a recording contract will vary widely, depending on the individual artist and the particular record company, and may be as low as 12% on albums for a new artist or in excess of 20% for a top-line artist.

Separate royalty rates are commonplace. A company may agree one royalty rate for singles and another (higher) royalty rate for albums. Similarly, one royalty rate may apply to a designated territory, and another royalty rate to territories outside the designated territory.

Normally a royalty is calculated as a percentage of a Royalty Base Price on Net Sales of records. The Base Price is frequently published dealer price (PDP) less discounts. All discounts should be expressed to be customary trade, bona fide arm's length discounts.

Net Sales

Net Sales are frequently defined as 90% or 85% of sales of records less those returned during any period. There are historical reasons for accounting for 90% of records sold (or 85% in North America). The original 10/15% allowance was permitted to compensate the record companies for breakages back in the days when manufactured records were made of shellac and highly fragile.

For many years, however, the record industry has operated on the basis of sales less "returns" (records which were either returned as faulty or returned because they were supplied on a sale or return basis and remain unsold). It is

17

therefore generally unsatisfactory for a record company to account to an artist on 85% or 90% of Net Sales and the royalties should be payable on 100% of Net Sales.

Packaging Deductions

A further area where care needs to be taken is the treatment of packaging deductions*. In many contracts, a packaging deduction is made from the Royalty Base Price before calculating the amount of the royalty. Many companies have standard packaging deduction rates and, at the beginning of negotiations they may claim these rates range between 15% and 25%. Obviously a 25% packaging deduction from the Royalty Base Price is, in financial terms, exactly equivalent to a 25% reduction of the royalty. It is therefore usually worthwhile for the Artists to negotiate the highest possible reduction in the packaging deductions. Care should also be taken to ensure that the packaging deduction are deducted from the Royalty Base Price itself and not from the royalty: if a packaging deduction is deducted from the royalty, the likelihood is it will create a negative royalty.

Duration of Royalty Obligation

The period during which the royalty is to be paid is also of crucial importance. Although the Artists are only required to render services during the term (see Paragraph 1.3) the Company will have the right to exploit the records worldwide for the full period of copyright in the recordings (see Paragraph 1.5). It is completely unacceptable for the Artists if the royalty payment provision applies only during the term. The provision should apply to all sales by the Company and its licensees of records during the entire copyright period.

A number of specific royalty breaks are set out below.

CD Reduction

"Where Records are sold in compact disc form or pre-recorded cassette form the rate specified is 50% of the rate for vinyl records."

This provision was commonplace in the early days of compact discs, but would now be unacceptable to the Artists.

Club Royalty Rate Reduction

"Where Records are sold to a club or similar operation, the rate is 50% of the rate otherwise applicable and no royalties are payable in respect of any Records received by members of a club operation as part of an introductory offer or as free or bonus records or on terms pursuant to which the record club or similar operation does not receive payment."

The Artists will generally seek to prevent the Company from effecting club sales or similar sales for a period of 24/36 months from first release of a record. The Artists will also seek to prevent the giving away of any free records.

Library Royalty Rate Deduction

"Where Records are sold to libraries or educational institutions or the armed forces, the rate is 50% of the rate otherwise applicable."

This provision is often accepted without amendment.

TV Promotion Royalty Rate Reduction

"Where Records are promoted by television advertising, the rate should be 50% of the rate otherwise applicable."

This break should only apply if the records are promoted by a major television advertising campaign (rather than mere promotion) and the Artists' advisors may wish to specify that the campaign must be not less than a minimum amount.

Discount Royalty Rate Reduction

"Where Records are sold at less than the Company's top line label price, the royalty rate shall be 50% of the rate otherwise applicable."

It may be more appropriate for the Artists to agree a separate royalty rate for mid-price labels and budget price labels, rather than suffer a 50% deduction.

Club Royalty Base Price Reduction

"In respect of Records sold to any club operation the Royalty Base Price shall, at the election of the Company, be the amount received by the Company or such club operation."

The Artists will generally want the Company not to effect club sales for a period of 24/36 months after initial release. If premium records are also excluded (see below) there may be some benefit to the Artists permitting the Company to sell to club operations—provided that the Company accepts that the arrangements are to be on bona fide, arm's length terms.

Premiums

> "In respect of Records distributed or licensed to third parties in
> connection with any promotional or advertising operation or for so-
> called 'premium' use, the Artists shall be entitled to royalties of [ ]%
> of all net sums actually received by the Company from third parties
> in respect of such exploitation in lieu of any other payment".

A "premium" is an item which is given away free in order to encourage
consumers to buy another piece of product. It is clearly inappropriate for the
Artists' records to be used to stimulate sales of some other item of product. The
Artists may wish to exclude all so-called premium sales altogether.

Compilation Reduction

> "In respect of Records incorporating material that is not derived
> from the Master Tapes the Royalty Base Price and the Royalty Rate
> payable to the Artists shall be that proportion of the Royalty Base
> Price and the Royalty Rate otherwise applicable and shall be
> computed by a fraction the numerator of which is the total of all
> material derived from the Master Tapes and the denominator the
> total of all material contained on such Records".

The Artists may wish to exclude the Company's right to couple the Artist's
tracks with other material without the Artists' consent. The use of a fraction
whose denominator is the total number of recording artists is an other area the
Artists would wish to look at. It might be fairer to have the fraction relate to the
total number of tracks contributed by other people and the total number of tracks
contributed by the Artists.

Discount Reduction

> "The Royalty payable in respect of sales of Records to dealers,
> traders, wholesalers, trading groups or other multiple groups or
> chains at a discount shall be reduced in the same proportion as the
> discount bears to the usual price to such customers."

This means that where the Company agrees (say) a 25% discount to any
customers, it will also reduce the royalty by 25%. This provision is unlikely to
be acceptable to the Artists.

Flat Fee Reduction

> "The Company shall have the right to license Records and Master
> Tapes to other parties on a flat fee basis as opposed to a royalty basis

and the Company shall pay to the Artists royalties of 50% of all net sums received by the Company pursuant to any such flat fee."

A "flat fee" deal is one where the Company receives one single outright sum and does not receive any further royalties. A provision such as this is open to abuse in that the Company could sell rights to an associated company for a nominal sum (say, US$1). The Company would then account to the Artists for 50 cents. Meanwhile its associated company would be free to sell the records indefinitely without paying any royalty obligation to the Company or the Artists.

Flat fee deals are generally undesirable and should preferably be excluded altogether. On those occasions where they are agreed, it should be made clear that the Company has an obligation to enter into such deals on the best reasonably obtainable bona fide arm's length terms. Where such an obligation is imposed on the Company and the Company enters into an arrangement on terms which are not arm's length terms, the Artists will have a right of action against the Company which would could be found liable to the Artists for the Artists' losses.

Promotional Copies

"No royalty shall be payable in respect of Records which are distributed to radio stations or television stations or ships or airlines or distributed to promote or stimulate the sale of records or are distributed free as samples or as 'cut outs', discontinued goods or deletions."

The Artists will normally try and limit the quantities that may be given for promotional purposes and eliminate altogether the giving of free samples. The arrangements relating to remuneration for cut outs and deletions are subject to negotiation.

Licensee Reductions

"Where the Company's licensees, lessees, sub-licensees, or sub-lessees apply further or greater reductions, deductions, decreases or negations of any kind to the royalties or other sums payable to the Company then these should be applied for the purposes of calculating the royalties owed to the Artists under this agreement and under no circumstances shall the Artists be entitled to receive more than 50% of the net sums received by the Company from any such licensee, lessee, sub-licensee or sub-lessee by way of royalty in respect of any country or territory."

This provision deals with a situation where the Royalty Breaks operated by the Company's licensee are more onerous than those operated by the Company towards the Artists. In such circumstances, the Company could be entitled to receive less money from its licensee than the amount which it owes, the Artists by way of royalty. If the Company is licensing on arm's length terms, then the provision may be acceptable. The Artists may, however, take the view that it is the responsibility of the Company to ensure that it can sub-license the Records at the same Royalty Base Price on which it is obliged to pay the Artists.

Exclusion of Receipts

> "Royalties shall not be payable until the Company has itself received payment in sterling in the United Kingdom and foreign currency shall be converted at the same rate of exchange as the Company was paid in."

The Artists will normally wish royalties to be payable when any associate of the Company has received payment, whether that is in the United Kingdom or not.

Reserves

> "The Company shall have the right to make reserves for returns, credits and exchanges from the Royalties which reserves shall be determined by the Company in its entire discretion."

The Artists will normally wish to see reserves limited to not more than 20% in any accounting period. The reserves ought to be liquidated in the course of two to four accounting periods. Additionally, the Artists may wish to provide that the reserves are to be maintained in an interest-bearing account.

Recoupment

> "The Company shall have the right to recoup from all Royalties payable to the Artists all advances paid by the Company and all sums deemed to be advances and all recording costs."

Whether or nor recording costs are recoupable from the royalties is a major commercial point. The position of the Artists may be that the Company is to recoup the recording costs out of its own share of revenues.

Other Deductions

There are some circumstances where the Company will look to the Artists to pay any royalty due to the producer* of the records. Whether or not this is acceptable will depend on the circumstances.

Because the record producer may have made a copyright contribution in the sound recordings and because the producer may in any event have been engaged by the Company, the contract may provide that the Company has the right to deduct from the Artists' royalties the amounts of royalties payable to the producer.

If it is agreed that the Artists will bear the producer's royalties, then there is nothing wrong with this provision, although the Artists should obtain a copy of the producer's contract for the purpose of determining precisely what royalty obligations exist before agreeing to such a provision.

1.11 Royalty Accounting

All recording contracts should provide dates for statements of account to be rendered, showing sales of records, accrued royalties, the amount of the advance unrecouped etc. Each statement is normally accompanied by the amount it shows to be owing.

Whether the contract provides for payments to be made on a half-yearly basis 90 days after 30 June and 31 December in each year, or on a quarterly basis 45/60 days after 31 March, 30 June, 30 September and 31 December, is to be negotiated. The Artists would clearly prefer the latter, the Company, the former.

It would be normal for a recording contract to oblige the Company to maintain full and proper books of account at its principal place of business. The Artists or the Artists' advisors should have the right to inspect, audit and take copies of the books provided the Artists give reasonable prior notice. Inspections are frequently limited to occur only during normal business hours and the Company may well wish to limit the number of inspections to one per year. Clearly, such a limitation is not reasonable if an inspection has revealed errors or inconsistencies previously.

Frequently, companies wish to ensure that persons auditing them are not engaged on a contingency basis—ie if they find underaccounting of £10,000, they receive a certain percentage of it—and many companies require the auditor not to be engaged at the same time on another inspection of the company's books. Whether these restrictions are acceptable is a matter for negotiation.

If an audit inspection reveals underaccounting to the Artists, it is normal for the Artists to be able to recover the reasonable costs of such audit and inspection, if the amount of underpayment exceeds a certain amount. In many cases the error margin is required to be 10%, although, on occasions, a 5% margin is agreed. The amount of the margin is obviously a matter for commercial negotiation.

A record company will normally wish to have the right to deduct and withhold from royalties any sums which are deductible in accordance with local law. Normally, the only deductions relate to withholding taxes* and the Company will be under a legal obligation to make these deductions.

Where the Artists are represented by an agent or business manager, that person will normally wish the royalties to be directed to him or her. Royalty accounts clauses therefore frequently contain a payment direction clause irrevocably directing the Company to pay all sums to the Artists' agent or representative whose receipt will be a full and sufficient discharge to the Company of its liability to make the payment. From the Artists' point of view, however, it is preferable to direct the Company to pay the agent his or her percentage and for the Company to distribute the royalties direct to the Artists. This speeds up the process and eliminates the possibility of the Artists losing all their royalties if their agent becomes insolvent.

1.12 Controlled Compositions

When a record company manufactures records which contain performances of songs, the record company has to pay copyright royalties to the owners of the copyright in the songs. Normally song copyrights are owned by music publishers, who acquire their rights through publishing agreements which they enter into with the composers of the songs (see Paragraph 2).

A commercial practice has evolved over the years where record companies seek to pay a reduced rate for the use of compositions which are written by the artists who are signed to them. They do this by means of what is generally referred to as a "controlled composition clause".

This clause effectively says that if the Artists have written any compositions, or own or control any compositions, then the Company will have the right to use those compositions on records, but will only be required to pay 75% of the statutory or mechanical royalty payment. Obviously a provision like this, not only saves money for the record Company, but also loses money for the Artists. It will also lose money for the Artists' publisher which may be a company linked to the record company. In some cases, record companies will agree to escalate the controlled composition rate percentage to 87.5% on sales of 500,000 records and 100% on sales of 1 million, or other figure.

Where the Artists write all their own material, a controlled composition clause is likely to cause them significant loss of income and should be resisted as far as possible. Where the Artists do not write their own material, the controlled composition clause is likely to be of little commercial relevance.

It is particularly important for the Artists' advisors to ensure that, in those circumstances where the Artists concede a controlled compositions clause, the Artists' music publisher has agreed in their contract with the Artists that they will abide by the controlled composition clause and license the compositions to the record company at the rate required by the record company. If the appropriate provision is not inserted in the Artists' publishing contract, the publisher may refuse to grant the record company the licence at the reduced rate, which would lead to the record company claiming from the Artists the extra which it was required to pay to use the controlled compositions by way of reducing the Artists' royalties—not a happy situation.

1.13 Credit

The credit clause in a record contract specifies the type of credit which the Artists are entitled to receive on records made by the Company. The clause may also provide that the Company is not liable for any casual or inadvertent failure to accord credit. This is a regular provision. The failure to give credit is one of the few provisions which would entitle the Artists to injunctive relief to restrain the distribution of the records.

1.14 Conduct

Some recording contracts contain a provision to the effect that the Artists will not do any act which would bring the Artists into public disrepute or offend the community or public morals or prejudice the Company or the exploitation of the records. The Artists may be required to undertake and agree to respect public conventions and morals during the term.

In practice, not many record companies appear to require this type of protection and a morals clause is likely to meet with justifiable resistance from Artists.

1.15 Suspension

A recording contract may give the Company the power to suspend the term and the engagement of the services of the Artists on certain grounds. Grounds will include failure or refusal by the Artists to perform their services or breach of their undertakings and obligations in the agreement.

Failure of the Artists to submit to a medical examination (if the Company requires insurance, for example) will also normally constitute grounds for suspension.

Normally, the Artists will wish to limit the circumstances where the contract might be suspended to fundamental material breaches by the Artists which have not been remedied within 30 days from receipt of written notice specifying the breach.

If the Artists are prevented from performing services by injury, illness or mental or physical disability or are incapable of performing the services for a number of consecutive days, this may also constitute grounds for suspension. Whether or not the Company is to have power to suspend as a result of a change in the appearance or personality or voice of the Artists is a matter for discussion. In practice, such a provision may well be unacceptable to the Artists. The Company may require a right to suspend on account of the occurrence of an event of force majeure, and the Artists will normally wish to resist this.

1.16 Effect of Suspension

The effect of suspension in a recording contract is normally to stop time running for the duration of the event for which notice was given, plus any time required by the Company in order to resume the services of the Artists.

If the Artists have accepted a provision giving the Company the right to suspend on the occurrence of an event of force majeure, if the event continues beyond a reasonable period, the Artists should be entitled to give notice requiring the Company to resume the engagement or terminate the agreement.

Normally, during any period of suspension, the Company is relieved of any obligation to make payment to the Artists of remuneration. The Artists' advisors will, however, normally wish to clarify that, if the Artists are abroad or on tour or staying in a location at the request of the company, the obligations of the Company to provide hotel accommodation and meals and fares for the Artists shall continue. The same should also apply to accrued royalties due on sales of records.

Provisions which state that during the period of suspension the Artists will comply with obligations which are not affected by the suspension and that the Company will remain entitled to rights granted to it are perfectly regular.

1.17 Termination

The contract will normally provide that the Company has the right to terminate it or accept the repudiation of the contract by the Artists if the Artists fail or refuse to perform any of the services or are otherwise in breach of any of their obligations and undertakings.

Normally the Artists should require a certain period of time in which to remedy any alleged breach before the Company has the right to terminate.

If the Company accepts the repudiation by the Artists of the contract, this would effectively bring the contract to an end but would enable the Company to recover consequential losses or damages from the Artists. Where the Company terminates, it will not normally be able to recover consequential losses. The Artists, may therefore wish to amend the termination provisions accordingly.

Normally the Artists will want some form of assurance that the Company will continue to perform the Company's obligations under the agreement—in particular, the payment obligations. This assurance frequently takes the form of a right on the part of the Artists to terminate the agreement if the Company has failed to make payment of sums shown due (or render accounts) within a specified period after having received notice from the Artists specifying such failure and requiring it to be remedied.

The agreement may also provide that the Artists have the right to terminate the agreement if the Company should become insolvent or have a receiver or administrator or administrative receiver or liquidator appointed or go into liquidation other than voluntary liquidation entered into for the purpose of reconstructing.

1.18 Effect of Termination

A recording contract may specify what happens on termination of a contract.

Normally the Company will wish to ensure that the Artists will continue to comply with obligations on their part which are intended to survive termination—for example, the recording bar (see Paragraph 1.10).

Similarly the Company will wish confirmation that it remains entitled to all rights granted or assigned to it by the Artists during the term of the agreement and all rights relating to the services of the Artists.

The contract may also specify that the Artists are entitled to receive only that remuneration which is accrued due payable at the date of termination. A provision like this may cause the Artists some difficulty, because the Artists will wish to make it explicit that the Company remains obliged to pay royalties to the Artists in relation to future exploitation by the Company of records made during the term. This point therefore needs to be dealt with explicitly.

A provision along the lines that any claim which either party has against the other in respect of any breach which occurred prior to termination or suspension will not be affected or prejudiced is entirely regular.

1.19 Boilerplate

The boilerplate section of a typical recording contract will contain the following provisions:

- No obligation (see Paragraph 52.6)
- Notice (see Paragraph 52.8)
- Severability (see Paragraph 52.10)
- Entire agreement (see Paragraph 52.3)
- Waiver (see Paragraph 52.11)
- No partnership (see Paragraph 52.7)
- Governing law (see Paragraph 52.5).

2 Term Publishing Agreement

2.1   Description of a Publishing Agreement

The publishing agreement* is one of the two principal transaction documents in the music industry, the other being the recording contract* (examined in Chapter 1).

The parties to this particular transaction are:

- the composer or composers being signed up by the publishing company (collectively referred to in this Chapter as the "Composer"); and
- the publishing company signing up the Composer (referred to in this Chapter as the "Publisher").

A publishing contract normally provides that the Publisher has the exclusive right to the composing services of the Composer for a period of time which is calculated as a term* of years. The Composer will assign the entire copyright in all compositions written by the Composer during the term to the Publisher, and the Publisher will acquire the right to exploit the compositions in all media throughout the world for a period. The duration this period will normally be negotiated, and will range from the term of the agreement, plus a so-called "retention period*" of 15 to 20 years, up to the full period of copyright (life of the composer plus 70 years).

A distinction should be made between a term publishing agreement which relates to all works written during a term of years, and a publishing agreement for a single work or a number of specified works which is examined in Chapter 12. Sometimes publishing agreements are referred to as composers' agreements.

This Chapter examines the provisions of a term publishing agreement from the point of view of the Composer or the Composer's legal advisors.

2.2   Transaction Analysis

A typical publishing agreement might be expected to contain the following clauses:

- Engagement (see Paragraph 2.3)
- Options* (see Paragraph 2.4)
- Grant of rights (see Paragraph 2.5)
- Advances* (see Paragraph 2.6)
- Composer's warranties and obligations (see Paragraph 2.7)
- Publisher's obligations (see Paragraph 2.8)
- Royalties* (see Paragraph 2.9)
- Royalty Accounting (see Paragraph 2.10)
- Joint compositions and new lyrics (see Paragraph 2.11)
- Collaboration (see Paragraph 2.12)
- Copyright notices (see Paragraph 2.13)
- Group provisions (see Paragraph 2.14)
- Suspension (see Paragraph 2.15)
- Effect of suspension (see Paragraph 2.16)
- Termination (see Paragraph 2.17)
- Effect of termination (see Paragraph 2.18)
- Termination by composer (see Paragraph 2.19)
- Boilerplate* (see Paragraph 2.20).

2.3 Engagement

Term

The key element of a term publishing agreement is for the Publisher to acquire the composing services of the Composer for the term of the agreement. Normally, the term comprises at least two parts, an initial period and then one or more successive options, as in the case of a recording contract (see Paragraph 1.4). As in the case of a recording contract, the precise length of the term will vary according to the circumstances and it is important that a balance be struck between, on the one hand, providing the Publisher a term of years sufficient to enable the Publisher to recoup their investment and on the other hand, not tying the Composer down for an oppressively long period of time (see Paragraph 1.3).

In some cases, the agreement may provide for a one-year contract period which may be extended by three or four one-year option periods. During each period, the composer may be expected to write a minimum number of compositions.

Interrelationship between Publishing Agreement and Recording Contract

In some cases a publishing agreement is linked to a recording contract. Some record companies may wish their associated publishing companies to enter into publishing agreements with artists who are signed under recording contracts. In such circumstances, care must be taken to ensure that the term of the publishing agreement is co-terminous with the term of the recording contract. The reason for this is that it is not uncommon for publishing agreements to contain writing commitments, in much the same way as recording contracts contain recording product commitments (see Paragraph 1.3). In some cases, however, a publishing agreement will specify that the writing commitment is met only when the compositions have actually been recorded and released by a major record company.

Obviously, in these circumstances, if a Composer's/Artist's recording contract is terminated throughout the period that the publishing agreement remains in effect, the Composer/Artist may well be unable to interest another major record company and therefore be unable to fulfil the Composer's writing commitment under the publishing contract—since without a record company, the Composer will simply be in no position to ensure that all the Composer's compositions are recorded and are released by a major record company.

Where the Publisher decides not to exercise an option to extend the publishing agreement, but an associated record company exercises its option to extend the recording agreement, the rights in any new compositions written by the Composer after the end of the publishing agreement will be controlled by the Composer and the Composer will therefore be able to ensure compliance with any controlled composition clause in the recording contract (see Paragraph 1.12).

Where the record company does not exercise its option to extend the initial term, but the Publisher chooses to extend the initial term, the Composer/Artist may find it difficult to secure another record company unless the publishing agreement obliges the Publisher to consent to mechanical payments on controlled compositions* at a reduced rate, not just in favour of the Publisher's associated record company but any third party record company.

Exclusivity and Scope of Services

Normally the services of the Composer are acquired on an exclusive basis. This means that the Publisher has the exclusive right to all compositions written by the Composer during the term.

Compositions are frequently defined as meaning any lyrics and/or musical compositions and/or other musical or literary or dramatic works written by the Composer, whether they are written alone or in collaboration with others (but in such cases, only to the extent of the Composer's share of co-written works) whether they are written in conventional manuscript or on the keyboard or other instruments and whether they are stored in electronic format or recorded on tape or annotated in the conventional manner. Works which are orchestrated or arranged will normally also count as compositions.

In some cases, the Publisher may acquire existing compositions written by the Composer before the commencement of the publishing agreement as well as all future compositions written by the Composer between the commencement of the agreement and its expiry.

Writing Commitment

The Publisher may require the Composer to write not less than a specified number of compositions in each year of the term. Often the number of compositions will be linked to the number of tracks required to comprise an album and the publishing agreement may contain an obligation on the Composer to ensure that the compositions which form the writing commitment are recorded and released by a record company. Obviously, the Composer will only be able to do this if (s)he is signed to a record company and these provisions need to be considered carefully for the reasons stated above.

Delivery of the Compositions

In order to be able to determine whether the Composer has met his or her writing commitment, and in order to be able to exploit the compositions, the Publisher obviously needs to know when they have been written.

It is therefore normal for a publishing agreement to provide that the Composer will deliver to the Publisher copies of all scores, lyrics, vocal, instrumental or orchestral parts, demo tapes, floppy disks or other material on which the compositions are written or stored, together with a short one-page confirmation of assignment of copyright. This can be used for registering the compositions with the Performing Right Society Limited and the Mechanical Copyright Protection Society Limited, avoiding the need to disclose the commercial provisions of the agreement.

Some publishing agreements require the Composer to maintain duplicate copies of all material sent and contain an acknowledgement on the part of the Composer that, if the Publisher loses any such material, the Composer will have no claim against the Publisher. These provisions are perfectly usual.

Right to make Composer's Services Available

Some publishing agreements contain a provision permitting the Publisher to make the Composer's composing services available to third parties. Whether or not this is appropriate will depend both on the type of material usually written by the Composer and also on the terms of the arrangement between the Composer and Publisher.

If the Composer has written film and television music in the past, it may well be reasonable for the Publisher to make the Composer's services available to third parties for the purpose of composing new film and television material. In such circumstances, the method of apportionment of any income which the Publisher receives for the Composer's services (as distinct from income received by the Publisher for granting a synchronisation licence* to use the Composer's work) will need to be considered.

Promotional Services

Some publishing agreements acquire the right to use the services of the Composer for promotional and publicity purposes. Whether or not such a provision is appropriate will depend on the circumstances. Where services are provided for publicity or promotional purposes in the entertainment industry, it is normal for them to be made available without any payment of any fee other than reimbursement of expenses. In many cases, such a provision is made subject to the Composer's prior professional engagements, of which the Publisher has notice.

2.4 Options

Option provisions in publishing agreements are not dissimilar to the provisions contained in recording contracts, and a number of the factors referred to in Paragraph 1.4 will be relevant. Exercise of an option normally requires payment of an additional advance (see Paragraph 1.6). If the Publisher exercises its first option, it will normally be entitled to exercise a second option, and so on.

There may be circumstances, however, where the Composer has not met the writing requirement. In such circumstances, the Publisher will clearly be unable to determine whether or not it wishes to exercise its option, and the time for exercise of the option may be extended until 90 or 180 days following delivery of the writing commitment.

2.5 Rights

Copyright Assignment

The agreement will provide for an assignment to the Publisher of the entire copyright in all compositions written by the Composer during the term. The assignment will normally be for a period to be negotiated. The length of the period may range from the term, plus a retention period of 15 to 20 years up to the full period of copyright including all renewals, reversions and extensions throughout the world.

Where existing compositions are included in the assignment, if the existing compositions are subject to agreements with third parties, the assignment may be expressed to be subject to these agreements. If it is intended that the Publisher should also get the benefit of any income stream arising from the existing agreements, the contract should provide not only that the rights are assigned subject to the existing agreements, but also with the benefit of the existing agreements. Otherwise, the cash flow will remain the Composer's property.

Performing Rights

The right to perform the compositions in public and to authorise their broadcast and/or transmission will be controlled by a performing right society if the Composer is a member of any such society. These societies are responsible for the collective administration of the performance right in musical works and the collection of fees and royalties from broadcasters, concert halls, places of entertainment as well as shops, restaurants, bars, airports, shopping malls—anywhere, in fact, where music is played in public.

Each country has its own performing right societies. There are three principal societies in the United States of America: the ASCAP*, the BMI* and the SESAC*. In the United Kingdom, the collecting society is the Performing Right Society Limited (PRS). Reciprocal arrangements exist between performing rights societies in all countries, under which they collect and pay over income arising from the exploitation of works of members of their affiliated societies, as well as works written by their own members.

The PRS has the right to issue licences for the performance and recording of compositions before they are published, where such performance is related to synchronisation with any cinema or television film intended for exhibition in the United States of America. For this reason, many publishing contracts acknowledge that the PRS has this right in order to clarify that it is not a right which is controlled by the Publisher.

Performing rights organisations have two categories of member: publisher members and composer members. They collect the income arising from public performance of works written by their composer members and divide them up in the proportions agreed to between the composers and their publishers in their publishing agreements.

Under the rules of the PRS, the Composer may receive not less than 6/12ths of performing rights income—ie 50%—and the balance will be received by the Publisher. The PRS and all other performing rights societies pay their income direct to their composer members and publisher members. For this reason, income derived by the Composer from the PRS is normally not directly referred to in the publishing agreement, since the Composer will receive this money direct from the PRS, not through the Publisher. Traditionally, the performing rights societies account 45 days after 30 June and 31 December in each year—ie 15 August and 15 February.

Because the terms of membership of the PRS and other performing rights organisations require composers to assign to them the performing rights in their music, it is necessary for the copyright assignment contained in the publishing agreement to exclude rights previously assigned to performing rights organisations.

Mechanical Rights

Where a record company wishes to use the performance by a recording artist of a composition on a record, the record company must obtain a licence to use the composition from the copyright owner—normally the music publisher. The Publisher will grant the record company a licence to use the composition in return for the payment of a fee which is normally referred to as a "mechanical fee" or simply "mechanical".

A mechanical fee authorises the mechanical reproduction of a musical work. In the early days of music publishing, mechanical reproduction was effected by means of piano rolls, and the like before the use of the term was extended to records, long-playing records and, nowadays CDs, CD-Roms,

33

video cassettes, video discs etc. Mechanical royalties are collected on behalf of music publishers by so-called mechanical collection societies.

In the United States the principal mechanical collection society is the Harry Fox Agency. In the United Kingdom the principal mechanical collection society is the Mechanical Copyright Protection Society Limited (MCPS). In many European countries one collecting society deals with both mechanical income and performing rights income and in the United Kingdom both the MCPS and the PRS have recently decided to merge their operations, which are now known as the Music Alliance.

Moral Rights

Four moral rights exist under United Kingdom law. Two are of little relevance to publishing agreements (the right not to have a work falsely attributed to oneself and the right to privacy for photographs or films commissioned for domestic use) and two are relevant (the right to be identified and the right to object to a derogatory treatment of a work).

Normally publishing agreements will contain an absolute irrevocable waiver on the part of composers of their moral rights. Since most publishing agreements contain provisions under which the Publisher agrees to accord credit to the Composer, there is generally no difficulty in the Composer waiving their statutory right to be identified, since the contract gives the Composer a contractual right to be identified. The credit obligation is generally limited to printed copies of the compositions, since record label copy will be outside the publisher's control.

The right to prevent one's work being subjected to a derogatory treatment* is, however, a somewhat delicate matter. It will be remembered that it is the business of the music publisher to exploit the compositions in as many different ways as possible throughout the world. In practice, this means authorising the production of cover versions both in the original language and in local languages in foreign countries, as well as authorising the use of compositions in synchronisation with motion pictures (as part of the soundtrack of films) or in synchronisation with commercials.

There is clearly a potential conflict here between the Publisher's desire to exploit the compositions freely and the Composer's desire (for example) not to have the compositions used in commercials or used with foreign language versions which change the subject matter of the song. A further complication arises by virtue of the fact that if an artist other than the original artist performs a song, it is likely that the new artist will do so in a manner completely different from the original artist. If the original artist is also the composer of the song (s)he may find the cover version* artistically unacceptable and may also wish to retain a monopoly on his or her own performance—especially if a work acquires cult status. This might increase sales of the original record, but it would reduce publishing income which might be unacceptable to the Publisher.

There are two possible variations to a composer's agreement which may be of relevance. First, the Publisher may agree to consult with the Composer and give good faith consideration to the Composer's views before authorising the exploitation of foreign language versions or before licensing the use of the compositions for films or commercials. On this basis, the Composer may feel comfortable with an absolute moral rights* waiver, since the Publisher would have a contractual obligation to consider the Composer's reservations about uses of the Composer's material—although it does not guarantee that the Publisher will actually follow them.

The second possibility is to give the Composer the right to block certain types of exploitation. An absolute right of approval in relation to commercial use may also be acceptable to the music Publisher in some circumstances.

Name and Likeness

Most publishing agreements will contain a provision entitling the Publisher to use the name likeness and biography of the Composer for the full period of the Publisher's rights in the compositions in order to assist the Publisher to exploit the rights granted under the agreement. Restrictions should be placed on the Publisher having any merchandising rights for the reasons stated in Paragraph 1.5.

Covenant for Further Assurance

The final provision which is frequently encountered in a grant of rights clause is what lawyers refer to as a "covenant for further assurance". This is an undertaking on the part of the Composer to do any acts and execute any documents which may be necessary in the future to transfer the rights assigned or granted to the Publisher. Again, this is a regular provision and one that may be accepted by the Composer.

Covenants for further assurance are frequently backed up by powers of attorney. Although a power of attorney limited to the specific subject area of the contract is acceptable, a general power of attorney should never be given by a Composer—and there is no legitimate business reason for a Publisher to ask for one (see Paragraph 53.13).

2.6 Advances

All publishing agreements should provide for the payment of advances. It is normal for publishing agreements to provide that advances are recoupable from royalties—in other words, the Publisher has the right to suspend payment of a royalty until such time as the total royalties payable equal or exceed the advance. The advances are normally, however, recovered from the Composer's share of royalties alone, not the Publishers (see Paragraph 2.9).

There may be a number of advances payable during the term of the agreement. The amounts and the instalments, and the events linked to the instalments are, of course, entirely negotiable. The amounts of the advances may be fixed for each period. Alternatively, a "rollover*" advance may be paid of, say, £50,000 each time the previous advance has been recouped. In this case, the agreement will not need to contain a fixed writing commitment. A further alternative would be a minimum/maximum advance equal to two-thirds of the composer's royalty income in the preceding period, subject to a minimum of £x and a maximum of £y.

Where further advances are payable on the exercise of options (as would be normal), the dates on which these are payable are similar to the dates on which the first advance was payable—and again entirely negotiable. (See also Paragraph 1.6)

2.7 Composer's Warranties

There are a number of warranties* that the Publisher will wish to obtain from the Composer. These include the following matters.

Majority

The Publisher will normally want assurance that the Composer has attained the age of 18—because contracts with minors are unenforceable in certain circumstances (see Paragraph 54.3).

Ability to Contract

The Publisher will want to know that the Composer is free to enter into the agreement and is not under any restriction or prohibition which might interfere with the Composer's obligations under the contract.

Authorship and Ownership

The Publisher will wish to ensure that the Composer is the sole absolute unincumbered legal and beneficial owner of the copyrights assigned to the Publisher and will be the sole author of the compositions, unless the Publisher consents to collaboration.

Restrictions and Prior Rights

The Publisher will wish to ensure that there are no restrictions relating to the compositions which the Composer is legally able to write and, where existing compositions are assigned, the Publisher will wish to be reassured that they are not the subject of any prior licence or grant of rights (other than to the PRS) and that they have not been exploited by any third party prior to the agreement.

Originality etc

The Publisher will wish to ensure that the compositions and the services of the Composer are original and do not infringe any right of copyright or any other right of any other person.

PRS Confirmation

The Publisher will wish to ensure that the Composer will sign collection agreements and division of fees forms required by the Publisher.

Control

The Publisher will have full and complete control over the manner and extent of exploitation and advertisement of the compositions and the right, without the Composer's consent, to transfer assign or grant licences in the compositions. This provision may obviously need to be modified in the light of the comments in relation to moral rights in Paragraph 2.5.

Authorisation

The Publisher is authorised to make alterations, adaptations and additions to the compositions and provide translations of new words or lyrics in other languages. This provision may obviously need to be modified in the light of the comments in relation to moral rights in Paragraph 2.5.

Non-publishing Exploitation

The Company will not disclose any confidential information in relation to the agreement. The Composer acknowledges that the Publisher shall not be required to print a published edition of the compositions. Published editions of works generally generate only a small part of the income on which royalties are paid (see Paragraph 2.9).

Copyright Status

The Composer is a "qualifying person" within the meaning of the Copyright, Designs and Patents Act 1988. This warranty is essential to guarantee to the Publisher that the product of the Composer's services is capable of being protected by copyright legislation throughout the world. Most persons living or working in the western world are qualifying persons.

Non-disclosure

The Composer will not disclose any confidential information in relation to the agreement. Most publishing agreements contain a confidentiality provision requiring the Composer not to disclose information. The obligation is normally amended to permit disclosure to professional advisors.

Insurance

Some agreements require a warranty that the Composer is in a good state of health coupled with an undertaking that the Composer will comply with the requirements of the Publisher's insurers. Whether or not this provision is appropriate will depend on the circumstances.

Dangerous Pursuits

Some publishing agreements may contain restrictions excluding the Composer from pursuing dangerous hobbies. In many cases, such an exclusion is inappropriate and provisions of this type need to be considered in the context of the relevant transaction.

Whereabouts

An obligation to keep the Publisher informed of the Composer's address, telephone number and whereabouts may also be included and is not unreasonable.

Tax Residency

The Publisher may also wish the Composer to notify the Publisher of any change of tax status. This could require the Publisher to deduct withholding tax* from sums payable to the Composer.

Legal Advice

The Publisher is normally concerned to see that the Composer has obtained legal advice from a solicitor specialising in this type of agreement. This provision is designed to insulate the Publisher from claims that the contract is voidable.

Indemnity

Some publishing agreements seek to impose indemnity obligations on Composers. It is reasonable for a Publisher to wish to be indemnified in relation to copyright status, ownership, and originality, but indemnity protection in relation to other matters may be unfair and oppressive and should be resisted for the reasons referred to in Paragraph 53.16.

2.8   Publisher's Obligations

Publishers will generally be reluctant to undertake extensive exploitation obligations, since even where they are dealing with an established Composer, they have no guarantee as to the future nature of the Composer's work or its popularity.

The Publisher will generally undertake to register all compositions with performing right and mechanical societies and since the interest of both Publisher and Composer is to generate the maximum amount of income from the compositions, the Publisher should, in normal circumstances, feel able to agree to use all reasonable endeavours in their reasonable commercial discretion to exploit the compositions. The Composer should obtain at least this level of commitment from their Publisher.

2.9   Royalties

Remitted or Source Income

The royalties payable under publishing contracts are normally calculated as a percentage of receipts (which may sometimes be referred to as gross receipts). Receipts may be calculated either on a "remitted" basis or on a "source" basis.

Remitted receipts include all sums actually remitted to and received by the Publisher arising directly and identifiably from the use and/or exploitation of the compositions. Source receipts will mean all income arising at source (ie the money paid by end users) less only commissions, fees and expenses paid to or deducted by sub-publishers, administrators and standard commissions deducted by the PRS and mechanical rights societies (see Paragraph 2.5).

Whichever basis is used, the Publisher will normally wish to leave out of account certain excluded items. These will include, not only VAT, sales taxes and withholding taxes, but also the cost of conversion and transmission of currency, commissions of sub-publishers and administrators (which the Composer will normally wish to limit to 25% of source income), commissions of the PRS and mechanical rights societies and other agencies, amounts paid by way of remuneration to arrangers, adaptors and translators, advances and guarantees received by the Publisher, unless and until earned, and so-called "black box" income.

Black Box Income*

If a Publisher receives an advance or a guarantee or a security deposit and it is non-returnable, it is reasonable for the Composer to require that this money should be brought into account. The same applies to "black box" income which is unidentifiable income and there may be circumstances where the amount of "black box" income can be apportioned in an equitable way between all compositions represented by the Publisher.

Double Deductions

Where sums are provided to be deducted, great care should be taken to ensure that there are no double deductions*. For example, if a contract provides that "gross receipts" are income remitted to the Publisher, such income will have already suffered the prior deduction of commissions from sub-publishers, mechanical societies etc. If the contract provides that these commissions are to be deducted from "gross receipts" as defined (ie remitted income) they will have been deducted twice and the Composer's income stream will have been unfairly manipulated to his or her detriment.

Duration of Payment Obligations

The period during which the royalty is to be paid is also of crucial importance. Although the Publisher only requires the copyright in compositions written by the Composer during the term, the Publisher will have the right to exploit such compositions worldwide for the term and an additional period which may be as long as the full period of copyright. It is therefore completely unacceptable for the Composer if the royalty payment provision applies only during the term. The provision should apply to all exploitation by the Publisher and its licensees of the compositions during the copyright period.

Royalty Percentages

The percentage of royalties which a Composer receives from a Publisher's gross receipts will depend both on the status of the Composer and on the relationship between the Composer and the Publisher.

If the Publisher is a company which is owned by the Composer and which has been set up to exploit the Composer's compositions, then, depending on the Composer's tax arrangements, the publishing contract may provide for a very high percentage. Normally, the minimum percentage of the various types of income is 50%, but in the case of a top-class Composer their share may be as high as 70–80%. Any advance paid is normally recouped only from the Composer's share of 50–70%, not the whole income stream

The categories of receipts and normal minimum percentages payable to the Composer are set out below:

- PRS income which is received direct by the Composer and the Publisher individually (see Paragraph 2.5): 50%
- Mechanical fees and royalties from original records: 50%

- Mechanical fees and royalties from cover records: 50% after deduction of additional sub-publisher's percentage
- Synchronisation licences*: 50%
- Sale of printed copies: 10%
- Other income: 50%.

Normally, a Publisher is exempt from paying royalties on the first 350 copies of printed editions and is exempted from paying royalties on complimentary copies of printed musical editions or on orchestral or band parts or copies sold at or below cost.

2.10 Royalty Accounting

The publishing agreement should provide dates for statements of account to be rendered, showing accrued royalties, the amount of the advance unrecouped etc. Each statement is normally accompanied by the amount it shows to be owing.

The Publisher may be asked, in some cases, to bring into account money receivable from overseas affiliates for the purpose of calculating whether advances have been recouped and further advances are payable, even though the money receivable may not actually be received for a further six to eighteen months.

The standard payment dates in the music industry are 30 June and 31 December in each year and it is normal for the statements to be issued 90 days after these dates. It would be normal for a publishing agreement to oblige the Publisher to maintain full and proper books of account at its principal place of business. The Composer or the Composer's advisor should have the right to inspect, audit and take copies of the books provided the Composer gives reasonable prior notice. Inspections are frequently limited to occur only during normal business hours and the Publisher may well wish to limit the number of inspections to one per year. Such a limitation is not reasonable if an inspection has previously revealed errors or inconsistencies.

If an audit inspection reveals underaccounting to the Composer, it is normal for the Composer to be able to recover the reasonable costs of such audit and inspection if the amount of underpayment exceeds a certain amount. In many cases, the error margin is required to be 10%, although, on occasions, a 5% margin or fixed sum is agreed. The amount of the margin is obviously a matter for commercial negotiation.

A Publisher will normally wish to have the right to deduct and withhold from royalties any sums which are deductible in accordance with local law. Normally, the only deductions relate to withholding taxes and the Publisher will be under a legal obligation to make these deductions. The clause is therefore regular.

Where a Composer is represented by an agent or business manager, that person will normally wish the royalties to be directed to him or her. Royalty accounts clauses, therefore, frequently contain a direction clause irrevocably directing the Publisher to pay all sums to the Composer's agent or representative, whose receipts will be a full and sufficient discharge to the Publisher of its liability to make the payment. From the Composer's point of view, however, it is preferable to direct the Publisher to pay the agent his or her percentage and for the Publisher to pay the balance to the Composer. This accelerates the process and eliminates the possibility of the Composer losing all his or her royalties if their agent becomes insolvent.

Some contracts contain a provision to the effect that, if the Publisher fails to pay any royalties, the Composer is required to give 30 days' notice of such failure and the Publisher then has a further 30 days to make good any payment during which time the Publisher shall not be deemed to be in default. This type of provision should be resisted by a Composer, since it effectively gives the Publisher carte blanche to deliver a late account every time and the Composer has no right to receive any money until (s)he gives notice.

2.11 Joint Compositions and New Lyrics

Because a song comprises two separate elements (the words and the music) it is necessary for a publishing agreement to determine how receipts from a song are to be divided up. For this reason, many publishing agreements provide that, where the music and the lyrics contained in any composition are written by different people, that each will be treated as a separate composition and in the absence of written agreement, the percentage of receipts allocated to each separate part shall be 50% to the music and 50% to the words. This is perfectly reasonable in most circumstances, but may not be acceptable in every situation.

Where the "Composer" consists of a combination of persons of musical and literary/dramatic ability, it may be necessary to consider to what extent the respective contributions are free-standing, to what extent they are collaborative and to what extent they are perceived to be important or essential to the final work. In the case of a group, these are all matters which should be discussed in the agreement between the various artists (see Chapter 15).

There are also occasions where original music in a composition is exploited with new lyrics, or original lyrics are exploited with new music and some publishing agreements provide that the percentage of gross receipts payable is to be reduced by up to 50% to permit the payment of a share of gross receipts to the person who wrote the new lyrics or music. This provision is not unfair, but there may be circumstances where a Composer would require consultation or approval rights.

Many compositions are written by more than one person and, for this reason publishing agreements will normally contain a provision which specifies how the entitlement to gross receipts is to be calculated in respect of each contributor to the music and the lyrics. One way of effecting the division is to provide that all contributors are entitled to the same share, but this is likely to be unfair to the principal contributors.

Only the contributors can agree between themselves what percentage they are entitled to and it may, therefore, be reasonable for a publishing agreement to provide that the share will be calculated pro rata to the total number of composers/writers, unless the Publisher has received a joint written direction to the contrary signed by all relevant parties. Obviously, there will be many occasions where a straight division of income will result in a situation which fails to recognise individual effort or contribution and will result in an inequitable decision. It is possible for composers to set out contractual provisions which deal with these situations.

2.12 Collaboration

Most publishing contracts will require a Composer to obtain the consent of the Publisher before the Composer collaborates with somebody else. At first sight this may seem to be unfair, but the reason such a provision is included in contracts is because, if the collaborator is under contract to a different publisher, the Publisher alone will not be able to authorise the exploitation of the jointly written work.

In practice, joint publishing arrangements do not cause much of a problem, but Publishers generally prefer to own 100% of their works and the Composer will therefore need to agree with the Publisher a suitable procedure for ensuring that rights are obtained in relation to material written with collaborators— because, where copyright is co-owned, the consent of all owners is required in order to authorise its exploitation.

2.13 Copyright Notice

It is normal for publishing agreements to provide that the name of the Composer will appear on the outside cover or title page or first page of every printed copy of the compositions. Agreements should also provide that the Composer should receive credit on all disks, films, video recordings and other sound or audiovisual carriers incorporating the compositions.

If the agreement contains a provision entitling the Publisher to the benefit of the Composer's services for the purposes of writing commissioned music for films, the credit provision will also need to extend to the precise screen and advertising credit to be accorded to the Composer in relation to films for which the Composer contributes the music.

2.14 Group Provisions

See Paragraph 1.8.

2.15 Suspension by the Publisher

See Paragraph 1.15.

2.16 Effect of Suspension by the Publisher

See Paragraph 1.16

2.17 Termination by the Publisher

See Paragraph 1.17.

2.18 Effect of Termination by the Publisher

See Paragraph 1.18.

2.19 Termination by the Composer

Normally, a Composer will want some form of assurance that the Publisher will continue to perform the Publisher's obligations under the agreement—in particular, the payment obligations. In publishing agreements, this assurance frequently takes the form of a right on the part of the Composer to terminate the agreement if the Publisher has failed to make payment of sums shown due (or has filed to render statements of account) within a specified period after having received notice from the Composer specifying such failure and requiring it to be remedied.

The Composer should also have the right to terminate the agreement if the Publisher should become insolvent or have a receiver or administrator or administrative receiver or liquidator appointed, or go into liquidation.

What happens to the rights acquired by the Publisher if the agreement is terminated is a matter for discussion. If the rights in the compositions have been assigned to the Publisher, they will be owned by the Publisher outright and termination of the agreement will not automatically re-assign rights in the compositions to the Composer. One consequence of termination, however, would be that future compositions unwritten as of the date of the termination would not, of course, be assigned to the Publisher because the term of the agreement would end on termination.

The issue of what happens to rights in existing compositions if the Publisher was in fundamental material breach is frequently a vexed one. Some agreements provide that in such event the rights in all compositions are re-assigned to the Composer, subject to and with the benefit of, licences negotiated by the Publisher with third parties.

A linked question is the issue of assignability. A provision re-assigning to the Composer the Publisher's rights in compositions will be of limited effect if the Publisher has already assigned these rights to a third party. The question of assignability of contractual rights and rights of copyright is dealt with in Paragraph 53.1.

From the Composer's point of view, however, it is possible to include contractual provisions which will protect the Composer in the event of the Publisher's insolvency, even if the Composer has assigned (not licensed) rights to the Publisher.

2.20 Boilerplate

The boilerplate section of a typical publishing agreement will contain the following provisions:

- No obligation (see Paragraph 52.6)
- Notice (see Paragraph 52.8)
- Severability (see Paragraph 52.10)
- Entire agreement (see Paragraph 52.3)
- Waiver (see Paragraph 52.1)
- Partnership (see Paragraph 52.7)
- Governing law (see Paragraph 52.5).

3   Master Acquisition Agreement

3.1   Description of a Master Acquisition Agreement

A master acquisition agreement is used in circumstances where a record company is acquiring rights in master tapes which have been recorded by another party.

The parties to this particular transaction are:

- the record company acquiring the rights in the master tape (referred to as the "Company"); and
- the company or individual which has made the master tape (referred to in this Chapter as the "Licensor".

The purpose of the master acquisition agreement is to transfer rights in the master tape made by the Licensor to the Company which will pay the Licensor an advance* equal to the cost of production together with a royalty*. The obligation to pay all artists and other persons who rendered services in relation to the master tape (such as producer etc) will remain with the Licensor.

This Chapter examines the provisions of a master acquisition agreement from the point of view of the Company or its legal advisors.

3.2   Transaction Analysis

A typical master acquisition agreement might be expected to contain the following clauses:

- Delivery (see Paragraph 3.3)
- Grant of rights (see Paragraph 3.4)
- Licensor's warranties* and obligations (see Paragraph 3.5)
- Advance (see Paragraph 3.6)
- Royalties (see Paragraph 3.7)
- Royalty Accounting (see Paragraph 3.8)
- Compositions (see Paragraph 3.9)
- Other Product (see Paragraph 3.10).

3.3 Delivery

Delivery Material

The delivery of the actual master tape(s) by the Licensor to the Company is obviously the main objective of the agreement. The agreement will contain a detailed specification of the master tape(s), identifying the artists, the compositions and other relevant persons (producer, etc) and will normally provide that the master tapes are to be of such technical and artistic quality as may be acceptable to the Company.

If the Licensor fails to deliver acceptable material, the agreement may contain a provision giving the Licensor a grace period of 30 days from notice of rejection to deliver acceptable material without being in breach of its obligations. From the Company's point of view, it is important not to pay over any large sum until receipt of acceptable material.

Letters of Confirmation

The Company may require signed copies of contracts* with the relevant artists and record producer. These may contain information which the Licensor considers sensitive, so alternatively, letters of confirmation from the artists and producer may be provided. The purpose of such confirmations is to verify the scope and extent of the rights acquired by the Licensor in order to protect the Company from having its right to manufacture and exploit records derived from the master tapes being challenged by any person whose rights or consent should have been acquired by the Licensor.

3.4 Grant of Rights

Copyright

The agreement will normally provide that the Company is entitled to the exclusive right to manufacture and exploit records derived from the master tape for a specified term of years. The term of years may be the full period of copyright in the master tapes or some shorter period. The agreement will also specify the territory for which the Company acquires rights.

Whether the Company obtains the rights by way of assignment or exclusive licence is a matter for negotiation. The basic difference is that licences may generally be terminated and assignments generally may not (although they may be drafted in such a way that they can be terminated). For an explanation as to the differences between assignments and licences, see Paragraph 53.2.

The Company will be relying on the Licensor's warranty that it is the owner of the copyright in the master tapes. If there is any doubt on this score, the Company should obtain corroboration before entering into the agreement, because the consequences of even innocent infringement of copyright may be the payment of substantial damages.

Name, Likeness and Biography

The Company will normally require the right to use the name, likeness and biography of all Artists and other persons who services are contained on the master tapes. The unauthorised use of a person's likeness constitutes a criminal misdemeanour in some states of the USA. Once again, the consequences of violation of these rights could be financially damaging and the Company should not proceed if there is any doubt.

Moral Rights

The Company will normally require confirmation that the Artists have waived their moral rights* (to the extent they have any) in relation to any copyright works on the master tapes (see Paragraph 1.4). It should be noted that United Kingdom legislation currently does not provide for producers of sound recordings to have moral rights in the sound recordings. The World Intellectual Property Organisation (WIPO) has recently agreed a treaty which proposes to give performers moral rights in their performances, but no state has yet provided legislation to protect such rights.

Promotional Services

The agreement may also require the Licensor to make available to the Company the services of the Artists for the purposes of making audio-visual promo material and for publicity and promotional purposes. Whether or not the Licensor has the right to make these services available will depend on the Licensor's own contract with the artists. In order to secure its right to require the services, the Company may insist on an inducement letter from the Artists (see Paragraph 51.2).

Right to Commence Proceedings

In some contracts, a provision may be inserted expressly providing that the Company has the sole and exclusive right to commence proceedings in the Company's own name for infringement of copyright and similar matters. Such a provision may be necessary if the Company obtains a licence of copyright as opposed to an assignment (see Paragraph 53.2) since in some jurisdictions a licensee does not have the right to sue in its own name without joining the owner of copyright to the court proceedings.

Under United Kingdom law, an exclusive licensee does have the right to sue in their own name, so the provision is not strictly necessary. However, it is advisable in cases where the territory of the agreement extends beyond the UK.

Further Assurance

The contract may also contain a "covenant for further assurance". This is an undertaking on the part of the Licensor to do any acts and execute any documents which may be necessary in the future to transfer the rights granted to the Company. This is a normal provision which may be accepted by the Licensor. Frequently covenants for further assurance are backed up by powers of attorney (see Paragraph 53.13).

3.5   Licensor's Warranties and Obligations

There are a number of warranties that the Company will normally wish to obtain from the Licensor. These include the following matters.

Consents

The Company will want confirmation that the Licensor has obtained all necessary performer's consents from Artists and pre-paid all equitable remuneration in relation to their performances (see Paragraph 51.6). The making and/or exploitation of a recording without the consent of all relevant artists is unlawful (see Paragraph 1.4).

Ability to Contract/Ownership

The Company will wish confirmation that the Licensor is free to enter into the agreement and is the sole absolute unincumbered legal and beneficial owner of all rights granted to the Company and is not under any restriction or prohibition which might interfere with the Licensor performing its obligations under the contract.

No Conflict

The Licensor will normally be required to warrant that the Licensor has not entered into any arrangement which might conflict with the agreement.

Originality etc

The master tapes and the delivery material are original and not obscene, blasphemous or defamatory.

Ownership and Control

The Licensor controls all rights necessary to grant to the Company the rights under the Agreement and has no notice of any defect or restriction in such rights.

Copyright Status

The Licensor is the owner of the copyright in the master tapes which are protected by copyright throughout the world.

Non-infringement

The master tapes and other material delivered will not infringe any right of copyright or any right of any other person.

Quality

The master tapes and other material will be of first-class technical and artistic quality suitable for the production of records in all configurations.

No Liability

The Company will not incur any liability to any person in relation to the master tapes or the records or the use of the logos or trademarks of the Licensor.

Contractual Credits

The records and the delivery material comply with all contractual credit and other obligations made by the Licensor and do not violate any moral rights of any person. This provision is important because non-compliance with credit obligations may give persons entitled to a written credit the right to prevent distribution of the product.

No Liabilities

The Licensor will deliver the master tapes and delivery material free from any liabilities to make payments. The contract may specifically contain warranties that no recording, synchronisation, mechanical or distribution royalties are payable—other than possibly mechanical copyright royalties at a specified rate in relation to compositions incorporated in the records. The contract may specifically provide a warranty that the Licensor has paid or will pay out of the Licensor's share of income all sums payable to the American Federation of Musicians*, including sums payable pursuant to the Phonograph Record Trust Agreement, the Phonograph Record Manufacturers Special Payment Fund Agreement and the American Federation of Musicians Pension and Welfare Fund.

Distribution

The Company is to have absolute discretion as to whether to produce or continue or discontinue the production of records. In practice, the Licensor may require some undertaking on the part of the Company to market the records effectively.

No Liability

All consents which are necessary for the sale of the records have been obtained by the Licensor. The Company will not incur any liability to any third party other than the payment of royalties as specified to the Licensor.

Non-disclosure

The Licensor will not reveal or disclose any financial or other confidential information in relation to the agreement.

Exclusivity

No other person, firm or company will have the right to manufacture, import or distribute in the territory, any records in any configuration, derived from the master tapes in whole or in part at any time during the term*.

Label

The Company shall have, at all times, the discretion as to label or labels on which the records are released and the pricing level of such records and the Company shall be entitled to issue records at special low prices, or as special low budget price items. In practice, the agreement may specify a designated label or labels.

As to pricing of records on initial release, the agreement may provide that the Company is obliged to release the records on a top-line label initially and restricted from issuing records at mid-price or budget-price for pre-specified periods of time.

Indemnity

The contract may well contain an indemnity provision from the Licensor to the Company. If both entities are corporate entities, indemnity provisions may be acceptable. The Licensor may, however, wish to limit the indemnity provisions for the reasons specified in Paragraph 53.16.

3.6 Advances

The advance payable to the Licensor should normally at least equal the cost of production expended by the Licensor on a master tape. See also the provisions of Paragraph 1.5.

3.7 Royalties

See Paragraph 1.9.

3.8 Royalty Accounting

See Paragraph 1.11.

3.9 Controlled Compositions and Recording Restrictions

See Paragraph 1.8.

3.10 Other Product

The master acquisition agreement may contain a provision giving the Company the option to acquire future master tapes produced by the Licensor. These options are frequently referred to in the media industry as "first refusal" rights and are often supported by a matching offer or "last refusal" right. (See Paragraph 52.7.)

3.11 Boilerplate

The boilerplate section of a typical master acquisition agreement will contain the following provisions:

- No obligation (see Paragraph 52.6)
- Notice (see Paragraph 52.8)
- Severability (see Paragraph 52.10)
- Entire agreement (see Paragraph 52.3)
- Waiver (see Paragraph 52.11)
- Partnership (see Paragraph 52.7)
- Governing law (see Paragraph 52.5).

4 Master Licence Agreement

4.1 Description of a Master Licence Agreement

The master licence agreement is used by the owner of copyright in a sound recording for the purpose of licensing the sound recording to third parties. It contains provisions which are normally designed to protect the position of the person granting the rights. It may be contrasted with the provision of a master acquisition agreement (see Chapter 3) which contains terms which are drafted from the point of view of the person acquiring the rights.

The parties to this particular transaction are:

- the owner of the sound recording being licensed (referred to as the "Company");
- and the company distributing the records (referred to as the "Licensee")

The Chapter examines the provisions of a master licence agreement from the point of view of the Company or its legal advisors.

4.2 Transaction Analysis

A typical master licence agreement might be expected to contain the following clauses:

- Grant of Rights (see Paragraph 4.3)
- Company's Warranties* (see Paragraph 4.4)
- Remuneration (see Paragraph 4.5)
- Licensee's Undertakings (see Paragraph 4.6)
- Royalties* (see Paragraph 4.7)
- Royalty Accounting (see Paragraph 4.8)
- Force Majeure (see Paragraph 4.9)
- Determination (see Paragraph 4.10)
- Effect of Determination (see Paragraph 4.11)
- Boilerplate* (see Paragraph 4.12).

4.3 Grant of Rights

The Agreement needs to specify the precise rights granted to the Licensee. It should therefore specify the territory and the term of the Licensee's rights. If the Licensee is being granted the right to manufacture records, the definition should provide which formats apply, and also specify that the Licensee's rights exist in relation to audio product only.

The Agreement may provide that the Licensee has the non-exclusive right to manufacture records in the territory, but the exclusive right to sell and distribute them in the territory. There will be many instances where this is inappropriate, but some countries may lack competitive or technically acceptable manufacturing capacity and companies in those territories may need to manufacture records in another territory. If the Company has given the exclusive manufacturing rights to a Licensee in that other territory, that Company may find difficulty in licensing the adjoining territory.

The agreement may also provide that the Licensee has the non-exclusive right to use certain publicity material, subject to terms and conditions from time to time notified by the Company (such as credit requirements etc). This is perfectly normal.

Additionally, the agreement will need to provide for the Licensee to receive master tapes in order to permit the Licensee to manufacture records. The method and place of delivery should be specified, together with provisions relating to customs and excise, import duties etc.

Following the expiry of the term by effluxion of time (but not termination) the Licensee will have the right to sell off the stock of records previously manufactured by the Licensee during the term for three to six months.

The Company may wish to limit the sell-off* period to a three month period, although six month periods are common. The Company may also wish to eliminate the possibility that the Licensee may build up a stockpile of records during the latter part of the term and then flood the market with them during the sell-off period, damaging the market for any future licensee. The Company may achieve this by limiting the number of records which the Licensee may manufacture during the last year of the term to the same number as those manufactured by the Licensee during the previous year. In practice, however, ensuring compliance with this obligation may prove difficult.

4.4 Company's Warranties

The Licensee will require a number of warranties from the Company in relation to rights granted to the Licensee, including the following.

Ability to Contract

The Company is free to enter into the agreement and grant the Licensee the rights.

No Conflict

The Company has not entered into and shall not enter into any arrangement which may conflict with the agreement.

Third Party Liabilities

All sums payable in relation to the production of the recordings (other than mechanical royalties—see Paragraph 2.5) are to be paid by the Company.

There may be a number of additional matters in relation to which the Licensee may wish to obtain a warranty from the Company—such as the warranties given to a person acquiring rights as specified in Paragraph 3.5. These will obviously be matters of commercial negotiation.

4.5 Remuneration

Advance and Royalties

The agreement will provide for the Licensee to pay the Company an advance. It may provide for a percentage to be paid on signature and for the balance to be paid on delivery. The advance will normally be expressed to be non-returnable and recoupable from royalties.

It would be normal to expect the master licence agreement to be supplied and drafted by the Company. It is therefore likely that it will provide for the Licensee to pay royalties based on published dealer price, less only normal arm's length bona fide discounts given by the Licensee.

It is unlikely that the Company would permit the Licensee to take packaging deductions* or make any other royalty deductions or 'breaks' (see Paragraph 1.10) although, if the Licensee commits itself to a major television advertising period in the territory during the term, the Company may reduce the actual royalty percentage rate during the period of the term when such advertisements are actually running. It will be normal for the Company to provide that the expenditure actually incurred by the Licensee should be in excess of a minimum amount and to require receipts and invoices as proof that the Licensee had incurred such expenditure.

Mechanical Royalties

It is normal for a licence agreement to contain a provision for the Licensee to pay mechanical royalties.

4.6 Licensee's Warranties

There are a number of warranties which a master licence agreement will require from the Licensee. These include the following matters.

55

Reservation of Rights

The Licensee confirms all rights, other than those expressly granted in the master tapes, are reserved to the Company.

Mechanicals

The Licensee agrees to pay all mechanical royalties before manufacturing records.

Copyright Protection

The Licensee agrees not to do anything which would threaten the copyright protection of the master tape.

Delivery of Material

The Licensee undertakes to return to the Company the delivery material on the expiry of the term or, if sooner, the termination of the agreement.

Promotional Material and Artwork

The Licensee will agree not to create any promotional material or artwork without the consent of the Company and agrees that the copyright and all other rights in such material will belong to the Company.

Statements

The Licensee agrees to provide the Company with a monthly statement of shipment and net sales of records.

Sale or Return

The Licensee agrees not to sell any records on a sale or return basis.

Claims

The Licensee will give the Company full particulars on the claim being made.

Payment

The Licensee will promptly pay the Company all sums that are due.

Alienation

The Licensee will not assign or license or sub-license any of the rights acquired by it.

No Copying

The Licensee will not copy or duplicate the master tape otherwise, for the purpose of manufacturing records.

Import Charges

The Licensee will pay all costs, fees, duties and other expenses relating to the dispatch and/or import of the master tape.

Possession of Delivery Material

The Licensee shall keep all delivery material in a safe and secure place in the Licensee's possession.

Damage to Delivery Material

The Licensee will pay the Company the cost of repair or replacement of any damaged or lost delivery material.

Acceptance of Delivered Material

The master tape and all material is deemed to have been accepted by the Licensee, unless it notifies the Company of any damage within 48 hours of receipt.

Insurance

The Licensee undertakes to effect and keep in place adequate insurance in relation to the delivery material and name the Company as the named insured and loss payee.

Collective Bargaining Agreements

The Licensee agrees to conform with all local industry, trade union and guild collective bargaining and other agreements relating to the manufacture and distribution of records.

Release

The Licensee agrees to release the records throughout the territory within three to six months from delivery and maintain the records on continuous release within the territory throughout the term.

Advertisement

The Licensee agrees to advertise the records throughout the territory in the same manner and with equal prominence to other records distributed by the Licensee.

Best Endeavours

The Licensee will agree to exploit the rights granted to the best of the Licensee's skill and ability in order to ensure that the highest possible royalties result.

Non-discrimination

The Licensee agrees that the records will receive fair and equitable treatment and will not be discriminated against in favour of any other records which the Licensee distributes.

Stock Disposal

The Licensee agrees that on the expiry or determination of the agreement, the Company will have the right to purchase from the Licensee all unsold stocks of the records at cost price and if the Company elects not to purchase them, the Licensee will destroy all such records and provide a certificate of destruction to the Company.

No Agency

The Licensee may warrant that it is not the agent from an undisclosed third party. It is important for the Company to know exactly with whom it is dealing.

Under the general law of agency, it would be possible for the Licensee to be acting as the undisclosed agent of another corporation. From the Company's point of view the identity, of all its licensees is important and this may therefore be a warranty which the Company will wish to insist on.

Indemnity

The Licensee agrees to indemnify and keep the Company fully indemnified in relation to any and all costs and expenses incurred by the Company as a result of any breach of or non-performance by the Licensee of its obligations under the Agreement.

4.7 Royalties

Royalty Rate Breaks

The Company will wish to keep the royalty rate constant and permit as few "breaks" as possible (see Paragraph 1.10).

Withholdings

The Licensee will normally be prohibited from withholding or deducting any tax or making any reserve any against returns or credits. Where withholding taxes* are payable, the Licensee may be required to produce evidence of such a fact before making any deduction.

If any withholding taxes are required to be deducted, it will be the responsibility of the Licensee to ensure that no improper deductions are made and that the Company is provided with all necessary receipts, certificates and other documents and other information in order to permit the Company to claim any relevant tax credit.

Payment

The Company may require the Licensee to effect payment of royalties by telegraphic transfer.

Currency Conversion

If the Licensee is in a foreign country, the Agreement will need to provide for a procedure for calculating the relevant exchange rate, as well as specifying the currency in which payment is to be made. US dollars are often used as a currency for foreign transactions.

Blocked Funds

If the Distributor is in a different country from the Company and is outside the European Economic Area, the agreement may contain a provision that, if the Distributor is unable to transfer any money payable or receivable under the agreement as a result of exchange control restrictions, the Distributor will notify the Company and transfer sums into an account designated by the Company (subject to such transfer not violating local laws).

4.8   Royalty Accounting

The Agreement will normally provide that the Licensee is to account on quarterly accounting periods ending on the usual accounting period dates and that a statement of account will be rendered 45 days after each prolonged period.

The Agreement may well specify the details to be included in the statement of account which may show records manufactured, stored, shipped, returned and sold. It is normal to provide that each accounting statement will be accompanied by a payment of all sums due without the Licensee making reserves.

Books of Account

The Licensee will agree to keep full and proper books of account and permit the Company or its representative to inspect, audit and take copies of them upon reasonable notice during normal business hours.

If any inspection of the Company discovers any error to the detriment of the Company in excess of 5% of the amount owed at any one time, the reasonable costs and expenses of the Company's audit are payable by the Licensee. The Licensee may wish to amend the margin of error to 10% rather than 5%. Whether this is acceptable or not is a matter for negotiation.

Confidentiality

The Licensee will keep confidential and not disclose to any third parties other than its professional advisers, where necessary, any matters relating to the Agreement or the business of the Company.

4.9   Force Majeure

The Agreement may contain a force majeure provision exempting the Company from any liability for failing to supply the Licensee as a result of circumstances beyond its control. For the effect of force majeure provisions generally, see Paragraph 52.5.

4.10 Determination

The Agreement will normally contain a provision determining or terminating the Agreement, if the Licensee is in breach of its obligations or becomes insolvent. The Licensee may wish to insert similar provisions permitting the Licensee to determine if the Company is in breach.

This may, however, not be appropriate, since the Company's main obligation is to provide the delivery material. Once delivery has been effected, the only continuing obligations on the part of the Company are its warranties and if there is a claim against the Company for breach of warranty, the Licensee will probably not wish to terminate the Agreement—since it terminates the Licensee's rights—and would be more likely to sue the Company for breach of warranty.

4.11 Effect of Termination

The Agreement may contain a provision which provides for what happens if the Agreement is terminated by the Company. In such event, it would be normal for the Company to retake possession of the master tape and any stock of the records of the Licensee and also to take the benefit of any agreements entered into by the Licensee relating to the records.

4.12 Boilerplate

The boilerplate section of a typical recording contract will contain the following provisions:

* No obligation (see Paragraph 52.6)
* Notice (see Paragraph 52.8)
* Severability (see Paragraph 52.10)
* Entire agreement (see Paragraph 52.3)
* Waiver (see Paragraph 52.11)
* Partnership (see Paragraph 52.7)
* Governing law (see Paragraph 52.5).

5 Pressing and Distribution Agreement

5.1 Description of a Pressing and Distribution Agreement

The pressing and distribution agreement* provides an owner of copyright in sound recordings an alternative to leasing the master tape to a record company. In a master licence agreement, the record company acquiring rights in such an agreement, pays the owner of the master tape an advance* and a royalty*. In a pressing and distribution agreement, the owner of the master tape is entitled to receive 100% of receipts from manufactured records after the owner has paid the distributor a distribution fee, distribution expenses and the cost of manufacture.

A pressing and distribution agreement is inherently more risky than a master licence agreement, since it is possible that if sales of the records perform badly, the gross receipts will not be sufficient to cover the distributor's fee, expenses and the cost of manufacture of the records. Conversely, however, if the records are successful, the owner of a master tape may generate more profits through a pressing and distribution agreement than through a master licence arrangement.

The parties to this particular transaction are:

* the owner of the sound recording being distributed (the "Company"); and
* the entity distributing the records (referred to in this Chapter as the "Distributor").

This Chapter examines the provisions of a pressing and distribution agreement from the point of view of the Company or its legal advisors.

5.2 Document Breakdown

A typical pressing and distribution agreement might be expected to contain the following clauses:

* Grant of rights and delivery obligations (see Paragraph 5.3)
* Delivery and prices (see Paragraph 5.4)
* Advertising and promotion (see Paragraph 5.5)

- Company's warranties* and undertakings (see Paragraph 5.6)
- Distribution fee and application of receipts (see Paragraph 5.7)
- Accounts and payments (see Paragraph 5.8)
- Returns (see Paragraph 5.9)
- Property and risk (see Paragraph 5.10)
- Credit risk (see Paragraph 5.11)
- Other Product (see Paragraph 5.12)
- Manufacture and distribution (see Paragraph 5.13)
- Breach and insolvency (see Paragraph 5.14)
- Consequences of termination (see Paragraph 5.15)
- Boilerplate* (see Paragraph 5.16).

5.3   Grant of Rights and Delivery Obligations

Exclusive Rights

The agreement will give the Distributor the sole and exclusive right to manufacture records (and, if relevant, CDs, CD-Roms etc) throughout a specified territory. Some agreements create an exclusive territory and a non-exclusive territory. The Distributor may have the exclusive right to sell records, CD-Roms etc in the exclusive territory and the non-exclusive right to do so in the non-exclusive territory.

   The Company will need to ensure that it reserves the right to distribute promotional records, CDs etc free of charge in the exclusive territory, because the grant of exclusive rights to distribute and sell will prevent the Company from doing similar activities, unless the agreement expressly provides for it. If the Company were to grant the Distributor sole rights, the Distributor's rights would not be exclusive, and the Company would have the right to sell and distribute without violating the Distributor's rights.

Extent of Rights

The Distributor will normally require the exclusive right to sell, distribute and otherwise exploit the records, CD-Roms etc together with the right to collect all income derived from their sale and the right to initiate proceedings for infringement etc.

   The Company should examine carefully the rights granted to the Distributor. It will probably be appropriate for the Company to restrict exploitation of the sound recordings in multimedia format over the Internet.

Name, Likeness and Biography

The Distributor will normally require the right to use the name, likeness and biography of all artists and other persons whose services are contained on the master tapes. This provision is perfectly acceptable although the Company may wish to clarify that the Distributor will not have the right to use the name and likeness of the artists for general merchandising purposes and that the Distributor's rights will be limited to uses specifically connected with the distribution. The unauthorised use of a person's likeness constitutes a criminal misdemeanour in some states and this right is essential to the Distributor.

Right to Commence Proceedings

In some contracts, a provision may be inserted expressly providing that the Distributor has the sole and exclusive right to commence proceedings in the Distributor's own name for infringement of copyright and similar matters. Such a provision may be necessary if the Distributor obtains a licence of copyright as opposed to an assignment (see Paragraph 53.2) since, in some jurisdictions, a Licensee does not have the right to sue in its own name without joining the owner of copyright to the proceedings.

Under United Kingdom law, an exclusive licensee does have the right to sue in their own name, so the provision is not strictly necessary, but it is advisable in cases where the territory of the agreement extends beyond the UK.

Name and Logo

The Distributor will normally wish to have the right to insert its name, logo and trademark on the records, CDs etc and on associated packaging. This is perfectly acceptable.

Records Subject to the Agreement

A pressing and distribution agreement normally covers a period of time which might be anything from 12 months to a number of years. In some cases, pressing and distribution agreements are limited to specific records. In other cases ,where an arrangement exists for a term* of years, it will normally include the existing sound recordings owned by the Company, together with any future sound recordings acquired by the Company during the term.

The Company may wish to limit the future obligations to sound recordings which the Company intends to distribute on a particular label, or featuring specific artists and any limitations of this order obviously need to be specified.

5.4   Delivery

The agreement will provide that the Company is to deliver tapes and other materials to the Distributor. In the case of existing tapes, the delivery date will be on or shortly after the signature of the agreement. In the case of future tapes, the delivery date will be a specified number of days after the Company has completed recording. Normally, the Distributor will want advance notice of delivery dates and the agreement may link the delivery date to the anticipated release of the record.

The Company should ensure that the Distributor examines the material for technical defects and will wish the Distributor to do so within a specified number of days after delivery. Failure by the Distributor to specify any technical defect within a stated period will constitute acceptance. If the Distributor spots any defect, the Company should require the Distributor to give notice to the Company in writing and the Company will normally require 30 days to remedy the defect.

Orders

The agreement will specify the procedure under which the Company orders copies of records etc from the Distributor. It will specify the price, the notice period for orders and the delivery date. The Distributor will wish to have the right to change its price from time to time during the term of the agreement. The Company should negotiate to fix the price or, if possible, require the Distributor to match quotations obtained by the Company from third parties.

The order price for materials manufactured by the Distributor will be recoverable by it from the gross receipts it collects from the sales of records etc.

Materials and Stock

The agreement will provide that delivery materials will be returned to the Company after the Distributor has no use for them. The agreement may also provide that at the end of the term, the Distributor can require the Company to remove its existing stock of records (and pay the Distributor if the Company has not already paid). The Distributor may frequently reserve the right to destroy any uncollected stock of records on its premises after a certain period. The Company should consider the length of the period and ensure that, before doing so, the Distributor gives the Company notice of its intention.

The Agreement will also need to say who is to provide inlay cards, labels, slip boxes etc. Either these will be manufactured by the Distributor or they will be supplied by the Company, but the agreement will need to specify exactly what is to happen.

Risk

The agreement will provide that risk in materials delivered to the Distributor will remain at all times with the Distributor and will require the Distributor to insure the materials against risk. This means that, if anything happens to the materials while they are in the Distributor's possession, the Distributor will have no liability.

The Company should additionally require the Distributor to note the Company's interest on the Distributor's policy of insurance by making the Company the named insured and loss payee. This will give the Company the right to recover money direct from the insurance company in some circumstances. The Company should also consider whether the Company requires confirmation from the Distributor's insurers of the terms of its cover. If this is required, and the agreement is to last for a term of years, then the agreement could require the Distributor to direct its insurance brokers to send confirmation to the Company of the cover terms on an annual basis.

Price

If the agreement is drafted from the point of view of the Distributor, it may provide that the Distributor has the right to sell and distribute records etc at whatever prices the Distributor determines in consultation with the Company. A consultation right does not require the Distributor to enter into detailed or prolonged discussions with the Company. The Distributor is merely obliged to notify the Company of the proposed price and if the Company remonstrates, the Distributor is permitted to end its consultation at any time and the price will be fixed.

The Company should negotiate for the Distributor to distribute at prices specified by the Company, after consultation with the Distributor. Alternatively, a more reasonable compromise would be for the prices at the three main levels (top-line, mid-line and budget) to be agreed, relative to the prices of other labels.

5.5   Advertising and Promotion

Number of New Records

Where the pressing and distribution agreement relates to a catalogue, the Distributor will wish to ensure that the catalogue continues to expand and for the Company to introduce a specified new number of titles every year. It may also require the Company to replace any deleted titles with new titles. Whether these provisions are appropriate will depend on the commercial circumstances.

Promotion

The agreement will normally require the Company to promote the titles and records and to bear the cost of advertising and promotion. Demand for the records etc will obviously be stimulated by advertising and promotion and this is therefore an important provision for the Distributor because, if the sales are low, the proceeds remaining after payment of the Distributor's distribution fees, commission and expenses may be insufficient to pay the Distributor's manufacturing price.

In such circumstances, the Distributor will be left to recover the amount of the shortfall from the Company. Its chances of recovery of money are likely to be slim if the Company's main business is the exploitation of records and the Distributor is the Company's exclusive distributor—since, in these circumstances, the Company will not be receiving income from other sources and its ability to pay the Distributor will depend entirely on the value of its assets.

The agreement may provide that the Company is to use its best endeavours to promote the titles. Best endeavours obligations may imply an open-ended obligation to spend money. These obligations are frequently negotiated down to reasonable endeavours, or reasonable endeavours in the Company's reasonable discretion. In the circumstances that have been described, there may be little point in the Company negotiating a best endeavours obligation down to a reasonable endeavours obligation, since if the Company fails to promote the records adequately, it may well become insolvent anyway.

Minimum Expenditure

The agreement may provide that, during each year of the term or during the first six months or some other period, the Company is to incur expenditure of a certain minimum amount in connection with advertising and promotion of the titles. It may also require the Company to deliver invoices or receipts or vouchers to the Distributor evidencing such expenditure if the Distributor requests.

In such circumstances, the Company will need to decide whether an obligation on the Company to effect minimum expenditure is appropriate or not, and if it is, to negotiate the amount to spend. If the Company is able to obtain discounts (for example, on air time rate card rates for advertisements etc) it may negotiate for the expenditure to be calculated at rate card rates. That way the amount of the Company's discounts will reduce its cash outlay.

If the Company is required to deliver receipts and invoices etc, it should make sure that the requirement is only to deliver copies. If the Distributor requires a right to inspect and audit the Company's books of account, it should limit their audit right the same way as they will limit the Company's (see Paragraph 1.11).

5.6 Company's Warranties and Undertakings

There are a number of warranties that a Distributor may wish to obtain. They include the following matters.

Ability to Contract

The Distributor will wish to have confirmation that the Company has the right to enter into the agreement and that the Company has not entered into any other arrangement or done anything which would interfere with the rights the Company is giving the Distributor under the agreement.

Ownership and Control

The Distributor will want the Company to warrant that the Company is the sole exclusive absolute unincumbered legal and beneficial owner of all right and title in the records. This is normal. If the Company has granted any rights to third parties they should be disclosed.

Obscenity etc

Nothing contained in the delivery materials or the records is obscene or libellous or defamatory. This is normal.

Originality etc

The exercise by the Distributor of the rights granted to it will not infringe any copyright, right of privacy, right of publicity performer's right, moral right* or any other right.

Quality of Materials

The materials to be delivered to the Distributor will be in first-class condition and of first-class technical quality. The Company will normally wish the Distributor to inspect all materials within a specified number of days after delivery and to give the Company a 30-day period to replace any machines which are defective.

Logo, Trademark and Publicity Material

The Distributor will not incur any liability for use of the Company's name, logo or trademark or the use of any publicity material the Company supplies to it. The Company should doublecheck that there are no restrictions relating to the Company's publicity material. If there are, the Company will have to pass them on to the Distributor.

Credit

The records and publicity material comply with all contractual credit and other obligations owed by third parties. The Company should doublecheck that this is the case. It may be worthwhile for the Company to negotiate a provision to cover the Company in the event of inadvertent failure to comply (along the lines specified in Paragraph 1.13), if circumstances are appropriate.

Refer Orders

Since the Distributor is the Company's exclusive distributor, it will wish the Company to refer any order and enquiries which the Company receives in its exclusive territory to it. This is normal.

Import Duties

The Distributor will not assume liability for import duties and associated costs relating to the delivery of master material. This is normal, but, if the Company is in a different country from the Distributor and the Distributor is responsible for the physical arrangements relating to import, the Company should exclude liability for subsequent costs, including warehousing and transportation fees since these may be exceptional.

Synchronisation and Mechanical Fees

The Distributor will not be liable for any mechanical or synchronisation fees other than at the standard MCPS* or statutory rate. The Distributor may well wish to deduct and pay such mechanical fees direct to the relevant society in order to guarantee that the Company will pay these sums.

Consents and Waivers

All performer's consents and moral rights waivers which are necessary have been obtained and the delivery material records and publicity material comply with all applicable statutory provisions. This is normal.

Copyright Notices

All records and publicity material will contain full and accurate copyright notices. This is normal.

Indemnity

The contract* may contain an indemnity provision. If both parties are corporate entities, an indemnity provision may be acceptable. The Company may, however, wish to exclude or limit the indemnity provisions for the reasons referred to in Paragraph 53.16.

5.7   Distribution Fee and Application of Receipts

The agreement will normally provide that the Distributor is entitled to deduct and retain from all gross sums that it receives from the sale of records, the following sums in the following order:

- Distribution fee (frequently around 20%)
- Distribution expenses
- Manufacturing price.

The Company will wish to control the nature of the distribution expenses and the amounts on which they are expended. Normally, these will be limited to actual direct costs* incurred by the Distributor. If any of these are incurred by the connected party, it should be specified that they are to be calculated on a bona fide arm's length basis. As regards the manufacturing price, the Distributor may reserve the right to change this, but this is a negotiable point.

After the deduction of the above expenses, the Distributor will pay to the Company the balance remaining. Some contracts make the Distributor's obligation to pay the balance conditional on full and continuing performance of all obligations and warranties. This means that, in the event of a non-material breach, the Distributor may be justified in withholding payment of all money. This could obviously be extremely serious for the Company if the breach was incapable of being remedied. The Company should ensure, therefore, that the Distributor's obligation to pay is not conditional. If the Distributor argues that it may suffer loss if the Company is in breach, the Company will point out that the Distributor can recover from the Company for any breach of the Company's warranties.

5.8   Accounts and Payments

Payment Dates

The precise dates on which payments are to be made are a matter of commercial negotiation. They may be payable 15 or 30 or 45 days from the month end to which they relate. The Distributor will wish there to be a lengthier delay. The Company will wish accounting to be as soon after the month as possible.

Statements

The agreement will provide that when payment is made, the Distributor will send statements calculating the balance of gross receipts at the same time.

The Company should enquire as to the precise form of statement the Distributor intends to use, ensure that it contains all the information the Company needs and include it in the agreement as an exhibit.

Some contracts provide that the amounts shown due in statements are conclusive and binding on the parties. Other contracts provide that, if the money is banked, then the statements are binding on the parties. Provisions like this are not normal and are unreasonable. The Company should not accept them.

Books of Account

The agreement should provide that the Distributor will keep full and proper books of account and authorise their inspection and audit. Audit access rights are frequently limited to not more than once per year, subject to reasonable prior notice. This is normal.

A requirement to give not less than 60/30 days' written notice of audit is not reasonable. The Company should resist this. A provision which states that the Distributor will not be in breach if it has failed to account unless it receives a further 30 days' written notice, is also unreasonable and should be resisted.

Confidentiality

The Agreement may provide that the person carrying out the audit will enter into a confidentiality obligation with the Distributor, which may be acceptable, but, if the clause requires the Company to indemnify the Distributor from breach of confidentiality by the Company's professional advisor of their agreement with the Distributor, this is unreasonable.

Value Added Tax

The Agreement should provide that Value Added Tax is payable on sums payable by the Distributor to the Company on receipt of the Company's VAT invoice. The Company must ensure that the contract contains such a provision. If it does not, sums received by the Company will be deemed to include VAT— which will lose the Company about one-third of its turnover.

5.9   Returns

The agreement will contain provisions dealing with goods which are returned on the grounds that they are faulty, or that they have been sent out by the Distributor in error, or because they have been sent out on a sale or return basis. These goods are frequently referred to as "returns".

Reserves

The agreement will provide that the Distributor has the right to reserve a percentage of gross receipts on account of returns. The Company will wish to ensure that the percentage is fixed to a pre-specified amount (ideally no more than 15–25%), that the amounts reserved are held in an interest-bearing account and that the reserves are liquidated and paid to the Company (to the extent they have not been applied towards reimbursement of returns) within a reasonable period of time.

The period during which the reserve is to be liquidated will depend on what is negotiated. It would be normal to expect this period to be between six months and twelve months. The precise length will depend on the balance struck between the parties. An factor which is obviously related will be the actual percentage retained by the Distributor. In this regard, the Company may wish to enquire as to the Distributor's returns history over all its operations in the preceding 12-month period. If this indicates a figure of 15–16%, then a lower reserve percentage may be appropriate. If the money is held in an interest-bearing account, the Company may tolerate a slightly longer period.

The manner in which reserve funds are held may also be of relevance to the Company. If the Distributor is a major international distributor, the Company may take the commercial view that the prospect of its insolvency is remote. If the Company is dealing with a smaller distributor, it needs to think about the possibility that it may become insolvent. If this does happen and the reserve which the Distributor is holding for returns under the agreement is maintained in the Distributor's general bank account, then the reserve is likely to be removed by the Distributor's bank (which may be one of its principal creditors) or even if this is not the case, it will be available for the Distributor's secured creditors.

If the reserved sums are likely to be substantial, it would be strongly advisable for the Company to persuade the Distributor to deposit them in a trust account opened in joint names. If the account is designated as a trust account, the Distributor's bank will have notice of the Company's interest. It is unlikely that the Distributor will agree that the account may be operated only on the joint signature of both parties. A suitable compromise might be for the bank mandate to provide that the account may be operated solely by the Distributor, unless an insolvency type event occurs, at which point, the transfer of any funds from the account would require joint signatories both on the Company's behalf and on the Distributor's behalf. This would preserve funds in the account and should prevent any receiver or liquidator from removing funds without the Company's consent.

Returns Limit

There may be some situations where distribution of the records etc on a sale or return basis might not be appropriate. Equally, this method of distribution might be acceptable up to a specified limit and in this situation, the Company should specify the maximum number of records etc which the Distributor may consign on a sale or return basis during any accounting period.

Commission

Where goods are consigned on a sale or return basis, the Company will need to look at what happens to the commission (or distribution fee) the Distributor has charged if these goods are subsequently returned. Ideally the Company should ensure that the agreement provides that any distribution fees or expenses incurred by the Distributor in relation to these goods are credited to the Company's account. The Distributor, for its part, may wish to make an administration charge to cover the cost of processing the returns. The amount of such a charge is a matter for commercial negotiation. The Company should ensure that no administrative charge is made by the Distributor for dealing with the return of records etc sent in error or returned as faulty goods.

Post-Termination Returns

The agreement may provide that if records etc are returned to the Distributor after the termination of the agreement the Company will pay the amount of any credit to the Distributor on invoicing. Ideally, the Company should amend the agreement to provide that goods will only be accepted for return within a pre-specified date from their original consignment (three to six months). If the agreement ends as a result of the Company terminating because the Distributor is in breach, then the Company may wish to provide that the cost in relation to any returns received after the date of termination is to be borne by the Distributor. Whether this is fair or not will depend on the circumstances. The Company should certainly seek to have the entire amount of any reserve repaid to the Company on termination and this is a further matter for inclusion in the Distributor's bank mandate (see the Reserves section of this paragraph).

5.10 Property and Risk

We have already examined risk in relation to the delivery materials in Paragraph 5.4. From the Company's point of view, one of the key areas in the distribution agreement is the area which deals with the transfer of title (ie ownership) in the manufactured goods (records etc). The Distributor will wish title in all manufactured goods to belong to it until it has received payment in full. If the Distributor is manufacturing goods at its sole expense and is recovering its costs out of gross receipts collected by it from the sale of the manufactured goods, this is not an unreasonable position for the Distributor to take.

The difficulty, however, is that if the Distributor becomes insolvent, the Company's goods will be the property of the Distributor's creditors, and if these creditors are secured, they will receive all the proceeds from the Company's goods and the Company will receive nothing. There is no use in the Company's providing that, if the Distributor becomes insolvent the goods become the Company's, because insolvency immediately transfers all property which the Distributor owns to the Distributor's receiver or liquidator.

The position is further complicated by the fact that the Distributor will be supplying manufactured goods to its customers and these customers themselves may become insolvent. This part of the problem is easy, all that is required is for the Distributor to retain title to the goods it provides its customers, under the terms of its agreement with them. The Company must ensure that the Distributor actually does this and, although it will not be possible for the Company to monitor each and every transaction the Distributor enters into, the Company can at least examine the Distributor's standard terms and conditions of trading to see that these do effectively retain title until the Distributor has received payment for all goods supplied to any customer. This aspect will then be covered, if the agreement contains an undertaking on the Distributor's part that it will only supply goods pursuant to its standard terms of trade.

Insolvency

This leaves the Company with the problem of the Distributor's own insolvency. This is not a paranoid concern on the Company's part, nor is it a remote theoretical possibility. Recent years have seen a number of cases where the insolvency of a distributor has a domino-like effect on its suppliers, who may suddenly be plunged into liquidity through no fault of their own—other than the error of failing to negotiate an adequate distribution agreement. It is therefore vital from the Company's point of view that the Company's agreement with the Distributor satisfies the Company's legitimate concern on this point. If it does not, any mishap which befalls the Distributor might be the Company's undoing as well. If the agreement fails to meet the Company's concern on this point, it will pose an unacceptable commercial risk and, however good the Company feels the Distributor's distribution might be, the Company should think very hard before entering into such a situation.

The solution may be for the Company to agree a credit limit with the Distributor for its manufacturing costs. So long as the Distributor's invoices for manufacturing costs are paid within (say) 90 days and/or so long as the total outstanding manufacturing costs and distribution expenses owed by the Company to the Distributor remain below £/$x (the Company's estimated figure for (say) a calendar quarter) property and title in and to the goods will remain the Company's. If the Company falls behind the Distributor's payment terms or goes over its credit limit, then property in all goods passes to the Distributor, until such time as the Company's outstanding debts are brought back within the agreed terms. If the Company is late or over-runs the Distributor may wish to reduce the total amount of credit or payment time on future instalments, and this line of reasoning might be difficult for the Company to resist. Payment of the Company's distributor's costs and expenses should, however, be one of the Company's top priorities and there is a compelling argument for the Company's bankers to provide the Company with the necessary funds to pay off the Company's manufacturer in order to ensure that the market value of the Company's manufactured stock falls within the scope of the Company's own bankers' security interests, rather than the Company's suppliers' bankers.

Recovered Stock

When the Distributor sells its stock of records etc, it deducts the amount of its distribution fee and distribution expenses from the gross receipts and pays the Company the balance. Because the Distributor's retention of title provisions in its terms of trade are likely to be "all money" provisions (ie retain title to the Distributor until its customers have paid all sums owed), non-payment by one of the Distributor's customers, in theory, entitles the Distributor to repossess all that customer's stock of records etc which have been supplied by the Distributor. Obviously, that stock would include not just the Company's own titles, but all other titles distributed by the Distributor.

There is, therefore, the possibility that even though the Distributor may have paid the Company for all records sold to a particular customer (thereby passing title to the Distributor), the Distributor repossesses copies of the Company's records etc supplied to a customer because of non-payment by the customer of invoices relating to other records etc supplied by the Distributor. The agreement may, therefore, provide that the Distributor is free to sell such items of recovered stock without paying the Company again. This is quite reasonable.

Insurance

The agreement may provide that the Distributor has the right to effect insurance on all records etc at full replacement value, that the cost of such insurance is to be treated as a distribution expense and that the proceeds of the insurance will belong to the Distributor.

It may be more appropriate for the records etc to be insured at their open market value. The Company should negotiate for the Company's interest to be noted on the Distributor's insurance policy as named insured and loss payee. It is not reasonable for the Distributor to state that the proceeds of insurance should belong to the Distributor absolutely. The Company clearly has an interest in the records etc which will be the Company's property subject to the Distributor being paid.

Where the insurance provides that both the Company and the Distributor are to be noted on the insurance, it is unlikely that insurers will effect payment if there is any dispute between the parties. It might, therefore, be sensible for the agreement to specify that the Distributor will have the right to recover out of the insurance proceeds of any goods destroyed, the cost of manufacture of such goods and those distribution expenses which relate to storage, and that the balance is to be paid to the Company.

Inspection

It is normal for a distribution agreement to provide that the owner of the product distributed has the right to inspect warehouses where goods are being stored and carry out a stock inspection on reasonable prior notice.

5.11 Credit Risk

There may be circumstances where the Distributor refuses to supply goods to a customer who, in the opinion of the Distributor, is not a good credit risk. If the order is of a significant size and the Company's assessment of the customer's creditworthiness is different from the Distributor's, the Company might wish to instruct the Distributor to supply the goods.

In such circumstances, the Distributor may require the Company to pay it the invoice value, if the customer fails to pay within the credit limit period, without prejudice to the Distributor's right to recover the invoice value out of the gross receipts remaining after the Distributor has deducted its distribution fee and distribution expenses. This provision is not unreasonable.

It is in both the Distributor's and the Company's own mutual interests for the Distributor to maintain tight credit control over goods supplied. The Company should therefore familiarise itself with the Distributor's credit control procedures.

5.12 Other Product

The agreement may contain a provision giving the Distributor the right of first refusal and a matching offer right in respect of other future product acquired by the Company (see Paragraph 53.7). Whether this is acceptable or not will depend on the circumstances.

5.13 Manufacture and Distribution

The agreement may provide that the Distributor has the right to opt out of distributing any record etc, if it has reasonable grounds for believing that such distribution would constitute or give rise to a breach by the Company of the Company's undertakings in the agreement. Such possible breach could cover a wide variety of matters, such as non-payment of mechanical royalties, infringement of copyright by the goods, obscenity, blasphemy etc.

It is reasonable for the Distributor to have the right to cease distribution of records etc in such terms, although the Company should examine the precise provisions to ensure they are fair. If the Distributor suspends distribution, it would be prudent for the Company to reserve the right to have the goods distributed by a third party or, alternatively to compel the Distributor to distribute the goods if the Distributor's grounds for concern are shown to be inapplicable.

Force Majeure

The agreement may also contain a provision permitting the Distributor to cease distribution on the occurrence of an event of force majeure. If it does, the Company will need to consider the matters referred to in Paragraph 52.5.

Blocked Funds

If the Distributor is in a different country from the Company and is outside the European Economic Area, the agreement may contain a provision that, if the Distributor is unable to transfer any money payable or receivable under the agreement as a result of exchange control restrictions, it would notify the Company and transfer sums into an account designated by the Company (subject to such transfer not violating local laws).

5.14 Breach and Insolvency

The agreement should contain provisions relating to breach or insolvency on behalf of either party. The Company should consider the matters referred to in Paragraph 5.10.

5.15 Consequences of Termination

The agreement may contain a specific clause which deals with the consequences of termination. Practical matters which may be covered are reserves for returns, disposal of existing stock (see Paragraphs 5.10 and 5.11) and the collection of outstanding payments from customers. The Company may also need to consider other matters referred to in Paragraph 53.15.

5.16 Boilerplate

The boilerplate section of a typical distribution agreement will contain the following provisions:

* No obligation (see Paragraph 52.6)
* Notice (see Paragraph 52.8)
* Severability (see Paragraph 52.10)
* Entire agreement (see Paragraph 52.3)
* Waiver (see Paragraph 52.11)
* No partnership (see Paragraph 52.7)
* Governing law (see Paragraph 52.5).

6   Producer's Agreement

6.1   Description of a Producer's Agreement

The agreement pursuant to which a record company engages the services of
a Producer is, after the artist's recording contract (examined in Chapter 1), the
most important agreement* relating to the production of sound recordings.
The parties to this particular agreement are:

- the individual producer* being engaged to collaborate with an artist or group
  in the production of sound recordings (referred to as the "Producer");
- and the company engaging the Producer (referred to as the "Company").

This Chapter examines the provisions of the Producer's Agreement from
the point of view of the Producer or the Producer's legal advisors.

6.2   Transaction Analysis

A typical Producer's contract* might be expected to contain the following
clauses:

- Engagement (see Paragraph 6.3)
- Grant of Rights (see Paragraph 6.4)
- Producer's warranties* and obligations (see Paragraph 6.5)
- Advances* (see Paragraph 6.6)
- Royalties* (see Paragraph 6.7)
- Royalty accounting (see Paragraph 6.8)
- Credit suspension (see Paragraph 6.9)
- Effect of suspension (see Paragraph 6.10)
- Termination (see Paragraph 6.11)
- Effect of termination (see Paragraph 6.12)
- Boilerplate* (see Paragraph 6.13)

6.3 Engagement

The first issue falling to be considered from a Producer's point of view is: who engages the Producer? In some situations, the offer to engage the Producer may come from the artist. It is more advantageous if the Producer is engaged directly by the artist's record company. In circumstances where the Producer is required to be engaged direct by the artist, the Producer should insist on the record company entering into a contractual obligation to pay the Producer direct. The Producer should also ensure that advances paid to the artist are not recouped from royalties payable to the Producer.

The terms of the engagement normally require the Producer to render services to the record company. The scope and nature of the services should be defined and if the Producer is required to render services on an exclusive basis it may be advisable, from a Producer's point of view, to insert a maximum number of days or weeks, in order to avoid the Producer being tied into the contract for a long time because of difficulties with the artist completing their recordings.

A Producer will normally be required to render their services in accordance with a recording schedule. Obviously, the Producer should approve this schedule. The Company may reserve the right to specify the location at which the services are to be rendered. It is to be expected that the Producer will have fixed views over what studios are acceptable or suitable and they may, therefore, wish the contract to identify specific studios or require the Company to engage studios in the town or city in which the Producer resides.

Since the Producer alone will not be in a position to ensure completion of the recordings within the time limit specified in the recording schedule, the contract should make it clear that the Producer is not liable for any failure to complete within the scheduled time, if such failure is attributable to the artists whom the Producer is producing.

The agreement may require the Producer to use their best endeavours to ensure that the sound recordings are produced in accordance with the recording schedule and that the costs of production do not exceed the budget. Because such matters are likely to be outside the Producer's control, the Producer may wish to specify that any such obligation will be without financial liability on the Producer's part.

The final matter relating to the engagement of the Producer's services is the question of producing remixes. It is common for records to be remixed a number of times and it may be appropriate for the Producer to insist on a contractual obligation on the Company to use the services of the Producer if remixes are required. Quite apart from the artistic grounds which the Producer may have for requesting such a clause, there are commercial reasons justifying it, since many Royalty Break* provisions reduce the Producer's royalties pro rata to the number of tracks produced (see Paragraph 6.7).

6.4   Grant of Rights

The agreement will normally provide that the Company is the owner of the entire copyright in the services of the Producer. Frequently, Producers' agreements contain an acknowledgment that the work carried out by the Producer has been effected on a *"work made for hire"* basis. This is a concept which exists under US copyright law and will effectively mean that the Company is the first owner of any copyright work produced by the Producer's services. Whether these provisions are acceptable for the Producer will depend on the circumstances. If the Producer is contributing to the arrangement or revision of musical works, then the Producer may be the co-author of the music written by the artist. If this is the case, although it may be perfectly acceptable for the Company to own the copyright in the sound recordings, the Producer might not wish to have the copyright in the musical works written by the Producer assigned to the Company. The agreement should be amended to reflect the fact that such rights are reserved to the Producer. In practice, they may be dealt with by a separate music publishing arrangement (see Chapter 2).

The agreement may also contain an acknowledgment from the Producer that the Company has been responsible for making all arrangements for the production of the sound recordings. The purpose of this provision is to confirm the ownership of copyright in the sound recordings belongs to the Company. Under the laws of the United Kingdom, the "author" of a sound recording is the person by whom the arrangements for the making of the sound recording were made and the author is the first owner of copyright. Any provision confirming this fact should be acceptable to a Producer.

The grant of rights clause may also contain a provision pursuant to which the Producer will be asked to waive all their moral rights in relation to the sound recording. Again, there is no objection to such a provision from a Producer's point of view because, in fact, moral rights do not subsist in sound recordings. Where a Producer is contributing to the writing of musical works, moral rights* will exist in relation to the compositions which have been co-written or arranged by the Producer and they should consider carefully the matters referred to in the moral rights section of Paragraph 2.5.

Most Producer's Agreements will contain a provision entitling the Company to use the name, likeness and biography of the Producer for the full period of copyright in the sound recordings in order to assist the Company to exploit the sound recordings. The Producer may wish to place restrictions on the Company having any merchandising rights.

6.5   Producers' Warranties and Obligations

There are a number of warranties that the Company will wish to obtain from the Producer. These include the following matters.

Ability to Contract

The Company will want to know that the Producer is the sole and absolute owner of all rights granted to the Company and that the Producer has the capacity to grant the rights to the Company and is not under any restriction or prohibition which might interfere with the Producer's obligations under the contract.

Copyright Status

The Company will generally want to ensure that copyright subsists in the Producer's services. This is normally determined by the Producer's nationality or residence and is very rarely a problem for anyone living or working in the western world.

No Conflict

The Producer will normally be required to warrant that they have not entered into any arrangement which might conflict with the recording contract. Any recording (see Paragraph 1.9) will, therefore, need to be disclosed.

Originality etc

The contract will normally contain a warranty that the services of the Producer are not obscene or defamatory and are original to the Producer.

Non-infringement

The contract will normally contain a warranty that the services of the Producer and their product do not infringe any right of copyright or any other right of any other person.

Right to Use/Adapt

The contract will normally contain a warranty that the Company has the right to use, adapt, change, delete from, add to/rearrange material produced by the Producer to the extent it wishes. The Producer may have concerns in relation to derogatory treatment (see Paragraph 1.5)

Rearrangement

Some contracts contain an acknowledgement on the part of the Producer that, if the Producer rearranges any work, they will not be entitled to receive performance royalties from the Performing Right Society Limited (see Paragraph 1.7).

Return of Property

Some contracts contain provisions requiring the Producer to return any property of the Company lent to the Producer or which is in the possession of the Producer at the end of the recording schedule.

No expenditure

Although a Producer's contract does not normally give the Producer the right to make expenditure on behalf of the Company, some contracts contain a specific provision excluding this possibility—presumably in the light of experience.

Unions and work permits

Many Producers' contracts contain a warranty that the Producer is a member of the appropriate union (Musicians Union or Equity etc) and confirm that the Producer will obtain all the necessary work permits required in order to enable the Company to make use of the Producer's services. If the Producer is engaging in foreign travel at the request of the Company, it may be reasonable for the Producer to shift the burden of obtaining work permits onto the Company.

Non-disclosure

Most Producers' contracts will contain a confidentiality provision requiring the Producer not to disclose information, except to their professional advisors.

Publicity

Some contracts contain an express restriction, preventing the Producer issuing any publicity relating to records. This type of restriction may be reasonable pre-release. A general restriction on the Producer participating in any interview or any other publicity without the Company's consent is, however, unreasonable.

Whereabouts

An obligation to keep the Company informed of the Producer's address, telephone number and whereabouts may also be included and is not unreasonable.

Legal Advice

The Company is normally concerned to see that the Producer has obtained legal advice from a solicitor specialising in this type of agreement. This provision is designed to insulate the Company from claims that the contract is voidable.

Indemnity

Some recording contracts seek to impose indemnity* obligations on the Producer. These obligations are capable of being unfair and oppressive and should always be resisted by individuals for the reasons referred to in Paragraph 53.16.

6.6 Advances

The Producer's agreement will normally provide that the Company is to pay the Producer an advance against a royalty entitlement. From the Producer's point of view, the advance represents a fee payable to the Producer for the work carried out in producing the recordings.

If the Producer is engaged directly by the record company, they will view the remuneration payable to the Producer as part of a total remuneration package payable in connection with the sound recordings being produced. This remuneration package will also include advances payable to the artists and the cost of production.

For budgetary purposes, the Company may wish to ensure that the Producer is to be responsible for any overcost in producing the sound recordings. The Producer will normally wish to resist any such provision In those circumstances where a Producer concedes that the Company has the right to recover excess costs of production, the Producer will need to ensure that the Company does not have the right to recover the entire excess cost both from the artists and the Producer. Additionally, the Producer may wish to limit the Producer's responsibility to the proportion of the excess costs represented by the Producer's share of advance royalty, over the total advance in royalty payable to the artists and all other persons. Finally, since the position of the Producer will be that any overcost is normally the result of the artists or factors beyond the Producer's control, once the excess cost has been recovered, the Producer will wish the royalty entitlement to be restated retrospectively in such a way that the amount of royalty income which the Producer has deferred, while the Company is recovering, the excess cost is paid to the Producer as soon as the excess costs have been recovered. In practice, this may require the Company ensuring its agreement with the artists permits the Company to deduct this type of payment to the Producer from the artists' royalty payments.

It is, however, normal for the Company to expect any advance it pays to the Producer to be recoupable from royalties. It is, therefore, important, from the Producer's point of view to ensure that the amount of their advance bears the same proportion to the total advance payable to the artists as the proportion borne by the Producer's royalty to the total royalty.

If the proportions are different, a situation will arise where the Producer has an advance which has been recouped before the artists' advance and this may cause difficulties, since the record company may object to paying the Producer royalties when it has not recouped the artists' advance.

To illustrate this, if we suppose the artists receive an advance of £150,000 against a 15% royalty, and the Producer receives an advance of £30,000 against a 3% royalty, there will be no problem because recoupment will occur at exactly the same point. Even where the Producer, and the artists' advances and royalties are proportionate to each other, a complication may arise if the Company has the right to recover "overages*" in production costs from the artists, but not from the Producer. This is a further area which needs to be considered.

6.7 Royalties

The royalty rate which may generally be expected by a Producer is normally between 1% and 3%. There will, however, be circumstances where it may be appropriate for the Producer to be paid a flat fee, as opposed to a royalty, or to receive a royalty rate higher than 3%. Record companies generally include in their royalty provisions a number of royalty breaks, these are examined in Paragraph 1.10.

The standard pro rata break is a particular importance to the Producer. This is the provision which provides that, if not all the tracks on the sound recordings have been produced by the Producer, then the Producer's royalty entitlement will abate rateably. In the case of a single, this means that, if the Producer produces the 'A' side but not the 'B' side, (s)he will receive only 50% of the royalties. From a Producer's point of view, this is unfair since most people will buy a single for the 'A' side, not for the 'B' side, and the Producer will generally wish to ask the Company for 'A Side Protection' which will guarantee the Producer the full royalty entitlement, irrespective of whether all tracks on the album or single have been produced by the Producer.

6.8 Royalty Accounting

See Paragraph 1.12.

6.9 Credit

See Paragraph 1.14.

6.10 Suspension

See Paragraph 1.16.

6.11 Termination

See Paragraph 1.18.

6.12 Effect of Termination

See Paragraph 1.18.

6.13 Boilerplate

The boilerplate section of a typical recording contract will contain the following provisions:

*   No obligation (see Paragraph 52.6)
*   Notice (see Paragraph 52.8)
*   Severability (see Paragraph 52.10)
*   Entire agreement (see Paragraph 52.3)
*   Waiver (see Paragraph 52.11)
*   No Partnership (see Paragraph 52.7)
*   Governing law (see Paragraph 52.5).

7 Promo Production Agreement

7.1 Description of a Promo Production Agreement

A promo production agreement* is used in circumstances where a record company is commissioning an audio-visual producer* to produce a promo video.
The parties to this transaction are:

- the production company being commissioned to produce the promo video by the record company—referred to as the "Producer"; and
- the recording company entering into the agreement with the Producer—referred to as the "Company".

This Chapter examines the provisions of a promo production agreement from the point of view of the Producer or its legal advisors.

7.2 Transaction Analysis

A typical Promo Production Agreement might be expected to contain the following clauses:

- Production (see Paragraph 7.3)
- Rights (see Paragraph 7.4)
- Payments (see Paragraph 7.5)
- Producer's Obligations and Warranties* (see Paragraph 7.6)
- Company's Obligations and Warranties (see Paragraph 7.7)
- Boilerplate* (see Paragraph 7.8).

7.3 Production

The Agreement will normally specify what facilities and services are to be provided by the Producer at what locations or studio during a production period in accordance with an agreed production schedule, in order to produce and deliver to the Company certain delivery material.

The definitions of all these matters need to be examined closely by the Producer in order to ensure that the Producer can comply with their obligations. This is particularly important where, as is normally the case, the Producer is required to commit to produce prespecified material for a fixed budget. If there is any cost overrun, the Company will expect the Producer to bear the excess cost out of the Producer's own resources. It is obviously in the Producer's interests to identify those circumstances where additional costs may be incurred as a result of the actions of the Company, or the artists concerned, and make provision for such costs to be reimbursed to the Producer.

7.4   Rights

Copyright, Moral Rights and Performer's Rights

The agreement will normally provide that the Company is to be the owner of the entire copyright in the material produced and the product of the Producers' services. This provision is quite normal and acceptable.

Additionally, the rights clause will normally provide for a confirmation on the part of the Producer that it has waived any and all moral rights* and also obtained all necessary consents from performers. If, however, the services of performers and other artists have been available to the Producer by the Company, then this provision will be inappropriate and the Producer will normally look to the Company providing confirmation that it has obtained all necessary consents in relation to services of performances.

This provision is necessary because under the laws prevailing in the European Economic Area, performers are entitled to rights in relation to their performances and, where their consents have not been obtained, they may be able to restrain the distribution of recordings incorporating their performances.

Right to Use/Adapt

The agreement will normally contain an acknowledgement that the Company has the right to use, adapt, change, delete from, add to, amend or rearrange the material to the extent the Company wishes. Whether or not this provision is appropriate will depend on the circumstances. The Producer may in some circumstances wish to limit the Company's right to edit the material to time segmenting or censorship or foreign language provisions. Whether this is acceptable will depend on the circumstances.

Equally, the Producer may require the Company to give it the first opportunity to amend the video material. There may also be circumstances where the Producer's production agreement with the Director contains obligations (such as the director's cut etc) which need to be passed along to the Company.

Production Contracts

The agreement will normally provide that the Producer will use production contracts* which have been approved by the Companies. This approval right is required in order to reassure the Company that the Producer has obtained all necessary rights from third parties. The production contracts should contain an acknowledgement from all persons providing services or giving performances that the payment they have received constitutes equitable remuneration* (see Paragraph 53.6). The Company may also wish the principal director of the promo video to enter into a direct letter of confirmation with the Company confirming the transfer of various rights. This requirement is not unreasonable.

7.5 Payment

The agreement should provide that the Company will pay the Producer an amount equal to the budget in accordance with the agreed cash-flow schedule. The Producer will need also to ensure that the Company undertakes to pay the Producer VAT on the amount of the budget, since if the contractual agreement makes no reference to the VAT, amounts in the agreement are deemed to be inclusive of VAT.

7.6 Producer's Warranties and Undertakings

There are a number of warranties* that the Company will wish to obtain, including the following.

Ability to Contract

The Company will wish the Producer to confirm it has the right to enter into the agreement and has not entered into any other arrangement which might conflict with it.

Ownership of Copyright

The Producer is the absolute owner of copyright in the material and has obtained from the principal director an assignment of all rights of copyright. The Producer is the sole, absolute, unincumbered legal and beneficial owner of the copyright of the material.

Confidentiality

The Producer will not reveal any financial or other confidential information in relation to the promo video.

Copyright Notices

All copies of the promo video will contain a copyright notice in accordance with the Universal Copyright Convention provisions, naming the Company as the copyright owner.

Compliance with Directions

The Producer will consult with the Company and follow its directions at all times during the production schedule.

Originality

The promo video will be original to the Producer, except to the extent it is based on materials supplied by the Company, and will not be obscene libellous, blasphemous or defamatory or infringe any right of copyright or any other right.

Compliance with Regulations

The promo video will comply with all rules and regulations, including rules of studios, guilds, trade alliances etc.

Technical Standards

All delivery materials will be in first-class condition and of first-class quality suitable for exploitation without further expenditure.

Compliance with Guidelines

The promo video will not infringe any guidelines of the Independent Television Commission, the British Broadcasting Corporation, the British Board of Film Classification or any other relevant body.

Synchronisation of the Mechanical Fees

The Producer will deliver the material free and clear of any and all synchronisation and mechanical fees. Here, in practice, the Producer may require confirmation from the Company that the Company has licensed, the Producer the right to use performances of the artists (if they are signed to the Company) and the right to incorporate in the video all musical works whose copyrights may be controlled by the Company or its associated music publishing company.

Consents

The Producer has obtained all necessary waivers and consents in relation to the production of the material.

Credits

The promo video will contain only those credits approved by the Company.

Insurance

The Producer will take out and keep in force insurance policies approved by the Company.

Other Arrangements

The Producer will, if requested by the Company, produce copies of all agreements with studios, locations and facilities.

Indemnity

The contract may contain an indemnity provision. The Producer may, however, wish to exclude or limit such indemnity provision, for the reasons referred to in Paragraph 53.16.

7.7 Company's Warranties

There are a number of matters where the Producer will wish to obtain warranties on the part of the Company, including the following.

Rights

Where artists are signed to a record company and the record company's associated music publishing company controls rights in material written by the artists, the Producer will require the publishing company to issue a synchronisation licence* permitting the use of the material which it controls in the promo video. The Producer will also require the Company to consent to the making of recordings featuring the artist's services.

Ongoing Obligations

The Producer may be required to enter into agreements with persons rendering services in the promo which contain ongoing obligations on the part of the Producer. If this is the case, the Producer will require confirmation from the Company that it will comply with these ongoing obligations.

Confirmation

The Producer may require additional confirmations from the Company in relation to insurance matters and other practical arrangements relating to the production of the video.

7.8   Boilerplate

The boilerplate section of a typical distribution agreement will contain the following provisions:

*   No obligation (see Paragraph 52.6)
*   Notice (see Paragraph 52.8)
*   Severability (see Paragraph 52.10)
*   Entire agreement (see Paragraph 52.3)
*   Waiver (see Paragraph 52.11)
*   Partnership (see Paragraph 52.7)
*   Governing law (see Paragraph 52.5).

8 Promo Artist's Agreement

8.1 Description of a Promo Artist Agreement

The promo artist's agreement* provides the Company producing a promo video with the services of the artist and all necessary rights in the products of services.

Normally, a company making a promo video will acquire the services of the main featured artists direct from the record company entitled to their exclusive services. There will, however, be additional artists whose services need to be engaged, eg backing singers, musicians, dancers etc, and it is with such persons that the company producing the promo will wish to enter into a promo artist's agreement.

The parties to this particular transaction are:

* the artist or artists whose services have been required by the promo production company (referred to as the "Artist"); and
* the production company engaging the service of the artist (referred to as the "Company").

8.2 Transaction Analysis

A typical promo artist's agreement might be expected to contain the following clauses:

* Engagement (see Paragraph 8.3)
* Payment (see Paragraph 8.4)
* Rights (see Paragraph 8.5)
* Undertakings (see Paragraph 8.6)
* Boilerplate* (see Paragraph 8.7).

8.3 Engagement

The Company will need to specify the services required of the Artist, whether they are required on an exclusive or non-exclusive basis, the dates, times and venues at which the Artist is required to be present and, in some cases, it may be necessary to specify what works are to be performed in the promo video.

8.4   Payment

The agreement will need to specify the fee to which the Artist is entitled. The Company will wish the payment provision to confirm that the remuneration received by the Artist constitutes equitable remuneration (see Paragraph 53.6). Normally, the Company will wish the fee to be a flat fee paid on a buy-out* basis.

8.5   Rights

The Company will need obtain an assignment by the Artist of the copyright in respect of the product of the Artist's services and will need confirmation of the grant of all consents which are required in order to exploit the Artist's performances.

8.6   Undertakings

The Artist will normally be required by the Company to confirm that the Artist is free to enter into the agreement, to agree to keep all matters connected with the promo video confidential and to agree that the Artist is not entitled to any screen credit in relation to the performance. There may also be circumstances where it might be appropriate to impose on the Artist a recording bar*— effectively barring the Artist from re-recording any of the material recorded within a specified period.

8.7   Boilerplate

The boilerplate* of a typical promo artist's agreement will contain the following provisions:

*   Partnership (see Paragraph 52.7)
*   Governing law (see Paragraph 52.5).

9   Sub-Publishing Agreement

9.1   Description of a Sub-Publishing Agreement

A sub-publishing agreement is used in circumstances where a company wishes
to use the services of a sub-publisher in a foreign territory to oversee the
exploitation of music copyrights owned by the company.

The parties to this particular transaction are:

- the publishing company which owns the rights in compositions—referred to
  as the "Company"; and
- the foreign publisher who has agreed to assist the company exploit its
  compositions in the foreign publisher's territory—referred to as the "Sub-
  Publisher".

This chapter examines the provisions of a sub-publishing agreement* from
the point of view of the Company or its legal advisors.

9.2   Transaction Analysis

A typical sub-publishing agreement might be expected to contain the following
clauses:

- Engagement (see Paragraph 9.3)
- Grant of rights (see Paragraph 9.4)
- Cover versions* (see Paragraph 9.5)
- Reserved rights (see Paragraph 9.6)
- Warranties* (see Paragraph 9.7)
- Copyright (see Paragraph 9.8)
- Other composers (see Paragraph 9.9)
- Advance and royalties* (see Paragraph 9.10)
- Accounting (see Paragraph 9.11)
- Determination (see Paragraph 9.12)
- Effect of determination (see Paragraph 9.13)
- Previous publisher (see Paragraph 9.14)
- Boilerplate* (see Paragraph 9.15).

9.3 Engagement

The agreement will specify what services are to be provided by the Sub-Publisher, identify whether there are any key personnel who are to provide them and identify the territory and term* in which the services are to be provided.

The Company may also require that the Sub-Publisher and the personnel make themselves available for meetings and conferences and may make it a requirement that key personnel* are at all times engaged by the Sub-Publisher during the term.

9.4 Grant of Rights

The precise description of the rights to be granted to the Sub-Publisher will depend on the Company's arrangements. Generally, however, the Company will wish to retain control of exploitation of certain rights in the compositions it owns and the rights licensed by the Company may include the following:

Publication

The Sub-Publisher may be granted the exclusive right to print and publish printed copies of the compositions.

Mechanical

The Company will generally wish to give to the Sub-Publisher the non-exclusive right to grant licences for mechanical reproduction of compositions (on vinyl discs, video discs etc) in the territory.

Performing Rights

The performing rights in the compositions will normally have been assigned to the PRS* or one of its analogous organisations as a result of the composer's membership of such a society. It will not, therefore, be possible for the Company to give the Sub-Publisher the exclusive performing rights in the compositions in the territory. The Company may, however, grant the Sub-Publisher the right to grant non-exclusive licenses for public performance of compositions subject to the rights of the PRS and its affiliated societies. The Company will probably wish to exclude the Sub-Publisher having the right to grant licences for satellite broadcasting in the territory, since such broadcasting may extend into neighbouring Sub-Publishers' territories.

Synchronisation

Normally, the Company will wish to retain the right to grant synchronisation licences* of compositions, authorising their use in synchronisation with, and in timed relation to, moving pictures. The agreement may, however, provide that the Sub-Publisher is to have the right to issue synchronisation licenses for productions produced in the territory with the prior consent of the Company.

Cover Versions

The Sub-Publisher will generally have the right to make and publish cover versions* (see below).

9.5 Cover Versions

The provisions relating to cover versions are of extreme importance. A cover version is normally a foreign local language version or adaptation of the original composition which will have been procured by the Sub-Publisher.

Since the commercial objective behind the Sub-Publishing arrangement is for the Sub-Publisher to exploit the Company's compositions to the maximum in the Sub-Publisher's territory, the making of arrangements for cover versions is of fundamental importance.

Normally the Company will permit the Sub-Publisher to commission revised material, such as foreign language lyrics or (maybe) revised arrangements of the original compositions, but the Company will wish to limit the amount by which the performance income, in relation to the compositions, is reduced by their cover version use. For this reason, the Sub-Publishing agreement provides that where revised material is commissioned by the Sub-Publisher, the Sub-Publisher and any new composer will not be entitled to participate in more than two-twelfths of the public performance fees (following the rules of the PRS, these are always calculated in twelfths).

Similarly, the Company will need to provide a mechanism to enable a cover version which has been produced in one territory (say Spain) to be exploited in other Sub-Publishers' territories (say South America). For this reason the agreement may also provide that, where revised material is commissioned by the Sub-Publisher, the Sub-Publisher will ensure the transfer of all rights of copyright in that material to the Company, subject to the right of the Sub-Publisher to use the material for the Sub-Publisher's territory. The agreement assigning the rights will contain the usual warranties as to originality, non-infringement etc.

9.6 Reserved Rights

The Sub-Publishing agreement will normally provide that the Company will reserve exclusively a number of rights. The reserved rights will normally include:

- the exclusive right to make literary, dramatic and musical versions of the compositions and to license their exploitation (by way of musicals etc)

throughout the Sub-Publisher's territory;
- the exclusive right to license the use of the titles of the compositions throughout the Sub-Publisher's territory;
- the exclusive right to grant synchronisation licenses in relation to the compositions throughout the world, including the Sub-Publisher's territory.

It is also normal practice to reserve all rights other than those specifically granted.

9.7   Warranties

There are a number of warranties that a Company will wish to obtain from a Sub-Publisher, including the following matters.

Ability to Contract

The Sub-Publisher has the right to enter into the agreement, has not entered into any conflicting arrangement and is not under any contractual prohibition which will prevent the Sub-Publisher from rendering services.

Confidentiality

The Sub-Publisher will not disclose or reveal any information relating to the Company or the agreement.

No Assignment

The Sub-Publisher will not assign or sub-license or otherwise part with possession of the agreement.

PRS

A Sub-Publisher is, and will remain during the term, a member of the local performing right organisation and will be in good standing with that organisation.

Key Personnel

The Sub-Publisher will remain entitled to the services of the key personnel throughout the term.

No Poaching

The Sub-Publisher will not, within the three-year period following expiry of the term, enter into any arrangement with any composers of the compositions.

Statements

The Sub-Publisher will send the Company duplicate copies of all statements received from local mechanical and performing societies.

Enforcement

The Sub-Publisher will protect and enforce the copyrights in the compositions.

Prevailing Rates

The Sub-Publisher will not license exploitation of the compositions at less than prevailing rates.

Maximisation of Receipts

The Sub-Publisher will use its best endeavours to maximise the receipts derived from the compositions in the territory during the term.

Indemnity

The Sub-Publisher will indemnify the Company in relation to the performance by the Sub-Publisher of its obligations in the agreement.

9.8 Copyright

The sub-publishing agreement needs to contain a mechanism so that the Sub-Publisher is advised on a regular basis of any new copyrights acquired by the Company. The agreement may provide that the Sub-Publisher is to receive copies of lead sheets or demo tapes.

Conversely, where the Sub-Publisher publishes an edition or procures a recording, the agreement will provide that the Company is sent copies of the published edition or copies of released records or cassettes.

Another fairly fundamental copyright obligation is the registration of all compositions in the name of the Company by the Sub-Publisher with local performing right societies and mechanical collecting societies and other trade bodies or copyright registries in the territory. The agreement may provide that the Sub-Publisher has to effect such registrations within a stated period of time.

The final copyright obligation which is normally found in sub-publishing agreements is an obligation on the Sub-Publisher to print the name of the Company and the composer on each printed edition of the compositions and to ensure that such details appear on all records and discs released in the territory.

9.9 Other Composers

One provision which may be found in certain sub-publishing agreements is a provision relating to the acquisition by the Company of rights in compositions by new composers. There may be circumstances where a Company has the opportunity of acquiring rights in compositions from a composer on terms which are not compatible with the Company's agreement with its Sub-Publishers.

For this reason, it is sometimes useful to incorporate in sub-publishing agreements a provision under which the Company will give the Sub-Publisher notice of any adjustments which are required to be made in order to permit the Company to enter into an agreement with the relevant composer. If the Sub-Publisher fails within a stated time to consent to the amendment, the Company will have the right to seek another Sub-Publisher in the territory.

9.10 Advance and Royalties

The agreement will normally provide for the Sub-Publisher to pay the Company an advance in return for being appointed as Sub-Publisher for the territory.

The agreement will also require the Sub-Publisher to pay to the Company a percentage of receipts derived from various types of exploitation. The following percentages may be appropriate:

* in respect of printed editions, 10% of the marked retail selling price
* in respect of receipts from mechanical exploitation: 80%
* in respect of receipts from performance exploitation: 100% subject to a right on the part of the Sub-Publisher to receive 20% of performance income derived from the publisher's share of compositions remitted from the territory during the term.
* in respect of receipts from the exercise of the synchronisation rights: 20%
* in respect of receipts derived from cover versions: 50%
* in respect of all other receipts: 80%.

There are occasions where the Sub-Publisher may be in receipt of unidentifiable income (sometimes referred to as "black box" income*) and the agreement may provide for the Sub-Publisher to pay to the Company such proportion of black box income as is represented by a fraction, the numerator of which is the total derived from the Company's compositions and the denominator is the total derived from all compositions exploited by the Sub-Publisher during the relevant period.

9.11 Accounting

The agreement will normally provide that the Sub-Publisher has to maintain books of account which the Company can inspect, audit and take copies of.

If the Company discovers any error in the Sub-Publisher's books on inspection and the error is excess of 5% or 10% to the Company's detriment, it will expect the Sub-Publisher to pay the cost of the audit.

The agreement will also need to contain a currency conversion provision. If exchange control provisions prevent the remittance to the Company of money, the agreement will normally provide that the Sub-Publisher is to pay the money into an account in the name of the Company in the territory. Where withholding taxes* are deducted, the agreement may provide that it is the responsibility of the Sub-Publisher to ensure that no improper deductions are made.

A major consideration in any sub-publishing arrangement is the financial stability of the Sub-Publisher. If the Sub-Publisher becomes insolvent during the term of the agreement, in view of the fact that the music industry accounts on a bi-annual basis, the Company might risk losing six months' revenue. A possible solution is to require the Sub-Publisher to establish a collection account in the joint names of the Company and the Sub-Publisher, and direct all licensees to make payments into such account. The bank at which the account is maintained can be given standing written directions on how the income is to be applied (what percentage the Sub-Publisher may retain) or, alternatively, the Sub-Publisher and the Company can sign a joint direction when the accounts due to each party have been calculated twice per year. This procedure will at least ensure that the Company's money is not used for the benefit of the Sub-Publisher's creditors, even if it does not guarantee payment into the account of all relevant income.

9.12 Determination

The agreement will provide for a number of events entitling the Company to determine the agreement. Events entitling the Company to terminate are as follows.

Non-payment

Failure to pay on the due date and remedy within five days following notice.

Material Breach

Any breach by the Sub-Publisher of a material term which is incapable of remedy or any other term which is not remedied within 30 days of notice.

Misrepresentation

Any misrepresentation made by the Sub-Publisher at the time or before entering into the agreement is incorrect.

Disposal of Material Assets

Any disposal or threatened disposal by Sub-Publisher of a substantial part of its assets.

Abandonment of Business

The abandonment by the Sub-Publisher of the business of exploiting compositions.

Indebtedness

Any indebtedness is not discharged on the due date or the Sub-Publisher is in breach of any guarantee.

Insolvency

The Sub-Publisher is declared, or becomes insolvent, or convenes a meeting with its creditors or has a receiver or administrator or administrative receiver or liquidator or other similar officer appointed.

9.13 Effect of Determination

If the Company effects determination of the Sub-Publishing agreement all its rights previously licensed to the Sub-Publisher revert to the Company, normally without further formality, but the Sub-Publisher remains liable to account to the Company in relation to 100% of receipts received by the publisher after termination. Additionally, the Company will normally have the right to appoint another Sub-Publisher or agent in the territory immediately .

Where the sub-publishing agreement runs its full course and expires, as opposed to being terminated, it is normal for the Sub-Publisher to have a right to collect income which has arisen during the term for a period of 12 months after expiry of the term*.

9.14 Previous Publisher

Because it is normal practice to allow that, where a Sub-Publishing agreement expires, as opposed to being determined, the Sub-Publisher has the right to collect income arising in the territory during the term of the arrangement, when a Company appoints a new Sub-Publisher in a territory, it will need to make express provision in order to preserve the right of its former Sub-Publisher to collect income which arose before the date of appointment of the new Sub-Publisher.

9.15 Boilerplate

The boilerplate section of a typical sub-publishing agreement will contain the following provisions:

*   No obligation (see Paragraph 52.6)
*   Notice (see Paragraph 52.8)
*   Severability (see Paragraph 52.10)
*   Entire agreement (see Paragraph 52.3)
*   Waiver (see Paragraph 52.11)
*   No partnership (see Paragraph 52.7)
*   Governing law (see Paragraph 52.5).

10 Administration Agreement

10.1 Description of an Administration Agreement

An administration agreement* is an arrangement where the owner of copyright in musical works who lacks the expertise or the resources or time to exploit the musical works, appoints a third party administrator to manage and exploit the owner's musical copyrights.

An administration agreement differs from a sub-publishing agreement in that it is not uncommon for the owner of copyright in musical compositions to appoint one administrator to take care of the owner's copyrights on a world-wide basis, whereas a sub-publishing agreement is normally entered into on a territory-by-territory basis. Indeed, it may be that an administrator appointed in relation to a catalogue of compositions may then secure their exploitation by a series of sub-publishing agreements on a world-wide basis. The parties to this particular transaction are:

- the owner of the compositions being administrated—referred to as the "Company"; and
- the entity administrating the compositions—referred to as the "Administrator".

10.2 Transaction Analysis

A typical administration agreement might be expected to contain the following clauses:

- Engagement (see Paragraph 10.4)
- Authorisation (see Paragraph 10.5)
- Reserved Rights (see Paragraph 10.6)
- Administrator's undertakings and agreements (see Paragraph 10.7)
- Copyright (see Paragraph 10.8)
- Payment (see Paragraph 10.9)
- Accounts (see Paragraph 10.10)
- Determination (see Paragraph 10.11)
- Effect of Determination (see Paragraph 10.12)
- Boilerplate* (see Paragraph 10.13).

10.3 Engagement

The engagement will require the Administrator to render to the Company certain pre-specified services for the term* of the agreement. The Company will define the services which are to be performed by the Administrator, so that they fit in with the Company's requirements, and may require the services of the Administrator and certain specified key personnel* in connection with the recording, broadcasting, publication and exploitation by all means possible of compositions controlled by the Company in the territory specified in the agreement during its term.

The Company will require the Administrator and any key personnel to consult with the Company and give good faith consideration to the Company's views as to how the compositions will be exploited. It should be remembered here that the Company is relying on the Administrator's ability and knowledge of the industry and it may be inappropriate to require the Administrator to follow the directions of the Company at all times.

10.4 Authorisation

The agreement will specify the precise ambit of the Administrator's authority. The Administrator will normally have the exclusive right to negotiate licences to exploit the compositions which are the subject of the agreement. Whether or not the Administrator is empowered to execute agreements on behalf of the Company will depend on the terms negotiated between the parties. If the Administrator is empowered to execute agreements on behalf of the Company, it will normally wish the fact that it is acting as agent on behalf of the Company to be disclosed to the licensee. It is also advisable from the Administrator's point of view for all licence agreements to state the fact that the Administrator is acting as agent for the Company and for the attestation clause to read "Signed by [Name of Individual], for and on behalf of [Name of Administrator] acting as the lawfully appointed agent of [Name of Company]".

Where the Administrator is acting as agent on behalf of the Company, the Administrator itself will be immune from all legal actions brought against it as a result of any breach of warranty or non-performance on the part of the Company. This position should be contrasted with the situation where the Administrator itself acquires an assignment or licence of rights from the Company and then licences these rights to third parties acting in its own right, not as agent of the Company. In such circumstances, the Administrator will be liable for any breach or non-performance in relation to the rights.

The Administrator will also wish to have the right to inspect and audit books and records of licensees. As a matter of convenience, the Company will normally wish the Administrator to exercise these rights on its behalf, since it will be acting in reliance on the Administrator's expertise in managing rights portfolios and generating income. A separate, but linked, issue is whether the Administrator is to have the exclusive right to collect all income arising in respect of the compositions. This will depend on what provisions have been agreed between the Administrator and the Company in relation to the collection and distribution of income (see Paragraph 10.9).

There will be circumstances where the Company's copyrights may be infringed and the administration agreement will normally provide that the Administrator is to have the right to commence legal proceedings on behalf of the Company where the Company's rights are infringed. Normally, the Company will wish to have the right to approve the circumstances in which proceedings are issued and the terms and conditions on which actions are settled or compromises are reached. This is entirely reasonable. The Administrator, for its part, may wish to be appointed as the Company's attorney for the purpose of commencing proceedings. The Company may wish to limit the scope of the Administrator's power and grant a limited power of attorney relating solely to the commencement and maintenance and settlement of proceedings. From the Administrator's point of view, the grant of a limited power is acceptable, provided, however, that it covers all the steps which Administrator might wish to take in relation to the enforcement of rights and commencement and termination of proceedings.

10.5 Reserved Rights

The Administration agreement will normally provide that all rights which are not specifically granted to the Administrator are expressly reserved to the Company. This type of provision is entirely acceptable from the Administrator's point of view.

In fact, if the Administrator is appointed as the Company's sole and exclusive agent (see Paragraph 10.4), no rights will be granted to the Administrator. It is perfectly acceptable for the agreement to state that all rights are reserved to the Company, subject to the Administrator's exclusive right to act on its behalf.

10.6 Administrator's undertakings and agreements

There are a number of warranties that an administration agreement will normally contain. These will include the following matters

Ability to Contract

The Company will wish confirmation that the Administrator has the right to enter into the agreement and that the Administrator has not entered into any other arrangement or done anything which would interfere with or prevent the Administrator from observing or performing its obligations under the agreement.

Services

The Company will wish the Administrator to render the services to the best of the Administrator's skill and ability and to use its best endeavours to maximise gross receipts. Because "best endeavours" obligations may imply an obligation on the Administrator's part to expend significant sums of money, it may, therefore, be advisable from the Administrator's point of view, to clarify the fact that the extent of any such obligation is to be determined in the Administrator's reasonable commercial judgment.

Confidentiality

The Administrator will not reveal make public any financial or any other confidential information in relation to the agreement or the business of the Company. This type of provision is entirely normal.

No Right to Contract

The Administrator will not, on behalf of the Company, enter into any contract* with any third party. Whether or not this is acceptable depends on what has been negotiated. If the Administrator is appointed as the Company's agent, then it will require the right to enter into contracts. Whether or not the Company is to have the right to approve contracts is negotiable. If any approval right is granted, the Administrator will wish to ensure that approval is not unreasonably withheld or delayed and may wish to provide that if the Administrator has not received valid objection from the Company within a certain number of days of notifying a proposed contract, the proposed arrangement would be deemed to have been approved.

PRS Membership

The Administrator is, and will remain during the term of the agreement, a member in good standing of the Performing Right Society Limited*. Because a significant part of the income derived from the exploitation of rights in the compositions owned by the Company will be derived from public performance and broadcasting revenue administered by the PRS and its affiliated societies, membership of the PRS by the Administrator is likely to be necessary.

Key Personnel

The Administrator will remain entitled to the services of key personnel during the term. This type of provision will be relevant where the Company is entering into an agreement with the Administrator on the basis that the services will be performed by designated personnel. From the Administrator's point of view, where a key personnel clause is conceded, it is normally advisable to permit the services to be provided by any one of two or three individuals in order to prevent the Administrator losing its rights, if a named individual leaves its employment.

Gross Receipts

The agreement will provide that all gross sums received by the Administrator from the exploitation of the compositions are to be applied towards a designated account. Who this account is controlled by will depend on the terms agreed.

Exclusion of Agreement with Composers

The Company may well wish to prohibit the Administrator from entering into any contractual arrangement with the composers of any of the compositions for a period of three years or more following expiry of the term of the agreement. This type of provision is often referred to as a "no poaching" provision and is designed to protect the Company's legitimate business interests. Unless the Administrator has an established prior course of dealings with any of the composers, this restriction will normally be acceptable.

Statements

The Administrator will provide the Company with copies of all statements relating to the exploitation of the compositions received by the Administrator from performing right societies*, mechanical societies or other persons. This is an entirely normal provision. The time scale within which the Administrator is expected to comply with the arrangement will need to be fixed, but, otherwise, the requirement is normal.

Enforcement of Rights

The agreement may require the Administrator to take all steps necessary to enforce rights in the compositions and/or prevent their infringement in the territory. Unless rights have been granted to the Administrator on an exclusive basis, the Administrator will probably be unable to take steps in its own name. It may, however, be possible for the Administrator to take steps in the name of the Company if it is appointed as the Company's attorney for this purpose (see Paragraph 10.4). Any requirement for the Administrator to take steps and maintain proceedings at its own cost and expense is unreasonable and should be resisted. The enforcement and protection of copyrights is of direct commercial benefit to the Company and any costs incurred in doing so are a legitimate business expense of the Company and should be borne by the Company, not the Administrator.

Indemnity

The agreement may contain an indemnity provision. The Administrator may, however, wish to exclude or limit the indemnity provisions for the reasons referred to in paragraph 53.16.

10.7   Copyright

Notification of Compositions

The agreement should provide that the Company will notify the Administrator promptly of all Compositions owned or controlled by the Company and the amounts of royalties required to be paid to the composers of the compositions. The royalties received by composers are frequently referred to as the "Composers' share" of revenue.

Where an established catalogue is the subject of an administration agreement, the identity of the compositions and the share of income payable to the composers may be specified in the schedule. Where, however, the Company is in the business of acquiring rights on an ongoing basis or has songwriters signed to it under term composer's agreements (see Chapter 2), the list of compositions will grow during the term and it is important from the Administrator's point of view, for the Administrator to be notified of all new compositions so that their exploitation can be ensured and monitored.

The Administrator will normally require lead sheets together with demo recordings of compositions and the agreement may also provide that, where publication of foreign language editions or new editions of musical works is procured by the Administrator, the Company will receive a copy of each printed edition, together with a copy of all cover versions or new recordings procured by the Administrator during the term.

Copyright Registration

It is of vital importance, from the Company's point of view, to ensure that the copyrights in its compositions are protected. For this reason the agreement may impose on the Administrator an obligation to procure the copyright registration of compositions. Until recently, registration of copyright in the US copyright registry was a mandatory requirement if infringement proceedings were to be commenced. Renewal of copyright in the US was also required for works published pre-1 January 1978, but, following the USA's accession to the Berne Convention, renewal of copyrights in the US is no longer required.

The agreement may require the Administrator to ensure that a copyright notice in the form prescribed by the Universal Copyright Convention included on all printed editions of the compositions and that a notice in accordance with the Rome Convention for the Protection of Phonograms is included on all audio-visual recordings. This requirement is entirely acceptable.

Additionally, the agreement will probable require the Administrator to make sure that every composer/arranger/lyricist is credited and named on the various editions/sound recordings. The Administrator may well wish to ensure that any casual or inadvertent failure on its part to accord credit will not be deemed to be a breach of the agreement.

Registration with Performing and Mechanical Rights Societies

The agreement will normally require the Administrator to register the copyright of each composition with performing rights societies and mechanical societies in the territory. This is an entirely normal requirement.

10.8 Receipts and Payment

The agreement will contain provisions in relation to the collection and division of receipts derived from the exploitation of the compositions during the term. Generally speaking, the music industry is geared up towards payments calculated by reference to the half year—ie periods ending on 30 June and 31 December each year (see Chapters 1 and 2). As we have already seen, the principal revenue derived from the exploitation of compositions (see Paragraph 2.9) falls within a small number of categories.

From the Company's point of view it is important to ensure that the timing and routing of the payments is dealt with properly. For this reason, an administration agreement may well provide that the Company is to receive payment of all performing rights income direct from the relevant performing right society. Performing rights income distributions are normally made 45 days after the half year (on 15 August and 15 February). An Administrator will normally wish to resist a Company being accounted to direct by the PRS, since the Administrator will wish to have security over the payment stream to guarantee receipt of its commission. From the Company's point of view, receipt by the Administrator of income will raise the same concerns in relation to solvency as discussed in relation to a sub-publishing arrangement (see Paragraph 9.11).

Any concern which the Company may have in relation to the Administrator's solvency needs to be addressed and the solution should be considered carefully. It is important from both parties point of view to guarantee the security of the money collected and to guarantee the protection of each entitlement of each party to recover sums which are due to them. One possible solution is referred to in Paragraph 9.11.

Timing is also important in considering the receipt and distribution and income from mechanical exploitation and sub-publishing arrangements. Revenue from these types of exploitation is generally distributed 90 days after the half year (ie on 31 March and 30 September). The agreement should therefore ensure that the Administrator's accounting obligations are properly synchronised. The date the Administrator actually "receives" income is crucial for the purpose of determining the time for performance of its obligations. If the Administrator receives a statement of account and royalty cheque from a music publisher on 31 March, it is unlikely that the Administrator will have actually received clear funds in the collection account before 1 April. If the standard music industry half yearly reporting of the payment obligations are inserted in the administration agreement, the Administrator will be under no obligation to account to the Company in relation to the sums received until 30 September that year (ie 90 days following the end of the 1 January to 30 June period in which the sums were received). For this reason, the agreement may specify that income is to be applied by the Administrator within a stated number of days (30, 45 or 60).

10.9 Accounts

The Administrator will maintain true and correct books of account and records and provide the Company with statements of account promptly on the agreed accounting dates (see Paragraph 10.8). This is an entirely normal provision.

The Company or its authorised representative will have the right to inspect, audit and take copies of books of account maintained by the Administrator in relation to the compositions. The agreement may provide that if an error to the detriment of the Company in excess of 5% of the amount owed in any period is discovered, the Administrator is to pay the costs incurred by the Company in relation to such inspection or audit. These provisions are again quite normal. From an Administrator's point of view it would preferable, however, if the margin of error were 10% rather than 5%. The obligation to pay audit costs should in any event be limited to reasonable costs necessarily and properly incurred.

The agreement may also contain an obligation on the part of the Administrator to inspect and audit the books of account of licensees. This provision will generally be acceptable, provided that specific provision is made for the reimbursement of the costs incurred by the Administrator in performing such obligations. Since the obligation is carried out for the benefit of the Company, it would be normal and reasonable to expect the Company to bear the costs.

10.10 Termination

The agreement will normally contain a provision permitting the Company to terminate it if the Administrator is in breach of its obligations or becomes insolvent. The Administrator may wish to insert similar provisions permitting it to terminate if the Company is in breach.

10.11 Effect of Termination

The agreement may contain a provision which provides for what happens if the agreement is determined by the Company. In such an event, it will be normal for the Company to require payment of all sums received by the Administrator in relation to the compositions and for the Company to have the right to appoint another party to administer the Company's rights in the territory.

The Administrator may wish to insert a provision clarifying the fact that if the agreement expires by the passing of time, the Administrator will continue to be entitled to collect money arising in the territory during the term.

10.12   Boilerplate

The boilerplate section of a typical administration agreement will contain the following provisions:

* Notices (see Paragraph 52.8)
* Severability (see Paragraph 52.10)
* Entire agreement (see Paragraph 52.3)
* Waiver (see Paragraph 52.11)
* No partnership (see Paragraph 52.7)
* Governing law (see Paragraph 52.5).

11   Single Work Recording Contract

11.1 Single Work Recording Contract

A single work recording contract* is used in circumstances where a record company wishes to contract an artist or artists to record specific works rather than enter into a term* recording contract (see Chapter 1).

The parties to this particular transaction are:

- the recording artist or artists whose services the record company wishes to acquire (collectively referred to as the "Artists"); and
- the recording company (referred to as the "Company").

11.2 Transaction Analysis

A typical recording contract might be expected to contain the following clauses:

- Engagement (see Paragraph 11.3)
- Grant of rights (see Paragraph 11.4)
- Artists' warranties* and obligations (see Paragraph 11.5)
- Advances* (see Paragraph 11.6)
- Royalties (see Paragraph 11.7)
- Royalty accounting (see Paragraph 11.8)
- Credit (see Paragraph 11.9)
- Boilerplate* (see Paragraph 11.10).

11.3 Engagement

See Paragraph 1.3.

11.4 Grant of Rights

See Paragraph 1.5.

11.5 Artists' Warranties and Obligations

See Paragraph 1.7.

11.6 Advances

See Paragraph 1.6.

11.7 Royalties

See Paragraph 1.10.

11.8 Royalty Accounting

See Paragraph 1.11.

11.9 Credit

See Paragraph 1.13.

11.10 Boilerplate

See Paragraph 1.19.

12 Publishing Agreement for Specified Work or Works

12.1 Description of Specific Work(s) Publishing Agreement

This type of publishing agreement* is suitable for use in circumstances when a publisher wishes to acquire publishing rights and specified works, as opposed to works produced by a composer over a term* of years where a term publishing agreement (see Chapter 2) is more appropriate.

The parties to this particular transaction are:

- the composer of the various works (the "Composer") and
- the publishing company entering into the arrangement (the "Publisher").

12.2 Transaction Analysis

A typical specific work(s) publishing agreement might be expected to contain the following clauses:

- Grant of rights (see Paragraph 12.3)
- Advance* (see Paragraph 12.4)
- Composer's warranties and obligations (see Paragraph 12.5)
- Publisher's obligations (see Paragraph 12.6)
- Royalties* (see Paragraph 12.7)
- Royalty accounting (see Paragraph 12.8)
- Copyright notices (see Paragraph 12.9)
- Boilerplate* (see Paragraph 12.10).

12.3 Grant of Rights

See Paragraph 2.5.

12.4   Advance

See Paragraph 2.6.

12.5   Composer's Warranties and Obligations

See Paragraph 2.7.

12.6   Publisher's Obligations

See Paragraph 2.8.

12.7   Royalties

See Paragraph 2.9.

12.8   Royalty Accounting

See Paragraph 2.10.

12.9   Copyright Notices

See Paragraph 2.13.

12.10   Boilerplate

The boilerplate section of a typical specific work(s) publishing agreement will contain the following provisions:

- Notices (see Paragraph 52.8)
- Severability (see Paragraph 52.10)
- Entire Agreement (see Paragraph 52.3)
- Waiver (see Paragraph 52.11)
- No partnership (see Paragraph 52.7)
- Governing law (see Paragraph 52.5)
- Certificate of value (see Paragraph 52.2).

13   Tour Agreement

13.1   Description of a Tour Agreement

A tour agreement is used to formalise the financial and other commercial arrangements relating to a tour to be undertaken by a group of artists.
The parties to the particular transaction are:

- the company making the arrangements for the booking of venues and promotion of the artists (referred to as the "Promoter"); and
- the artists themselves. Normally, for the reasons examined in Chapter 15, artists will wish to make their services available through a company which they own and control (referred to in this Chapter as the "Company").

This Chapter examines the provisions of a tour agreement* from the point of view of the artists' company or its legal advisors.

13.2   Transaction Analysis

A typical tour agreement might be expected to contain the following clauses:

- Promoter's undertakings (see Paragraph 13.3)
- Company's undertakings (see Paragraph 13.4)
- Expenses, taxes and payments (see Paragraph 13.5)
- Box office and complimentary tickets (see Paragraph 13.6)
- Control of production (see Paragraph 13.7)
- Recording and photography (see Paragraph 13.8)
- Credit (see Paragraph 13.9)
- Subscription and sponsorship (see Paragraph 13.10)
- Merchandising (see Paragraph 13.11)
- Security and medical service (see Paragraph 13.12)
- Insurance (see Paragraph 13.13)
- Technical provisions (see Paragraph 13.14)
- Crew (see Paragraph 13.15)
- Artist's requirements (see Paragraph 13.16)
- Determination (see Paragraph 13.17)
- Boilerplate (see Paragraph 13.18).

13.3 Promoter's Undertakings

The Promoter will agree to make available to the Company designated venues on designated dates. The Company will normally require access to the venues for the purpose of carrying out sound checks and rehearsals and the agreement will therefore normally provide for this.

It is usual for the specifications of each venue to be set out in the agreement, principally, the capacity, the ticket price and the gross potential earnings for each venue.

Depending on the circumstances, the Company may also require the Promoter to make available certain facilities and equipment at each venue. If the artists have their own "show" which tours with them, the list of facilities may not be extensive and the financial provisions (principally, the percentage which the Promoter takes of gross box office receipts) will be weighted more in favour of the artists to reflect the fact that the Promoter is not required to provide extensive facilities.

The agreement will normally provide that the Promoter pays to the Company either an advance* against the whole tour or a guaranteed sum in respect of each venue. The guaranteed sum for each venue may be specified in a schedule to the agreement, along with details of the venue's specifications, ticket price, capacity etc. The Promoter will obviously wish to recover the expenditure which it has effected in acquiring each venue and publicising the tour. The agreement will therefore normally permit the Promoter to recover its expenses from the total gross box office receipts derived from each venue. It is in the interests of the Company to limit the expenses which may be recovered by the Promoter from each venue and the total amount of permitted expenditure on expenses for each venue may also be listed in the schedule.

After the Promoter has recovered its expenses from the gross box office receipts, it will wish to retain a percentage of the venue receipts by way of commission. Whether the percentage retained by the Promoter is a percentage of the gross box office receipts or the net box office receipts after the deduction of the expenses is a matter for negotiation. Obviously, from the point of view of the artists' company it is preferable if whatever percentage is deducted by the Promoter (and the amount may vary between 10% and 40% depending on the wide variety of circumstances) should be deducted from the net box office receipts. The Promoter would prefer it to be deducted from gross sums.

The agreement may also provide that the Promoter is to ensure that the venue owners and operators do not deduct any commission or require payment by the Company's licensees in relation to the sale of tour—or artist—related merchandising.

The agreement will also specify the dates on which the Promoter is to pay to the Company the various guaranteed sums. Because the Promoter is being required to guarantee that the proceeds from each venue will be not less than a specified amount, there will be a strong commercial incentive on the Promoter to promote the tour to the maximum. If sales exceed the guaranteed sum the artists' company will be entitled to receive the surplus, after the deduction by the Promoter of the expenses, guarantee and their Promoter's percentage.

13.4 Company's Undertakings

The obligations undertaken by the Company are actually quite simple. The Company is undertaking only to make available the services of the artists to perform in the venues on the venue dates. Whether or not the Promoter wishes the Company to specify the tracks which are to be performed by the artists is a matter for commercial negotiation. Normally, the artists, will want some degree of flexibility in their tour programme, but if the tour is to promote a recently released album, then obviously tracks from the album will feature on the artist's playlist.

Where an artist is signed to a record company, because of the direct benefit record sales are likely to receive from a tour, the Artist may receive financial support from the record company. Whether sums advanced by the record company are to be treated as advances made to the Artist under its recording contract will depend on the provisions agreed between the Artist and the record company. Alternatively, if the record company does provide tour support the application of the gross office receipts might provide for the record company to be reimbursed out of the net box office receipts received from the Promoter.

13.5 Expenses, Taxes and Payment

The agreement will normally provide that the Promoter is to produce receipts, vouchers or other evidence of expenditure supporting the total expenses reclaimed by the Promoter.

A balance needs to be struck between maximising profits from the tour and minimising expenses. It will not be in the interest of the artists' company for the Promoter to expend the total from its expenses on each venue if ticket sales have already exceeded the guarantee figure, because the expenses are deducted from the total gross box office receipts. The agreement may therefore permit the Promoter to spend less than the total expenses and give the Promoter the benefit of a percentage of the underspend provided that the number of tickets sold for each venue exceeds the guarantee.

It is extremely important, from the Company's point of view, that the Promoter should accept responsibility for the payment of all withholding taxes* and any other local taxes. The agreement may also contain a payment direction requiring the Company's receipts to be paid to the artists' agent or manager.

13.6 Box Office and Complimentary Tickets

The Promoter will normally be required to produce a ticket manifest by no later than a certain number of days before the first engagement, showing the number and price and colour coding of all tickets. It is normal for the agreement to provide that tickets should be consecutively numbered and, if more than one performance is to take place on any date, the tickets will be printed in a different range of colours for each performance. It is also usual to identify tickets sold in advance and tickets sold on the date of engagement.

118

The Promoter will be required not to print or sell or permit the printing of selling of tickets in excess of the number provided for on the ticket manifest or at prices other than those specified on the manifest without the consent of the artists' company.

The artists' company may require each ticket to be endorsed with a form of wording which indicates that persons entering the venue have consented to being filmed and recorded. The agreement may equally provide for a form of notice to be displayed at each entrance to the venue. The arrangements for complimentary tickets, and the numbers available to the artists' company will also normally be specified.

The agreement will normally provide that the Promoter is to provide the artists' tour manager with a seating plan of each venue on the date of the engagement, indicating the position of tickets sold, complementary tickets and tickets which are unsold. The Promoter will then be required to provide the artists' company or the artists' tour manager with a statement specifying the number of tickets sold by each venue and calculating the amount of gross box receipts within a specified number of hours after each concert. The artists' tour manager may also require all unsold tickets to be made available to the tour manager for verification purposes and the agreement will normally provide that the tour manager or other appointed representatives of the artist has a right to enter into the box office of any venue and inspect, audit and take copies of books and records relating to the concerts.

13.7 Control of Production

The artists' company will normally wish to retain control of the production, presentation and performance of each concert. This is normally acceptable from the point of view of the Promoter.

Whether the Company is to exclude liability in relation to non-performance as a result matters beyond the control of the parties, is a matter for negotiation. This aspect is linked with insurance (see Paragraph 13.13).

13.8 Recording and Photography

It is crucial, from the point of view of the artists, that neither the Promoter nor the venue owner or operator should permit the recording, filming or photographing of any of the concerts or rehearsals without the prior written consent of the Company. If the artists are under exclusive recording contract the artists' record company will have the exclusive right to film and or record the artists' performances (see Chapter 1).

The Company may wish to require each venue owner or operator and other relevant persons to sign a waiver of recording rights, confirming that they have no right to film or record any material and the Company may also require each venue owner or operator to restrict the admission of photographers other than those who bear passes issued by the Promoter. The procedure for approving passes will normally be specified in the agreement, since the artists' company may wish to control the issue of photography passes. The agreement will also provide that photographers' access to backstage areas is to be restricted.

13.9   Credit

The form of billing credit in advertising, programmes, lights and other publicity for each venue is normally specified. Whether there are to be support groups or not will depend on the circumstances and whether or not any support group is to receive billing is a matter for negotiation.

13.10   Subscription and Sponsorship

The Company will wish to ensure that its play dates have not been included in any subscription arrangement with any venue and that neither the Promoter nor any venue owner or operator has entered into any contract with any third party sponsor or advertiser which might associate the name or business of any third party directly or indirectly with the concerts or the artists. Equally, there may be circumstances where the artists the themselves have a sponsorship or advertising arrangement and they may wish the tour arrangements to reflect this.

   Where the artists have an existing logo, they may wish the advertising and promotion arrangements relating to the tour to use their logo. Equally, they may wish to have control or approval of advertising of publicity material, in which event the contract will provide for this.

13.11   Merchandising

The sale of artists' merchandising at the venues normally generates significant amounts of income. The artists will therefore wish to ensure that the exclusive right to sell artists' merchandising is reserved to the artists' company or its licensee. The contract should therefore provide that neither the Promoter nor any venue owner or operator will sell or advertise for sale any item which bears the name or logo or likeness of any of the artists or which directly or indirectly competes with the artist-authorised merchandising of souvenir programmes and other souvenir items, including photographs, records and videos.

   Additionally, the contract will normally impose a positive obligation on the Promoter and each venue owner or the operator to prohibit the sale of unauthorised merchandise in or around the venue on the concert dates.

13.12   Security and Medical

The artists will be looking to the Promoter to ensure that adequate arrangements are made in relation to their own security. The Promoter will be responsible for ensuring that only authorised persons are permitted in the backstage area before, during and after the concerts and will provide a designated number of security personnel. Depending on the circumstances, the agreement may provide for security personnel to be in place at designated points.

The artists will also wish to ensure that their own health and welfare is taken into consideration and the agreement will normally, therefore, require the Promoter to make advance arrangements for availability at short notice of dentists, doctors and, possibly, voice specialists in each relevant town or city. The contract may also require the Promoter to ensure the availability of "crash" medical personnel with resuscitation equipment.

13.13   Insurance

It is essential, from both parties' point of view, that adequate insurance arrangements are effected in relation to each concert and each venue for public liability and property. It is normal for the artists to expect the Promoter to take care of these arrangements and the Company will normally wish to satisfy itself that the insurance arrangements are in force by seeing written confirmation to this effect from the relevant insurance broker.

The possibility that a concert may not take place as a result of the cancellation or non-appearance of the artists also needs to be addressed, and the agreement will therefore provide not only that cancellation and non-appearance insurance must be effective in relation to each venue date but also that the artists will not have liability to the Promoter in the event of cancellation or non-appearance. From the Promoter's point of view it will wish its interest to be noted on the insurance policy, in order to recover sums expended in payment of the expenses and the guarantee.

13.14   Technical Arrangements

The technical arrangements will, of course, depend on each set of circumstances. The artists may wish the Promoter to provide a technical representative who will be present at each venue, from the beginning of set-up until the end of tear-down, who will be responsible for liaison between the artists' road crew, the tour manager and the technical staff of each venue. Where a foreign tour is involved, the representative must be proficient in both the English language and the language of the area when the venue is located.

The Company will also wish to obtain vehicle permits for each venue for vehicles designated by the artists' tour manager. The Promoter may be required to ensure that an office is available in the back stage area of each venue for the use of the tour manager and other personnel of the Company. The office may be required to be fitted out with PC, fax machine etc.

The agreement will normally provide that the artists will have access to the venue in order to effect a sound check and it will be the responsibility of the Promoter to advise the artists' company of local noise abatement, noise pollution and noise control regulations and other liabilities. The Promoter must also ensure that each venue complies with local regulations.

13.15 Crew

The Company will normally wish the Promoter to agree that each venue will make adequate provision for the group's road crew. The Company may wish to make a number of specific requirements such as the provision of shower facilities, food and refreshments. The extent of the provisions in relation to road crew requirements will reflect not only the status of the artists but also the size of their show.

13.16 Artists' Requirements

The artists will also generally have an established list of requirements which they themselves wish the Promoter to provide in each venue. Many established artists have what is known as a "tour rider"—ie a schedule of their requirements which may be annexed to the contract as a rider.

The artists will normally require dressing rooms and the hospitality room which will be stocked with clean crockery, glasses and food and drinks. The precise requirements of the artists in relation to beverages and food may be extensive. Additionally the artists may wish the contract* to contain provision for the services of an experienced wardrobe mistress.

13.17 Determination

The Company will normally wish the agreement to contain provisions entitling them to terminate the agreement if the Promoter is in breach of material obligations or fails to pay or becomes insolvent.

13.18 Boilerplate

The boilerplate section of a typical tour agreement will contain the following provisions:

- Notice (see Paragraph 52.8)
- Severability (see Paragraph 52.10)
- Entire agreement (see Paragraph 52.3)
- Waiver (see Paragraph 52.11)
- No partnership (see Paragraph 52.7)
- Governing law (see Paragraph 52.5).

14 Management Agreement

14.1 Description of a Management Agreement

The management agreement* is probably the third most common form of document in the music industry after the recording contract and the publishing agreement.

The relationship between manager and artist is unique in the media industries and management agreements have, in recent years, attracted considerable interest from the courts, so it is important, whether one is involved in the arrangement from the point of view of the artist or from the point of view of the manager to "get it right".

A manager's function under the management agreement is to promote and manage the career of an artist. Very often artists entering into management agreements are young and unknown in their industry, while the managers themselves are, almost by definition, experienced, well-connected individuals in the music industry.

This natural imbalance between, on the one hand, young, inexperienced artists with little knowledge of the music industry practice or the law of contract and, on the other hand, older, experienced managers familiar with the intricate and sometimes obscure practices of the music industry and who are experienced in negotiating contracts* as well as in the use of the law and lawyers, has led on a number of occasions to oppressive and unconscionable agreements being entered into between artists and managers.

The courts in England and Wales have shown considerable concern to ensure that inequitable agreements between artists and managers are not enforced. There is therefore little point from a manager's point of view in driving an unnecessarily harsh bargain with an artist, because of the likelihood that the courts would rule any unconscionable provision to be unenforceable.

Exceptional care, therefore, needs to be taken in relation to management agreements and legal advice must always be sought by both the manager and the artist. If the artist does not have sufficient financial resources to pay for the cost of legal advice, then the manager will need to agree to meet the artist's legal bill for obtaining advice from a specialist lawyer familiar with agreements of this type. Any restriction placed by the manager on the identity of the person advising the artist is completely unacceptable—the artist must be left free to choose his or her legal advisor. The amount of the artist's legal bill will to some extent be determined by the complexity and fairness of the manager's management agreement. For a short, fair agreement the total bill may be no more than £750. For a longer, more complex agreement negotiated aggressively by the manager, the amount could be ten or twenty times this.

From the manager's point of view, it is reasonable to require an upper limit or "cap" on the artists' legal expenses. The artists, however, should never agree what this cap figure might be without having received a copy of the proposed agreement and submitted it to their lawyers for review. As explained above, the cost of advising on and negotiating the final form of a management agreement will have a direct bearing on how fair and reasonable the agreement is to start with.

The parties to a management agreement are:

- the manager or management company (referred to as the "Manager"); and
- the artists or artist who are to be managed (referred to as the "Artist" or "Artists").

14.2 Document Breakdown

A typical management agreement might be expected to contain the following clauses:

- Appointment (see Paragraph 14.3)
- Manager's Undertakings (see Paragraph 14.4)
- Artist's Undertakings (see Paragraph 14.5)
- Group Provisions (see Paragraph 14.6)
- Artist's Obligations (see Paragraph 14.7)
- Gross Receipts (see Paragraph 14.8)
- Accounting (see Paragraph 14.9)
- Manager's Activities (see Paragraph 14.10)
- Consents (see Paragraph 14.11)
- Suspension (see Paragraph 14.12)
- Effect of Suspension (see Paragraph 14.13)
- Termination (see Paragraph 14.14)
- Effect of Termination (see Paragraph 14.15)
- Boilerplate* (see Paragraph 14.16)

14.3 Appointment

The agreement will normally appoint the Manager to act as the Artists' sole and exclusive agent during a term of years in relation to the negotiation and (possibly) execution of engagement agreements relating to services of the Artist throughout a designated territory.

Term

The term of the agreement should be of sufficient length to permit the Manager to recover money invested by the Manager and the Artist but not be so long as to unfairly prejudice the Artist's interests. Whether or not the Manager is to have the benefit of being able to extend the term, by the exercise of one or more options, is a matter for commercial negotiation between the parties. Normally the management agreement will be for a fixed term and will continue after that, unless and until determined by not less than six or 12 months' notice in writing.

Scope of Engagement

It is important, from the Artist's point of view, to clarify the scope of the engagement. The Manager may wish the management agreement to cover all services of the Artist in relation to the entertainment industry generally, throughout the world. The Artist may wish the arrangement to be limited to one territory or to exclude one or more territories and may wish to limit the type of services which be covered by it. For example, the Artist may wish to exclude the services of the Artist as a touring performer in order to reflect some pre-existing contractual commitment.

The Manager will generally wish the agreement to extend to all services of the artist relating to the entertainment industry including motion pictures, film, television, radio appearances, audio and audio-visual recording, live stage appearances, personal appearances, advertising, sponsorship, merchandising, as well as literature, art, music and choreography. From the Artist's point of view, if the Manager's principal area of activity is the music industry, the Artist may wish to limit the scope of the agreement to this industry.

Engagement Agreement

The agreement will also specify the precise scope and extent of the Manager's authority in relation to engagement agreements. It is perfectly acceptable for the Manager to reserve the exclusive right to introduce and negotiate agreements relating to services of the Artist. Whether or not the Manager should have the right to execute agreements on behalf of the Artist is a matter of negotiation. The Manager should, at the very least, consult with the Artist and give good faith considerations to the Artist's views in relation of proposed engagement agreements. From the Manager's own point of view it is important that the Artist will comply with the provisions of negotiated agreements. The Manager will obviously want the Artist to be aware of what these obligations are. Although the Manager may prefer to have the right to sign engagement agreements on behalf of the Artist, this right will obviously cause the Artist concern and the Artist will wish have to the right alone to sign engagement agreements.

In circumstances where the Manager is advancing substantial amounts of income to the Artist, the Manager may quite reasonably wish to protect its legitimate business interests and may require an undertaking from the Artist that the Artist will execute any engagement agreement negotiated by the Manager provided it is on the best reasonably obtainable commercial terms within a stated period of it being submitted to them.

The Agreement may provide that the Artist will not negotiate any engagement agreements and will refer all interest and enquiries to the Manager. These provisions are entirely reasonable.

Collection of Income

In some instances, the agreement may provide that the Manager is to have the sole and exclusive right to collect and receive all income arising in relation to engagement agreements. Whether or not this provision is reasonable will depend on the precise commercial circumstances.

For example, if the Manager takes a group of unknown individuals, grooms them for stardom, gives them singing lessons, dancing lessons, instrumental lessons, clothes them, feeds them and gives them a spending allowance over a period of 12 months to 18 months, by the time the Artists are in a state of readiness to sign a recording contract with a major record company, the Manager will have expended a significant, if not substantial, sum. In these circumstances, it would be permissible for the Manager to have the right to collect and receive all income arising under the engagement agreements—at least until the Manager had recouped its initial expenditure.

In circumstances where the Manager's function is less extensive and the outlay is less significant, there may be reservations from the Artist's point of view about letting the Manager receive the entire income stream under the engagement agreements. This type of arrangement may work fine in circumstances where the Manager is honest and solvent. Even where the Artist has complete faith in the Manager's integrity, insolvency is a well known risk area in the commercial world. If the Manager becomes insolvent at a time when the Manager is holding significant sums of money due to the Artists, there is a real risk that this money will be applied for the benefit of the Manager's creditors and not paid to the Artist.

For this reason, the Artist may prefer for the engagement agreements to contain "split" accounting provisions, directing the Manager's commission to be paid to the Manager and the remaining sums to the Artist. In practice, this may be difficult to achieve, since the Manager's entitlement will include the right to recover expenses incurred by the Manager on the Artists' behalf, as well as the right to recover commissions. Because the amount of the expenses in each accounting period will vary, a "split" payment direction may not always be practicable.

A further alternative from the Artists' point of view would be to establish a collection account which would be a designated trust account into which the Manager would pay all sums. This objective might be achieved by inserting into all engagement agreements a payment direction in favour of a designated account number rather than a split payment direction. The terms of the bank mandate controlling the operation of the account could provide either for a standing direction to the bank or for joint signatory of remittance instructions.

Legal Proceedings

The agreement may provide that the Manager is to have the exclusive right to initiate and maintain legal proceedings in relation to engagement agreements. Legal proceedings are capable of resulting in considerable cost exposure and, since this is deducted from the Artist's income, the Artist will generally wish to limit or control any right to commence proceedings in the Artist's name.

Execution of Employment Agreements

The management agreement may provide that the Artist will execute any documents required by the Manager under the agreement. For the reasons explained above, the Artists may wish to reserve the right to approve engagement agreements. A provision giving the Manager the right to execute engagement agreements on behalf of the Artists is also likely to be questionable for the reasons set out above.

Publicity and Interviews

The management agreement may provide that the Manager is to have the sole right to authorise and arrange interviews and co-ordinate promotion, advertising and publicity material in relation to the Artists. It is not unreasonable for the Manager to require this provision.

14.4 Manager's Undertakings

The management agreement should it contain a number of undertakings on the part of the Manager.

First, it should specify precisely what services the Manager will be required to perform during the term. The services might include advice and guidance in respect of the employment of the Artist, the selection of literary, dramatic, musical and artistic materials, the arrangement of publicity, public relations and advertising, the selection of booking agencies and theatrical agencies, the wardrobe and image of the Artist and the development and presentation of the talents of the Artist.

The agreement will normally provide that the Manager will use all reasonable endeavours to conclude engagement agreements on behalf of the Artist for the Artist's services during the term and to maximise receipts from such engagements. If the Manager is paying an advance to the Artist or spending significant sums on them, this is likely to increase the Manager's level of business activity, because the Manager will want to recover the advance and will wish to secure recording or music publishing agreements for the Artist to generate income. In circumstances where no advance* is paid and the Artist is not receiving significant sums from the Manager, the Artist may well wish the Manager's level of obligation to be higher and may wish the Manager to agree to undertake its best endeavours to procure engagement agreements on behalf of the Artist.

The agreement may also specify the times and dates during which the Manager is obliged to render services. Depending on the circumstances, it may be entirely acceptable to the Artist for the Manager to render services at reasonable times and places during normal business hours. Where, however, the Artist is entering into the management agreement on the basis of the skills and personal track record of one or two key individuals, then the Artist may wish the Manager to agree to procure that the services will be performed by the key personnel. Where key personnel are engaged, the Artist will normally wish to have the right to terminate the management agreement, if the Manager ceases to be entitled to the full-time services of at least one of the key personnel.

14.5 Artist's Undertakings

There are a number of warranties* that the management company will normally wish to obtain from the Artist. These include the following matters.

Majority

See Paragraph 1.7.

Ability to Contract

See Paragraph 1.7.

No Conflict

See Paragraph 1.7.

Unions and Works Permits

See Paragraph 1.7.

Non-disclosure

See Paragraph 1.7.

Publicity

See Paragraph 1.7.

Exclusivity of Services

The Artist will not render services during the term otherwise than pursuant to engagement agreements negotiated by the Manager. This provision is entirely reasonable. Where, however, the Artist is subject to existing contractual commitments in relation to the Artist's services, the agreement should refer to such commitments to prevent the Artist otherwise being in breach.

Professionalism

Pursuant to employment agreements, the Artist will render all services required to the best of the Artist's skill and ability, professionally and punctually in willing co-operation with others. This provision is entirely acceptable.

Appearance

The Artist will at all times pay due and proper attention to their personal appearance.

Insurance

See Paragraph 1.7.

Health

The Artist shall take all practical steps to preserve and maintain the Artist's health and to comply with the provisions of insurance companies who have agreed to provide insurance cover, in relation to the Artist, for the benefit of the Manager or other persons. This is a reasonable requirement, since the Manager will suffer loss if the Artist is unable to perform services as a result of illness.

Morals

See Paragraph 1.7.

Prior Agreements

The Artist will disclose to the Manager all prior agreements and arrangements relating to the Artist's services. This is again a wholly reasonable requirement for the benefit of both parties.

Dangerous Pursuits

See Paragraph 1.7.

Training and Instruction

The Artist shall undertake such training and instruction as the Artist and the Manager agree and shall do all reasonable acts or things as may be required for the fulfilment of obligations under any engagement agreement. These obligations are reasonable.

Referral of Enquiries

See Paragraph 1.7.

Professional Name

The Artist undertakes not to change the professional name without the consent of the Manager or perform under any other name. Again, these requirements are reasonable.

Whereabouts

See Paragraph 1.7.

Legal Advice

See Paragraph 1.7.

Indemnity

See Paragraph 1.7.

14.6 Group Provisions

See Paragraph 1.8.

14.7 Artist's Obligations

The management agreement may restrict the Artist from rendering any services, whether paid or unpaid, to any third party. This may be reasonable although the Artist may wish to make specific provision permitting them to take part in charity performances etc.

The agreement may impose an obligation on the Artist not to vary any term or condition of any engagement agreement without the consent of the Manager. There may frequently be situations where the terms of engagement agreements are varied simply to take account of practicalities and, from the Artist's point of view, any such provision should ideally be limited to material terms.

The agreement may contain a provision under which the Artist agrees not to employ or engage any person in respect of the Artist's career without the consent of the Manager. This type of provision is unreasonable and should not be tolerated.

14.8 Application of Gross Income

Order of application

In considering the order of application of gross income, the first thing which should be looked at is the definition of gross income. The management agreement may provide that the arm's length cash value of any goods received by the Artist, or any "in kind" arrangement, are added to the cash sums actually generated by the Artist's services, grossing-up the total amount of income on which commission is payable. Generally, this provision is unacceptable from an Artist's point of view, although if there are circumstances where, as a result of a Manager's intervention, a genuine benefit of a material amount is provided for the Artist, then it would not be unreasonable for provision to be made.

An obvious example of benefit negotiated by the Manager would be for example the provision of tour support by a record company. From an Artist's perspective the amount of the tour support should not be used to gross-up the Artist's income for the purpose of calculating management commission because the tour support is being applied in order to generate sales of records and airplay which would generate publishing income. This income would be shared between Manager and the Artists in the percentages agreed. If however, the Manager negotiates the Artist a new Aston Martin, as part of a product endorsement deal, it would be reasonable for the Manager to receive a commission on the cash equivalent.

The general order of application of gross income or gross receipts under a management agreement is the following:

- Manager's commission
- Expenses incurred by the Manager
- Advances paid to the Artist

In addition, the Manager may be entitled to recover interest on the unrecovered amount of expenses and Artist's advances. The rate at which the interest is recovered may be expressed to be at a rate 2.5% above the base rate of any designated bank. This may not be unreasonable, if this is the rate at which the bank would be prepared to lend to the Manager.

The agreement may also provide that the Manager is to have the right to deduct from the gross income or gross receipts a reasonable reserve on account of future expenses or Artists' advances. Again, depending on the circumstances, this provision may be acceptable, although normally, the Artist will wish to limit the percentage amount which may be reserved.

Commission

The rate of commission to be deducted by the Manager will vary widely depending on the circumstances, from anywhere between 10% to 25%. The higher figure will be appropriate where the Manager is making available substantial advances and the lower figure will be appropriate when dealing with an established Artist. When dealing with a supergroup, the figure may be even lower.

Expenses

Where an agreement provides that the Manager is entitled to recover expenses, an Artist will normally wish such expenses to be fully supported by invoices or vouchers as evidence of their expenditure. Additionally, the Artist will wish to exclude expenses on certain matters, such as entertainment and general office expenses, as well as transport, legal and accountancy fees unless these can be shown to have been expended solely in relation to the Artist.

Advances

Where the Artist has received advance payments from the Manager, the agreement will contain a provision entitling the Manager to recover the amount of such advances from the income or receipts. The amount of all advances and the dates of payment are matters which obviously will depend on the circumstances and are to be negotiated between the Artist, the Artist's advisors, the Manager and the Manager's advisors.

Application of Gross Receipts

A point of fundamental importance is which party should be responsible for collecting the gross income (see Paragraph 14.3). Is the income to be paid to the Manager's account or to the Artist's account or to some designated collection account?

14.9 Accounting

See Paragraph 1.11.

14.10 Manager's Activities

The agreement may provide that the Manager will have the right to act as agent or Manager for any other artist or group during the term. Whether this acceptable or not will depend on the circumstances. Certainly the Artist will not wish to see the Manager's time availability unduly diminished by reason of commitment to other persons. Additionally the Artist may wish the Manager not to be associated with any group of artists which might directly compete with them in their sector of the market. Equally, however, there will be occasions where the Manager may have long-standing commitments to other artists which must be respected. The precise formula of this clause will therefore depend on the particular circumstances.

The management agreement may contain a provision stating that the Manager is to have the right to acquire literary, dramatic or musical material from the Artist or to produce audio or audio-visual material featuring the Artist. These provisions are normally totally unacceptable, since they conflict with the Manager's obligation to acquire the highest reasonably obtainable sum in relation to the Artist's services. If the Manager is making use of some such service through its own trading activities, it will be able to derive profit from them without accounting to the Artist. This is clearly unreasonable and should not be permitted in normal circumstances.

14.11 Consents

The agreement may provide that the Manager is to have the right to grant performers' consents on behalf of the Artist. Whether this is appropriate or not may depend on whether it is to have the right to execute engagement agreements on the Artist's behalf or not. Equally, however, there may be circumstances where consent to film or record an Artist's performance (at, say, a live venue) may be required to be given by the Manager because of prevailing circumstances, and a provision of this nature may be acceptable.

14.12 Suspension

See Paragraph 1.16.

14.13 Effect of Suspension

See Paragraph 1.17.

14.14 Termination

See Paragraph 1.18.

14.15 Effect of Termination

See Paragraph 1.19.

14.16 Boilerplate

The boilerplate section of a typical management agreement will contain the following provisions:

* No obligation (see Paragraph 52.6)
* Notices (see Paragraph 52.8)
* Severability (see Paragraph 52.10)
* Entire agreement (see Paragraph 52.3)
* Waiver (see Paragraph 52.11)
* No partnership (see Paragraph 52.7)
* Governing law (see Paragraph 52.5).

15 Artist's Partnership/Service Company Arrangements

15.1 Description of Artist's Partnership/Service Company arrangements

Most of the chapters in this book provide a detailed description of documentation relating to specific transaction arrangements. The number of variable factors which are capable of affecting individual agreements between artists is, however, too wide and a standard form "one size fits all" solution for artists' arrangements between themselves is not practicable.

The evil to be avoided in inter-artist arrangements is the imposition of a ready-made arrangement, or an arrangement made for other persons. The important thing in dealing with agreements between artists is to match the solution to the various requirements of the artists and the relevant circumstances.

This chapter examines some of the key areas in which artists will need to take advice both from a suitably qualified accountant and a lawyer. The combination of separate legal and accountancy advice is not duplication, but a necessary prerequisite. The best possible combination is an international tax practitioner (either accountant or barrister) who is a specialist in devising tax-effective royalty* structures and a legal advisor who is experienced in implementing effective transaction structures.

15.2 Partnership or Corporate Structure

One of the basic matters requiring thought is whether the artists' affairs are best organised on partnership basis or a corporate basis or a mixture of the two.

The disadvantage of partnership is that each of the partners is liable for the acts and omissions of the others. If artists are organised as directors of a company, although they lose their self-employed schedule D status and become schedule E employees, they are generally not personally liable for the acts or omissions of the company (although they may, in practice, be required to sign inducement letters, see Paragraph 51.2). If the company becomes insolvent they do not themselves become bankrupt.

In circumstances, however, where the membership of a group is liable to change, each successive change in line-up could create a separate partnership.

The provisions relating to cessation of a partnership and commencement of a new partnership are extremely complex, as is the treatment of partnership tax. It is not necessary to have a formal written agreement to create a partnership, since the carrying on of a business in common with a view to profit automatically creates a partnership under the governing Act, the Partnership Act 1890.

In fact, by the time a group has performed their first paid gig, they have probably already created a partnership. A number of provisions contained in the 1890 Act automatically apply to partnership situations, such as ownership of assets, right to terminate, and liabilities on termination. It is highly desirable that artists whose business affairs are not organised through limited liability companies should seek advice from a media lawyer experienced in advising on matters of partnership law.

15.3 Taxation

It is a well-established principle of law that every individual has the right to organise his or her affairs in such a way as minimise or avoid the payment of unnecessary tax. Tax avoidance is perfectly legitimate. Tax evasion (failing to file tax returns or concealing income) is, however, illegal and a criminal offence.

It is important for all artists to consider how best they can minimise the payment of taxation. The methods chosen to do this will invariably affect the corporate structure of an artist's business affairs. For example, it may be tax-effective to organise an artist's performing activities outside the United Kingdom so that the artist's performing services are acquired by a company in Jersey or the Isle of Man, which will receive the proceeds of the artist's tours outside the UK. The artist's UK services might be made available through a UK limited liability company and the artist's recording services might be made available through yet another separate foreign entity.

15.4 Division of Income

Any arrangement between the artists should specify how the income from their various activities is to be divided.

Income might loosely be categorised under three heads being:

* recording income
* publishing income
* other income.

Recording income is normally the subject of an even division. Publishing income is not usually divided equally between all members of a group, unless each member of the group co-writes all songs. Normally, publishing income is divided between the composers and lyricists of the songs either equally or in proportion to the shares which they contribute to the writing of the songs. Some groups or artists, however, divide equally all publishing income. It is probably fairer on the artists who write music and lyrics for the publishing income to be apportioned directly in proportion to the contribution made by each individual member.

Other income may come from a variety of different sources, such as merchandising income, tour income, personal engagements and other performances. Whatever way this income is divided up, it is important that agreement is reached between the artists at an early stage to avoid disputes.

15.5 Group Name and Trademarks

In many cases, the name of a group of artists may be capable of protection by trademark legislation. Where a specific logo is designed for the name of a group, the logo may also be protected as trademark.

The cost of applying for and maintaining trademark registrations across the world is high. The benefit of applying for and obtaining trademark registration is of considerable significance in enforcing rights against merchandising rights infringers. A trademark effectively permits a group of artists to market so-called "official" souvenirs and merchandise, and, subject to financial resources, is a highly desirable step.

The issue of ownership of the group name and associated trademarks is of fundamental importance. Where the line-up of a group changes the continuing members of the group will wish to ensure that they alone have the right to authorise the use of the groups name and its trademarks. It is highly desirable from all parties' points of view that the question of ownership of group name and trademarks is resolved in a written agreement, so that when members leave the position is clear.

15.6 Morals and Disputes

For some groups of artists (like boy bands) it may be desirable to have a so-called "morals" clause. Although clauses of this nature are of little use in the world of grunge, they may be important if a group of artists has a squeaky-clean image which it wishes to preserve. In such circumstances, members of a group of artists may wish to expel one of their members from the group, if that member makes any public statement about drugs, is the subject of proceedings or is charged or found guilty of the commission of an act of moral turpitude.

Where expulsion provisions are included in group arrangements, they may also extend to other matters, such as persistent lateness at live gigs or recording studios, failure to turn up for dates on tour, falsification of information given to insurers etc.

15.7 Alternative Dispute Resolution

One final provision which should be inserted in all agreements between artists is a procedure in relation to the resolution of disputes.

Legal proceedings taken through the courts are often extremely expensive and may take considerable time. Arbitration proceedings are unsatisfactory in other ways. In some circumstances, their cost can equal or exceed the cost of legal proceedings and, unless the award of a panel of arbitrators flies in the face of reason and flaunts logic, a party who has suffered a manifest injustice at the hands of arbitration will be unable to appeal against it through the courts.

A far safer and more private means of resolving disputes, is alternative dispute resolution, which provides a quick, cost-effective and streamlined procedure designed to resolve disputes in an equitable manner by mediation without resort to the courts. If alternative dispute resolution fails, the parties will still be able to exhaust their rights through normal legal channels.

Because of the old music industry adage "where there's a hit, there's a writ" it is highly desirable that, whatever commercial arrangements are agreed between the artists, they should include a specific provision for alternative dispute resolution to be used, should they ever fall out.

B: Development and Production of Film and Television Projects

16 Submission and Confidentiality Agreement

16.1 Submission and Confidentiality Agreements

This Chapter examines, quite separately, the provisions of a submission agreement* and a confidentiality agreement.

A submission agreement is usually an agreement sent by a large corporation to a person who wishes to submit projects to it for consideration. Its purpose is to control and/or limit the liability of the corporation by excluding obligations of confidentiality etc.

A confidentiality agreement is intended to have the reverse effect, and is normally required by an individual who wishes to send material to a company. The purpose of the agreement is to provide that the company or corporation will treat information relating to the individual's project as confidential and will not disclose it to any third party.

This Chapter examines the provisions of submission agreements and confidentiality agreements, in each case from the point of view of the individual.

16.2 Submission Agreement

The following provisions may be found in a submission agreement.

Authorship and Ownership

The agreement may confirm that the person submitting the material is the author and owner of all rights of the submitted material. This is acceptable.

The agreement may also disclose whether or not the material is based on third party material which is protected by copyright. Again, this is acceptable.

Non-infringement

The material submitted does not infringe any rights of copyright, patent, trademark, rights of privacy, publicity, moral rights or other rights. This is an acceptable provision.

Relevant Contractual Arrangements

The material is not to be subject to any assignment or licence or other arrangement pursuant to which any third party has rights. This is an acceptable provision.

No Confidentiality

The submission is not being made in confidence and the corporation receiving the material has no obligation to keep the material confidential. Whether this is acceptable or not will depend on the circumstances.

Similar Productions

Receipt of the material will not prevent the corporation from making productions which are based on any part of the material which is not new or novel or which is in the public domain or in producing projects on a similar theme or projects based on other sources.

Normally, this provision is acceptable, but careful attention needs to be paid to the wording of the relevant provision.

Maximum Compensation

The maximum compensation payable to the person submitting the material will be the rates specified in the appropriate agreement between the Writer's Guild of Great Britain and Producers' Alliance for Cinema and Television or, if no agreement is in force, the agreement that is closest in type to the material. US studios will, of course, refer to the relevant American agreement.

Whether this provision is acceptable or not will depend on the commercial circumstances.

No Liability for Destruction

The corporation will not be liable in the event the material is lost or destroyed. This is a reasonable requirement and the individual should obviously ensure that copies are kept of all material.

Right to Copy

The corporation has the right to copy the material and make adaptations and submit the material to third parties. A provision permitting the corporation to copy material for internal circulation is reasonable, although the individual might wish to limit the rights of the corporation to adapt the material or send it to outside third parties.

Arbitration

In the event of any dispute between the corporation and the individual, the dispute will be submitted to an arbitrator or to an alternative dispute resolution procedure. This is a sensible provision and, of course, alternative dispute resolution is preferable.

Boilerplate Provisions

A submission agreement will also contain a provision indicating the governing law and stating that the corporation has a right to assign its rights.

Unacceptable Provisions

Provisions which require an individual to waive any right to remuneration whatever are clearly unacceptable, as are provisions which state that the corporation will have no liability to the individual if it uses their material.

Many of the terms in US submission agreements are completely unreasonable and some of them are of dubious enforceability. There is a story reportedly recounted by Lew Wasserman of MCA that a sharp eyed in-house studio attorney spotted the fact that the address given by a person submitting material to that studio was the state hospital for the criminally insane. This prompted the attorney to review the studio's submission agreement and insert a warranty* to be given by all persons submitting material in future that they had full mental capacity. It is, of course, well known (even among lawyers) that any contract purportedly entered into by an insane person is void, as will be any warranty contained in it.

16.3 Confidentiality Agreement

A typical confidentiality agreement may contain the following provisions.

Nominal Payment

The company will acknowledge the receipt of £1 paid for by the individual. Payment of consideration is a prerequisite for an enforceable contract*, which is why this provision is often included. It is acceptable.

Associated Companies

The undertaking is binding on the company and all associated companies. This is perfectly acceptable, although the definition of "associates" should be checked to ensure that it does not extend to entities over which the company has no control.

Confidential Information

The undertaking will extend to all information relating to the particular project, other than information which is in the public domain. The company will agree to keep the confidential information restricted and will take all steps necessary to prevent it from being disclosed by the company's employees, servants or agents. The company will use the confidential information solely for the purpose of determining whether or not it wishes to enter into an agreement with the individual. This is acceptable.

Possession and Circulation

The company will retain possession of the confidential information and will not circulate it, other than to persons approved by the individuals. This is acceptable.

Storage

The company will keep all material in a safe and secure place and return them to the individual at the end of discussions relating to the project. This is reasonable.

Indemnity

The company will indemnify the individual in relation to any breach by the company of its obligations. As to indemnities, see generally Paragraph 53.16. A confidentiality agreement is, however, one of those documents where it is reasonable to seek indemnity protection, in order to underline the serious nature of the obligations.

17 Option and Purchase Agreement

17.1 Description of Option and Purchase Agreements

An option agreement* giving a film producer* the exclusive right to purchase a work within a period of time is an extremely effective commercial compromise. This has emerged in the motion picture industry in order to reconcile two opposing needs.

From a producer's point of view, the acquisition of outright ownership in every project the producer wished to develop would be extremely uneconomical. Conversely, from the point of view of the author or owner of rights, it would be bad business practice to sell film rights in a work on an outright basis to a producer because, if the producer went into liquidation, lost interest in the project, was simply unable to raise the production finance or for any other reason the project was not made, the author or the owner would suffer commercial disadvantage.

It is therefore normal for a producer to negotiate with the author or the owner for an option to acquire rights at a point in a future, during a prescribed option* period, for an agreed purchase price. If the producer pays the agreed purchase price during the option period, the producer will own the rights. If not, the author or owner will be free to exploit the rights after the end of the option period.

The parties to an option agreement and purchase agreement are:

- the producer intending to acquire the rights (referred to in this paragraph as the "Producer"); and
- the owner of the rights (referred to as the "Rights Owner").

17.2 Mechanics of an Option Agreement

The following are the basic commercial provisions which are normally contained in an option agreement.

Option Period

The option period is generally an initial period of at least 12 months which may be extended by one or more further periods of 12 months, for which the Producer will pay additional sums.

Option Price

The option price is frequently 10% of the purchase price and it is usual to treat the option price as an advance against the purchase price. Depending on the terms* agreed between the parties, sums paid to extend the option period may or may not also be counted as advances against the purchase price.

Purchase Price

The amount of a purchase price for a particular work will obviously depend on what the work is and who its author is, as well as whether the audio-visual project is to be a film destined for theatrical release or a television film or a television series.

A purchase price may be either a fixed sum or a percentage of the budget (normally between 1.5% and 3%) or a combination limited to a fixed maximum amount or "cap").

In addition, again depending on the commercial circumstances, Rights Owners may be entitled to a percentage of profits in a film (see Chapter 24).

Remakes and Sequel Films

Where a Producer acquires the right to make remakes or sequels, the industry rule of thumb for calculating the remuneration payable to the Rights Owner is 50% for a remake and 33.33% for a sequel (although these percentages are often reversed).

Rights Optioned

The precise definition of the rights acquired by the Producer will depend on the project and the nature of the work. In addition to cinema and television rights, the Producer will require certain subsidiary and ancillary rights, such as the right to exploit recording and merchandising elements of the work and the right to publish limited synopses of the work. The Producer will also need the right to make adaptations of the work (such as screenplays) and the right to use the work with other material and use its title prior to exercise of the option.

Normally a Rights Owner will withhold publication, live-stage and radio rights from a Producer. The Producer will generally seek to impose a restriction preventing the exercise of the live-stage and radio rights, unless the option agreement relates to the film rights in a work which has been produced on the live stage.

Additionally, as a separate issue from sequel films which may be made by the Producer, there is a question of sequel works written by the author. If the Producer's film is successful, the Producer will suffer a serious loss of opportunity if a provision has not been negotiated giving the Producer an option or first refusal right over sequel books (whether existing or written in the future).

17.3   Form of Option Agreement

The form of many option agreements is extremely cumbersome. This is because each option agreement needs to define the terms and conditions on which the Producer will acquire rights in the work and each option agreement will therefore need to have annexed to it a long-form purchase agreement.

Many of the provisions contained within the option agreement are repeated in the purchase agreement and there is frequently an excessive amount of duplication. There is, however, a simple drafting solution, which is to incorporate (by reference in the option agreement) all necessary warranties* required from the purchase agreement. This will produce an option agreement that is one or two pages long with a slightly longer form of purchase agreement (ten or eleven pages) attached to it.

Another factor which has a bearing on the form of an option agreement is the procedure to be adopted for execution of the purchase agreement once the option has been exercised. A Producer is normally concerned to ensure that, once it has paid the Rights Owner the purchase price (or at least the cash amount payable on exercise), the Rights Owner will execute the purchase agreement. In order to protect against the possibility that the Producer might pay and the Rights Owner might refuse to execute the purchase agreement, some option agreements require purchase agreements to be pre-signed by Rights Owners and held by the Producer in escrow.

This is an unsatisfactory procedure from a Rights Owner's point of view. Even from the Producer's point of view it is less than desirable, since it may be impossible to determine whether a document bearing the Rights Owner's signature alone is held in escrow or whether the purchase price has been paid and the document is effective.

Some lawyers attempt to solve this difficulty by inserting a provision which states that the Producer is appointed as the Rights Owner's attorney and has a power of attorney coupled with an interest in the work which is, therefore, irrevocable. The idea behind this is that the Producer will be able to execute a purchase agreement as the attorney of the Rights Owner if the Rights Owner refuses.

Unfortunately, this does not work under English law since—even if a power of attorney is stated to be irrevocable, there may be circumstances when it is revoked. If the person giving the power of attorney loses mental capacity, the power of attorney is automatically revoked and it can, in any event, be expressly revoked. The solution is to provide that the Producer acquires a specific power of attorney by way of security (see Paragraph 53.13).

The remainder of this paragraph has been written on the assumption that a short-form option agreement is used, incorporating by reference warranties and other provisions set out in the purchase agreement attached to it. The main commercial terms of the option agreement have been examined in Paragraphs 17.2 and 17.3. It only remains to analyse the provisions of the purchase agreement (including those which will be incorporated by reference in the option agreement).

17.4 Analysis of Purchase Agreement

A typical purchase agreement might be expected to contain the following clauses:

- Assignment (see Paragraph 17.5)
- Warranties (see Paragraph 17.6)
- Remuneration (see Paragraph 17.7)
- Sequels (see Paragraph 17.8)
- Agency and payment (see Paragraph 17.9)
- Screen credits (see Paragraph 17.10)
- Accounting (see Paragraph 17.11)
- Assignability (see Paragraph 17.12)
- Turnaround (see Paragraph 17.13)
- Boilerplate* (see Paragraph 17.14).

17.5 Assignment of Rights

The agreement will contain an assignment of the rights acquired by the Producer. Alternatively, the agreement may provide for an exclusive licence of the rights to the Producer (see Paragraph 53.2). Whether the rights are assigned or licensed, there needs to be an acknowledgement that the Producer has the right to adapt, alter and cut the work the right to rearrange it and use it with other material. This is of fundamental importance, as is a waiver of moral rights* (see Paragraph 53.10).

17.6 Warranties

The purchase agreement will normally contain the following specific qualities.

Ownership

The owner is the sole, absolute, unincumbered owner of all rights granted throughout the world. This is normal.

Recitals

The facts contained in the recitals to the agreement (the preliminary clauses) are true and correct. This is normal. Recitals, however, should only be used where there is a long and complex history of ownership of the work. Their purpose is to assist people dealing with documents in the future to reconstruct the series of events forming part of the chain of title of the work, not to state the obvious (eg that the Producer and the Rights Owner wish to enter into an agreement).

Novelty

No other audio-visual work has been produced which is based on the work or based on the same real life facts as those contained in the work, or on public domain material. This is normal. Obviously, the terms of the warranty need to be adjusted to fit the circumstances.

Ownership

In circumstances where the Rights Owner is not the author, the agreement may contain a warranty that the Rights Owner has acquired all rights from the author and has paid all sums due. This is acceptable.

Acquisition Agreement

In circumstances where the Rights Owner has acquired rights from the author, the Producer may wish a copy of the acquisition agreement to be annexed, as well as a warranty from the Rights Owner that the terms of the acquisition agreement have not been amended.

No Knowledge of Breach or Waiver

Where the Rights Owner is not the author, the Producer may require a warranty that the Rights Owner has no actual or constructive knowledge of any breach by the author of any term of the acquisition agreement and has not waived any of the Rights Owner's rights under the acquisition agreement.

Restrictions

The Rights Owner will not permit the exploitation of certain restricted rights (such as live-stage or radio rights) during a designated restricted period (see Paragraph 17.2).

No Transfer

Neither the Rights Owner or the author has assigned, licensed or encumbered any rights, except pursuant to agreements which are listed in the schedule.

Non-infringement

The author is the sole author of the work which is original and does not infringe any right of copyright, moral right, right of privacy, right of publicity or any other right.

Obscenity and Blasphemy

The work is not obscene or blasphemous or defamatory.

No Restrictions

The Rights Owner has the right to enter into the agreement and has not entered into any arrangement which might restrict the exercise by the Producer of its rights under the agreement.

No Claim

There is no actual or prospective claim in relation to the rights.

US Copyright Renewal

The Producer will have the right to register the copyright and renew or extend copyright in the USA.

Qualifying Person

The author was at all times during the writing of the work a qualifying person for the meaning of the Copyrights Designs and Patents Act 1988. This will guarantee copyright protection in the United Kingdom and as a result, copyright in those countries throughout the world which are members of the Berne Convention and the Universal Copyright Convention (ie countries in the world).

Publisher's Release

The Rights Owner will provide the Producer, within 14 days of execution, with a publisher's release. The form of publisher's release is normally a consent to the Producer producing a synopsis of the work. Without such a consent, technically, the Producer might be infringing the publisher's exclusive right to print and publish the work.

Author's Release

Where the Rights Owner is not the author, the Producer may require the owner to deliver an executed document from the author, confirming that the author has been paid all sums due.

Validity of Copyright

Copyright in the work is valid and subsisting pursuant to the laws of the United Kingdom, the USA, the provisions of the Berne Convention and the Universal Copyright Convention.

Copyright Notice

All published copies of the work have borne copyright notices in the form prescribed by the Universal Copyright Convention. Compliance with this provision used to be necessary in order to procure protection under US copyright legislation, but the position of the US has subsequently changed.

Confidentiality

The Rights Owner will not disclose or make public any information relating to the agreement, except to the Rights Owner's professional advisors.

Moral Rights

The author has irrevocably and unconditionally waived all moral rights to which the author is entitled in respect of the work (see Paragraph 53.10).

Indemnity

The owner undertakes to indemnify the Producer in relation to breaches (see Paragraph 53.16).

17.7 Remuneration

For a summary of the likely remuneration provisions in purchase agreements, see Paragraph 17.2.

17.8 Sequels

For the reasons referred to in Paragraph 17.2, a Producer will generally wish to acquire rights in sequel books written by the author.

17.9 Agency and Payment

There may be circumstances where the Rights Owner has an agent, in which event, the agreement will contain a direction to a Producer to pay the agent.

17.10 Screen credit

The agreement will normally specify the form of screen credit which the owner is entitled to receive (see Paragraph 18.7).

17.11 Accounting

If the Rights Owner is to receive a percentage of net profits, the agreement will need to provide the dates on which the Rights Owner is to receive statements of account as well as stating the dates on which payments are to be made.

17.12 Assignability

See Paragraph 53.1.

17.13 Turnaround

The agreement may contain a so-called "turnaround*" provision if rights are assigned to the Producer.

A turnaround provision will normally give the Rights Owner the right to require the Producer to reassign the rights to the Owner if production has not commenced on an audio-visual project within a specified time, provided the Rights Owner pays the Producer a certain sum. The Producer will normally wish the Rights Owner to repay to the Producer the total amount expended by the Producer on developing the project (possibly with interest). The Rights Owner may wish to exercise the turnaround right simply by repaying to the Producer the sums which have been previously been paid to the Rights Owner by the Producer. The precise amount to be repaid to effect turnaround will obviously be the subject of commercial negotiations.

The time period before which the turnaround right may be exercised is also subject to negotiation. It is not in the Rights Owner's interest to impose an artificially short period on the Producer, since many worthwhile projects take a considerable amount of time to put into production.

17.14 Boilerplate

A purchase agreement will normally contain the following boilerplate provisions:

* No obligation (see Paragraph 52.6)
* Notices (see Paragraph 52.8)
* Severability (see Paragraph 52.10)
* Entire agreement (see Paragraph 52.3)
* Waiver (see Paragraph 52.11)
* No partnership (see Paragraph 52.7)
* Governing law (see Paragraph 52.5)
* Certificate of value* (see Paragraph 52.2).

18   Screenplay Agreement

18.1   Description of a screenplay agreement

The screenplay agreement* is the document pursuant to which a producer* of a film commissions a writer to write a screenplay. A screenplay may be entirely original to the screenwriter or it may be an adaptation of an existing literary work.

The parties to the particular transaction are:

- the production company commissioning the Writer (referred to in this paragraph as the "Producer"); and
- the screenwriter (referred to as the "Writer").

This Chapter examines a screenplay agreement from the point of view of the Writer.

18.2   Transaction analysis

The screenplay agreement might be expected to contain the following clauses:

- Engagement (see Paragraph 18.3)
- Assignment (see Paragraph 18.4)
- Warranties* (see Paragraph 18.5)
- Remuneration (see Paragraph 18.6)
- Credit (see Paragraph 18.7)
- No obligation (see Paragraph 18.8)
- Work permits (see Paragraph 18.9)
- Insurance (see Paragraph 18.10)
- Suspension (see Paragraph 18.11)
- Effect of suspension (see Paragraph 18.12)
- Termination (see Paragraph 18.13)
- Effect of termination (see Paragraph 18.14)
- Boilerplate* (see Paragraph 18.15)

18.3 Engagement

This clause will normally set out the precise terms relating to the engagement. The first point which needs to be specified is the basis on which the Writer will render the Writer's services. In most cases, the Producer will require the Writer's services on an exclusive basis to ensure that the Writer is available to work on the Producer's project full-time. There may be some circumstances, however, where the Producer is prepared to accept that the Writer will be available on a so-called "first call" basis—ie where the Producer has first call on the Writer's services. Normally, however, a Producer will expect to have the Writer's exclusive services.

The agreement will normally provide for the Writer to produce a first draft screenplay. The Producer will then have a reading period of a specified number of weeks in order to consider the screenplay, at the end of which, the Producer will make it known to the Writer whether the Producer requires revisions. If the Producer does require revisions, the agreement will provide that the Writer is to deliver a revised second draft screenplay. Following receipt of this, the Producer will then again have a further reading period and will be entitled to require the Writer to produce further revisions by a stated date. Following delivery of the revised second draft screenplay, the Producer may have the right to require a "polish" by the Writer or alternatively, the agreement may require that the Writer will remain available throughout the production schedule to advise the Producer and assist in relation to the shooting script.

The agreement will normally provide that each rewrite is to be produced on different coloured paper, so that the Producer may easily identify the revised elements of the screenplay.

18.4 Assignment

The rights clause will normally contain an assignment of copyright from the Writer to the Producer throughout the world. This is perfectly normal.

18.5 Warranties

The following warranties are normally found in a screenplay agreement.

Sole Author

See Paragraph 17.6.

Absolute Unencumbered Owner

See Paragraph 17.6.

No Transfer

See Paragraph 17.6.

Originality and No Infringement

See Paragraph 17.6.

Obscenity, Blasphemy, Defamation

See Paragraph 17.6.

Right to Enter Into an Agreement

See Paragraph 17.6.

No Claim

See Paragraph 17.6.

Storage of Materials

See Paragraph 17.6.

Qualifying person

See Paragraph 17.6.

Waiver of Moral Rights

See Paragraphs 17.6 and 53.10.

Confidentiality

See Paragraph 17.6.

Indemnity

See Paragraph 17.6.

Right to Adapt

The agreement will normally provide that the Producer has the right to adapt and alter the material written by the Writer. This is standard.

Work Made for Hire

The agreement may contain an acknowledgement that the work shall be considered to be a "work made for hire" for purposes of US copyright legislation. This is normal.

18.6 Remuneration

The remuneration provisions in the Writer's agreement normally take the form of a series of payments made on specified dates. A certain sum will be payable on signature, a further amount on delivery of first draft screenplay, another amount on delivery of second draft, if requested, and further amounts payable on receipt of further revisions.

Normally, the agreement will be drafted on the basis that the Producer is entitled to what is sometimes referred to as "cut-offs*". In other words, if the Producer decides not to commission the second draft, there is a "cut-off point" and the Producer is not required to pay further remuneration to the Writer.

The agreement may contain an acknowledgement that the fixed sum payable on signature and delivery of first draft constitutes equitable remuneration*. This is a concept which has been recently introduced by EU Directives and confirmations on this basis are normal and acceptable (see Paragraph 53.6).

Additionally, the agreement may provide that, if the film is produced and is based solely or principally on the product of the Writer's services, the Writer will be entitled to a participation in profits.

Depending on the level of the fixed remuneration paid to the Writer, the agreement may be expressed to be a "buy-out*" of all residual, re-use, repeat fees and other payments. Residual payments are payable under the Writers' Guild of Great Britain Agreement with the Producers' Alliance of Cinema and Television. Residual payments are calculated as a percentage of the minimum fee established in the WGGB* agreement for various types of exploitation such as US network television exploitation and world-wide videogram exploitation. Whether the fee payable to the Writer is to be inclusive of residual payments or not is a matter of negotiation.

The remuneration will normally not be increased if the Writer takes longer to perform a service than is originally contemplated, nor are additional sums normally payable by the Producer if the Writer works during evenings or weekends or on public holidays.

The remuneration clause will normally contain a provision permitting the Producer to deduct any withholding taxes payable to the Writer and may also contain a payment direction, instructing payments to be made to the Writer's agent.

18.7 Screen Credit

It will be normal to expect the agreement to provide for the Writer to receive a credit in a prestated form. In circumstances where more than one Writer performs services, the agreement should provide that the credit is to be determined in accordance with the Writers' Guild of Great Britain, the Screenwriting Credits Agreement 1973 or the appropriate arbitration proceedings of the Writers' Guild of America.

In addition to the Writer's screen credit, the Writer may also be entitled to receive credit in major paid advertising issued by the Producer or the Producer's distributor. There are a number of circumstances where the Producer will wish to be excused from the obligation to provide the Writer with credit such as advertising in newspaper columns of less than eight column inches, congratulatory advertisements in relation to awards, institutional group advertising, advertising not primarily relating to the film and in relation to certain sizes of poster.

In some agreements, there may be a provision relating to the size of the Writer's credit or its position. If there is a provision in the agreement relating to size of credit, it is usual to see the so-called "art-work exception*", which provides that where the name of a film is the subject of some form of art-work in advertising, the size of the Writer's credit is not linked to the art-work size.

Additionally, it is normal for all screen credit clauses to contain a provision excusing the Producer in the event of casual or inadvertent failure by the Producer or any third party to accord the credit.

The agreement may also provide that the Writer has the right to require the Producer to remove the Writer's name from the credits of the film if the Producer makes changes to the screenplay which the Writer finds objectionable.

18.8 No obligation

It is normal for screenplay agreements to contain a provision stating that the Producer is not obliged to produce the film and, in the event the Producer is unable to do so, the Writer's sole claim shall be to receive the payments provided on signature and on delivery of the first draft screenplay if the Writer has performed the Writer's obligations.

In such circumstance, it is perfectly normal for the Producer to require an acknowledgement from the Writer that the Writer will not have any claim for loss of opportunity to enhance the Writer's reputation or loss of profits.

18.9 Work Permits

Depending on the circumstances, it may be necessary for a producer to insert a provision stating that the Producer's obligations towards the Writer are dependent on the Writer obtaining whatever work permits are necessary to enable the Writer to come to the country where the work is to be carried out.

Provisions such as these are normally included by prudent Producers because difficulties with immigration authorities as a result of drug convictions are not unknown.

18.10 Insurance

Depending on the precise circumstances and the amount of the fee paid to the Writer, the Producer may wish to secure life insurance on the Writer. The agreement, in these circumstances, may contain an acknowledgement from the Writer that the Writer does not have any entitlement to sums paid under any insurance policy.

The agreement will also provide that the Writer will attend such medical examinations as may be required by the Producer and provide all information requested by insurers in the form of proposal forms etc which the Writer will complete in a prompt and truthful manner.

18.11 Suspension

See Paragraph 20.18.

18.12 Effect of suspension

See Paragraph 20.19.

18.13 Termination

See Paragraph 20.20.

18.14 Effect of termination

See Paragraph 20.21.

18.15 Boilerplate

The boilerplate section of a typical screenplay agreement will contain the following provisions:

* Assignability (see Paragraph 52.1)
* Notice (see Paragraph 52.8)
* Severability (see Paragraph 52.10)
* Entire agreement (see Paragraph 52.3)

- Waiver (see Paragraph 52.11)
- No partnership (see Paragraph 52.7)
- Governing law (see Paragraph 52.5)
- Certificate of value* (see Paragraph 52.2).

19   Development Agreement

19.1 Description of a Development Agreement

A development agreement* is normally used by a financier of a film or a broadcaster to commission a producer* to develop a screenplay and to carry out all other necessary work, in order to prepare the project for production.

The development agreement permits a financier or broadcaster to prepare a project for production without actually incurring expenditure up to the amount of the entire production budget.

The parties to this particular transaction are:

• a financier or broadcaster providing finance to the producer to develop the particular project (referred to as the "Company"); and
• the producer being engaged to carry out the development work (referred to as the "Producer").

19.2 Document Analysis

A typical development agreement might be expected to contain the following clauses:

• Development (see Paragraph 19.3)
• Grant of rights (see Paragraph 19.4)
• Producer's obligations (see Paragraph 19.5)
• Payment (see Paragraph 19.6)
• Producer's warranties* (see Paragraph 19.7)
• Production (see Paragraph 19.8)
• Boilerplate* (see Paragraph 19.9).

19.3 Development

The development agreement will normally specify in precise detail what the Producer is required to achieve. This will vary according to the circumstances of production and will also depend on whether any development work has already been undertaken.

It would be normal to expect at least an outline to exist in relation to the project. The development work may require the Producer to commission a treatment of not less than a certain number of pages or it may require the Producer to commission a named writer pursuant to a screenplay agreement (see Chapter 18) and produce a first-draft screenplay together with a second draft and revisions, if requested by the Company.

The development agreement will normally require the Producer to produce a draft budget and cash flow schedule, so that the Company will know how much the production of the project is likely to cost. Frequently, the Company will wish the financial estimates of the Producer to be cross-checked by a completion guarantor and will require a letter of intent from an approved completion guarantor agreeing to enter into a completion guarantee (see Chapter 25), which will guarantee the delivery of the film for the amount stated in the draft budget by the date specified in the draft production schedule.

19.4 Grant of Rights

It is normal for development agreements to require an assignment of all literary, dramatic, musical and artistic material created during the development period. If the Producer contracts a writer under a screenplay agreement, the writer will assign the copyright in the screenplay to the Producer and the development agreement will contain an assignment transferring all rights acquired by the Producer to the Company, thereby transferring rights in the screenplay.

The assignment of all rights does, however, raise an issue from the Producer's point of view, since, in the absence of any contractual commitment, the Company will be free to commission another Producer to produce the project, unless the development agreement contains an obligation on the part of the Company to use the services of a Producer. Normally the imposition of an absolute obligation will be unacceptable, but it is frequently acceptable for the Company to undertake to offer to engage the Producer to produce the project if the Company decides to proceed.

19.5 Producer's Obligations

A Producer will normally be required to expend the development finance as economically as possible, solely in connection with the production of the development material. The Company will normally require the Producer to keep full and proper books of account in relation to expenditure occurred on the development material and will have the right to examine the books and accounts.

The Company will normally require the Producer to be solely responsible for all costs incurred in connection with the development material, including payment of fees to writers and all other third parties. The Company may also obtain an acknowledgement from the Producer that the Company will not have any liability to pay to the Producer any sums in addition to those required to be paid under the agreement.

The Company may also require the Producer to follow all rights clearance procedures nominated by the Company from time to time, in order to ensure that all necessary consents and waivers have been obtained from third parties, so that the project can proceed freely if the Company decides to put it into production.

19.6 Payment

The payment provisions in the development agreement will depend on the circumstances of the transaction and will be determined, to some extent, by the cost of development material which the Producer is contracting to produce.

Normally, a development agreement contains a series of payment dates and instalments. The payment of the instalments by the Company may be conditional on delivery by the Producer of certain materials at each stage in development.

The total sum paid to the Producer will normally include a fee for the Producer's personnel and should also include allowance in the budget for legal costs.

19.7 Producer's Warranties

A development agreement may be expected to contain warranties from the Producer on the following matters.

Capacity

See Paragraph 20.121.

Ownership

See Paragraph 17.6.

No Restrictions

See Paragraph 17.6.

Non-infringement

See Paragraph 17.6.

Obscenity, Blasphemy and Defamation

See Paragraph 17.6.

Not to Pledge Credit

The Producer will not pledge the credit of the Company or hold the Producer out as the Company's agent in any dealings.

Storage of Material in a Secure Place

The Producer will keep all development material and research material in a safe and secure place.

Copyright Notice

See Paragraph 17.6.

Right to Cut and Adapt

See Paragraph 17.5.

First Class Standards

The Producer will use its best endeavours to ensure that the development material is produced in a first-class manner consistent with the standards expected of a first-class production company.

Approval

The Producer will advise the Company of the identity of proposed researchers, consultants and other third parties, and obtain the Company's consent before engaging such persons in connection with the production of development material.

Approval of Agreements

The Producer will obtain the Company's prior approval of all agreements which the Producer intends to enter into with the third parties.

Confidentiality

See Paragraph 17.6.

Indemnity

See Paragraph 17.6.

19.8 Production

The development agreement will normally contain an acknowledgement on the part of the Producer that the Company is under no obligation to expend production finance on the production of the project. The Producer may, however, wish to secure its own position in the event the Company decides to do so (see Paragraph 19.3).

19.9 Boilerplate

A development agreement may be expected to contain the following boilerplate provisions:

* Notices (see Paragraph 52.8)
* Entire agreement (see Paragraph 52.3)
* Assignment (see Paragraph 52.1)
* Waiver (see Paragraph 52.11)
* No partnership (see Paragraph 52.7)
* Governing law (see Paragraph 52.5).

20 Engagement of Producer, Director and Principal Cast

20.1 Engagement Agreement

There are a number of similarities between the agreements* used to engage the services of a producer, director or principal cast member in film and television projects. The principal differences arise in relation to the description of the services to be performed by the individuals. This Chapter therefore examines the terms generally applicable to all engagements of services, but also considers the definitions of the relevant services separately.

Frequently, the affairs of individuals who are active in the entertainment industries are arranged so that their services are provided through a service company which will lend the services of the individual. The engagement agreement, in this instance, is normally referred to as a loan-out* agreement and the service company (often described as the "lender") will agree to lend the services of the individual to the company making the film. Apart from this change, the form of engagement agreement used where an artist's services are made available through a loan-out corporation is virtually identical to the form of agreement used where a production company will directly engage the services of an artist. Because a production company normally wishes to have a direct contractual commitment with an artist, in those circumstances where a loan-out corporation is used, the artist will be asked to enter into what is known as an inducement letter with the production company (see Paragraph 51.2).

The parties to an engagement agreement are:

- the production company engaging the services of the individual producer, director or artist (referred to in this Chapter as the "Company"); and
- the individual director, producer or principal cast member whose services have been engaged (referred to in this Chapter as the "Individual").

20.2 Services of Producer

The term "producer*" is used in a number of different contexts in the audio-visual industries and, on occasions, this has been known to cause difficulties.

The first sense in which the term is used is to denote the production company. Frequently, legal documents refer to this entity as the "producer".

The second sense in which it is used is to designate a person who has been responsible for securing finance for a production which has been originated by another producer. These types of producers are frequently referred to as "executive producers". They may include people whose reputation alone is such that their support of a project will be sufficient to gain a "green light" (eg Steven Spielberg). Or they may be executives of corporations who have been responsible for giving a project the go-ahead and wish their name to be attached to it. Equally, they may be officers or directors of third party financiers who wish to have their name attached to the project.

Normally, the term "producer" is used to refer to the individual who originates a particular audio-visual project by commissioning an outline or treatment or buying an option on a book. This person is generally responsible for acquiring all literary material, obtaining commitment from the star artists, identifying a possible director and raising all the finance for the project. He or she will also be responsible for working out the budget and production schedule, making arrangements for hiring all personnel and equipment, and dealing with all the other aspects necessary for the completion of a production.

A distinction may be drawn on the one hand, between negotiating deals with the talent (cast and director), raising finance from distributors, broadcasters etc and, on the other hand, the nitty gritty aspects of being responsible for the physical aspects of production. The former type of function may be performed by an executive producer and the latter part of the function may be performed a line producer or an associate producer. In practice, however, on smaller productions, both the "executive "and so-called "line" function are very often performed by one producer.

The services of the producer are normally required from the commencement of pre-production until the end of post-production—ie the date on which the film is delivered to its principal distributor.

20.3 Director's Services

The definition of the services of a director is generally pretty straightforward. These will include developing a script in collaboration with the writer, assisting the producer of the film to produce the production schedule and budget, selecting artists, screenwriters, composers, lyricists, choreographers and other creative personnel and selecting a director of photography, cameraman, editor, production manager and other personnel.

Additionally, the director will direct principal photography of the film and be in charge of its assembly and editing during post-production. During the post-production process, the director will also be responsible for overseeing the production of all music required for the film soundtrack, dubbing and special effects. The director will normally produce the director's cut (see Paragraph 20.4) and will be responsible for ensuring the production of a music cue sheet containing details of all compositions and recordings used in the film.

The services of the director are normally required from the commencement of pre-production until the end of post-production—ie the date on which the film is delivered to its principal distributor.

20.4 Director's Cut

All director's agreements will permit directors to produce a first cut of a film. In practice, it is likely that a director will cut a film many times before producing a version which the director is satisfied with.

Most director's agreements require the director to show his or her cut to the film's principal financier and give the company the right to make changes requested by the principal financier.

If the director is extremely well known, the director may be able to insist on a provision in the contract guaranteeing the director with the right to produce the final cut of the film, but this type of concession is relatively rare.

20.5 Artist's Services

The time period during which the artist's services are required is not as extensive as the time period during which the services of the director and producer are required.

Normally, the Company will require the services of artists during pre-production for wardrobe purposes. The number of days will, of course, be determined by the type of production. Costume drama or sci-fi production will require more extensive preparation. During the pre-production period, the Company may also wish to have the services of artists for the purposes of publicity, photographs and interviews.

In the case of a musical production, the services of the artist will be required before principal photography, in order to record musical material which is to be used during the shooting of the film. During principal photography of musical films, the artists will generally mime to playback.

In addition, in the case of artists' services, it is normal for the agreement to provide that the artists will be available for up to three free days during post-production for post-synchronisation purposes, miniature shots etc.

In calculating the length of time for which the artist's services are required during production, the Company will normally wish to make provisions to deal with the possibility that the shoot may be extended by an event of force majeure etc. The artist's other professional commitments may be such that the artist may want to limit the number of weeks by which the engagement may be extended and require a "stop date", after which the artists will be unavailable. The Company's position in these circumstances is normally determined by the requirements of its completion guarantor (see Chapter 25) who will determine whether or not a stop date is acceptable.

Where the requirements of the role require an artist to perform services of a dangerous or hazardous nature or the film is to contain scenes of nudity or simulated sex, there are provisions in union agreements which the Company will be required to comply with.

20.6 Document Analysis

A typical engagement agreement (whether of a director, producer or artist) might be expected to contain the following clauses.

- Engagement (see Paragraph 20.7)
- Rights (see Paragraph 20.8)
- Remuneration (see Paragraph 20.9)
- Expenses (see Paragraph 20.10)
- Payment (see Paragraph 20.11)
- Warranties* (see Paragraph 20.12)
- Conditions precedent (see Paragraph 20.13)
- Credit (see Paragraph 20.14)
- Accounting (see Paragraph 20.15)
- Conduct (see Paragraph 20.16)
- Insurance (see Paragraph 20.17)
- Suspension (see Paragraph 20.18)
- Effect of suspension (see Paragraph 20.19)
- Termination (see Paragraph 20.20)
- Effect of termination (see Paragraph 20.21)
- Boilerplate* (see Paragraph 20.22).

20.7 Engagement of Services

The services of the Individual are engaged for the requisite period (see Paragraphs 20.1, 20.2 and 20.3) at such locations as the Company requires in accordance with the production schedule for the film.

20.8 Rights

The rights clause in contracts for the engagement of services of individuals may contain the following provisions.

Copyright Assignment

The Individual will assign to the Company the entire copyright in the product of their services throughout the world for the full period of copyright protection. Even though such a provision may not be essential in an artist's agreement, there are circumstances where an artist may make an original contribution to a script and it is therefore wise to include it.

Performer's Consent

The Individual will confirm all consents required to permit the Company to exploit the performance of the Individual throughout the world. Strictly speaking, this provision is not necessary in the agreements with directors or producers, but is often included, not only because there are instances where directors play cameo roles in their own films, but also because they may appear in a documentary film about the making of the film.

169

Moral Rights

The Company will require a waiver of moral rights* of the Individual. Because the right to be identified is replaced with a specific contractual right to a credit (see Paragraph 20.14), this provision will not, in practice, cause an artist, director or producer any problem.

In the case of derogatory treatment of one's work, a director will generally negotiate a separate contractual provision to apply to cutting of the film so, again, in practice, a waiver of the statutory right is not normally a difficulty.

Name and Likeness

The Company will wish to obtain confirmation that it has the right to use the Individual's name, likeness and biography in connection with any merchandising or other activities relating to the film. The Individual may wish to exclude any general merchandising activities.

Documentary Film

The Company may wish to secure the consent of the person being engaged to the Company making a documentary film which incorporates so-called "behind-the-scenes" activities featuring the Individual. The Company may also wish to obtain the Individual's consent in relation to the use of out-takes in the film.

Soundtrack

There may be circumstances where the Company wishes to obtain from artists an acknowledgement that the Company has a right to produce audio recordings derived from the soundtrack of the film.

Dubbing

In agreements with artists, the Company will normally wish to obtain the consent of the artist to dub the artist's voice into English or any foreign language, if required for the purposes of production. There are standard provisions in the PACT/Equity Agreement in relation to this procedure.

20.9 Remuneration

Generally, the fees payable for the producer and director will be fixed amounts payable in agreed monthly instalments during production.

Although the fee payable for artists is generally a fixed amount designed to compensate the artist for the period of principal photography (often six to twelve weeks but occasionally considerably longer) it is not unknown for principal photography to continue for a few days or even a few weeks beyond a scheduled date if there have been difficulties during production. For this reason, an artist's fee is sometimes broken down into a weekly rate and a daily rate.

Additionally, in the case of artists, various guild and union agreements provide for the payment of residual payments or repeat and re-run fees. Normally, a producer will wish to prepay all these residuals so that the film may be exploited in the various media and territories without any additional payment being due to the artists. In some circumstances, the budget may not be adequate for the producer to prepay all residuals. Where sums are paid in excess of basic guild or union rates, it is normally anticipated that residual payments will be "bought out" and no further payments will be due.

Equitable Remuneration

The European Union recently introduced a statutory right of "equitable remuneration*" for writers and performers in relation to the rental of physical copies of their works or performances. The Company will normally wish to obtain confirmation from the individuals that the fixed sums paid to them under the agreement constitute equitable remuneration (see Paragraph 53.6).

20.10 Expenses

A contract for the engagement of services of an Individual may contain the following provisions relating to expenses:

Travel Expenses

The guild and union agreements generally require the Company to pay travelling expenses only if the Individual is required to attend a studio more than 30 miles away from Charing Cross in London or a location more than 20 miles away. In these circumstances, the Company is required to provide transport and pay the artist during travelling time or, where public transport is available, repay the artist to the cost of travel and make payment for travelling time. In practice, the Company may provide transport for the artist to and from the location or studio. If the artist works late at the request of the Company beyond the time when public transport is available, the union agreements require the Company to provide the artist with transport free of charge. The agreement may also provide that, if the Individual cannot reasonably return to London (or whatever city is the principal production base) every night, the Company will provide the artist with suitable hotel or accommodation and reimburse the artist the reasonable pre-approved cost of accommodation and meals, excluding drinks.

Per diem

Where an artist is required to render services at a foreign location, in some cases, the artist may be entitled to a daily (or "per diem") payment to cover expenses such as meals etc.

Resting Time

The PACT/Equity agreement requires the Company to arrange transport to any oversees location by an airline operating scheduled passenger services and having safety standards acceptable to the Civil Aviation Authority. It also requires that, where the flight time exceeds four hours, the artist will not be required for principal photography on the date of the flight, and where the flight time exceeds eight hours, the artist will have a 24-hour rest period.

Car

Depending on the status of the artist, there may be a need for the exclusive or non-exclusive use of a car to take the artist to and from their residence and the place where their services are required.

Winnebago

Depending on the status of the artist, there may be a requirement for the company to provide the artist with a private dressing room, caravan or Winnebago.

20.11   Payment

The payment clause may contain the following provisions.

Payment Direction

Where a contract* is negotiated by an Individual's agent, the agent will normally insist that the contract contains wording where the Individual directs the Company to pay all sums to the artist's agent. The Company will wish to obtain an acknowledgement, in return, from the Individual that payment to the agent releases the Company from its liability. This is normal and reasonable.

Value Added Tax

If Value Added Tax is to be paid, the Company will require delivery of a VAT invoice before being liable to pay it. This is reasonable.

Withholding

The Company will also reserve the right to deduct and retain any withholding tax due to the Individual in relation to the fee paid to the Individual for their services. The Individual will authorise the Company to deduct and withhold any withholding taxes* that may be required to be paid by law. This is a perfectly standard requirement.

In practice, certain non-EU artists who are higher paid may be subject to the imposition of withholding taxes in the United Kingdom. In some cases, they may ask the company to "gross-up" the amount of the fee to ensure that the Individual receives what they would have been entitled to before the imposition of withholding tax. It should be noted that, if a non-resident Individual negotiates for the introduction for a gross-up provision in relation to their entitlement to net profits, this will considerably increase the amount of net profits required to pay the Individual's entitlement and the additional tax payment and may have an impact on other profit participants.

20.12 Warranties

An agreement for the engagement of services may contain the following specific warranties.

Majority

That the Individual has attained the age of 18. Where this is self-evident, such a warranty is not necessary.

Capacity

The Individual is free to enter into the agreement and grant the Company the various rights.

No Restriction

There is no restriction or prohibition which might prevent or interfere with the Individual providing their services to the Company.

Exclusivity

The services of the Individual have not been and will not be made available to any other person during the time when the Company has the right to such services.

No Conflict

The Individual has not entered into any arrangement which conflicts with the agreement.

Qualifying Person

The Individual is a qualifying person within the meaning of the Copyrights Design and Patents Act 1988. This provision is designed to ensure that copyright protection adheres to the Individual's services.

Originality and Obscenity/Defamation

The product of the services of the Individual will be original and will not be obscene or defamatory.

Work Made for Hire

The product of the services of the Individual will be considered works made for hire for US copyright purposes. Effectively, this means that the Company owns them as if it were an employer. The right to terminate assignments of copyright in the US is more limited for works made for hire.

Right to Adapt

The Company has the right to adapt and alter the contribution of the Individual.

Professionalism

The services of the Individual will be made available in a professional manner, in willing co-operation with others.

Time of Day

The services of the Individual will be rendered in accordance with the requirements of the Company at any time of day, including Saturdays, Sundays and public holidays.

Confidentiality

The Individual will not disclose or reveal any financial or any other information relating to the film without the written consent of the Company.

Health

The Individual is in a good state of health and will take all practical steps necessary to maintain it and do everything necessary to enable the Company obtain insurance.

Dangerous Pursuits

The Individual will not take part in any hazardous or dangerous pursuits and will not leave any location without the consent of the Company. Normally the insurance cover which the company's effects on personnel will exclude certain dangerous risks, and it is important that the Company obtains the agreement of all personnel not to take such risks.

Promotion and Advertising

In the case of artists, the Company may wish confirmation that, other than payment of expenses, the artist will not seek remuneration for promotional work.

Clothes

There may be circumstances where the Company requires the artist to make available their own clothes.

Appearance

The agreement may provide that the artist will not do anything to change their appearance or, alternatively, they will accept that the artist's appearance will be changed in order to with the requirements of the film director and the part.

Part and Script

The artist accepts the part as written and agrees to learn it to such extent that no delay will arise in production as a result of the artist's lack of familiarity with it.

Portrayal

The Company will have the right to decide on how the artist will be portrayed in a film, in particular, matters relating to their dress, make-up etc.

Double

In an agreement engaging the services of an artist, the Company will want to have the right to use doubles and stand-ins.

Third Parties

The Company will have the right to make the services of the Individual available to third parties and the Individual will co-operate with all such third parties. This is an essential provision since, if the completion guarantor takes over production, the Individual will be required to co-operate with the completion guarantor.

Whereabouts

The Individual will keep the Company informed at all times during the engagement of their whereabouts and telephone number.

No Agency

The Individual will not enter into any contract on behalf of the Company with any person. In practice, this may be acceptable in contracts for directors and actors, but this type of provision is obviously not practical to include in the agreement with a producer.

Rules and Regulations

The Individual will comply with all rules and regulations in force at any place where the Individual renders services.

No Sponsorship

The Individual will agree not to enter into any arrangement where any third party might acquire the right to advertise, promote or sell goods or services of any description using the Individual's name or any reproduction of the physical likeness of the Individual in association with their involvement with the film.

Restriction

If the film is of a famous play or opera, the Company may wish to ensure that none of the principal personnel involved will participate in any competing audio-visual version for a stated period of years.

Indemnity

The agreement may contain indemnity provisions (see Paragraph 53.16).

20.13 Conditions Precedent

The agreement may make it a condition precedent of any obligation on the Company towards the Individual that all necessary passports, visas and work permits are obtained. It may relieve the Company of any liability towards the Individual, if any of the same are withdrawn, revoked or cancelled.

Since entry visas may be refused to persons who have drug convictions etc, this is a sensible precaution for the Company to take.

20.14   Credit

Screen Credit

The agreement will normally entitle the Individual to a screen credit, subject to the film being made and the Individual substantially performing their obligations. The form of words should be specified, as well as their position in the opening or end credits and whether the size of the credit is linked to any other.

Advertising Credit

In addition to on-screen credits, individuals engaged in the film may be entitled to a credit in paid advertising issued by the Company. Normally, advertising of less than a certain number column inches is excluded. Advertisements of a congratulatory nature relating to awards or advertisements relating to general activities of the Company are also excluded from the scope of any advertising credit obligation, as are posters and billboards of certain sizes.

Artwork Exception

Where advertising uses an artwork arrangement for the title of the film, it is normal for contracts to include a provision which says that any reference to size of the advertising credit will relate to the ordinary or regular unembellished upper or lower case standard typographical lettering for the title, not the artwork version.

Casual or Inadvertent Failure

It is normal for a provision to be included which would excuse the Company from breach of any credit obligation if such breach arises as a result of casual or inadvertent failure.

20.15   Accounting

Net Profits

If the Individual is entitled to receive a participation in net profits (see Chapter 24), the agreement will provide that the Individual will receive a statement of net profits within a specified number of days after each accounting period.

The percentages of net profits payable to Individual creative personnel (director, producer and principal cast) may vary between 2.5% and 5%. In some cases, they will be greater, in some, they will be less. The negotiating position of some individuals may permit them to receive a percentage of gross receipts from a film, although this is somewhat rare.

Accounting Periods and Dates

Quarterly accounting is standard in the audio-visual industry. However, in many agreements, the accounting obligations after the first three years from release of a film are semi-annual, as opposed to quarterly.

Accounting dates in the audio-visual industry are normally 45 to 60 days after quarterly accounting periods. If accounting periods revert to a semi-annual basis, then the accounting dates will normally be 60 to 90 days after the end of the period.

Audit

The agreement will normally permit the authorised representative of the Individual to inspect, audit and take copies of books of account of the Company to the extent they relate to the net profits. The agreement may, however, impose an obligation on the Individual to procure that the accountant involved executes a confidentiality agreement in a form required by the Company and is not at the time of the audit engaged in another dispute with the Company.

20.16   Conduct

So-called "morals" clauses have been used in the audio-visual industry since the earliest days. These clauses state that the Individual will not at any time during the engagement do anything which might bring the Individual or the film into public disrepute or offend the community or public morals or prejudice the Company.

Whether this type of clause is appropriate or not will depend on the circumstances.

20.17   Insurance

It is important for the Company to effect insurance arrangements on all key members of the production. All individuals will undertake to submit in a timely manner to medical and other examinations and will undertake to complete in a truthful manner all necessary proposal forms.

The Company will also need to obtain confirmation from the Individual that he or she does not have any interest in the proceeds of insurance policies effected by the Company. Again, this is normal.

20.18 Suspension

Engagement agreements with individuals need to contain provisions permitting the Company to suspend or terminate the engagement in certain circumstances.

The Company will normally be entitled to suspend the engagement of an Individual if:

*   the Individual fails or refuses to perform any service or is otherwise in breach of any obligations;
*   the Individual has failed to submit to any medical examination or has made any untrue statements or inaccurate replies to proposals;
*   the Individual has been prevented from performing a service by injury or illness or mental or physical disability or is, in the opinion of the Company, incapable of performing the services for a specified number of consecutive days;
*   in the case of an artist, the appearance or personality or voice of the artist shall have deteriorated materially and such deterioration continues; or
*   an event of force majeure prevents the Company from making use of their services.

20.19 Effect of suspension

On suspension, it is normal for the Company's payment obligations towards the Individual to cease. Where suspension is caused by an event of force majeure, however, the Individual should be entitled to receive payment of expenses.

During the period of suspension, the Individual will be expected to comply with all their obligations in the agreement which are not effected by the suspension, and may be required to act in accordance with any dispute resolution proceedings contained within a relevant union agreement.

20.20 Termination

The Company will normally have the right to terminate the agreement at any time when it is entitled to suspend (see Paragraph 20.17) or if suspension has continued beyond a specified number of days.

It is normal for an agreement to provide that notice of termination will be given in writing to the Individual and, where a relevant union agreement contains dispute resolution provisions, the Company may undertake to be bound by these.

20.21 Effect of Termination

The agreement will normally provide that a number of provisions will apply on and after notice of termination, including the following.

Compliance

The Individual will continue to comply with all obligations which are not affected by termination.

Rights

The entitlement of the Company in relation to rights granted will not be affected.

Remuneration

The Individual will only be entitled to such remuneration as accrued, due and payable at the date of termination or suspension.

Claim

Any claim which either party may have in relation to breach occurring prior to termination or suspension will not be affected. All rights of termination or suspension are separate from, and in addition to, any other rights of the Company at law.

20.22   Boilerplate

The boilerplate section of an agreement for services may contain the following provisions:

- No obligation (see Paragraph 52.6)
- Notices (see Paragraph 52.8)
- Severability (see Paragraph 52.10)
- Assignability (see Paragraph 52.1)
- Entire agreement (see Paragraph 52.3)
- Waiver (see Paragraph 52.11)
- No partnership (see Paragraph 52.7)
- Governing law (see Paragraph 52.5).

C: Production and Financing of Film and Television Projects

21 Production, Financing and Distribution Agreement— Production Aspects

21.1 Description of Production, Financing and Distribution Agreement

The production, financing and distribution agreement* is, without any doubt, one of the most impressive and complex documents used in the media industries. The PFD agreement*, as it is known, has many variants and exists under many different forms and names. For example, the terms of trade of broadcasters within the United Kingdom who commission programmes from independent producers* are, in essence, reformatted PFD agreements, which are called something else.

The PFD agreement is most simply analysed by breaking it down into its component parts. This Chapter therefore examines production aspects from the PFD agreement, Chapter 22 examines financing and distribution aspects and Chapter 23 examines warranties*, take-over, default, abandonment and other general provisions.

The parties to this particular transaction are:

- the producer of the film (the "Producer"); and
- the company providing the finance for the production of the film (the "Company").

21.2 Transaction Analysis

The production elements of a production, financing and distribution agreement may include the following provisions:

- Production, delivery and essential elements (see Paragraph 21.3)
- Rights (see Paragraph 21.4)
- Production contracts (see Paragraph 21.5)
- Production reports (see Paragraph 21.6)
- Insurance (see Paragraph 21.7)
- Credit (see Paragraph 21.8)
- Censorship (see Paragraph 21.9)

- Rushes (see Paragraph 21.10)
- Company representatives (see Paragraph 21.11)
- Film, library and props (see Paragraph 21.12)
- Laboratory and optical work (see Paragraph 21.13)
- Consents and approvals (see Paragraph 21.14).

21.3 Production, Delivery and Essential Elements

Budget and Production Schedule

The Producer agrees to produce the film in accordance with the production schedule for the budget and to deliver the delivery material to the Company on the delivery date. The production schedule is normally attached to the agreement, as is the budget for the film, which provides a complete breakdown of all anticipated expenditure. The total budget of a production is worked out by adding up the cost of three separate areas:

- direct cost;
- indirect cost; and
- contingency.

The Direct Cost
The direct cost comprises *"Above the Line Costs"** and *"Below the Line Costs"**.

Above the line costs include all costs relating to the acquisition of underlying rights and all fees payable to the producers, director and principal cast of the production.

Below the line costs are studio and equipment costs, design and wardrobe costs, fees of members of the cast other than principal cast, travelling and accommodation costs, film stock costs, laboratory costs, special effects costs and all post-production costs.

The below the Line Costs are generally consistent and reasonably predictable, depending on the type of production involved. The above the line costs are capable of tremendous variation and reflect the artistic and creative qualities of the production.

The Indirect Cost
The indirect cost* includes the fee payable to the completion guarantor and any commitment fees or similar charges payable in respect of finance, legal fees and accountancy fees.

The Contingency
The contingency* element is an allowance normally of 10% of the direct cost of the production which is included to anticipate any unforeseen contingencies which may arise during the course of production. In order to produce a budget the producer or production manager of a film needs to know precisely how many days' availability he will require for each member of the cast, each member of

the production team and all equipment. A production schedule must, therefore, be created, itemising every single requirement.

In order to complete the production schedule, the production manager will require details of all locations to be used for the film. It is the task of the production manager to cost out every potential location, paying particular regard to travel distance and travel time (which will increase the labour costs), the requirement to construct sets, transportation accommodation and subsistence charges, per diems* for cast and crew, equipment transportation and storage, office facilities for location work, power requirements, dressing rooms and laboratory and rushes arrangements.

During production of the film, time is literally money and it is therefore vital to spend it in as an economical a way as possible. For this reason, a shooting script is broken down into composite elements and each member of the cast is assigned a separate number. Each scene of the script is numbered and all props and sets are catalogued. The results are then cross-plotted and the scenes with the highest number of common denominators are grouped together and shot in sequence in the most economical way possible following the judgment of the director, the producer and production manager.

Cross-plotting enables the release of major props and expensive cast members at an early stage in production and avoids tying-up elements for any longer than necessary.

Undertaking to Produce

In consideration of the Producer's undertaking to produce the film and deliver the delivery material, the Company will agree to pay to the Producer the budget in accordance with the cash flow schedule (which is normally part of the budget). The Company will also agree that the Producer is entitled to receive the production fee specified in the budget.

Laboratory Pledgeholder's Letter

The Producer will be required to execute and deliver to the Company a laboratory pledgeholder's letter (see Paragraph 51.4). The purpose of this letter is to ensure that all material held in the laboratory is retained by the order of the Company, not the Producer.

Screenplay/Shooting Script

The screenplay is to be approved by the Company and will comply with all recommendations of the Company's legal advisors. The Producer will comply fully with all title search and rights clearance procedures recommended by the Company's legal advisors.

The agreement will also normally provide that the film will not depart from the shooting script except for minor dialogue changes and other minor changes required to meet the exigencies of production.

Underlying Rights and Third Party Rights

The agreement will provide that any literary, dramatic, musical or artistic material created for the purpose of the film will have been written by persons who have entered into agreements approved by the Company. When existing third party material is used (such as music, lyrics or sound recordings) the terms of such agreements are required to be approved by the Company. This is to avoid exposing the Company to actions for infringement and also to ensure that the terms on which the rights acquired are commercially sensible.

Studios and Locations

The film will be photographed and recorded at the various studios and locations on the dates specified in the production schedule.

Essential Elements, Facilities and Technical Specifications

The film will incorporate the essential elements and facilities and will comply with the technical specifications. Normally, the agreement will list a number of essential elements, including literary material (books, screenplay, revisions), principal artists, director, producer and composer.

Where any special facilities or equipment or process is essential to the production values of the film, this will also be listed. The specifications which the film is expected to comply with, need to be set out. These include the duration, film gauge, film stock, colour process, aspect ratio, lenses, sound system and other technical specifications.

Language

The film will be recorded and photographed entirely in the English language, unless the approved screenplay or shooting script contains non-English language dialogue.

Quality

The film will be a feature-length colour cinema film of first-class, quality technically, artistically and in all other respects. For television productions, obviously, the reference to cinema films will be amended.

Dubbing

If any actor used in the film is unable to speak English fluently when required to do so for the purposes of the screenplay, the Producer will ensure that the actor speaks the actor's dialogue with lip movements set to the required English words. The English words will be dubbed by an English-speaking actor approved by the Company during post-production.

Sponsorship

The film will not contain any third party material or visually identifiable references to any merchandised goods or services and the Producer will not enter into any product placement arrangement or tie-in* arrangement, unless the Company has specifically consented in writing.

Code Compliance

The film will comply with codes of all relevant bodies, including the Independent Television Commission. As to censorship see Paragraph 21.9.

Other Regulatory Requirements

The Producer will comply with all applicable statutes, ordinances, rules and regulations and obtain and pay for all necessary permits, licences, consents etc. This provision is necessary where foreign location shooting is concerned, since a number of consents and licences may be required.

21.4 Rights

Copyright Assignment

The Producer will be required to assign to the Company the entire copyright in the film. The Producer will also be required to assign all rights which the Producer has in relation to any underlying rights material (such as the book on which the film is based, the screenplay, the music commissioned for the film, the design material for the film etc) and the entire copyright in the product of all the services of the production personnel engaged in connection with the film.

Because of a recent European Directive (Directive 93/98), under United Kingdom law, copyright in films is jointly owned from the moment of creation and belongs to both the producer and the principal director. It is probable that the assignment clause will, therefore, specifically refer to the fact that the producer has acquired all rights from the principal director of the film, pursuant to the agreement engaging the director's services (see Chapter 20).

Music

So far as music rights are concerned, most composers are members of performing rights societies, such as the Performing Right Society Limited* or its foreign equivalents, such as SACEM in France and ASCAP*, BMI* and SESAC* in the USA (see Paragraph 2.5). The rules of performing rights societies do not permit their composer members or publisher members to assign outright any copyrights in musical works which they own. The performing rights societies themselves control certain rights of copyright, principally, the right to authorise public performance and broadcasting.

These rights are licensed by the performing rights societies who collect annual license fees from television companies and radio broadcasters, and public performance fees from venues where music is played. These venues include not only concert halls, but also pubs, clubs, hairdressers, airports and shopping malls. The assignment of rights to a Producer in musical works is normally subject to the rights of the PRS and its associated organisations and also subject to the rights of Phonographic Performance Limited, which is an organisation analogous to the PRS and controls the public performance right in sound recordings.

The Producer will therefore need to obtain a synchronisation licence* in relation to all music used in the film. This licence will permit the unrestricted exploitation of the film in all media without payment other than to the PRS and its associated societies, subject to payment of mechanical royalties (see Paragraph 2.5).

Performer's Consents

The Producer will confirm that there have been granted to the Producer, the Company and their respective successors and assignees all consents required in relation to any performances incorporated in the film. This is an essential requirement from both the Producer's and the Company's point of view, since, if the consent of a performer whose performance is incorporated in the film has not been obtained, that person may be able to injunct and restrain the distribution of the film or claim damages for the exploitation of the film.

Waiver of Moral Rights

The Producer will confirm to the Company the irrevocable waiver of moral rights* on the part of all persons who have been engaged in relation to the film.

The question of waiver of moral rights of directors and producers and artists is addressed in Paragraph 20.8. The waiver of moral rights of screenwriters is dealt with in Paragraph 18.7.

Equitable Remuneration

The Producer confirms and warrants to the Company that all persons engaged in connection with the production of the film have confirmed that the fixed remuneration which is payable to them (ie exclusive of any profit participations etc) constitutes equitable remuneration. This provision is necessary following the introduction of EU Directive 92/100 and is not normally contentious (see Paragraph 53.6).

Name, Likeness and Biography

The Producer confirms that the Company and its successors, assignees and licensees will have the right to use name, likeness and biography of all persons appearing in the film and related publicity material and underlying rights material. The rights of the Company extend to having the right to use recordings of the voices and any films or photographs or recordings of the personnel.

This provision is required because, in some jurisdictions (at least three states in the USA), it constitutes a criminal misdemeanour to use the name or likeness or biography of a person without their consent.

Merchandising Rights

The Company and its successors and assignees have the sole and exclusive merchandising rights in and to the name and likeness of all persons appearing in the film, rendering services in connection with the film or providing underlying rights or publicity material including the right to manufacture, distribute and sell articles of all descriptions.

This is another essential right in view of the increasing importance of film-related merchandising. In circumstances where star artists or other persons have limited the scope of the merchandising rights which they can grant (in many cases, existing contractual requirements of advertisers or sponsors may necessitate this), the Producer will need to exempt existing contractual arrangements. Many artists will wish to exclude merchandising arrangements not directly linked to the film.

Copyright and Title Registration

The Producer confirms that the Company shall have the sole and exclusive right to register the copyright in the film in the US Library of Congress and other libraries, the title of the firm in the Motion Picture Association of America Title Registration Scheme and take such steps, as may be necessary in the discretion of the Company, to protect its rights.

Normally, titles of films are not protected by copyright, but the MPAA Title Registration Scheme is intended to prevent studios from producing similarly named motion pictures which might result in passing-off claims or unfair competition claims in certain states.

Right to Bring and Defend Proceedings

The Company has the exclusive right to bring and defend proceedings in relation to the film without prejudice to its right to join the Producer as a plaintive or defendant in any action.

Where, for example, a claim for infringement is brought against the Company by a third party, the Company might wish to join the Producer as a third party in the proceedings and, in this way, the Company will be able to recover damages from the Producer without starting a separate legal action against it.

The Producer acknowledges that it has no right or entitlement in relation to any money recovered by the Company pursuant to any proceedings. Obviously, if the Producer has suffered damages as a result of the actions of a third party, this would not prevent the Producer from bringing proceedings in its own right.

Further Assurance

The Producer undertakes to do any acts and execute any documents required by the Company to give effect to any provision of the agreement. As security for the performance of the Producer's obligations, the Producer appoints the Company as the Producer's attorney, pursuant to the Powers of Attorney Act 1971, s 4 (see Paragraph 53.13).

There are certain statutory steps that the Company may require the Producer to perform, such as giving notice to third parties, and this guarantees that, if the Producer does not take such steps, the Company may do so as its attorney.

21.5 Production Contracts

Form and Approval

The Producer will undertake that all production contracts entitle the Company and its licensees to exploit the film and its component parts in all media throughout the world. The Producer will also undertake that the production contracts will be in such form that has been approved by the Company. It will agree to seek the Company's approval for any amendments that are proposed to be made to the production contracts.

Assignability

The Producer will confirm that it has the right to assign the production contracts to the Company and/or any completion guarantor (see Chapter 25) and confirms that the benefit of all warranties and indemnities* in the production contracts is assignable.

Contracts with individuals are personal and it is essential, from the Company's point of view, that the completion guarantor has the right to enforce the production contracts against the various individuals in the event the completion guarantor is required to take over production of the film.

Third Party Limitations

The production contracts do not contain any limitations in relation to rights controlled by third parties or in relation to any dates, beyond which the services of the individuals are unavailable.

It is important to the Company that, if principal photography is extended for any reason, it should remain entitled to the services of personnel. The completion guarantor will also be concerned on this point.

No Termination or Variation

Once the Company has approved the production contracts, the Producer will not amend or terminate or suspend any of them or waive any rights granted to it without the prior written consent of the Company.

If any problems do arise in the production, the Company will wish to be fully apprised of what happens, and agree on an appropriate course of action with the Producer.

Exercise of Rights

The Producer will acknowledge that the Company is entitled to exercise any of the rights which the Producer has, pursuant to the production contracts including the right to suspend the services of persons and the right to require persons to have medical examinations etc. The Producer will agree to do any acts required by the Company in this regard.

There may be occasions where the Company has a view on whether a person should be suspended or contractual rights should be enforced against an individual. The Company's view may differ from the Producer's and it is for this reason that the Company will seek to have the right to exercise the Producer's contractual rights on behalf of the Producer.

Remuneration

The remuneration pursuant to the production contracts will not exceed the amounts allocated in the budget and will be payable on the dates and intervals specified in the cash flow schedule.

It is important for the Company to 'lock down' as far as possible the financial aspects relating to the production.

Minimum Rate

All remuneration payable under production contracts, other than contracts for principal personnel, will be at the minimum relevant union agreement rates. The

Producer will not undertake to pay any person living expenses unless payable pursuant to a specified union agreement. This provision is required in order to control the total production costs.

Relevant Union Agreements

The Producer will not pay any residual repeat, rerun or reuse fees, unless they are required to be paid pursuant to the provisions of the relevant union agreement. In such event, residual fees are required to be pre-paid to the maximum extent permissible and, inclusive of all equitable remuneration obligations (see Paragraph 53.6).

The reasoning behind this provision is that the Company wishes to limit as far as possible any additional sums which are to be paid on exploitation of the film. This provision is especially important where the subject of the production finance agreement is not a large budget feature film but a small programme. In some cases, licence fees payable for foreign territories may be less than the amounts of residuals required to be paid to production personnel, and this means that the programme can only be sold at a loss.

The PFD agreement may also identify which relevant union agreement applies to actors, musicians, writers, technicians etc.

Original Documents

The Producer may be required to deliver to the Company an original, fully executed copy of each production contract within a certain specified number of days from execution.

The Company requires copies of all principal production contracts in order to ensure that it has acquired all necessary rights.

No Interest

Neither the Producer nor any person connected with the Producer will have any direct or indirect interests in any production contract or any of the underlying rights material or any interest in gross receipts or net profits or the right to receive any deferment or participation, except as specifically provided under the PFD agreement.

The Producer will also undertake not to enter into any production contract with any connected person. The purpose of these provisions is to prevent the Producer making a secret profit at the expense of the Company.

Not to Pledge Credit

The Producer undertakes and agree, that all production contracts are entered into by the Producer in its own right. It will confirm that the Company will not have any liability as the undisclosed principal of the Producer and that the Producer does not have the right to pledge the credit of the Company.

It is important for the Company to exclude any possibility that the Producer may act as the Company's agent because, at law, the acts of an agent are deemed to be that of the principal who is liable for them (see Paragraphs 54.26 to 54.29).

21.6 Production Reports

Status Reports and Cost Statements

The Producer will prepare daily status reports, weekly cost statements and cash flow schedules and will deliver copies to the Company every week. The Producer will, at all times, keep the Company and its production representative informed of the progress and the production of the film.

It is obviously important for both the Company and the completion guarantor to monitor the progress of the film and the expenditure at each stage in the production.

Information and Meetings

The Producer agrees to provide the Company with information in relation to any matter relating to the production, where the Company needs further information, and will also agree to attend meetings with the Company and its production representatives to discuss matters relating to the production.

It is obviously in the interests of both parties for communications concerning the film to be effective.

21.7 Insurance

Insurance Policies

The Producer undertakes to effect insurance policies in relation to a number of matters, including cast, negatives, faulty stock/tapes, props, sets and wardrobe, equipment, extra expense, third party property damage, office contents, general liability and errors and omissions.

The amounts and principal terms, including exclusions for all policies, will be agreed by the Company. The contract may, however, provide that the Producer is responsible for ensuring that cover is adequate.

Exclusions and Deductibles

The Producer agrees to notify the Company if insurance is refused in relation to any of the principal cast or personnel (director, producer etc) or if insurers wish to exclude liability in relation to certain matters or apply a deductible higher than the standard deductible.

The exclusion of matters from cover will normally mean that the Producer—and consequently the Company—is being expected to bear commercial risk in a particular area. An increase in the amount of deductibles will, of course, be relevant if there is a claim, since the amount of the deductible will not be covered.

Period of Insurance

The production policies will normally be required to remain in effect until delivery of the film, but the errors and omissions insurance policy will normally be required to remain in effect for three years following first exploitation.

The Producer will ensure that the Company is noted as "sole loss payee" and as "named insured" or "additional insured" on all insurance policies. Since the Company is making available the finance necessary to make the film, the Company will wish to ensure that, if payment is made on any claim, the Company will receive the money direct, rather than payment being made to the Producer.

Premiums

The Producer agrees to pay all premiums under the insurance policies and will not do anything which may result in the policies lapsing or becoming void or voidable or uncollectible. Each insurance policy will provide that its terms may not be amended without the consent of the Company and the insurance company concerned will immediately notify the Company in writing in the event that any policy becomes voidable or there is an impending lapse of cover.

The purpose of this provision is to afford the Company a reasonable opportunity for preventing any insurance policy from lapsing.

Identity and Terms

The identity of all insurance companies and underwriters and all terms and provisions of the insurance policies will be subject to the prior approval of the Company.

This provision is designed to ensure that the insurance cover is underwritten by a reputable company.

Assignability

The benefits of all insurance policies will be assignable and will provide the Company and the completion guarantor with cover against all claims which may be instituted by the persons engaged by the Producer or by reason of accident, death or damage etc.

The reason for this provision is that, although the policies are taken out in the name of the Producer, they are intended to cover loss which the Company may incur or liability which the completion guarantor may incur if it has taken over production of the film (see Chapter 25).

No Compromise or Settlement

The Producer agrees not to compromise or settle any insurance claim without the approval of the Company and will follow the instructions of the Company in relation to all claims. This provision is designed to prevent a situation where an insurance company may offer a sum of money to settle a claim which is not, in the opinion of the Company, adequate.

Documentation

The Producer agrees to provide the Company with full information and documentation relating to all insurance policies and any modifications, additions, and extensions of policies and will promptly deliver the policies and all receipts for premiums to the Company.

In practice, the policies themselves may not be available for several weeks after they have been taken out, but the Company will at the very least wish to see the schedule of insurances produced by the broker, together with confirmation of receipt of payment of premium.

Supplementary Cover

If, any time after receipt by the Company of any documentation or policies, it considers that the policies do not provide adequate cover, it has the right to give notice to the Producer requiring the Producer to provide cover. If the Producer fails to effect the requisite cover within the stated time, the Company will have the right to effect it on its own behalf.

The purpose of this provision is to protect the Company in the event that the Producer unwittingly and in good faith fails to effect adequate insurance.

Claims

The Producer agrees to advise the Company immediately on the happening of any event which might give rise to a claim and provide the Company with copies of all correspondence and documentation relating the matter immediately. The Producer will also agree to procure the full co-operation of the individual producer, the director of the film and all relevant production personnel with the Company, the completion guarantor and any insurance company or loss adjuster.

The Company obviously has a material interest in monitoring how claims are dealt with and the agreement may also require the Producer to follow the Company's instructions in full.

Failure to Obtain Policy

If the Producer fails to obtain a policy, the Company has the right to effect cover in its own name at the Producer's expense and the Producer will pay to the Company the amount of all premiums paid by it. This provision protects the Company in the event the Producer fails to obtain an insurance policy.

Loss

If the Company is required to make payment for any loss which should have been covered under an insurance policy, but was not, the Producer will pay to the Company the proceeds of such insurance claim or such sums which would have been received under the policy of insurance.

This provision is intended to ensure that, if the Producer fails to provide for insurance policy and a claim is made under it, the Company will not suffer any loss.

21.8 Credit

Approval of Credits

The Producer agrees not to enter into any arrangement with any person for a screen credit or advertising credit without the prior consent of the Company.

It is important, from the Company's point of view, that all screen credit obligations are carefully monitored and controlled.

Excluded Credits

The Producer agrees that no contractual obligations in the production contracts relating to credits in advertising of films will apply to teaser or special advertising or award or congratulatory advertisements. It will agree that, in relation to advertising occupying eight column inches or less or outdoor advertising below a certain size, the paid advertising obligation will be excluded.

Screen and advertising credits are often areas of dispute and it is most important both from the point of view of the Company and the Producer that the contractual credit provisions should be correctly drafted.

No Casual or Inadvertent Failure

The Producer agrees that all credit provisions in contracts will contain a provision stating that no casual or inadvertent failure on the part of the Producer or the Company to comply with the credit obligation will be deemed to be a breach.

This is an important provision, since failure to give a person a credit could lead to them losing an opportunity to enhance their reputation. This is a situation where the award of damages would not necessarily provide sufficient compensation for the person and an injunction might be a more appropriate remedy. It is essential for the Company and the Producer to attempt to eliminate any possibility of their film being injuncted for this reason.

Schedule of Credits

The Producer agrees to deliver to the Company a schedule containing full details of all credits, both on-screen and in advertising. The schedule will specify any size requirements and any position requirements.

The Company needs the Producer to provide this information, since a schedule of paid and on-screen advertising credits is a standard item of delivery material which the Company will be required to be delivered to foreign licensees and distributors in order to exploit the film.

Copyright Notices

The Producer undertakes that the film will contain copyright notices in accordance with the Universal Copyright Convention, designating the Company as the owner of the film, and will agree to register the Company as the owner of the film in the US Copyright Registry in the Library of Congress.

The form of the notice designated by the US Copyright Convention is: ©[name of copyright owner] [year of publication]. Inclusion of a notice in this form will guarantee that the film will benefit from copyright protection in all those countries which are members of the Universal Copyright Convention.

Independent Television Commission

The agreement will also provide that the final form of all screen and advertising credits will comply with any code of the Independent Television Commission and any civil authority in the USA, if appropriate.

Producer's Credit

The agreement will specify the exact form of credit to which the Producer is entitled to, both on-screen and in paid advertising.

21.9   Censorship

Rating

The Producer agrees that the film will be eligible for a rating no more restrictive than (say) 15 from the British Board of Film Classification and the equivalent rating from the Motion Picture Association of America.

The rating of a film is particularly important in some cases, eg films which are intended for general release, where a rating more restrictive than U may, for example, eliminate all children under the age of 12.

Cover Shots

Because certain television networks in the US require that broadcast programmes should be suitable for so-called 'family' audiences, the Producer may be required to produce cover shots in the form of visual and sound recordings capable of being used as an alternative to any scenes or dialogue which might be unacceptable for family viewing.

21.10   Rushes, Previews and Editing

Access to Rushes

The Producer agrees to accord the Company's production representative access to all screenings of rushes of the film and to permit the representative to view all negative and positive prints, cut sequences and rough cuts etc.

The object of this provision is to permit the Company's representatives to view the progress of the film.

Restriction

The Producer agrees not to permit any person, other than the production personnel or the authorised representatives of the Company or completion guarantor, to view any material relating to the film.

The object of this provision is to ensure secrecy.

Preview

The Producer will not make any arrangements for the preview of the film without the consent of the Company.

The Company will obviously wish to determine at what times and in which locations the preview showings of the film will occur and whether they are to occur with full sound recorded or library music.

Editing

Editing by the Producer will be carried out only on a positive print of the film and it will not make any changes to the original negative material without the consent of the Company.

The purpose of this provision is to ensure that the original negative of the film is preserved uncut, until the final cut of the film is finally determined.

Rough Cut

The Producer will ensure that, after principal photography, the director of the film assembles a rough cut of the film to be screened to representatives of the Company and the completion guarantor.

What happens after the viewing of the rough cut and the director's cut depends on what provisions have been agreed between the director and the Producer in relation to the director's cut (see Chapter 20).

21.11 Company's Representatives

The Company has the right to designate persons as production representatives and the Producer will agree to permit such persons access to all studios and locations and to advise the representatives of the dates and times of screening of rushes, rough cuts and previews.

The Producer agrees to provide the production representatives with documents and information relating to the film and answer any questions relating to any matter connected with the production of the film.

21.12 Film Library/Props

Film Library

The Company has the right to exploit any out-takes, music tracks, sound effects tracks, background plates and any other surplus film or sound material by means of film library or other form of exploitation. Whether this is permissible or not will depend on the relevant production contracts relating to such material.

Props

Following completion of production of the film and delivery, the Producer agrees to sell all wardrobe, props, materials and supplies for the best price and remit the proceeds of the sale to the Company within seven days from the date of the transaction.

Obviously, this provision will not be appropriate in circumstances where a sequel is planned.

21.13   Laboratory Optical House and Effects

The Producer will deliver all negative sound materials produced in relation to the film to the laboratory and ensure that all negative development and printing and sound transfers are carried out at the laboratory. The Producer will agree not to enter into any commitment with the laboratory in relation to the future striking of internegative materials or the making of release prints. Obviously, the Company wishes to control these matters itself.

The Producer will ensure that the laboratory executes a laboratory pledge-holder's agreement in favour of the Company before any materials are deposited with the laboratory. This form of document is an essential part of the Company's security arrangements (see Paragraph 51.4).

The Producer will ensure that all titles and optical work and special effects in the film are carried out by such companies and at such locations as the Company has previously approved.

21.14   Consents and Approvals

Division of Responsibility

The production and delivery of the film will be the sole responsibility of the Producer, but the agreement may provide that all decisions, whether business or creative, are made by the Company and the Producer jointly, with the Company's decision being final in the event of any dispute.

Consent or Approval

The agreement may provide that any matter requiring the consent or approval of the Company is to be given in writing. Approval by the Company of financial terms relating to any element will not be deemed to be approval of the terms and conditions of engagement or other contractual arrangements in relation to such an element.

Pre-approvals

The agreement will normally contain a list of persons, firms, companies and items which have been pre-approved by the Company.

Suspension and Termination

The agreement may contain an acknowledgement on the part of the Producer that the Company has the right to suspend or terminate the use of services and personnel or discontinue production of the film, on giving notice to the Producer.

Substitution and Alteration

The agreement may provide that, in the event any substitution for, or alteration from, any of the essential elements is made or is required, whether as a result of death, default, incapacity, failure to select or any other reason, the Company will have the right to take over or abandon production at its discretion.

Subsequent Change

The agreement may provide that approval by the Company of one or more of the essential elements shall be deemed withdrawn in the event of subsequent change or substitution of any other essential elements or if any approval of the Company was based on an assumption which may prove subsequently to be incorrect.

The point of this provision is that the Company will wish to protect itself from being in a position where approvals are obtained on a piece-meal basis and the Company finds itself with a number of elements, which taken individually, might have been acceptable if combined with other elements, but, taken collectively, fall short of the Company's requirements. An example where approval might be predicated on an assumption later proved incorrect would be where the Company has approved a studio in a foreign country on the basis of a given exchange rate, which subsequently moves to a significantly adverse position, increasing the Company's sterling or dollar expenditure in that country.

22 Production Financing and Distribution Agreement— Financing and Distribution Aspects

22.1 Description of Financing and Distribution Obligations

This Chapter examines the financing and distribution provisions of a production financing and distribution agreement. Production and related elements are examined in Chapter 21 and warranties*, take-over rights and general provisions are examined in Chapter 23.

22.2 Transaction Analysis

The financing and distribution elements of a production, financing and distribution agreement* may include the following provisions:

- Conditions Precedent (see Paragraph 22.3)
- Provision of Budget (see Paragraph 22.4)
- Banking (see Paragraph 22.5)
- Security (see Paragraph 22.6)
- Books and Records (see Paragraph 22.7)
- Remuneration (see Paragraph 22.8)
- Accounting (see Paragraph 22.9)
- Sales Policies (see Paragraph 22.10).

22.3 Conditions Precedent

Normally, the PFD agreement* will contain a number of conditions precedent which are required to be satisfied before the Company is obliged to provide finance. In the PFD agreement, the Company will make an absolute commitment to provide the Producer* with production finance up to the amount specified in the budget. The Company will wish to ensure that, before it is liable to pay any money, the Producer will have complied with a number of basic minimum requirements.

For this reason, it is normal to find that a PFD agreement contains a clause which contains conditions precedent. Conditions precedent are obligations or conditions which are required to be satisfied as a precedent to any liability of the Company to provide money. These types of provision need to be examined carefully by the Producer and its advisors to ensure that they are capable of being complied with.

These may include the following.

Production Contracts

The Company will wish to ensure that the individual producer and director of the film and principal cast and production personnel will enter into production contracts and associated inducement letters (see Paragraph 51.2). The Producer will be required to deliver original or certified copies of such documents.

In practice, there may well be a delay in finalising the terms of the agreements with principal cast and the Company may be required to release funding during the pre-production period before the contracts* have been finalised with principal Artists, but normally, the finalisation of contracts with the principal producer and director is an absolute obligation.

Production Account

The Producer will be required to open a production account with a bank approved by the Company. This is the account in which all sums paid by the Company towards the production of the film will be maintained by the Producer. The Company will normally make available funds in accordance with the cash flow to meet the weekly needs of the production and will normally require the account to be a trust account on which the Company's interest is noted.

Exclusion of Set-off Letter

The Producer will deliver to the Company an exclusion of set-off letter signed by the bank at which the production account is maintained. This requirement is designed to protect the Company from a situation where the bank might seek to exercise its right to set-off a debt owed to it by the Producer against sums maintained in the production account and claim such sums to the detriment of the Company and the production.

Chain of Title

The Producer will fulfil all requirements relating to underlying rights and third party rights which are intended to be in the production of the film and will deliver to the Company a satisfactory chain of title of all rights in the film.

Execution of Assignments and Licences

The Producer will have procured the execution of any assignments and licences required to authorise the production of the film. This provision would, for example, cover a situation where the Producer bases a film on an existing work. In such an instance the Producer will normally have obtained an option to acquire motion picture rights in the work (see Chapter 17). The Company is obviously interested to ensure that the Producer has obtained a valid assignment or licence of the motion picture rights in the work following the exercise of the option.

Production Personnel and Essential Elements

The Company will have approved the proposed terms of engagement of production personnel and proposed contractual terms relating to other essential elements.

Completion Guarantee

The Producer will deliver to the Company an executed copy of the completion guarantee. The completion guarantee is a document which guarantees to the Company the completion and delivery of the film in accordance with the budget or the repayment by the Company of all sums advanced by it in relation to the film in the unhappy event that an event of force majeure occurs which prevents the film from being completed (see Chapter 25).

Insurance Policies

The Producer will have delivered to the Company copies of all the insurance policies. In practice (see Paragraph 21.7) the Producer may not be able to deliver the policies themselves until some weeks after pre-production has commenced. Normally, the Company will accept a letter from reputable insurance brokers indicating the terms of the cover and confirming that insurers are 'on risk'.

Laboratory Letter

The Producer will deliver to the Company an executed laboratory pledge-holder's agreement (see Paragraph 51.4). This provides that the Company (or the completion guarantor) will have access to all original picture and sound materials relating to the film deposited with the laboratory.

This gives the Company security over the physical materials produced in the course of production and also permits the completion guarantor to get access to these materials if the guarantor has to take over production (see Chapters 23 and 25).

Approvals

All approvals required to satisfy conditions precedent in the completion guarantee or required pursuant to the terms of the completion guarantee security agreement have been obtained.

Although the Producer may have delivered the Company an executed copy of the completion guarantee, the guarantor itself may not be 'on risk' if its obligations are themselves subject to conditions precedent being satisfied. The Company should, therefore, require confirmation that these conditions have been satisfied.

22.4   Provision of Budget

Company to Provide Budget

The Company will agree subject to the fulfilment of the conditions precedent and provided no event of default has occurred (see Paragraph 23.4) to provide the budget (see Paragraph 21.3) in accordance whit the cash flow schedule by making available funds to the production account.

Cost of Production Excess

Normally, the Company will be under no obligation to provide additional funds if the cost of production exceeds the amount stated in the budget. The PFD agreement may, however, contain a provision which permits the Company to advance additional funds without giving it any obligation to do so.

In practice, if the Company has obtained the benefit of the completion guarantee, it will already have 'capped' the maximum cost of production of the film and any additional sums will normally be required to be advanced by the completion guarantor.

Surplus Funds

The Producer will hold any surplus funds and any sums derived from the liquidation of props and equipment acquired for the film on trust for the Company and will pay such sums to the Company within 14 days from delivery of the film or from the date of the surplus arising, if earlier.

Application of Finance

The Producer will undertake to apply all finance received from the Company and/or other facilities or services made available by the Company solely in connection with the production of the film.

Non-approval

Provision of finance by the Company to the Producer, in the absence of any approval or consent, is without prejudice to the right of the Company to elect not to provide any additional finance by reason of absence of approval etc.

This is a sensible provision for a company to include in the PFD agreement, since, frequently, there are delays in finalising contractual arrangements which may lead to the Producer being unable to satisfy all conditions precedent at a time when it is imperative that the Producer receives funds to enable the film to continue production. If the Company advances funds in such circumstances, this provision ensures that it is not committed to advance the entire production budget.

In practice, however, once a Company has begun advancing money towards production of a film, then, even if has not signed, a PFD agreement with a Producer, it may soon reach the stage that the amount of money advanced by it is so substantial that any choice on its part is ruled out and it will have to continue to advance the remainder in order to have any prospect of recovering any of the sums previously advanced.

22.5 Banking

Withdrawals

Withdrawals from the production account are to be made solely in connection with the production of the film in accordance with production reports made by the Producer. Withdrawals are to be made only on the written authorisation of one named signatory on the part of the Producer, accompanied by the counter-signature of one representative nominated by the Company. This provision ensures that the Company's representative is fully apprised of all withdrawals from the production account.

Production Account

All sums maintained in the production account are to be held on trust by the Producer for the Company (see Paragraph 22.3) and all payments to the production account are to be in accordance with the budget and cash flow schedule. No payment is to be made to the Producer or any associate of the Producer except as expressly specified in the budget. This latter provision prevents the Producer, or any associate, from making a secret profit out of the film or unlawfully withdrawing funds from the production account.

No Commingling

Only money which is to be applied towards the production of the film is to be placed in the production account and the Producer shall not permit the money in that account to become commingled with any other money payable to the Producer or any associate of the Producer or anyone else.

In practice, if the Company's funds have become commingled with other funds, it may be difficult to determine which funds are held on trust and, if other peoples' money is deposited in the production account, the question of whose money was spent on what may become difficult to determine.

Reports

The PFD agreement normally provides that the Producer is to give the Company reports on all expenditure made in each week, cumulative expenditure to date and an estimate of the likely final cost of production of the film.

Where a completion guarantor is involved, normally, the completion guarantor will also require direct access to this information.

Cash Flow Adjustment

Although the Company will, in principle, commit to provide funds to the entire amount specified in the budget, the contingency element of the budget (see Paragraph 21.3) and the possibility of savings of various items specified in the cash-flow schedule may mean that the actual amount required by the Producer to complete production of the film is less than that specified in the budget and cash-flow schedule.

For this reason, it is normal to find that the PFD agreement will provide that the Company's liability is reduced by the amount of any savings to date made in the budget and further reduced by any unspent contingency money. The PFD agreement will also provide that, if surplus funds are provided to the Producer, these sums are considered to be a loan repayable on demand.

Bank Instructions

The Producer will agree to issue irrevocable instructions to the bank at which the production account is maintained, requiring the bank to provide the Company (or its representative) copies of all statements and other information required in relation to the production account.

22.6   Security

Depending on the circumstances, the Company may require the Producer to execute a mortgage. If a security interest has been given to the completion guarantor (see Chapter 26), the Company may also require the Producer to enter into a deed of priority, so that it can be established whose security interest has priority over the others.

22.7   Books and Records

Maintenance of Books and Records

The Producer will agree to maintain full and accurate and proper records and books of account relating to the production of the film and to retain all invoices, vouchers, receipts and other records as evidence of expenses incurred in the production of the film. The Producer will normally agree to maintain such records for a number of years following delivery of the film to the Company.

Right to Audit

The Company will have the right to inspect, audit and take copies of all books and records relating to the film. The Producer will agree to maintain such books and records at the Producer's principal place of business.

Cost of Production

The Producer will agree, during a specified period following delivery, to prepare and submit to the Company a statement of the cost of production of the film, containing a full and detailed itemisation of all sums actually expended on it. The statement may be required to be certified by a firm of accountants familiar with the motion picture industry and approved by the Company.

22.8   Remuneration

The PFD agreement will normally provide the Producer with some remuneration for its services. Often the remuneration takes the form of a production fee which is specified in the budget. In such cases, the agreement may permit the Producer to draw the production fee on dates specified in the cash-flow schedule.

Because the possibility exists that the Producer may not be able to effect completion and a completion guarantor may have to take over production, it is common to find that PFD agreements provide that the Producer's entitlement to the production fee accrues on a daily basis across the entire period of production of the film.

Participation

The PFD agreement may also entitle the Producer to a participation in net profits derived from the film, in which event, the matters referred to in Chapter 24 may be of relevance.

22.9 Accounting

The Company will agree to submit to the Producer copies of statements of account, normally on a quarterly basis for the first three years following initial commercial exploitation and, after that, on a six-monthly basis. It is normal to provide that statements are deemed to be binding on the parties, unless, within a specified period, notice has been given of an error or omission.

22.10 Sales Policies

Control

The Producer will acknowledge that the Company has complete authority and control over distribution, exhibition and other exploitation of the film throughout the world.

Prints and Advertising

The amount to be expended in relation to prints and advertising of the film and its release pattern and all other matters relating to distribution are to be determined by the Company in accordance with its business policies from time to time in its entire discretion.

No Representation

The Company has not made any representation or warranty as to its business practices or the exploitation of the film or the amount of net profits or gross receipts of the film (if any) which may result from distribution.

This provision is intended to protect the Company from any claim by a Producer that a collateral contract or warranty exists, guaranteeing the Producer a certain minimum return.

Non-distribution

The Company may or may not distribute the film in any territory in accordance with the Company's business practice. There may be situations due to war or business embargo where the Company will wish not to distribute the film. This provision is intended to protect the Company from any claim by the Producer in such circumstances.

Industry Subsidies and Quotas

The Producer will agree to give the Company all necessary assistance to enable the Company to apply for and obtain any national or local industry subsidies or quotas.

22.11   Advertising and Publicity

Producer's Entitlement

The Producer will have no entitlement to make arrangements for advertising or publicity relating to the film or to engage any unit publicist, press officer or other advertising or public relations personnel without the prior written consent of the Company. It is quite reasonable for the Company to wish to ensure that it is in complete control of all advertising, public relations and publicity matters.

Press and Publicity

The Company will have the right to make arrangements for press and publicity personnel and photographers to take photographs, carry out interviews and perform other press- and publicity-related activities during the production of the film at the studios or any other locations. The Producer will agree not to allow other persons to take photographs or make recordings or interviews without the prior consent of the Company.

Closed Set

Control of the set and photographs and recordings made during production is extremely important. There are some circumstances where closed sets may be required in order to prevent any information or photographs being made available to the public. Equally, there are circumstances where the Company may wish to produce a documentary film of the making of the film and this will require access to production personnel, studios and facilities.

23 Production Financing and Distribution Agreement— Warranties, Take-over Rights and General Provisions

23.1 Description of Warranties, Take-over Rights and General Provisions in the PFD agreement

Chapter 21 has examined the production and related provisions contained in the PFD agreement*. Chapter 22 has examined provisions relating to finance and distribution. This Chapter examines the warranties*, take-over rights and general provisions of the PFD agreement.

23.2 Transaction Analysis

The general elements of a production financing and distribution agreement* may include the following provisions:

*   Warranties* (see Paragraph 23.3)
*   Default (see Paragraph 23.4)
*   Take-over (see Paragraph 23.5)
*   Effect of take-over (see Paragraph 23.6)
*   Boilerplate* (see Paragraph 23.7).

23.3 Warranties

The Producer* will warrant and undertake with the Company in relation to a number of matters concerning the production of the film. These will include the following.

Agreement Binding

The agreement constitutes a valid legal and binding obligation enforceable in accordance with its terms against the Producer.

Non-contravention

The agreement does not contravene any law or the Producer's corporate byelaws.

Proceedings

No litigation, arbitration or other proceedings are presently pending, proceeding or threatened against the Producer.

Authorisation

The signature and execution of the PFD agreement and all associated documents has been duly and validly authorised by all appropriate persons.

Ownership

The Producer was, prior to the assignment contained in the agreement (see Paragraph 21.4), the sole, absolute, unincumbered, legal and beneficial owner of the film, the delivery material and the publicity material and has acquired all rights free from any encumbrances subject only to restrictions imposed by relevant union agreements and the rights controlled by the PRS* and PPL (see Paragraph 21.4).

The Company requires the Producer to warrant that no other person controls any of the rights which the PFD agreement contemplates the Producer will acquire and assign to the Company. So far as restrictions imposed by various union agreements are concerned, in many cases, there will be none.

The rights controlled by the PRS and PPL (and their associated bodies) will principally include the right to perform music in public. It is important for the Company to obtain confirmation that any right the PRS has in relation to the synchronisation of music in the film has been expressly waived. This means that where music specially commissioned for inclusion in the film from a PRS member, a form of licence from the PRS is obtained.

Non-infringement

Nothing contained in the film or the delivery material will infringe any right of copyright, right of trademark, right of privacy, right of publicity or any other any other right of any person or be obscene or blasphemous or libellous or defamatory.

The Company must ensure that it has the right to exploit its rights in the film without any claims from third parties.

Names and Likenesses

The Producer has acquired the right to use any names, professional names, likenesses and biographies of production personnel, as well as voices and photographs taken during the course of production, for the full period of copyright. The agreement may also specifically require the Producer to confirm that it has acquired the sole and exclusive merchandising rights in and to the services and product of the services of the production personnel in connection with the film (but not otherwise). This provision is intended to ensure that the Company will have the right to manufacture and sell articles of all descriptions which may include reproductions or representations of any characters in the film as played by the principal personnel.

No Incumbrances

The Producer confirms that there are not, and shall not be, any liens or incumbrances in relation to the film, the delivery material or the publicity material which might inhibit or restrict the free and unrestricted exercise by the Company, its successors and licensees of rights granted under the agreement. In practice, this warranty might be limited so as to exclude liens arising in the ordinary course of business (such as the laboratory's right to exercise a lien over materials if its fees remain unpaid).

Peaceful Enjoyment

The Company's successors and licensees will have the right to quietly and peacefully enjoy and remain in possession of all rights relating to the film. This warranty is designed to ensure that the Company does not suffer any interference with the exploitation of its rights.

Completion Guarantor Approval

The completion guarantor has approved the screenplay, shooting script, production, schedule, budget and cash-flow schedule.

Accuracy of Budget

The budget is a complete, bona fide and accurate estimate of the total cost of production of the film and includes adequate provision for all expenses, including music and other licences, pre-release publicity, public relations expenses, interest charges etc.

Production Contracts

All production contracts and other contractual arrangements relating to studios, locations etc will be entered into in a timely manner in accordance with the production schedule.

Participations, Contingencies or Deferments

The Producer will not agree to pay any person a percentage of gross receipts or net profits or other income or any contingent compensation or any deferred payment without the consent of the Company.

It is obviously in the Company's interests to ensure that the income stream it is expecting from the film is not diminished by the Producer giving it all away.

Qualification for Copyright Protection

The Producer and the principal director of the film will be the sole 'authors' and will be the qualifying persons within the meaning of copyright legislation. These basic warranties ensure that the film will benefit from copyright protection throughout the world.

Laboratory

All delivery material is located at the laboratory, all future material will be placed at the laboratory and no other laboratory will be used without the consent of the Company.

Necessary Rights

The Producer has acquired all rights of copyright and other rights necessary for the production, distribution and exploitation of the film throughout the world and has paid all sums due, save where expressly indicated in the budget or where the consent of the Company has been obtained.

Limitations

There are no limitations which might restrict the Company's right to exploit the film or any third party material used in the film freely.

No Variation of Production Contracts

None of the production contracts has been varied or modified and each of them is assignable to the Company and the completion guarantor.

The Company needs to ensure that the completion guarantor has the unfettered right to take over the production of the film. In the event that it does so, it will need to be able to call directly on the persons engaged by the Producer to perform their services. This is why it is important for the contracts used by the Producer to be assignable.

No Security Interest

No person has any security interest in relation to the film or any material relating to it. In practice, this warranty may be amended to refer to any lien enjoyed by the laboratory (see above).

Defect

The Producer has no actual or constructive notice of any defect in the Producer's rights in the film or the underlying rights.

Notice

The Producer will promptly notify the Company of the occurrence of any event which might adversely affect the financial condition of the Producer or the production of the film.

Technical Quality

The film will be of first-class technical quality suitable for commercial exploitation and will comply with all screen and advertising credit obligations and other obligations to third parties.

Title

The Producer knows of no reason which might lead to any liability in relation to the use of the title or any working title of the film.

Copyright Protection

The film shall be protected under statutory and common law copyright in all countries adhering to the Berne Convention and the Universal Copyright Convention.

Copyright Registration

The Producer will procure copyright registration of the film in the name of the Company in the United States of America and will comply with all formalities which are required in any territory to protect the copyright and other rights in the film.

In practice, these formalities may be limited to the inclusion on all copies of the film of a notice in the form prescribed in the Universal Copyright Convention:

© [name of the producer] [year of publication].

Essential Elements

The film will contain and comply with all essential elements (see Paragraph 21.3).

Other Remuneration

Neither the Producer nor any associate of the Producer will receive any remuneration, except as provided in the budget. This protects the Company from the Producer or persons or companies associated with it making a secret profit from the production.

Non-distribution

Neither the film nor any part of it will have been exhibited, distributed or released to the public in any form, by any medium, anywhere in the world, prior to delivery.

No Prior Incumbrance

Neither the Producer nor any of its predecessors in title in relation to any of the underlying rights has in any way incumbered the film or any of the rights required to exploit it.

No Incumbrances

The Producer will not create any security interests in relation to any of the Producer's assets without the consent of the Company. This provision is intended to determine that the Producer does not lose any of its own assets, which the Company may regard as important to enable the Producer to comply with obligations under the agreement.

Compliance With Completion Guarantee

The Producer has complied and shall comply fully with all obligations under the completion guarantee and completion guarantee security agreement.

No Take-over Exclusion

None of the production contracts prevents the taking over and delivery of the film by the completion guarantor or imposes any restrictions on the power of the completion guarantor or the Company including any restriction to cut and edit the film.

No Breach

Neither the Producer nor to the Producer's knowledge, the completion guarantor is in breach of their respective obligations under the completion guarantee or the completion guarantee security agreement.

Non-alteration

The Producer will not alter or permit the alteration of the screenplay or the shooting script without the prior written consent of the Company.

Timely Payment

The Producer will make payments of all sums due to any persons engaged in relation to the film in a timely manner.

Music Fees

No fees will be paid in respect of any music contained in the film otherwise than to the PRS or its affiliated organisation.

Contempt

Nothing contained in the film might breach any duty of confidence or constitute a contempt of court or contravene the provision of any statute relating to broadcasting or any code made by any competent authority.

Compliance with Relevant Union Agreements

The Producer will, at all times, comply with all relevant provisions of relevant union agreements relating to the film.

Confidentiality

The Producer will not disclose or make public any information relating to the agreement or the film or the business of the Company without the consent of the Company.

Indemnity

The Producer will indemnify the Company in relation to any breach by the Producer of its warranties and obligations in the agreement.

23.4   Default

The PFD agreement will normally set out a number of events which will be considered to be events of default on the part of the Producer. The occurrence of an event of default will permit the Company to exercise certain rights against the Producer, such as its right to takeover production or abandon production.

If a Company exercises its right to takeover production, the Producer will effectively be 'off the case' and the Producer's rights under the production contracts will be exercised by the completion guarantor. The PFD agreement will not, therefore, need to contain express termination provisions, as do many other agreements. Many PFD agreements do, however.

The following events may constitute events of default under a PFD agreement. Default on the part of the Producer in relation to any obligation under the PFD agreement, the completion guarantee, the completion guarantee security agreement or any other agreement executed in relation to the PFD agreement or in relation to the film.

Representations

Any representation or warranty made by the Producer in the PFD agreement is untrue in any material respect.

Levy of Execution

The property of the Producer has a levy of execution against it which is not removed within 14 days.

Winding Up

A resolution is passed or petition served for the winding up of the Producer.

Final Judgment

Final judgment against the Producer is obtained in relation to a matter which is likely to materially affect the Producer's financial condition.

Insolvency

The Producer declares a moratorium or becomes insolvent.

Cessation of Trade

The Producer ceases to carry on, or threatens to cease, in the whole or any material part of its business.

Disposal or Dissolution

Any material part of the assets of the Producer is sold or disposed of or any partnership in which the Producer is a partner is dissolved.

Invalidity of Security

Any part of the security created pursuant to the PFD agreement fails or ceases in any respect to have full force or effect.

Control

Control of the Producer changes.

Associate

Any of the above matters happen in relation to any associate or subsidiary or holding company of the Producer.

23.5   Take-over

The take-over rights of the Company are normally exercisable at any time by notice in writing after the occurrence of the following events:

- the total expenditure incurred in connection with the film exceeds 110% of the budgeted cost for the stage of production that the film is then at; or
- the production of the film has fallen materially behind the production schedule; or
- the Company has reasonable grounds to believe that the actual cost of the film will exceed the budget or progress is likely to fall materially behind the production schedule.

If the Producer fails to carry out instructions given by the Company or the completion guarantor or an event of force majeure occurs or an event of default occurs, the Company will also be entitled to exercise its take-over rights.

23.6 Effect of Take-over

The exercise by the Company of its right to take-over production, or the take-over by the completion guarantor under the powers which it obtains in the completion guarantee security agreement (see Paragraph 26) would normally constitute an extremely serious event for the Producer.

On the exercise by the Company of the take-over rights the Producer will normally be required to place at the Company's disposal all persons and equipment employed or used by the Producer in connection with the film. The Company will have the right to immediately assume supervision and control of the production of the film and the PFD agreement will contain an acknowledgement that all rights of the Producer automatically end.

The exercise of take-over rights, in the motion picture industry is, however, very much a rarity.

23.7 Boilerplate

The boilerplate section of a typical production financing and distribution agreement may contain the following provisions:

- No obligation (see Paragraph 52.6)
- Notices (see Paragraph 52.8)
- Severability (see Paragraph 52.10)
- Assignability (see Paragraph 52.1)
- Entire agreement (see Paragraph 52.3)
- Waiver (see Paragraph 52.11)
- No partnership (see Paragraph 52.7)
- Governing law (see Paragraph 52.5)
- Certificate of value* (see Paragraph 52.2).

24 Receipts and Profits in the Audio-visual Media

24.1 Purpose of this Chapter

The purpose of this Chapter is to provide a brief analysis of some of the financial aspects of transactions in the media industry. It may be helpful if this Chapter is read in conjunction with Chapter 31, which deals with distribution arrangements in the audio-visual media.

24.2 "Profit"

As with many terms used in the entertainment industry, there is no such thing as a standard definition of "profit". Profit is a variable and its value depends on the definition which it is given in each agreement*. Additionally, the profits for distributors, financiers, producers* and artists are all calculated out of different levels of income and expenditure. In many cases, the expenditure actually incurred differs substantially from that used in the profit calculation.

24.3 Distributor/Exhibitor Relationships

While it is common for the negotiation and documentation of distribution arrangements to involve legal advisors, the negotiation and documentation of agreements between theatrical distribution companies and exhibitors in the United Kingdom is commonly effected on one of the exhibitor licence forms. These have evolved in the course of practice and incorporate standard provisions which have been approved by the Society of Film Distributors and Cinema Exhibitors' Association.

A licence is required for the showing or performing of a film or sound recording in public or its inclusion in a broadcast or cable programme, as these acts are restricted by the United Kingdom copyright legislation.

24.4 Exhibitors' Expenses and 'House Nut'

The main expense incurred by theatrical exhibitors is on film rentals (the licence fees paid by exhibitors to distributors of films). The percentage of film rentals payable to a distributor by an exhibitor will vary from film to film and even from week to week on the same film. It would be normal to expect the film rental figure to account for between 40% and 60% of the exhibitors' operating expenses and between 35% and 70% of the weekly total of gross receipts, but there is no absolute norm and these figures are capable of wide variation. In addition to film rentals, the remaining categories of exhibitors' expenses are national insurance, advertising, administration, utilities, repairs, supplies, insurance, rent and other charges.

The categories and amounts of exhibitors' expenses are relevant to a distributor, since these expenses are used as a starting point for calculating the "house nut*". The house nut is the notional point at which an exhibitor has recovered its operating expenses. It is the point beyond which all income received by the exhibitor will constitute profit. The amount is notional because it invariably includes a 'cushion' or profit element for the exhibitor. The house nut for any one exhibitor will frequently vary from distributor to distributor and may be lower for established distributors than for independent distributors.

24.5 Box Office Receipts

The number of screens, number of seats per screen and ticket prices of exhibitors in the United Kingdom are known to theatrical distributors. Many exhibitors have one fixed price per seat, although concessionary rates are available for old age pensioners. The calculation of box office gross receipts is effected by means of daily returns which a distributor receives from each theatre (or cinema) screening the distributor's film. Where tickets are sold on a roll, the returns will indicate the opening and closing numbers of each ticket roll per day. The difference will constitute the admission figure. The gross receipts figure will be the number of admissions multiplied by the seat price after the exclusion of value added tax and any other local industry levy. In the United Kingdom, the levy on ticket admissions (which was known as the Eady Levy) was abolished in 1985.

It is normal for the distributor to be advised of all price increases in a screen or a circuit. A distributor will, in addition to daily returns, receive weekly returns from an exhibitor, which will contain a calculation showing the amount of film rentals owed to the distributor. The distributor will invoice the exhibitor after receipt of the weekly returns and expect to receive payment of film rentals 28 days from the end of the week to which the payment relates.

It is common to find provisions relating to the allocation of film rentals between first feature films and second feature films. The split of rentals between double main features and "short" films will also be specified and the distributor may establish ticket "floors", below which price, the exhibitor may not sell tickets for screenings. Where short films are shown with a first feature film, it is usual in the United Kingdom to apportion between 5% and 6% of gross box office receipts to the short film.

Where a film is shown on more than one screen semi-simultaneously by means of linked projection, an exhibitor will negotiate with a distributor on the apportionment between the two house nuts for each screen, since the exhibitor will frequently regard the second screen as an overflow capacity. A distributor may be prepared to accept the exhibitor's normal house nut for the additional screen if the distributor wishes the film to show on two screens for a specified period, and may negotiate with an exhibitor, terms which provide that, if the exhibitor wishes to continue exhibiting the film on two screens after the initial period required by the distributor, the exhibitor will be entitled to a reduced house nut on the second screen or, alternatively, pay to the distributor a minimum percentage of gross receipts arising from that screen without the deduction of the nut.

Income received by the exhibitor from the cinema concessions, arising from sales of sweets, soft drinks and other miscellaneous ephemera, is never included in the statement of gross box office receipts when calculating film rentals. Concession income belongs to the exhibitor alone and, in many cases, will represent the difference between an operating loss and a small profit for the exhibitor.

24.6   Exhibition Agreements

The following basic types of exhibition arrangement exist.

House Nut 90/10

Under this arrangement, the exhibitor will recover the house nut from gross box office receipts. The excess above the house nut is split 90% to the distributor and 10% to the exhibitor.

Example 1

House nut	= £100.00
Gross box office receipts	= £500.00
Exhibitor recovers house nut of	£100.00
The remaining £400 is split 90/10	
Distributor will receive	£360.00
Exhibitor will receive £40.00 + £100.00	= £140.00 in total

Example 2

House nut	= £100.00
Gross box office receipts	= £125.00
Exhibitor recovers house nut of	£100.00
The remaining £25 is split 90%/10%	
Distributor will receive	£22.50
Exhibitor will receive £2.50 + £100.00	= £102.50 in total

House Nut 90/10 with a Floor

On a straightforward house nut 90/10 deal, it is possible, in theory, for the distributor to receive nothing if the exhibitor does not recover the house nut (see Example 2). For this reason, it is common to specify that if the house nut is not recovered, the receipts will be split in an agreed percentage. This gives the exhibitor an incentive to make sure that the film will generate enough response locally to be a financial success. The floor level is generally between 60% and 75% of gross box office receipts.

On a house nut 90/10 deal with a floor of 75, if the exhibitor fails to recover the house nut, then 75% of gross box office receipts will be payable to the distributor and the exhibitor will have an operating deficit. The same figures from Example 2 above applied to a 75 floor deal give very different results.

Example 3

House nut	= £100.00
Gross box office receipts	= £125.00
Exhibitor recovers house nut of	£100.00
The remaining £25 is split 90/10	
Distributor will receive	£22.50
Exhibitor will receive	£102.50
but Distributor's share may not be reduced below 75% of gross box office receipts	
Distributor takes	£93.75
Exhibitor takes	£31.25

Sliding Scale Arrangement

A sliding scale arrangement is a variable percentage split of gross box office receipts payable by the exhibitor to the distributor without the recovery by the exhibitor of any house nut. The percentage of receipts payable depends on the level of gross box office receipts. At a very low level, the exhibitor will pay the distributor 25% and retain the balance of 75%. As the amount of gross receipts rises, so too does the percentage payable to the distributor. It is normal for the percentage film rental to increase in steps of 2.5% or 1% between 25% and 50%.

Where a distributor is making arrangements for a film which the distributor feels to have above average commercial prospects, the distributor may feel that the maximum percentage return of 50% of gross box office receipts is inadequate and may wish to negotiate to receive a higher percentage from the exhibitor. In such cases, the distributor may increase the maximum percentage figure payable to it to 60% and additionally negotiate with the exhibitor a figure above which the distributor will be entitled to between 75% and 90% of gross box office receipts.

Four Wall and Flat Fee Deal

A distributor is entitled to 100% of gross box office receipts, but pays the exhibitor a flat fee for making the four walls of the cinema, the front of the house and box office available to the distributor for the purpose of screening a film.

Under a flat fee arrangement, an exhibitor buys the right to exhibit a film for a specified period of time for a flat fee. In such a case, 100% of gross box office receipts belongs to the exhibitor who will pay for all advertising. Flat rentals may apply only on second feature or final run films which are not capable of being sold in any other way.

Holdovers and Pullouts

A distributor may wish to negotiate a holdover* figure with an exhibitor. A holdover figure will be a minimum level of gross box office receipts at which the exhibitor will agree to continue to show the film on the same agreed terms. Generally, in the United Kingdom, films are acquired on terms which permit the exhibitor to review a film's performance and decide whether or not to extend the engagement over an initial agreed period. If, however, a holdover is agreed, it may be accompanied by a "pull out*" arrangement where an exhibitor will be able to extricate itself from a holdover by paying a pull out fee. The pull out fee will be equivalent to what the distributor estimates the film might have earned if the holdover arrangements for the film had been adhered to.

Alignments and Barring

For historical reasons which originated in the days when the so-called US "majors" owned subsidiary companies in the United Kingdom, a system of alignments came into being where the product of a US major would be offered to the exhibition chain in which the major had an interest. The economic reasons for such alignments have long since disappeared.

The theatrical exhibition practice in the United Kingdom used to involve a complicated system of barring* arrangements, pursuant to which one cinema would be able to prevent a competing cinema within the same area from showing a film until a specified number of days from the first showing. The system of barring in the United Kingdom was extremely sophisticated and each cinema used to be subjected to a fixed distribution practice which would give it unvariable advantages and/or disadvantages over its neighbours.

Although it is still permitted for distributors and exhibitors in the United Kingdom to negotiate exclusivity arrangements on a film-by-film basis, the previously existing blanket barring arrangements have been declared anti-competitive.

24.7 Non-theatrical distribution

The market for non-theatrical distribution is extremely specialised and, although the sums generated are significant, they are generally not substantial. For this reason, non-theatrical distribution rights in films are normally acquired as an adjunct to theatrical distribution rights or television or home video rights, rather than as a primary medium. The traditional non-theatrical distribution market is being fragmented by the development of technology. In addition to the competing overlap between non-theatrical and video markets, there is also an overlap with the cable and satellite distribution markets, since persons acquiring cable and satellite rights in the United Kingdom wish to have the rights to license hotels and motels which have traditionally fallen within the non-theatrical market.

24.8 Types of Theatrical Release

The following are the basic categories of theatrical release:

- a limited release in a small number of cinemas confined usually to one key centre. By restricting availability of the film, a demand in a particularly identified sector is created and, as the word of mouth reputation of the film expands, the release pattern is widened.
- a regional release in a particular area or region may be tried to test the marketing and advertising strategy of a film, and may be followed either by a national release or limited release for which the regional advertising campaign may be varied.
- national release, which involves releasing a film in all regions nationally and simultaneously.

The final category is saturation release which is a very wide or intense national release. Saturation release involves the production of the maximum number of prints which the theatrical exhibition market is capable of bearing at any given moment. In the United States, a saturation release of a film would involve the distribution of one print of the film for every 100,000 people approximately. The combined population of the US and Canada totals approximately 250 million people, which would generate a total of around 2,500 prints, but for demographic reasons, 2,000 prints of a film is generally considered to be saturation point, although recent major releases have exceeded this number.

24.9 Distribution Expenses

The major items of expenditure in distributing films are the costs of manufacturing and distributing prints and the costs of advertising. Advertising and publicity costs extend from the initial conception of an advertising campaign until its final execution, starting with market research surveys and tests of advertising concepts and research evaluations. Following the conception of the campaign, the distributor incurs costs in preparing artwork, plates, transparencies, colour separations and mechanicals. It also incurs the cost of the salaries and expenses of advertising and publicity personnel and expenses and payments to actors and persons connected with a film who may undertake tours and make personal appearances, attend previews and other promotional events. Direct mail materials, printed advertising materials, promotional accessories, press books, press kits, tickets, invitations to premieres and screenings, manufacture of show reels, trailers stills and press and publicity releases, all need to be produced. Advertising allowances may be made to cinemas or other exhibitors and co-operative advertising costs may be incurred. The most expensive medium of advertising is advertising time bought on broadcast media.

24.10 Prints and Advertising

It is important, from the point of view of a producer entering into a presale agreement with a distributor in a territory, to limit the distributor's expenditure on prints and advertising. If these costs are monitored closely by the producer, the distributor may be encouraged to eliminate waste. It is also in the interests of the producer to ensure that a minimum amount is spent on publicising the film and the producer may therefore require the distributor under a presale agreement to expend a certain minimum sum on prints and advertising.

The position where a distributor is obliged by contract to spend a certain amount on advertising of a film, but expends only half that amount, should also be considered. What are the producer's remedies in such a situation? The distributor is clearly in breach of its contractual obligations, but how is it possible for the producer to quantify damages? What is the potential loss suffered by the producer? If the film has performed badly, the distributor's argument will be that the decision not to spend the entire amount which the distributor was contractually obliged to spend has actually saved the producer money. How can the producer prove that, if the distributor had spent the entire amount as specified in the contract, the film would have become successful and the producer would have gained additional income from the film? The producer may not be able to show this, but is always free to incorporate a liquidated damages provision in the agreement which will provide that, if the distributor under a presale agreement fails to spend the full contractual amount on prints and advertising, then the distributor must reimburse the producer the shortfall or a multiplier of the shortfall.

24.11 Types of Distribution Arrangements

Besides the production financing and distribution agreement, which has been previously estimated (see Chapters 21, 22 and 23), there are six basic types of distribution arrangements which are capable of a large number of variations.

Net Distribution Agreement

Under a net distribution agreement, the gross receipts derived by a distributor from a film are applied in the following order.

First, the distribution fee is retained by the distributor. Second, distribution expenses are deducted and retained by the distributor. Third, the balance remaining (if any) is paid back to the producer. Because the costs incurred by the distributor in respect of prints and advertising are likely to be significant, it may be some time before the distribution expenses have all been recovered. Until the point of recovery is reached, the producer will not receive any distribution income and the financiers will not have started to recoup their investment in the production itself.

Gross Distribution Agreement

In the case of a gross distribution agreement, there is no specified order of recoupment and the distributor's gross receipts are split between the distributor and the producer from the very beginning. The distributor will expect, under this arrangement, to take 65% or 70% of the receipts, the remaining balance of 30% or 35% being payable to the producer. The costs of prints and advertising will be borne by the distributor out of its share of gross receipts. The advantage for the producer of this type of arrangement is that there is a flow of income from the first pound or dollar. This type of arrangement will, in the case of a successful film, be extremely advantageous to a distributor, who will be entitled to a higher percentage of gross revenue than would be applicable under a normal net deal. This disadvantage, from the point of view of the producer can, however, be mitigated by negotiating a diminishing sliding scale of receipts payable to the distributor.

Variations of the Gross Distribution Agreement

One variation is for the distributor to account to the producer on "adjusted gross receipts" rather than on the basis of remitted gross receipts. The cost of co-operative advertising is deducted from the receipts, leaving the distributor to pay for the cost of prints alone out of the distributor's share, recovering the costs of advertising out of the receipts and leaving the balance to be remitted to the producer in the normal way. Because the cost of prints and advertising in relation to film rentals, varies in direct proportion to the success of the film in the box office (although the adjusted gross agreement accelerates the point at which the producer will receive income flow), the rate of return for a successful film is likely to be considerably less favourable than a net distribution arrangement. Under a net distribution agreement, once a distributor has recouped the cost of prints and advertising, all the profits will be payable to the producer, whereas, in a gross agreement the distributor will be entitled to deduct a greater percentage.

Flat Fee Theatrical Distributor's Agreement

In a flat fee arrangement, a distributor is paid a flat fee to cover all expenses in connection with the theatrical release of a film and agrees to remit 100% of gross income received from the film to the producer. This type of arrangement is only suitable for films which are to be given a limited theatrical release.

Flat Fee Acquisition Agreement

A further alternative exists in the form of a flat fee basis acquisition by the distributor of rights in a film in a number of different media. In return for paying the producer a flat fee, the distributor will retain all income derived from the exercise of the rights in the film and will also bear all expenses.

Off-The-Top Arrangement

Another possibility is an arrangement where the gross receipts of a film are applied first towards the recovery of distribution expenses incurred by the distributor and the balance is then applied in the agreed percentage and shared between the distributor and the producer. Any advance paid by the distributor can be recovered either in the same way as distribution expenses or out of the revenue payable to the producer; the former method is favourable to the producer, the latter to the distributor.

24.12   Distribution Fees

The amount of distribution fees payable under film distribution agreements will vary between 30% and 50%, depending on the medium and territory. A distributor may occasionally agree to vary the fee income by deferring part of a fee until a pre-specified point or, alternatively, a distributor may agree to a fee calculated on a sliding scale which reduces as income from the film rises.

24.13   Distribution Expenses

Depending on the type of distribution agreement, the expenses of a distributor may be deducted out of the producer's share (as in the net agreement), out of the distributor's share (as in the gross agreement), or "off-the-top*" (as in an adjusted agreement). Whatever way the distribution expenses are recovered, it is in the interests of the producer to ensure that these expenses relate only to actual direct costs incurred by the distributor on the film in question, and do not include any overhead-type items or any expenses payable to companies associated with the distributor (except where these expenses are calculated on an arm's length basis at a competitive rate).

The question of rebates and credits from connected laboratories and advertising agencies and other companies should also be considered as there may be a significant difference between arm's length rates and best obtainable commercial rates.

Distribution expenses in a production financing and distribution agreement should include as many delivery items as possible, since if these items are included in the negative costs of the film, they will probably be subject to an overhead charge and will certainly bear interest.

It may also be important to establish precisely what advertising/marketing services are included in the distribution fee and what services are permitted to be deducted as distribution expenses.

24.14   Prints and Advertising Commitment

From a producer's point of view, it is also important to obtain from the distributor a commitment to spend a predetermined amount on advertising the film and to provide a certain number of prints for theatrical release. A producer will, wherever possible, obtain a commitment from a distributor to release the film theatrically on a specified number of screens; this will involve the distributor in a substantial financial commitment to the film, which can only be recovered if the film is successful.

24.15   Sub-distributor's Fees

A producer will normally seek to limit the total of all fees and commissions paid to all distributors and all sub-distributors to a maximum percentage of remitted gross receipts. Where a sub-distributor is involved, a producer will normally seek to limit the amount recoverable by a distributor. The distributor's fee should also be calculated with reference to remitted income and not income received at source by the sub-distributor. Otherwise, it would be calculated on the higher amount. Provisions allowing for the deduction by the distributor of sub-distribution expenses from net income (ie a double deduction, since they will already have been deducted by the sub-distributor) are obviously not desirable from the point of view of the producer.

24.16   Distribution Accounting

The standard method of distribution accounting is to bring revenue into account at the time it is actually received, even though it may have been receivable much earlier, and to bring expenses into account at the time they are incurred, even though they may be payable at some point in the future. The policy of including only remitted money in distribution statements means that, at any one time, the distributor will be owed substantial amounts from third parties. Not all of these amounts will, in fact, be paid and some will constitute bad debts. Whilst the instinct of the producer or its representative may be to bring 'receivables' into account whether or not the sums are actually received, this may, in some circumstances, be to the detriment of the producer. It will result in a distribution fee being levied on moneys never received, the amount of the bad debt could be deducted by the distributor from the producer's share of net receipts and the producer will actually receive less as a result of an amendment intended to work in its favour.

24.17   Advances and Guarantees

Advances* (which may be returnable) and guarantees (which are generally non-returnable) are sometimes not brought into account unless and until they are wholly earned. In the case of an advance for videogram rights payable against a royalty on the sale of videograms, the point at which the advance is earned will be the point at which the total royalties payable will have equalled the advance and the distributor becomes entitled to receive royalty income. Because many distributors never recoup their advances, the exclusion of money paid by way of advance or minimum guarantee unless and until wholly earned can create a profit centre to the distributor and consequently cause loss to the producer.

24.18   Apportionment of Fees

A similar point arises on the calculation of television licence fees where these may be apportioned not only between different films, but also between different repeat showings of the same film. What, for example, is the position where a television station pays an advance entitling it to three showings of a film and only screens it twice? Assuming the licence fee is apportioned equally in respect of each screening, at which point can the producer require the distributor to bring the final one-third of the fee into account?

24.19   Interest

A by-product of the exclusion of advances and guarantees from receipts is that, under a production financing and distribution agreement, a distributor will very often continue to charge the producer interest on money which has been expended by the distributor, even where it has been recouped by the distributor. As accounting may be carried out on a quarterly basis in the case of both the pre-sale (or negative pick-up) agreement and the production financing and distribution agreement, if a distributor receives funds just after the beginning of a quarter he may not bring them into account until the end of the quarter. The producer may, therefore, wish to negotiate the suspension of interest charges at the moment any advance or guarantee is received by the distributor, whether or not it is earned or returnable, as well as the imposition of an obligation to pay distribution receipts into an interest-bearing account.

24.20 Distributor's Profit under a Production Financing and Distribution Agreement

Unlike a simple distribution agreement which permits the distributor to take only a distribution fee by way of profit, the production financing and distribution agreement gives the Company financing and distributing the film an interest in the profits of the film, as well as in all subsidiary and ancillary rights. The producer's right to participate in profits derived from subsidiary and ancillary areas will normally be postponed until the Company has recouped the cost of production of the film from its distributor's net receipts.

It is not uncommon to find that part of the finance required to complete and produce a film may be made available by the Company providing finance in the form of studio facilities, personnel or equipment. These facilities will be charged out at the current rate of the Company providing them, which evidently will be greater than their direct cost. A producer will be concerned to ensure that the costs attributable to personnel employed by the Company providing finance and facilities, pursuant to a production financing and distribution agreement, will be properly attributed to the production such personnel are working on. For this reason the producer will normally wish the audited certified cost statement of the film to be prepared within a relatively short period after the film has been completed and will want to vet this extremely carefully to determine that all items included on the statement are correct and accurate.

24.21 Application of Distribution Income

Although there is no universally standard method of applying the distribution income, the receipts of the Company under a production financing and distribution agreement might be applied in payment of the following sums in the following order:

* distribution fees;
* distribution expenses, including residuals and repeat fees;
* cost of production;
* interest on the cost of production;
* sums payable to the completion guarantor;
* interest on the completion guarantee;
* deferments and contingent fees;
* percentage participations in profits.

24.22 Derivation of Profits

Under a production financing and distribution agreement, the company providing finance may derive profits from the following different areas.

Distribution Fees

These have already been discussed. See Paragraph 24.12.

Share in Net Profits

A rule of thumb, which is often used as a rough starting point in negotiating the level of profit to which an investor is entitled, is that a person providing 100% of the finance for a film should receive 50% of the net profits—in other words, 0.5% of net profits for each 1% of the budgeted production costs. The remaining 50% of net profits is often divided between the financier and the producer leaving the producer with a 25%–40% share. Out of its share the producer will be expected to bear all participations in profits payable to actors and creative talent. For this reason, it is important for the producer to ensure that the definitions of participations payable to such persons are no more favourable than those payable to the producer. Usually a producer will seek to limit the reduction in its profit participation by inserting a provision to the effect that the participation cannot be reduced below a certain level or 'floor'.

Overhead Charges

Overhead charges like the theatrical exhibitors' house 'nut' (see Paragraph 24.4) do not always relate to the actual cost of heat, light, rates etc but more to the cost of being engaged in a highly speculative business. Overhead charges are a way of recovering losses incurred in developing projects which are not made or recovering lost money out of projects which are developed and are not successful.

Interest

Because interest is charged on the cost of production and the cost of production may be calculated by reference to the value of facilities provided by the company providing finance, interest is frequently charged on money which has never actually been spent. In view also of the length of accounting periods, interest may also be charged on money which has already been recovered by the company.

Facilities and services provided under a production financing agreement are charged at the most competitive rate for the company providing them, not the producer. They will be subject to an overhead charge and, additionally, will in some cases, have so-called 'fringe' payments (which are health pension and welfare payments payable under applicable US guild and union agreements) added on to them. The 'fringes' are normally added on before the overhead calculation in order to increase the value of the overhead.

Rebates and Commissions

A company which is a party to a production financing and distribution agreement may seek to trade on an arm's length basis, as opposed to trading on the best obtainable commercial terms, and may hold off out of account all rebates or credits received. Volume discounts from laboratories and advertising agencies may be substantial.

Exchange Rate Variations

If fluctuations in the international exchange rate move in favour of a company providing finance and obtaining distribution rights, pursuant to a production financing and distribution agreement, the producer is unlikely to benefit.

Subsidiary Profits

In addition to subsidiary rights, a company acquiring distribution rights under a production financing and distribution agreement may have subsidiary home video publishing or advertising companies which may exploit the rights in the film or its subsidiary or ancillary rights. Whether or not these rights remain available to the subsidiary on arm's length terms or on the best obtainable commercial terms, the subsidiary will make a profit out of this exploitation, which will not normally be passed back to the producer.

Double Add-Back

As an incentive towards a producer to stay within the budget for a film, a production financing and distribution agreement may, sometimes, contain a "double add-back" provision, which will increase the negative cost of the film by twice the amount of any excess over the budgeted cost, thus deferring the moment at which the producer may anticipate receiving profits. Such a provision may also be combined with a reduction in the amount of the production fee payable to the producer and the amount of the double add-back itself will also carry interest and overhead, even though the money has never been spent.

Excluded Income

Income arising from subsidiary and ancillary rights may be excluded from the profit calculation altogether and, if it is included at all, only a proportion of it will be brought into account. This will obviously not apply in the case of a pre-sale/negative pick-up arrangement. Where a company has publishing or video interests, the gross receipts of the subsidiary will not normally be included, but a definable royalty will be admitted in the accounts instead and, whilst distributors insist that their exhibitors include screen advertising revenue in statements of gross box office receipts, these items are frequently excluded in accounting to producers. Other sums excluded will be amounts receivable by way of taxes (such as sales tax and VAT), amounts received from the disposal of sets, costumes and equipment, sale of stock footage, sound material and publicity material, screen plays or other literary material, sums received from the disposal of prints and sums received arising as a result of tax-shelter type refinancing.

Deductions

Occasionally, items appear on statements of account to producers where the cost should prima facie be borne by the company distributing the film. Provisions which state that expenses will be borne by the company which has the right to deduct these (plus of course overhead and interest) out of sums payable to the producer need to be examined carefully.

24.23 Distributor's Profits under Pre-sale or Negative Pick-up Agreement

The profits of a distributor in this sort of arrangement will lie in the following areas.

Distribution Fees

These have already been discussed. See Paragraph 24.12.

Overhead

Although a distributor is not normally permitted to charge an overhead, some do succeed in charging one and most will find a way of claiming at least part of their ordinary running expenses back as allowable distribution expenses.

Interest

A distributor will not pass back to the producer the benefit of interest which the distributor may receive on funds belonging to the producer over which the distributor will have control and use for periods of up to six months.

Rebates and Commissions

A distributor may trade on an arm's length basis, as opposed to trading on the best obtainable commercial terms, and may not bring into account any rebates or credits received.

Exchange Rate

See Paragraph 24.22.

Deductions

See Paragraph 24.22.

24.24 Financier/Distributor's Profit

The areas in which a financier/distributor may be expected to derive profits under a production financing and distribution agreement have already been mentioned. See Paragraph 24.22.

24.25 Financier's Profit

The net receipts of a distributor, after the deduction of whatever sales agency fees and expenses are applicable, are generally remitted to the financiers of a film until the financiers have recouped their investment. It is normal to provide for a distributor's net receipts to be apportioned between the financiers in the proportion of their respective contributions (ie pro rata) and it is also normal, though by no means always the rule, for all the financiers to receive income progressively in their entitlement from the first sums remitted (ie pari passu).

After recoupment by the financier of its contribution towards the cost of production, the financier will normally be entitled to recover interest at a fixed rate above base rate or prime (usually 2.5% above). This interest rate constitutes a profit centre to the financier. Additionally, a financier will normally be entitled to participate in profits in proportion to the sum invested. See Paragraph 24.22.

24.26 Producer's Profit under the Production Financing and Distribution Agreement

A producer's profit under the production financing and distribution agreement is very straightforward to assess. There is only one person reporting and remitting income to the producer—the company which is a party to the production financing and distribution agreement—and the income reported will be all income received from the primary areas of exploitation, as well as the exploitation of the subsidiary rights (to the extent that such exploitation is not excluded from a calculation of net profits). After recoupment by the company of those elements already referred to, the producer may receive net profits.

24.27 Producer's Profit in Independently Financed Product

Unlike a production financing and distribution agreement where a producer has one system of accounting and one barometer to indicate whether the are in profit or loss, in the case of an independently financed film, the primary exploitation of the film may be carried out on a territory-by-territory basis with a number of different distributors. In some cases different media will be licensed to different parties in the same territory and, where a film is exploited on a piecemeal basis each theatrical distribution agreement and each videogram distribution agreement will be negotiated separately and may have different accounting dates, different accounting procedures and different definitions of distributors' net receipts. Additionally, in the case of independently financed product, a producer may have retained control of recording income, music publishing income, publishing income and merchandising income. All of these subsidiary areas of exploitation need to be integrated before a complete picture is available. Additionally, there are important commercial points relating to prints and advertising which need to be considered (see Paragraph 24.10).

24.28 Individual Artist's Profit

Because 'profit' is such an arbitrary term, the extent and degree of any individual profit participant's right to share in the profits depends on the terms negotiated. In any film, although it is probable that all net profit participants would have initially been offered the same definition, they may all have been negotiated differently and the producer may have to work out a different set of figures for each individual. This can lead to curious situations where a film may, for a short period, be in profit as far as one participant is concerned, and still have to recoup where others are concerned.

24.29 Favoured Nations

The so-called "favoured nations*" provisions automatically pass on to any profit participant any more favourable accounting position that has been negotiated by any other participant. Favoured nations clauses have a 'domino' effect and are generally not lightly conceded by any producer.

24.30 Producer's Net Profits and Net Profits

The distinction between net profits and producer's net profits is similar to that between an override royalty and a royalty based on receipts. If it is supposed that a film is financed 100% by an independent financier who is entitled to participate in 50% of the net profits by virtue of having provided the finance, then, if such financier agrees that the producer is to receive 50% of the remainder (ie 25% of 100% of net profits from a film), and the producer has to pay a participation of 2.5% of net profits of the film to an artist, the producer's share will be reduced to 2.5%. If, however, the producer is liable to pay to the artist 2.5% of 100% of net profits derived by the producer from the film, the producer's participation will be reduced by 2.5% of 25% (or 0.625%) to 24.375%. For obvious reasons, most profit participants seek to negotiate a percentage of net profits (ie profits of the film), as opposed to a percentage in the producer's share of profits derived from that film.

24.31   "Soft floors"

A producer will normally seek to limit the extent of third party participations to be deducted from his share of profits by providing that the producer's share of net profits may not be reduced below a certain level or "floor", and any excess participations are to be deducted 'off the top' (ie in first position from the figure which was previously net profits).

　　Assuming that a film makes profits of £2,000,000, out of which the producer is entitled to 25% (subject to the producer's share being reduced by third party participations to a floor of 20% with the excess to come "off the top"), what will the position of the producer be if there are third party participations of 15% payable? The producer's contract says that the participation cannot be reduced below a floor of 20% and therefore the producer should be entitled to £400,000 (ie 20% of £2,000,000). But the contract also says that any excess third party participations are to be deducted "off the top". The excess in this case is 10% (ie out of the 15 points payable only 5 can be met out of the producer's share of 25% before reducing it to the floor of 20%). The figure produced by the initial calculation of net profits (£2,000,000) must, therefore, be reduced by the 10% payable by way of excess participations. The new adjusted net profit figure will therefore be £1,800,000. Out of this, the producer is entitled to receive 25%, reduceable by third party participations to a floor of 20%, which works out at £360,000. The loss to the producer on the calculation is £40,000.

24.32   "Hard floors"

In order to avoid re-calculations along the manner of the soft floor, a provision is sometimes made for a producer's participation to be reduceable only to a hard floor by providing that the amount of net profits payable to the producer is that amount which is arrived at by the first application of the formula. If the example in Paragraph 24.31 above were applied to a hard floor situation, the producer would, nonetheless, receive £400,000.

24.33   Profit Deductions

Where any shares of profits payable to an individual are subject to the prior deduction of all other profit participations, that individual's entitlement will be recalculated after taking into account the cost to the producer of these. If all profit definitions allow the deduction of all other profit percentages before arriving at a final definition, the result will be a profit centre to the producer.

24.34 Accounting and Recoupment

A producer is unable to monitor the performance of a distributor under either a production financing and distribution agreement or a straightforward distribution agreement or presale* agreement, unless the producer has full powers of audit and inspection. Some agreements only permit the producer the right to demand a certificate of the distributor's auditors and this certificate is deemed to be conclusive proof of the accuracy of the accounting statements.

The viewpoint of the auditors of any distributor or even an independent expert must inevitably be different from that of a producer. Many film audit investigations disclose errors and a producer will normally wish to have the right to audit distributor's records. Additionally, the producer will wish to have access to the terms of all sub-distribution agreements, so that the producer may determine whether or not the distributor is exploiting the film to the best of its reasonable ability on the best reasonably obtainable commercial terms. The producer will normally also request copies of sub-distribution statements.

25 Completion Guarantee Agreement

25.1 Description of a completion guarantee

A completion guarantee is a contractually enforceable undertaking that a designated film will be completed for a sum not exceeding the budget and delivered to its principal financier within a specified period (normally three months) of the producer's* contractual delivery date.

The function of the completion guarantee is to provide a film's principal financier with certainty that, after having provided the producer with a considerable amount of money, the principal financier will have a film delivered to it. The completion guarantor will not normally accept responsibility for the artistic quality of the film nor will the guarantor give any assurance that the film as delivered will generate profits. The principal financier will, however, receive the assurance that, if the film is not completed and delivered within the requisite period, the principal financier's money will be returned to it.

Additionally, if the cost of production of the film exceeds that specified in the budget, the completion guarantor will pay the additional sums. The guarantor will normally have the right to recover sums advanced by it towards overcost, but only after the principal financier has itself recovered its investment in the budget from the revenue derived from the film.

A completion guarantee is only necessary where the principal financier is cash-flowing the production of a film, and making payments before delivery—this is normally done by a principal financier under a PFD agreement* (see Chapters 21, 22 and 23). Where a financier is paying on delivery (under a so-called negative pick-up* or pre-sale* agreement—see Chapter 31), the financier will not normally require the benefit of a completion guarantee, since, if the film is not completed and delivered to the financier, the financier will have no payment obligation (if it is the usual term of the negative pick-up/pre-sale agreement, that payment is made on delivery).

The parties to this particular transaction are:

*   the completion guarantor (referred to in this Chapter as the "Guarantor"); and
*   the principal financier or financiers of the film, collectively referred to in this Chapter as the "Beneficiaries".

Although the producer of the film (the "Producer") is not a direct party, the Guarantor is guaranteeing performance of the Producer's obligations and the Producer is, implicitly, involved in the arrangement. Because the Guarantor is assuming substantial liability in relation to the Producer's actions, it will require the Producer to enter into a completion guarantee security agreement (see Chapter 26) before it can give the guarantee.

25.2 Document Breakdown

A typical completion guarantee might be expected to contain the following clauses:

*   Guarantee (see Paragraph 25.3)
*   Guarantor's maximum obligation (see Paragraph 25.4)
*   Exclusions (see Paragraph 25.5)
*   Repayment and interest (see Paragraph 25.6)
*   Abandonment (see Paragraph 25.7)
*   Conditions precedent (see Paragraph 25.8)
*   Rights (see Paragraph 25.9)
*   Insurance (see Paragraph 25.10)
*   Subrogation (see Paragraph 25.11)
*   Actions against Guarantor (see Paragraph 25.12)
*   Boilerplate* (see Paragraph 25.13).

25.3 Guarantee

The Guarantor will normally guarantee completion and delivery of the film in accordance with a specified agreement between the Producer and the principal distributor of the film, although more than one agreement involving different parties may also be guaranteed. Obviously, the precise obligations under the main distribution agreement* will be vetted carefully by the Guarantor, as will the budget and the production schedule, before the Guarantor will agree to issue a guarantee.

Frequently, the Guarantor will require a formal financial undertaking from the Producer requiring the Producer to pay any sums in excess of those specified in the budget in relation to fees or living expenses of actors, additional delivery requirements pursuant to delivery agreements, publicity requirements and legal fees. This is often referred to as a "casting to budget undertaking".

Subject to the above terms, the Guarantor will normally agree to guarantee completion and delivery of the film in accordance with the budget and the production schedule. The guarantee is capable of being performed in a number of alternative ways. Either the Guarantor will advance to the Producer any sums in excess of the budget required to meet the cost of completing the film or the Guarantor will take over production of the film from the Producer in accordance with the Guarantor's powers under the completion guarantee security agreement (see Chapter 26). Alternatively, the Guarantor may elect to abandon the film, at which point the Guarantor will become liable to pay to the Beneficiaries the amount advanced by them towards the production of the film (to the extent expended by the Producer), plus unpaid sums, pursuant to existing contractual arrangements of the Producer.

25.4 Guarantor's Maximum Obligation

The Guarantee may specify the maximum amount for which the Guarantor is liable under the agreement. Normally, however, the Beneficiaries will be reluctant to accept any maximum obligation on the part of the Guarantor, since if additional sums are required to complete production and delivery of the film and the Guarantor's liability is less than the amount of such additional sums, the Beneficiaries may not receive delivery of the film, unless they make further funds of their own available.

The Guarantor will normally seek to make its liability conditional on the Beneficiaries and any other financiers making payment in full of all sums which they have contracted to provide for the production of the film. This is entirely usual.

The guarantee may also provide that the Guarantor's liability is limited to payment of any sums in excess of payments due under any insurance policies. Again, this requirement is not unreasonable, since, normally, the Beneficiaries will have the right to receive sums payable under the insurance policies. The issue remains as to who will fund the deductible under any insurance policies. Whether this is borne by the Guarantor or the Beneficiaries, is a matter for negotiation.

25.5 Exclusions

The guarantee will normally exclude liability on the part of the Guarantor in relation to a number of areas.

Intellectual Property Rights

Failure on the part of the Producer to obtain intellectual property rights or breach of copyright, trademark, right of privacy, right of personality, moral rights*, or performance rights, passing off or unfair competition.

Misrepresentation and Breach

Any misrepresentation or breach of warranty*, covenant, or defect or imperfection in rights to be granted by or to the Producer.

Censorship

Failure of the film to qualify for any rating or censorship requirement.

Artistic Quality

The artistic quality of the film.

Changes

Any changes in the budget or the production schedule or otherwise in relation to the film, including expenses for making changes, other than those agreed to by the Guarantor, which result from a departure or variance from the shooting script.

Extra Expenses

Extra expenses incurred in providing delivery items not required by the principal financing agreement or distribution agreement.

Stop Dates

Difficulties encountered as a result of the Producer's or director's or any principal actor's services being unavailable beyond a stop date. It will be appreciated that this type of provision could effectively prevent a completion guarantor from completing or delivering a film.

Insurance Policies

Areas of cover specified in insurance policies may be excluded from the scope of the guarantee because the Beneficiaries/Producer already have cover pursuant to the insurance policies.

Dishonesty or Fraud

Normally, any dishonest or fraudulent or criminal act on the part of the Producer or any of its servants, representatives or agents will exclude the Guarantor from liability.

Funding

If sums totalling the amounts specified in the budget have not been remitted to the production account within the relevant time specified in the cash-flow schedule, the Guarantor will not normally incur liability.

243

Delay

Normally, the Guarantor will not be liable in relation to delay in delivery caused as a result of force majeure.

Nuclear Contamination

Nuclear contamination and/or radioactivity are standard exclusions in most insurance policies. Since most completion guarantees are underwritten by insurers, they are also excluded in completion guarantees.

War

War, invasion, act of foreign enemies, hostilities (whether war is declared or not), civil war, rebellion, insurrection etc are normally excluded under insurance policies. Since most completion guarantees are reinsured, these events are normally excluded under completion guarantees also.

25.6 Repayment and Interest

The completion guarantee will normally provide that the Guarantor is entitled to be paid back any sums it expends in the performance of the guarantee, plus interest. The standard rate of interest in the film financing contracts is the base rate of a main bank plus 2.5%—which is the usual rate at which banks are prepared to lend.

The point at which the Guarantor becomes liable to receive the income stream from a film is also important. The Beneficiaries will normally wish to recover their financial contribution before the Guarantor recovers additional overcost sums paid by it. Normally, the Guarantor will recover its contribution to the cost of production in final position.

25.7 Abandonment

There will be occasions when the Guarantor may wish or be forced to declare abandonment of a film because it is unable to complete it.

Sometimes a declaration of abandonment may be caused by the death of an artist during principal photography. The artists Natalie Wood and Brandon Lee have died during principal photography. The film being made when Natalie Wood drowned was never completed but the film in which Brandon Lee died as a result of a munitions accident ("The Crow") was subsequently completed and released.

The guarantee may provide that, on a declaration of abandonment, the Guarantor will repay to the Beneficiaries the amount of finance advanced by them to date, plus any unpaid or non-cancellable contractual obligations which the Producer has incurred, up to the amount of any pre-specified maximum obligations.

25.8   Conditions Precedent

The guarantee will normally specify a number of conditions precedent which must be satisfied before the Guarantor will assume liability. Conditions precedent may include.

Finance

 The Beneficiaries will deposit in the production account sums equal to the full amount of the budget.

Completion Guarantee Security Agreement

The Guarantor will require security over the Producer and the various contracts* entered into by the Producer in order to produce the film. The Guarantor needs to have control over these aspects in order to be able to take-over production, and will normally obtain control through the medium of a completion guarantee security agreement between the Guarantor and the Producer. Execution of this agreement is normally a condition precedent to any liability of the Guarantor under the guarantee, since, if the Producer does not give the Guarantor the controls it requires, the Guarantor will be unable to comply with its obligations.

Completion Guarantee Fee

The Guarantor will normally exclude liability until it has been paid the completion guarantee fee. This is an item in the production budget for the film and will normally be payable by the Producer. There may be circumstances where the Beneficiaries will pay the fee direct to the Guarantor, in order to ensure satisfaction of this condition.

Collection Agreement

Because the Guarantor may advance* funds to the enable completion of the film, the Guarantor will normally want to ensure that it is permitted to recover these. Frequently, film production agreements appoint trusted third parties (such as the National Film Trustee Corporation Limited) to collect and administer payment obligations relating to films. The Guarantor may therefore wish the Beneficiaries and the Producer to enter into a collection agreement with a party, such as the NFTC, to secure the Guarantor's ability to recover any money or advances paid by it to complete the film.

25.9   Rights

If the Beneficiaries of a guarantee are the principal financiers under a PFD agreement* (see Chapters 21–23) they will normally have acquired all rights in relation to the film. If the Guarantor, therefore, takes over production of the film without the consent of the rights owners, it may be infringing various copyrights. For this reason, the guarantee may provide for the Beneficiaries to license the Guarantor all necessary intellectual property rights required to enable it to complete and take-over production of the film.

25.10   Insurance

The producer of a film normally takes out certain insurance policies (see Chapters 21–23). As has been seen (see Paragraph 25.4), the Guarantor will normally wish to limit its liability to sums in excess of those payable under the insurance policies. It may also wish to secure its position by providing that all sums payable under the insurance policies are payable to the Guarantor and not the Beneficiaries or the Producer.

   In the event of any insurance claim, since the Guarantor is liable to pay additional costs, the Guarantor will wish to provide that the Beneficiaries will not settle or compromise any claim without the consent of the Guarantor.

   The Guarantor will also wish the Beneficiaries to provide it with details of all cover and modifications, receipts of premiums and copies of insurance policies when they are available.

Amount of Cover

 The Guarantor may wish to address the possibility that the amount of cover under the insurance policies may subsequently become inadequate and provide that the Beneficiaries will increase the amount of cover, if requested to do so, within a prespecified period.

Continuation of Policies

The Guarantee will normally provide that the Beneficiaries will not do anything which may cause the insurance policies to lapse or become void or voidable.

Failure to Maintain Policies

In the event the Beneficiaries fail to maintain adequate insurance policies, the Guarantor will normally reserve the right to take out such policies and recover the cost of doing so as a contract debt from the Beneficiaries.

Liability

If the Guarantor incurs any liability and makes any payment in relation to any matter which should have been covered under the insurance policies, and, either the insurance policies have lapsed or are void, or the Guarantor is unable to recover such sum, it may reserve the right to receive repayment from the Beneficiaries as a contract debt.

Assignment

The Guarantor will normally require the assignment of the benefit of any insurance policies effected by the Beneficiaries and/or the Producer, in order to enable the Guarantor to control the cash-flow of the film.

Claim

The Beneficiaries will agree to give the Guarantor immediate notice of any matter which might give rise to any claim and to co-operate fully with the Guarantor in relation to any claim or other matter relating to the insurance policies.

25.11   Subrogation

The concept of subrogation may require some explanation. It normally arises in insurance contracts and operates as follows. If the Insurer makes a payment in relation to loss caused to the insured by a third party, the insurer automatically acquires the insured's rights against the third party and may bring proceedings against the third party to recover the losses occasioned by it to the insured.

A completion guarantee may contain a subrogation provision permitting the Guarantor to commence proceedings and recover sums which it has paid to the Beneficiaries as a result of some third party's breach. It will also contain a provision preventing the Beneficiaries from prejudicing any of the Guarantor's rights against such third parties. It will be appreciated that a Guarantor's subrogation provision may not, of course, apply where an insurance policy covers the matter where the loss has been incurred, since the insurance company will become liable for such loss and no payment will have been made by the Guarantor.

25.12   Actions Against the Guarantor

The guarantee may provide that no legal proceedings may be taken against the Guarantor by the Beneficiaries, unless and until, they have fully complied with all terms of the agreement. It may also provide that no party other than the

Beneficiaries will be entitled to bring or maintain any legal proceedings, since the guarantee will have been effected for the sole benefit of the Beneficiaries and not for any other persons.

25.13 Boilerplate

The boilerplate section of a typical completion guarantee may contain the following provisions:

- Notices (see Paragraph 52.8)
- Severability (see Paragraph 52.10)
- Entire agreement (see Paragraph 52.3)
- Waiver (see Paragraph 52.11)
- No partnership (see Paragraph 52.7)
- Governing law (see Paragraph 52.5).

26 Completion Guarantee Security Agreement

26.1 Description of a Completion Guarantee Security Agreement

A completion guarantor requires a completion guarantee security agreement before it can enter into completion guarantees (see Chapter 25).

Because a completion guarantee requires a completion guarantor to guarantee the performance by a producer* of the producer's obligations under a production financing and distribution agreement, the completion guarantor requires certain contractual rights with the producer, in order to ensure that the completion guarantor can control the producer and compel it to do all acts necessary, both to meet the producer's obligations under the production financing and distribution agreement*, as well as the completion guarantor's own obligations to the beneficiaries under its completion guarantee.

The parties to this particular transaction are:

- the completion guarantor (the "Guarantor"); and
- the producer whose obligations under the relevant production finance and distribution agreement have been guaranteed (the "Producer").

The persons receiving the benefit of the completion guarantee (the "Beneficiaries") are not a party to the completion guarantee security agreement, although, clearly, they are implicitly involved in it.

26.2 Transaction Analysis

A typical completion guarantee security agreement might be expected to contain the following clauses:
- Guarantee (see Paragraph 26.3)
- Conditions precedent (see Paragraph 26.4)
- Production of the film (see Paragraph 26.5)
- Commitment fee (see Paragraph 26.6)
- Recoupment (see Paragraph 26.7)
- Representations and warranties* (see Paragraph 26.8)

- Production account (see Paragraph 26.9)
- Insurance (see Paragraph 26.10)
- Security (see Paragraph 26.11)
- Production representative (see Paragraph 26.12)
- Attorney (see Paragraph 26.13)
- Default (see Paragraph 26.14)
- Take-over (see Paragraph 26.15)
- Effect of take-over (see Paragraph 26.16)
- Power on take-over (see Paragraph 26.17)
- Abandonment (see Paragraph 26.18)
- Guarantor's remedies (see Paragraph 26.19)
- Boilerplate* (see Paragraph 26.20).

26.3 Guarantee

The Guarantor will agree with the Producer to enter into the completion guarantee with the Beneficiaries, subject to the performance by the Producer of its obligations in the agreement.

The Guarantor and the Producer will agree that the Guarantor may exercise its rights under the completion guarantee security agreement and discharge its obligations under the completion guarantee by advancing to the Producer sums in excess of the budget required to complete the film or by exercising the take-over rights (see Paragraph 26.15) or by abandoning production of the film in accordance with the completion guarantee security agreement or by any combination of the above.

26.4 Conditions Precedent

The security agreement may contain a number of conditions precedent to the Guarantor's liability to the Producer including the following.

Provision of Budget

The deposit in the production account of sums equal to the full amount of the budget, plus any additional sums required to be deposited in relation to approved changes (see Paragraph 26.5).

Documentation

Execution and delivery of all ancillary documentation required, pursuant to the security agreement. This will include a charge or mortgage (possibly an inducement letter), certain insurance documentation and other documentation specified below.

Laboratory Arrangements

The Guarantor will normally require execution of a laboratory pledgeholder's agreement* and possibly a laboratory access letter* (see Paragraph 51.3), together with a takeover letter to be executed by the bank at which the production account is maintained, permitting the Guarantor to take-over and administer the production account.

Ancillary Documentation

The Guarantor will normally require certain ancillary documentation to be produced, such as copies of all underlying rights agreements, confirmation from the director of the film that the budget and production schedule are adequate, confirmation of approval by the principal financiers of the shooting script, production schedule, budget and cash-flow schedule, executed letters of acknowledgement from individual executive producers, producers, directors and production managers, confirmation from the principal financiers that they will accept delivery of the film from the completion guarantor as if it were effected from the Producer, power of attorney from the Producer and executed copies of a charge and deed of priority to protect the Guarantor's security interest.

26.5   Production

The completion guarantee security agreement will normally contain a number of specific provisions relating to production of the film, including possibly, the following.

Compliance

The Producer will produce the film fully in accordance with the agreement being guaranteed and in accordance with the shooting script, the budget and the production schedule. It will not make any variation to any of the foregoing without the consent of the Guarantor and all principal financiers.

Changes

If the Guarantor and all relevant financiers approve in writing, there may be circumstances in which the Producer may make changes which do not result in a potential increase in the cost of production of the film. Where changes do result in a potential increase, the Guarantor may require the Producer to make deposit of additional sums in the production account.

Production Personnel

All contracts* with production personnel will be subject to the prior approval of the Guarantor and none of them will contain stop dates (see Paragraph 20.5) without the Guarantor's prior consent.

Guarantor's Directions

The Producer will comply promptly with all Guarantor's directions and instructions, provided they do not require a breach of any of the provisions of the agreements being guaranteed.

Assignability

All production contracts and other agreements entered into by the Producer will provide that the contracts and their benefit may be assigned to the Guarantor. This means that, if the Guarantor takes over production, it will be able to require direct performance of their obligations by the relevant parties.

Adherence to Budget

All obligations in relation to the film will contain financial provisions in accordance with those provided in the budget. Budgeted amounts will not be exceeded by the Producer, without the prior written consent of the Guarantor.

Reports

The Producer will provide the Guarantor with daily status reports and weekly cost statements and cash-flow schedules and shall keep the Guarantor and its production representative fully informed in all matters.

Information

The Producer will provide, in a timely manner, any information required by the Guarantor or its production representative in relation to any matter in connection with the production of the film, and will attend any meetings requested by the Guarantor.

26.6 Fee

The security agreement will normally provide that the Producer will procure the payment of the completion guarantee fee and that the Guarantor has no obligation, unless and until, the fee is paid in full.

Where changes to a film are proposed to be made, the agreement may contain provision requiring the fee to be increased by a percentage amount of the cost of any such changes.

Additionally, the security agreement may contain a provision excluding the Guarantor from liability in the event that the Guarantor signs an agreement with the Producer, but is subsequently unable to agree the terms of the completion guarantee itself with the Beneficiaries. Normally, both documents will be executed contemporaneously but there may be occasions where one may be executed in advance of the other and if it is the completion guarantee security agreement which is executed first, this provision is not unreasonable.

If the Guarantor exercises the right of termination in pursuance of such a provision, it is obviously essential for the Producer to ensure that any amount of the completion guarantee fee previously paid is returned by the Guarantor as a condition precedent to the Guarantor avoiding liability.

In some circumstances, the Guarantor may be prepared to rebate a percentage of the fee if no claim is made by the Producer or the Beneficiaries on the guarantee. In such circumstances, an appropriate provision will need to be inserted in the agreement. Normally, the Beneficiaries will expect to receive the full amount of any rebate of the completion guarantee fee and will resist any claim on the part of the Producer to such sums.

26.7   Recoupment

Money which is advanced by the guarantor to enable completion of the film is normally recovered after the financiers of the film have recouped their own investment. The Guarantor will wish to ensure that its right to recover the sums it has advanced is referred to both in the security agreement and the completion guarantee itself. Since the Producer is not a party to the completion guarantee, a statement by the Beneficiaries and the Guarantor as to how the receipts of the film are to be applied will not necessarily bind the Producer.

26.8   Representations and Warranties

A completion guarantee security agreement will normally contain a number of representations and warranties, which may include the following.

Distribution and Financing Agreement

The Producer will warrant that the distribution agreement or PFD agreement* which the Guarantor is guaranteeing has been fully executed and delivered unconditionally free from any escrow, is in full force and effect and that it has not been in any way varied or modified and that the copy which the Guarantor has had is true, accurate and correct.

Approval

The Producer will also confirm that the various parties, distributor, financiers etc have approved the shooting script, production schedule, budget and cash-flow schedule for the film.

Rights

The Producer has acquired all rights, including copyright, performer's rights, and other rights in relation to the production of the film.

Adequacy of Budget

The budget includes adequate provision for all expenses relating to the film.

Compliance with Budget

The Producer will enter into written agreements with all necessary third parties in accordance with the budget and the production schedule and will provide copies of them to the Guarantor.

Production Contracts

The Producer has obtained, or will obtain, before principal photography, copies of enforceable agreements with individual producers, directors, production personnel, writers, composers etc.

Status of Producer

The Producer is validly incorporated and existing under the laws of whatever jurisdiction it is situated in.

Veracity

All the information and facts contained in the recitals are true and correct.

Corporate Authorisation

The Producer has procured all necessary steps to authorise the execution and performance by the Producer of the agreements relating to the film.

Disclosure

Copies of all agreements entered into by the Producer previously in relation to the film have been disclosed to the Guarantor.

Security Interest

Other than persons approved by the Guarantor, no person has any security interest or mortgage in relation to the film, the rights, or any of the film materials.

No Liability

Nothing contained in the film will infringe any copyright or constitute a libel or slander, or violate any rights of privacy or publicity or moral rights or performers' rights or constitute a contempt of court or otherwise infringe or violate any rights of any person.

Books and Records

The Producer will procure that full and accurate books and records are maintained in relation to the film.

Taxes

The Producer will pay, when due, all taxes, assessment and charges imposed on it and its properties and assets.

Corporate Existence

The Producer will maintain its corporate existence and rights and privileges necessary to the proper conduct of its business and comply with the requirements of all applicable laws.

Duty to Inform

The Producer will promptly advise the Guarantor of the occurrence of any event which might materially adversely affect its financial condition and shall advise the Guarantor of any claims or proceedings threatened or commenced against the Producer.

Statements and Accounts

The Producer will deliver copies of all statements and accounts, with respect to the film received by the Producer, in the event the Guarantor incurs any liability to pay additional costs of production.

Title

Neither the Producer nor any of its predecessors in title has sold, assigned or transferred or otherwise disposed of any rights in the film in a manner which would conflict with the production financing agreement or distribution agreement.

Incumbrances

The Producer will not purport to create or permit any mortgage pledge, lien, charge or security interest or other incumbrance to exist in relation to any of the rights or physical material. Normally, however, in the course of production, the laboratory will obtain a lien on materials and this provision frequently excludes any lien obtained by the film laboratory.

Waiver

The Producer will not waive any right which it has in relation to the production of the film without the consent of the Guarantor.

Indemnity

See Paragraph 53.16.

26.9   Production Account

The Producer will agree to open and maintain a production account and agree to pay into it all sums received from principal financiers/distributors.

The Producer will agree that, sums in the production account will be applied solely towards the production of the film in accordance with the budget and the cash-flow schedule.

The Producer will also agree that the Guarantor's representative or representatives will be joint signatories for the production account and that the bank at which the account is maintained will execute a take-over letter, giving the Guarantor the right to take over the account in the event the take-over rights (See Paragraph 26.15) become exercisable.

26.10 Insurance

The Producer will agree to take out effective insurance policies in accordance with the production financing and distribution agreement.

The Producer will agree not to make or advance or compromise or settle any insurance claim without the Guarantor's prior written approval. It will agree to follow the instructions of the Guarantor in relation to any claim, as well as providing the Guarantor with full information and documentation on all insurance matters.

There may be circumstances where the Guarantor is of the view that the insurance cover effected by the Producer is inadequate and the agreement may therefore give the Guarantor the right to require the Producer to effect additional insurance cover.

The Producer will agree not to do or fail to do any act which may result in the insurance policies lapsing or becoming void or voidable. To give further security to the Guarantor, the agreement may require the insurance policies to provide that their cover will not lapse until a number of days after notice in writing has been given to the Guarantor, which will have the right to pay any additional premium or remedy any other event which would have made the policies lapse or become voidable.

The Guarantor will normally be looking to receive the benefit of the insurance policies, since if a major claim arises, there will be a real possibility that the Guarantor may become liable under its completion guarantee. For this reason, the security agreement may provide that the benefit of all insurance policies is to be assignable.

26.11 Security

The Guarantor will normally require a mortgage or charge or other security interest to protect its liability and its right to recover any contribution it makes towards the production of the film. As has been described above (see Paragraph 26.7) the Guarantor's right to recover sums advanced towards the cost of production of the film is normally deferred until the financiers have recovered their contribution.

Because the financiers themselves will probably acquire security interests, this gives rise to a situation where the priority of the mortgages or charges in relation to the film will vary. Normally, the Guarantor will require priority during completion of the film. Once the film has been completed and delivered in accordance with the PFD agreement or distribution agreement, it is normal to expect the financiers to assume priority until they have recovered their investment. If, at this point, additional sums advanced by the Guarantor remain outstanding, then the Guarantor will reassume priority. It may, therefore, be necessary for the third party financiers and the Guarantor to enter into a deed of priority to reflect the state of affairs.

26.12   Production Representative

Normally, a Guarantor will have the right to ensure that one or more production representatives are present at all relevant times during the production of the film. Whether or not the costs of lodging, meals and expenses of the Guarantor's representative should form part of a budget is a matter which needs to be decided.

Normally, the Guarantor's representative will have unrestricted access to all stages, sets and locations and will be invited to see all rushes and screenings of the film. The representative will be provided with full reports and cost statements and have the right of full consultation with the individual producer and production manager and other production personnel. The representative may also be a counter-signatory to the production account for the purpose of drawing funds and may approve any variation to the cash-flow schedule for the film.

26.13   Attorney

Normally, the agreement will contain a provision for further assurance, appointing the Guarantor as the Producer's attorney (see Paragraph 53.13).

26.14   Default

See Paragraph 23.4.

26.15   Take-over

See Paragraph 23.5.

26.16   Effect of Take-over

See Paragraph 23.6.

26.17   Guarantor's Power on Take-over

See Paragraph 23.6.

26.18   Abandonment

See Paragraph 23.7.

26.19 Guarantor's Remedies

It will be normal, as stated above (see Paragraph 26.11) to expect the Guarantor to take some form of mortgage or security interest in relation to the film. The security agreement may, therefore, provide that if the Producer is in default under the agreement or the Guarantor is entitled to exercise its take-over rights, the rights of the Guarantor pursuant to the mortgage or the security agreement shall become exercisable.

26.20 Boilerplate

The boilerplate section of a typical completion guarantee security agreement will contain the following provisions:

- Notices (see Paragraph 52.8)
- Severability (see Paragraph 52.10)
- Entire agreement (see Paragraph 52.3)
- Assignment (see Paragraph 52.1)
- Waiver (see Paragraph 52.11)
- No partnership (see Paragraph 52.7)
- Governing law (see Paragraph 52.5).

27 Discounting/Loan Agreement

27.1 Description of Discounting/Loan Agreement

This type of agreement* is entered into where a producer* has a binding contractual commitment from a distributor or a number of distributors to pay to the producer a sum equal to the total cost of production of the film on delivery of the film to the distributor(s). Because the producer lacks the resources to pay for the cost of production of the film from commencement of production until delivery, the producer needs to obtain finance during production.

In these circumstances, the producer may obtain finance by assigning to a bank the producer's right to receive payment of the sums payable by the distributor(s) on delivery. Before making any loan available, the bank will wish to receive some form of guarantee that the film will actually be produced and delivered to the distributor(s) in accordance with the provisions of the distribution agreement(s). For this reason, the producer will normally procure that a completion guarantee (see Chapter 25) is issued to the bank and, on the basis of a completion guarantee and the assignment of all distribution advances, the bank may be prepared to lend the producer the cost of the production of the film.

The parties to this particular transaction are:

- the producer of the film (the "Producer"); and
- the bank or other entity lending the Producer the cost of production ("Lender").

27.2 Transaction Analysis

A typical discounting/loan agreement might be expected to contain the following clauses:

- Loan (see Paragraph 27.3)
- Interest (see Paragraph 27.4)
- Advances* (see Paragraph 27.5)

- Fees and costs (see Paragraph 27.6)
- Repayment (see Paragraph 27.7)
- Conditions precedent (see Paragraph 27.8)
- Warranties* and undertakings (see Paragraph 27.9)
- Changes in circumstances (see Paragraph 27.10)
- Expenses and duties (see Paragraph 27.11)
- Events of default (see Paragraph 27.12)
- Overdue payments (see Paragraph 27.13)
- Amount owing (see Paragraph 27.14)
- Set-off (see Paragraph 27.15)
- Boilerplate* (see Paragraph 27.16)

27.3 Loan

The Lender will agree that, provided no event of default has occurred, it will make the loan available to the Producer. The loan will normally be available to the Producer during a prespecified period and any amount of the loan which remains undrawn at the end of the period will cease to be available.

The amount of the loan will be the total sum(s) payable by the distributor(s) pursuant to the distribution agreement(s), less sums payable to the Lender by way of interest and by way of facility fee. From the Producer's point of view, it will be receiving a discounted amount of the distribution agreement(s), since the cost of interest on the borrowing and the facility fee and the bank's legal expenses will be deducted from the amount receivable from the distributor(s). For this reason, the agreement is often referred to as a "discounting agreement".

27.4 Interest

The loan will normally specify the rate of interest payable, either by reference to a designated bank or by reference to the offered rate at the London Interbank Market (known as 'libor'). If the loan is in pounds sterling the number of days in the year for calculating interest will be 365. If the loan is for a dollar sum, the number of days will be 360.

27.5 Advances

The Lender will agree to make the loan available to the Producer in certain preagreed tranches or advances, provided no event of default has occurred.

27.6 Fees and Costs

The Lender will normally have the right to deduct and retain from sums to be advanced the total amount of interest and facility fees and legal cost of the loan. The Lender may also wish to maintain an additional reserve to cover the possibility that the film may not be completed and delivered strictly in accordance with the distribution agreement obligations.

In practice, the reserve might cover the period between the delivery date in the distribution agreement and the long-stop delivery date specified in the completion guarantee (often three months later). If a reserve is retained by a Lender, the agreement should contain a provision for such amount of the reserve remaining after payment of interest to be rebated to the Producer in full. This will mean that, if the Producer delivers the film on its contracted delivery date, 100% of the reserve will be returned to it.

27.7   Repayment

The loan agreement will specify a repayment date. In practice, this may be the earlier of actual delivery by the Producers to the Distributor or the long-stop delivery date specified in the completion guarantee. The Lender will be the beneficiary of the completion guarantee, which will provide that, if the Guarantor abandons production of the film, the Lender will be paid out in full on the date that the film is abandoned.

The repayment provision will normally specify the currency in which the Lender is to be repaid, the account to which repayment is to be directed and the date on which payment is deemed to be received. Additionally, the Lender will require the Producer to ensure that no withholding taxes* are deducted from the repayment of any loans and will in return undertake to release* and reassign to the Producer any rights acquired by the Lender pursuant to any mortgage or charge or other security arrangements upon repayment.

27.8   Conditions Precedent

Normally, the Lender will require a number of conditions to be fulfilled before making the loan available to a Producer. These conditions will include: delivery to the Lender's lawyers and approval by them of memorandum and articles of association or corporate by-laws of the Producer; receipt of all necessary board resolutions; and executed copies of all ancillary documentation, such as completion guarantee security agreements, security assignments, charges, deed of priority copies of existing security agreements, laboratory pledgeholders agreements and various opinion letters.

27.9   Warranties and Undertakings

The loan agreement will normally contain a number of warranties and undertakings on the part of the Producer. These might include the following provisions.

Binding Obligation

The agreement is a legal, valid and binding obligation enforceable against the Producer.

Non-contravention

The signature execution of the performance of the agreement will not contravene any law or regulation or provision of the producer's corporate byelaws.

No Litigation

At the date of the agreement, there is no litigation, arbitration or administrative proceeding in force against the Producer in any court and no such proceeding, is so far as the Producer is aware, is pending or threatened.

Authorisation

Signature and execution of the agreement and associated documents has been duly authorised.

Veracity

All information set out in the agreement and associated documents is true and correct in all material respects.

Contingent Remuneration

The Producer has not made any arrangement for any person to be paid out of gross or net receipts of the film, except as disclosed in the budget.

Information

The Producer will provide the Lender with such financial and other information in relation to the Producer as the Lender requires.

Copyright Ownership

The Producer is and shall be the sole copyright owner of the film. This provision may need to be amended to reflect the fact that copyright in the film may have been assigned to the distributor.

Delivery Material

All delivery material is situated at the designated laboratory and all future delivery material will be placed at the laboratory.

Copyright and Obscenity

Nothing contained in the film or delivery material will be obscene, libellous or defamatory or will infringe any right of copyright, patent, trademark, privacy right, publicity right or any other right.

Rights Agreement

The Producer has entered into all necessary agreements with owners of rights. It has obtained all consents which might be required for the production and/or exploitation of the film.

No Notice of Defect

The Producer has no actual or constructive notice of any defect in its rights.

Quality

The film and delivery material will be of first-class quality, suitable for commercial exploitation.

Compliance with Credits

The film and delivery material will comply with all screen and advertising credit obligations of third parties.

No Incumbrances

The rights in the film and the delivery material are and shall be free from all liens, charges, security interests and encumbrances.

Film

The film will be a new feature-length, talking motion picture in colour, fully synchronised with dialogue, music and sound, originally photographed and recorded in the English language.

Copyright Protection

The film will be protected under statutory and common law copyright throughout all countries adhering to the Berne Convention and the Universal Copyright Convention.

Registration

The Producer shall ensure that copyright registration of the film is effected in the USA and other territories where registration is desirable.

Application of Funds

The Producer will apply all funds received from the Lender solely in connection with the production of the film.

Budget Approval

The budget has been approved by the completion guarantor and the distributor(s).

Distribution Agreement(s)

True and correct copies of the distribution agreements are annexed and the Producer shall not permit any changes or variations to be made to them without the prior written consent of the Lender.

Compliance

The Producer has complied and shall comply with all existing or future obligations under the distribution agreement(s).

Insurances

The schedule of insurances has been approved by the completion guarantor and the Producer shall insure that the relevant policies remain in full force and effect and shall not do or fail to do anything which may cause cover under the policies to be prejudiced.

Insurance Claims

If any claim arises under the insurance policies which may prejudice the Lender's position, the Producer shall assign to the Lender, subject to the prior rights of the completion guarantor, any rights the Producer has in respect of such a claim.

Lapse of Policies

If the Producer fails to keep the insurance policies in full force and effect and pay any premiums, the Lender shall have the right to pay the same and recover these from the Producer as part of the loan.

Cuts and Changes

The cost of any cuts or changes required under the distribution agreement(s) is not to be deducted from sums payable by the distributor(s) to the Lender under the distribution agreement(s). It will be remembered that the Producer has assigned to the Lender the right to receive all payments which the Producer is entitled to receive under the distribution agreement(s).

No Exclusion of Take-over

None of the production contracts prevent the taking over and completion and delivery of the film by the completion guarantor.

No Breach of Security Agreement

The Producer is not in breach of any of its obligations under the completion guarantee security agreement.

Irrevocable direction

The Producer shall issue irrevocable directions to the distributor for it to pay all sums into the collection account maintained by the Lender.

No Alteration

The film will not depart from the script without the prior written consent of the distributor(s) nor shall the Producer alter or permit the alteration of the script in any way.

No Variation

The Producer will not vary the terms of any agreement relating to the film without the Lender's prior written consent.

Compliance

The film will comply with all requirements of the distribution agreement(s).

No Other Agreements

The Producer has not entered into and shall not enter into any other arrangements or agreements in relation to the film

Rebate and/or Shortfall

The Producer shall pay into the collection account any rebate received from the completion guarantor, together with any short-fall in the cost of production of the film.

Notification

The Producer shall notify or procure that the completion guarantor shall notify the Lender immediately on completion and delivery of the film to the distributor(s) in accordance with the distribution agreement(s).

Confidentiality

The Producer shall not disclose or make public any information relating to the agreement or the Lender.

Cost of Production

The Producer shall deliver to the Lender a statement of the cost of production of the film, certified by a firm of reputable chartered accountants, within a specified number of days from delivery.

Application of Funds

All proceeds made available to the Producer by the Lender shall be applied solely towards defraying the direct cash negative cost of the film.

Indemnity

See Paragraph 53.16.

27.10 Changes in Circumstances

The loan agreement may contain a provision which requires the Lender to obtain compensation from the Producer in the event that any circumstances change in such a way as to give rise to additional liability of the Producer to the Lender under the loan agreement.

27.11 Expenses and Duties

It is normal in loan agreements for the Producer to pay the costs incidental of the agreement incurred by the Lender, including costs of drafting and stamping agreements, cost of default, duties and fines etc. So far as concerns legal costs, a Producer will normally wish to limit the amount which it is required to pay to the Lender. Whether this is acceptable or not will depend on the circumstances. The amount of the Producer's maximum liability will be a matter for negotiation.

27.12 Events of Default

The loan agreement will normally specify a number of events of default which permit the Lender to call in the loan and exercise any security interest it may have, including the following matters.

Non-Payment

Non-payment by the Producer of the loan on the repayment date.

Default

Default by the Producer in the observance or performance of any provision of the agreement.

Winding-up

Any resolution is passed for the winding up of the Producer or any petition is filed for its liquidation, or it ceases or threatens to cease to carry on business.

Distress

Any distress or execution is levied on any part of the property of the Producer.

Mortgage Enforceability

Any mortgage, charge or any other security agreement created by the Producer becomes enforceable against it.

Breach

The Producer fails to observe or is in breach of the loan agreement or distribution agreement(s) or any ancillary agreement.

Misrepresentation

Any representation or warranty proves to be incorrect or untrue in any material respect.

Judgment

Any final judgment is obtained against the Producer which is likely, in the Lender's opinion, to materially affect the Producer's financial condition.

Moratorium

The Producer agrees to declare a moratorium or becomes or is deemed to be insolvent or is unable to pay its debts.

Disposal

Any material part of the assets or revenue of the Producer is sold or disposed of or threatened to be sold or disposed of.

Failure of Security

Any part of the security created pursuant to the loan agreement or ancillary documentation fails or ceases to have full force and effect.

Change of Control

Change of control of the Producer occurs.

Associates

Any associate, subsidiary or holding company of the Producer suffers the occurrence of any of the events referred to above.

Rights Agreements

Any of the rights agreements is terminated, cancelled or becomes subject to any significant litigation.

Non-Delivery

The film is not delivered to the distributor(s) in accordance with the distribution agreement(s).

In the event of default, the loan will normally become due and payable on demand and the Lender will be relieved from the obligation to make any further advances available.

27.13   Overdue Payments

The loan agreement will normally contain a provision entitling the Lender to recover a higher interest rate on overdue payments and obliging the Producer to pay additional sums incurred by the Lender as a result of late payment.

27.14   Calculation of Amount Owing

Where proceedings are commenced against a Producer, there may be circumstances where the Lender is entitled to recover interest at a rate fixed by court. For this reason, some agreements include a provision to the effect that in those circumstances, the Lender is entitled to recover the higher of the rate payable under the agreement or the rate fixed by or payable under any court judgment or order.

Similarly, where any judgment or order is expressed in a currency other than the one in which the loan is drawn, the Lender will wish to be indemnified in relation to any variation between the rate of exchange in which the other currency is converted to the loan currency and the rate of exchange at which the Lender is able to purchase the loan currency with the amount of the other currency actually received.

27.15   Set-off

The loan agreement will also contain a provision entitling the Lender, after any event of default, to combine, consolidate and merge any other liabilities of the

Producer and to set-off or transfer any sums owed by the Lender to the Producer for the satisfaction of the liabilities of the Producer under the loan agreement.

27.16 Boilerplate

The boilerplate section of a typical loan agreement may contain the following provisions:

- Notices (see Paragraph 52.8)
- Assignment (see Paragraph 52.1)
- Waiver (see Paragraph 52.11)
- Entire agreement (see Paragraph 52.3)
- Governing law (see Paragraph 52.5).

28 Film Mortgage

28.1 Description of a Film Mortgage

The purpose of a film mortgage is to give a lender, or party providing finance for production of the film, security over it.

A great deal of confusion exists (even in legal circles) between the rights granted by a mortgage and the rights granted by a charge. A mortgage transfers legal title to the mortgaged asset (here the film) but a charge merely creates a security interest over a film which cannot be enforced without an order of the court. It is for this reason, that charges contain lengthy provisions relating to their enforcement, mainly referring to sections of the Law of Property Act 1925. These provisions are completely unnecessary where a mortgage has been created, since the right of ownership has already been assigned.

In some circumstances, a document will mortgage a film (ie assign rights of the film absolutely by way of security) and at the same time create a charge over the other assets of the producer*. In these mixed documents, provisions relating to enforceability are necessary. They remain, however, completely unnecessary in mortgages.

The parties to this particular transaction are:

- the lender which has agreed to advance* a loan to the producer to make a film (the "Lender"); and
- the producer of the film (the "Producer").

28.2 Transaction Analysis

A typical film mortgage might be expected to contain the following clauses:
- Mortgage (see Paragraph 28.3)
- Book debts and other money (see Paragraph 28.4)
- Future distribution (see Paragraph 28.5)
- Enforcement (see Paragraph 28.6)
- Warranties* (see Paragraph 28.7)
- Grant of time (see Paragraph 28.8)
- Dispositions (see Paragraph 28.9)
- Protection of third parties (see Paragraph 28.10)

- Protection of lender (see Paragraph 28.11)
- Other security (see Paragraph 28.12)
- Boilerplate* (see Paragraph 28.13)

28.3   Mortgage

The film mortgage will normally provide that the Producer assigns to the Lender, by way of security, the entire copyright in the film. Where the film does not exist, the copyright which will be created in the future will be assigned by present assignment of future copyright. The mortgage will also assign to the Lender absolutely the entire interest of the Producer in and to all film and sound material now and in the future created and all plant and machinery relating to the film owned by the Producer.

The Lender may in addition require the Producer to execute a floating charge over the entire business and other rights of the Producer. Whether this is required or not will depend on the circumstances, but, in the absence of any charge provision in the film mortgage, it is not necessary for the Lender to include the extensive enforcement provisions referred to in Paragraph 28.1.

28.4   Book Debts and Other Money

The Lender will normally require the Producer to undertake that it will not charge or assign in favour of any other person any money which it may receive in respect of book debts or other property. This type of provision is known as a negative pledge.

28.5   Future Distribution

Because the Lender has acquired rights from the Producer in the film by way of security, the mortgage needs to create some form of mechanism to allow the Producer to exploit these rights by entering into future distribution agreements.

The film mortgage may, therefore, provide a mechanism where rights are granted back to the Producer to enable the Producer to enter into distribution agreements with future distributors, requiring the income from these agreements to be paid to the Lender.

From the Lender's point of view, it is important that the Producer should enter into the distribution agreements, rather than the Lender, because the Producer will be making certain warranties about facts relating to the production of the film which only the Producer is aware of. Breach of any warranty would, of course, expose the person granting the distribution rights to legal proceedings. It is obviously unacceptable for the Lender to assume risk of proceedings in relation to defaults or breaches of the Producer, even though the Lender will be assuming indirect risk for breach of warranty on the part of the Producer, since a serious breach might entitle a distributor to terminate a distribution agreement, withhold payment of money due, and sue for damages.

28.6 Enforcement

If the mortgage also contains a charge (see Paragraph 28.1) it will be necessary for the Lender to include provisions relating to enforcement.

Normally, a charge may be enforced once an event of default has occurred. This event will usually permit the Lender to appoint a receiver who will have the power to take possession of and sell the property charge, subject to certain statutory provisions contained in the Law of Property Act.

28.7 Warranties

A film mortgage will normally contain a number of warranties, which may include the following matters.

Ownership

The Producer has the right to enter into the mortgage and is the sole, absolute and unincumbered owner of the film and the rights.

Maintenance

The Producer will maintain the film in good and serviceable condition.

No Modification

The Producer will not make any modification or permit any modification to be made to the film or the rights which might have an adverse effect on the Lender's security interests.

Laboratory Pledgeholder's Agreement

The Producer will not permit the laboratory pledgeholder's agreement to be varied without the consent of the Lender.

Taxes

The Producer will promptly play all taxes, licence duties, registration charges, insurance premia and other matters relating to the film.

Certification

The Producer will obtain all necessary certificates, licences, permits and authorisations required for the manufacture and use of the film and the protection of the rights.

Notification

The Producer will notify the Lender immediately of any material loss, theft, damage or destruction.

Information

The Producer will give the Lender information relating to the condition, location and use of the film and other information the Lender may require.

Protection

The Producer will do all in its power to protect and preserve the rights and shall, as soon as possible, ensure that one or more protection negatives of the film are struck.

No Counterclaim

The Producer will not allow any counterclaim, set-off or other equity in respect of any other sum to arise in relation to the film or the rights.

Distribution

The Producer will not enter into any agreement relating to the distribution or exploitation of the film or the rights without the prior written consent of the Lender.

No Modification

The Producer will not modify or vary or waive any rights under any distribution agreement without the consent of the Lender.

Performance

The Producer will observe and perform at all times all obligations and warranties on its part, pursuant to all agreements relating to the film.

Insurance

The Producer will maintain any and all insurance policies required to be maintained, pursuant to the loan agreement or any other agreement relating to the film.

28.8   Grant of Time

It is a standard provision in most security interest documents to provide that, if the Lender gives additional time to the Producer to comply with any obligation, the giving of such additional time will not effect or prejudice any of the Lender's rights.

28.9   Dispositions

The Producer will normally consent to the Lender having the right to assign or transfer its rights under the film mortgage agreement.

28.10   Protection of Third Parities

The film mortgage will normally provide that, if the Lender is required to sell any of the rights assigned or charged by way of security, any purchaser of the rights from the Lender will not be required to enquire whether the Lender's right to sell the assets has arisen. The receipt by the Lender of any purchase price shall be an absolute and conclusive discharge to the purchaser who will not be required to see how the sums paid are applied (ie whether they are paid to the Lender or any receiver or the Producer).

28.11   Protection of the Lender

If the agreement also provides for a charge over property, it is normal to provide an acknowledgement, on the part of the Producer, that neither the Lender nor any receiver will be liable in respect of any loss or damages which arises out of the exercise or attempted or thwarted exercise of their powers.

28.12   Other Security

The film mortgage will normally provide that the security created by it will be in addition to any other security interest owned by the Lender and will remain separate from it.

28.13   Boilerplate

The boilerplate section of a typical film mortgage will contain the following provisions:

- Notices (see Paragraph 52.8)
- Governing law (see Paragraph 52.5).

29 Security Assignment

29.1 Description of a Security Assignment

The purpose of a security assignment is to transfer to a lender the producer's right to receive advances*, minimum guarantees and other sums payable pursuant to distribution agreements*.

The parties to this transaction are:

*   the producer entitled to receive payment of sums, pursuant to distribution agreements (the "Producer*"); and
*   the lender to whom the producer is assigning the right to receive the payments (the "Lender")

29.2 Transaction Analysis

A typical security assignment might be expected to contain the following clauses:
*   Assignment (see Paragraph 29.3)
*   Producer's warranties* (see Paragraph 29.4)
*   Delivery of documents (see Paragraph 29.5)
*   Attorney (see Paragraph 29.6)
*   Boilerplate* (see Paragraph 29.7).

29.3 Assignment

The Producer will assign to the Lender the right to receive all sums, pursuant both to all existing distribution agreements and to all future distribution agreements.

Legally, the right to receive sums under future distribution agreements is known as a future chose (or thing) in action and, in order for the assignment of the future thing in action to be valid, consideration (see Paragraph 54.7) is required, even where the document is under seal. For this reason, it is important that the document should acknowledge that the Producer has received payment of a nominal sum of £1 from the Lender.

29.4 Warranties

The security assignment may normally be expected to contain the following warranties.

Validity of Distribution Agreements

The distribution agreements are valid, binding and have not been amended or altered.

Non-assignment

The Producer has not assigned, charged, pledged or otherwise incumbered its right to receive payment of sums under the distribution agreements.

No Equities

There are no equities or claims in existence between the Producer and the other parties to the distribution agreement which could diminish the sums payable under them.

Authorisation

The Producer has taken all corporate action necessary to authorise the execution and performance of the agreement.

Payment

The Producer will ensure that all sums assigned to the Lender will be paid to the Lender (or as it directs) from time to time.

No Variation

The Producer will not agree to any variation to the distribution agreements or release any of the distributors or other parties from any of their obligations.

Performance

The Producer will perform in a timely manner its obligations under the distribution agreements.

Notices

The Producer shall send the Lender copies of all notices and accounts received by it under the distribution agreements.

29.5 Delivery of documents

In order for the Lender to create a legal obligation on the part of the distributors to pay to the Lender sums which the distributors were previously obliged to pay to the Producer, the Lender needs to deliver notice of the security assignment to the distributors.

The security assignment may, therefore, contain a provision under which the Producer undertakes to deliver notice of assignment to all distributors. In practice, the Lender itself may prefer to send the requisite notices for certainty.

29.6 Attorney

As further security for the payment by the distributors to the Lender of the secured sums, the Producer will agree to appoint the Lender as its attorney by way of security for the performance of its obligations (see Paragraph 53.13).

29.7 Boilerplate

The boilerplate section of a typical film mortgage will contain the following provisions:

- Notices (see Paragraph 52.8)
- Assignability (see Paragraph 52.1)
- Governing law (see Paragraph 52.5).

30 Co-Production Agreement

30.1 Description of a Co-Production Agreement

The function of a co-production agreement* is to specify the terms and conditions on which one or more co-producers will agree to co-produce and deliver a film or television programme. There are a number of different types of co-production agreement which are encountered in the film and television industries.

It is difficult to generalise about co-production agreements because their form and substance varies so widely, depending on the number of parties, their location, their function and, of course, the commercial terms. Co-production agreements tend to be tailored to specific circumstances. The comments in this Chapter are, therefore, an indication of some general terms which may be found in co-production agreements.

The first problem in dealing with co-production agreements is that of nomenclature. Each of the parties is technically a "co-producer" and there may be ten or more co-producers. For simplicity we shall assume that there are two co-producers, one in the United Kingdom (the "Company") and the other, a foreign entity (the "Co-Producer").

30.2 Types of Co-Production Agreements

A true co-production agreement involves total co-operation between two (or more) entities, each of which is involved in the development, principal photography and post-production of a film or programme. Principal photography of the film or programme may take place in both countries. Normally post-production will be carried out in one country. A full co-production arrangement may be a treaty co-production or a non-treaty co-production.

Treaty Co-Production

A treaty co-production is an arrangement between a company in the United Kingdom and a company or corporation which is resident in one of the seven countries with which the United Kingdom has co-production treaties, namely, Australia, Canada, France, Germany, Italy, Norway and Spain.

A treaty co-production is eligible for national benefits given to cinema films in each of the participating countries and, in order to qualify for treatment as a treaty co-production, the minority partner must contribute at least 30% of the film's finance. There are also a number of provisions relating to ownership of the film negative and access to it which need to be incorporated in the agreement.

Most of the United Kingdom co-production treaties permit only bilateral arrangements (ie between companies from two countries), but, in practice, the bilateral treaty structure may accommodate multi-party co-productions. This may be achieved by means of a licence from the majority partner of certain rights to a distributor in a third country.

Rights Licence

A further type of co-production is where a producer or distributor will wish to obtain a licence of distribution rights for certain territories in return for payment of an agreed advance*. In these types of arrangements, the Co-Producer's role is closer to that of an ordinary licensee under a pre-sale agreement for a limited territory (see Chapter 31). The Co-Producer, in these cases, will have no control of the physical aspects of the production. It will commit to paying an agreed fee on delivery of delivery material. Normally, at least a percentage of the Co-Producer's fee is payable on signature of the agreement.

Facility Co-Production

The final type of co-production arrangement is a facility arrangement. This may be appropriate where a studio has facilities which are suitable for use in production of the film and which may be made available by the studio at a cost lower than might be obtained by the Company on the open market. In return for making the facilities available, the studio will normally expect to be granted distribution rights in the film in its own country and adjoining territories. Whether, in addition, the Co-Producer will be entitled to participate in the profits of the film is a matter for negotiation.

30.3 Transaction Analysis

Although the terms of co-production agreements vary widely and are generally determined by the circumstances, a full co-production agreement might contain some of the following clauses:

- Production (see Paragraph 30.4)
- Central elements (see Paragraph 30.5)
- Provision of budget (see Paragraph 30.6)
- Rights (see Paragraph 30.7)

- Company's warranties* (see Paragraph 30.8)
- Co-Producer's warranties (see Paragraph 30.9)
- Production contracts* (see Paragraph 30.10)
- Residuals (see Paragraph 30.11)
- Insurance (see Paragraph 30.12)
- Records (see Paragraph 30.13)
- Distribution (see Paragraph 30.14)
- Accounting (see Paragraph 30.15)
- Marketing (see Paragraph 30.16)
- Credit (see Paragraph 30.17)
- Censorship (see Paragraph 30.18)
- Rushes and Editing (see Paragraph 30.19)
- Termination (see Paragraph 30.20)
- Boilerplate* (see Paragraph 30.21).

30.4 Production

A full co-production agreement will specify what elements of the film are to be made by the Company and what elements are to be made by the Co-Producer. It will also identify any facilities to be provided and locations and studios to be used, as well as identifying the respective contributions of the Company and the Co-Producer to the budget.

Although principal photography of a film might take place in two or more countries, it is usual for one laboratory to be appointed and for all post-production work to take place in one country.

30.5 Essential Elements

The Company and Co-Producer will normally specify the essential elements of the film which are similar to those specified in a production financing and distribution agreement (see Chapter 21).

The agreement will normally specify the screenplay and shooting script for the film and provide that the film will not depart from these. It will also specify what studios and locations are to be used, specify a production schedule and state required technical specifications.

Normally, the language of the film will follow the language of the shooting script, but in cases where double dialogue recording is required, two language versions, scenes may be shot "back-to-back". In other words after each scene is set up, it is shot first in the English language version and then in the foreign language version. The agreement will normally provide that each actor's words will be lip-synched to the required English (or other language) dialogue. This is because productions where actors speak words in their own languages, as in spaghetti westerns, are generally not acceptable to modern audiences.

The agreement will also normally provide that there will be no visual identifiable references to any merchandise or goods. Neither party will enter into product placement agreements (see Chapter 44) without the consent of the other. The agreement will also specify that each party will comply with all relevant applicable laws, rules and regulations relating to the production.

30.6   Provision of Budget

The agreement will normally provide precise details of what payments are to be made by the Company and the Co-Producer. These will be linked with a cash-flow schedule for production of the film.

The question of what will happen if the cost of production exceeds the budget needs to be addressed. If a completion guarantee has been issued in relation to the film (see Chapter 25) the completion guarantor may assume liability for excess costs unless these have arisen in relation to matters expressly excluded in the completion guarantee, such as changes in the production schedule, changes in the specification or even currency fluctuations.

Fluctuations and exchange rates are a real difficulty in co-productions and these can have a particular importance where the film is a treaty co-production and the Co-Producer's contribution is only marginally more than the 30% minimum contribution required by most treaties. An adverse currency movement might have the effect of, not only of creating a cash-flow pressure in the budget, but also making the film ineligible for national treatment in the Co-Producer's country therefore removing national subsidies.

30.7   Rights and Money

A co-production agreement will normally provide that each Co-Producer will own rights in the film for their territory. How the rights in the rest of the world are to be dealt with is a matter for negotiation and depends on a number of circumstances.

If the Company is the major financier, the Company may wish to control distribution rights for the world outside the Company's own territory and the Co-Producer's territory. If this is the case, then, because normally copyright is vested in the parties jointly, both parties will need to agree to license to the Company the right to exploit the film for the territory outside their own countries—frequently referred to as the "rest of the world territory".

The question of how income arising in each party's territory is treated also needs to be considered. Does this income belong to each party outright, or is each party to bring into account the receipts they have received from their territory for the purpose of recouping the total investment.

A further alternative is to provide that revenue from each party's territory belongs to that party outright, but if the other party has not recouped their investment from the rest of the world territory within a stated time then the revenue from the first party's territory is "pooled" until the other party has recouped.

There are many additional variations on this basic theme.

30.8   Company's Warranties

The agreement will normally contain a number of warranties on the part of the Company, including the following.

Capacity

The Company is free to enter into and perform the agreement and has not made any conflicting arrangements.

Confidentiality

The Company will not reveal or make public any financial or other confidential information in connection with the film.

Consultation

The Company will consult with the Co-Producer at all stages of production and all sums payable under these shall be as specified in the budget.

Obscenity

The material produced by the Company for the film shall not be obscene or libellous or defamatory or infringe any right of copyright, privacy, publicity, moral right, performer's right or any other right.

Copyright Status

The Company shall be a qualifying person for copyright purposes and shall together with the principal director of the film, be the 'author' of the film and shall have acquired the entire copyright in the film from the principal director.

Relevant Union Agreements

All material produced by the Company shall be produced in accordance with all relevant union agreements.

Quality

All material produced by the Company shall be of first-class technical and artistic quality.

Third Party Interests

All material produced by the Company shall be free and clear of all third party interests, recording, synchronisation and mechanical and other fees.

Credits

All material produced by the Company shall comply with all contractual, credit and other obligations.

Budget

The budget, so far as the Company is aware, is a full, comprehensive and bona fide estimate of the cost of production of the film.

Indemnity

See Paragraph 53.16.

30.9 Co-Producer's Warranties

The agreement will normally contain a number of warranties on the part of the Co-Producer, similar to those on the part of the Company (see Paragraph 30.8).

30.10 Production Contracts

The agreement may provide that production contracts ought to be in the name of one company which will be responsible for obtaining all necessary assignments of copyright, performers' consents, waivers and moral rights and other contractual confirmations. If the Company is to be responsible for organising all contractual documentation, it may require that the Co-Producer will not vary, rescind or terminate any of the production contracts without the prior consent of the Company.

Equally, there will be circumstances where each party is required to contract certain elements in its own territory and the agreement may, therefore, provide that all contracts are to be approved jointly by both parties. In such cases, in order to eliminate any delay, the agreement may require comments or amendments to be communicated within a specified number of working days.

It is also normal to require that whatever remuneration is payable, pursuant to the production contracts, should be limited to the amount specified in the budget. Obviously, terms and provisions of union agreements will vary from country to country and in many cases, it is not possible to contract out of (or avoid

285

compliance with) union agreements, which may have a bearing on residual payments (see Paragraph 30.11).

It is also normal to provide that no Co-Producer will act as agent of any other Co-Producer or pledge their credit or create any other liability on their part, or, without the consent of the others, acquire any underlying rights material. This type of provision ensures that no one party makes a secret profit at the expense of the others.

30.11 Residuals

The terms and provisions of relevant union agreements may provide that certain residual repeat, re-run or re-use fees or payments are required to be made in relation to the exploitation of the film in certain media.

It is normal practice for film production companies to buy-out future exploitation of films in all media and prepay to the maximum extent possible all residual liabilities. There may be some circumstances where buy-out transactions and pre-payments are not possible. This is a very important area of all film production arrangements, since, if residuals and other liabilities are not prepaid, the film may not be exploited in certain media or territories. Where overseas distributors or sub-distributors are involved, they will require the Co-Producers to confirm that all residual liabilities have been pre-paid. It is very rare to find a distributor which will agree to bear residual liabilities out of their own resources, and there is a very real risk, from the Co-Producer's point of view, that the residual liabilities arising on a sale to a particular territory or a medium might exceed the amounts received from that territory or medium. Care is needed here.

A point which is linked to liability for residuals is the right to equitable remuneration of rental or lending of films (see Paragraph 53.6). Normally, the position of the Company and Co-Producer is that all equitable remuneration entitlements will be prepaid, but persons who have such entitlement may seek to assert their right to collect it through a collection society.

30.12 Insurance

The co-production agreement will normally contain detailed provisions relating to production insurances and errors and omissions insurance. These provisions are very similar to those which may be found in production financing and distribution agreements (see Paragraph 21.7).

30.13 Records

The production agreement will normally contain provisions relating to the keeping of books of account and records and relating to the production and the delivery of an itemised statement of the cost of production of the film. These provisions are very similar to those which may be found in production financing and distribution agreements (see Paragraph 22.7).

30.14 Distribution

The co-production agreement will normally specify exactly how the film is to be distributed. Normally, each party will retain some or all rights in their own territory (see Paragraph 30.7) and distribution throughout the remaining territory will be effected either by one or more third parties through existing pre-sale arrangements or by the party which is providing the most co-production finance.

The agreement will normally specify what distribution fees and distribution expenses are to be deducted (see Paragraphs 24.12 and 24.13) and will specify how the net receipts are to be applied—normally towards the recoupment of the investment made by each party on a pro rata basis. In some transactions, the income arising from each party's territory may also be brought into account.

30.15 Accounting

The co-production agreement will normally contain accounting provisions which are analogous to those to be found in a production financing and distribution agreement (see Paragraph 22.9).

30.16 Marketing

The question of how the film is to be marketed throughout the world other than in the Parties' territories will normally follow on from the distribution arrangements. If the Company is itself effecting world-wide distribution arrangements the agreement may provide that the company will consult with the Co-Producer(s) and give good faith consideration to any views expressed, but all decisions in relation to exploitation shall be determined by the Company in its entire discretion.

30.17 Credit

The co-production agreement will normally contain credit provisions which are analogous to those to be found in a production financing and distribution agreement (see Paragraph 21.8).

30.18 Censorship

The co-production agreement will normally contain censorship provisions which are analogous to those to be found in a production financing and distribution agreement (see Paragraph 21.9).

30.19   Rushes and Editing

Editing provisions are also normally linked to the distribution issue. In co-production agreements, it is normal to permit each co-production party to have some control over the version to be shown in their territory (although the distributor of the film may have views on this issue).

So far as the world version is concerned, it is normal to provide that the dominant co-production party (or its distributor) will have the final say over the version of the film selected for international exploitation.

If versions widely differ, the issue of which version is entered in competition in Cannes and other festivals may also need to be dealt with in the agreement.

30.20   Termination

The co-production agreement may contain a termination clause, but, in circumstances where there is a completion guarantor, a termination provision may not always be necessary. A force majeure clause is, however, advisable for the reasons referred to in Paragraph 53.8.

If the agreement does contain a termination provision, it will normally be mutual and entitle either (or any) party to terminate in the event of the other commiting a material breach of an obligation which is irremediable or which is not remedied within a certain amount of days or becoming insolvent.

30.21   Boilerplate

The boilerplate section of a typical co-production agreement may contain the following provisions:

*   Assignment (see Paragraph 52.1)
*   Force majeure (see Paragraph 52.4)
*   Notices (see Paragraph 52.8)
*   Severability (see Paragraph 52.10)
*   Entire agreement (see Paragraph 52.3)
*   Waiver (see Paragraph 52.11)
*   No partnership (see Paragraph 52.7)
*   Governing law (see Paragraph 52.5)
*   Certificate of value* (see Paragraph 52.2).

D: Acquisition, Distribution and Licensing of Film and Television Projects

31 Film and Television Distribution Generally

31.1 Purpose of this Chapter

The purpose of this Chapter is to provide a brief description of the principal commercial and legal factors affecting film distribution and exhibition. It may be helpful if this Chapter is read in conjunction with Chapter 24.

31.2 Distribution Generally

General

There are approximately 40 major distribution territories in the world, accounting between them for around 20 languages. The most important distribution territory is the United States of America. The high cost of dubbing films into foreign languages prohibits the production of foreign language versions for every territory. The main dubbing languages are French, German, Italian and Spanish.

The earnings potential of a film is maximised if distribution arrangements are made on a territory-by-territory and medium-by-medium basis. However, because theatrical distribution is the only medium of exploitation where a large negative cash-flow can be created by virtue of the large initial expenditure incurred on prints and advertising, a distributor will normally acquire distribution rights for television or home video in order to be able to offset the potential loss from theatrical distribution.

31.3 Worldwide Distribution Arrangements

A worldwide distribution agreement* is unlikely to be favourable to a producer, although it is a quick source of money, as the producer will initially obtain a large advance or minimum guarantee. The distributor may, however, elect for a 'safe' distribution pattern which will maximise the distributor's chance of recouping the distribution advance*, at the expense of allowing some territories to remain unprofitable, if their bad performance is offset by good performance of the film in other territories. Because a distributor is normally able to cross-collateralise revenue from territories and media on a worldwide basis (off-setting losses in some territories and media against gains in others), it is not forced to make the film perform well in every territory. Furthermore, distribution on a worldwide basis may be carried out by local subsidiaries of the main distributor, who may hesitate about challenging distribution policies or advertising campaigns originated by their overseas holding companies, whereas independent distributors would have no such qualms.

If the appointment by a producer of a single distributor world-wide in all media has its disadvantages, the disposal by a producer of worldwide videogram rights in a film to one source is likely to cause extreme difficulties to a producer. Not only will it make it almost impossible for a producer to negotiate theatrical release in many territories (since videogram rights will be denied to a theatrical distributor as a means of possible recoupment of the losses incurred in theatrical distribution), but the world-wide video distributor may simply refuse to exploit rights in minor territories where local language versions may be needed if the producer's theatrical distributor is not prepared to make these.

31.4 Order of Exploitation

The conventional order of exploitation of cinema films (as opposed to television films) is, initially, theatrical distribution followed by either pay television/satellite or videogram (depending on various commercial factors) and then by broadcast television exploitation. The distributor's aim will be to extend the duration of each form of distribution for as long as profitable. A successful theatrical release of a film considerably enhances its videogram exploitation value whereas television exploitation of a film will severely diminish it.

Because the initial theatrical release of film product is capable of generating large losses, it is normal for a company wishing to effect theatrical release of a film to have also acquired the videogram rights and/or television rights, since the value of these rights is enhanced by theatrical exhibition.

31.5 Residuals

It is important for the producer to take into account the amount of any residual re-run or foreign use payments which may be required, pursuant to union agreements or contractual commitments, in respect of the exploitation of audio-visual programming in particular territories or in particular media. It will obviously not be in the producer's interests to contract for a sale, where the net revenue is likely to be less than the amount of fees payable to artists, in order to acquire the exploitation rights granted by the agreement.

31.6 Laboratory Arrangements

The arrangements relating to laboratories are of crucial importance in the production and distribution of films. Two different types of laboratory letters are in common use. The first type is a pledgeholder's letter which is used to secure the position of a financier (see Paragraph 51.4). The second type is a laboratory access letter* which is frequently used to effect delivery of materials (see Paragraph 51.3). The producer of a film will not want to part with possession of a negative but may need to make the negative available to several distributors. This is effected by delivering the physical materials to a laboratory and instructing the laboratory to permit access by the distributor to those materials.

31.7 Theatrical and Non-theatrical Exhibition

General

Theatrical distribution involves the renting out and supply of prints of films for theatrical exhibition in cinemas. Non-theatrical distribution consists of the selling of rights to exhibit films in prisons, hospitals, schools, educational establishments and other institutions, as well as aeroplanes, ships, trains, military bases and oil and marine installations. There is an element of overlap between the non-theatrical and home video markets.

As the amount of income derived from the exploitation of films by means of home video and pay cable and satellite television continues to increase, the emphasis on theatrical exhibition of films is changing and such exhibition is, in some cases, viewed more as a means of generating publicity to ensure a high value on the sale of pay cable and satellite rights and a high return on videogram distribution rather than as a means of generating revenue in its own right.

31.8 Non-theatrical Distribution

The market for non-theatrical distribution is extremely specialised and, although the sums generated are significant, they are not substantial. For this reason, non-theatrical distribution rights in films are normally acquired as an adjunct to theatrical distribution rights or television or home video rights, rather than as a primary medium. The traditional non-theatrical distribution market is being fragmented by the development of technology. In addition to the competing overlap between non-theatrical and video markets, there is also an overlap with the cable and satellite distribution markets, since persons acquiring cable and satellite rights in the United Kingdom wish to have the rights to license hotels and motels which have traditionally fallen within the non-theatrical market.

31.9 Videogram Distribution

United Kingdom Videogram Market

The majority of transactions taking place in the UK videogram industry are between software renter and software supplier. The videogram rental income generated by these transactions generally belongs to the rental outlet and is not normally passed back to the distributor of the videogram. If videogram rental income were received by the distributor of a film, the distributor would normally be required to pay a percentage of the income received to the producer of the film being distributed.

The videogram rental outlets in the United Kingdom acquire their product from video wholesalers who are in turn supplied by the distributors who contract with videogram duplication facilities in order to meet anticipated orders. The videogram rental outlets expect to receive videogram copies of films within a six to nine month period following their initial theatrical release in the United Kingdom and before their exploitation by means of free television. Since television transmission affords the film-renting public the opportunity of making their own video copy off-air (which is permitted under the copyright legislation for the purposes of time-shifting), this destroys videogram rental potential of a particular title. The price at which the videograms are sold to rental outlets reflects the fact that the distributor will not generally receive a percentage of the rental income, which will be retained by the rental outlet. It also reflects the fact that the product is, in many cases, new and has often has only recently ended its theatrical exhibition run.

In addition to the supply of videograms to rental outfits via wholesalers, a separate market exists for the videogram distributor in the supply of videograms for resale direct to high street multiple stores. Instead of making product available for rental, the videogram distributor makes product available for sale through the high street multiples and this type of arrangement is frequently referred to as 'sell-through' videogram distribution, in order to distinguish it from distribution through rental outlets. Videogram product is made available to such rental outlets at higher prices than the sell-through market and at an earlier date, in order to enable the rental outlets to derive income by making the product available for rental before it is available for purchase and to enable the distributor to maximise income in the early stages by releasing the product at higher prices in comparatively small numbers.

The sell-through videogram market is especially important in the areas of childrens' programmes, 'how to' type videos and movie classics, the sales of which do not appear to be greatly affected by previous television exploitation.

31.10 Hold-backs and Windows

The order of exploitation of a film in the various media is of crucial importance, since both producer and distributor wish to maximise revenue earning potential in each separate medium before making the film available for use by other media.

The conventional release order of a film requires, first, for the film to receive theatrical release. After the initial period of theatrical release, a distributor will wish to procure videogram distribution in order to take advantage of the publicity generated by theatrical exhibition. After the videogram release, the film may be made available for pay cable exploitation or satellite transmission use. After this, the film may be made available by means of free television, but exploitation of a film by means of television is likely to have a materially adverse effect on videogram sales to rental outlets. It should be noted, however, that the sales of some types of videograms at sell through levels do not appear to be affected by television exploitation since many of the films and programmes sold in the sell-through medium have been transmitted by means of television.

The order of exploitation of audio-visual product is frequently varied. For example, television mini-series may never achieve theatrical release, pay cable and satellite channels may wish to acquire product before videogram release, or television companies may wish to effect limited theatrical release of made-for-television product. Generally speaking, however, the order is as set out above and the interval between first theatrical release and first videogram release may be expected to be between six and nine months. The videogram distributor will normally require a television hold-back during which it is guaranteed that the film will not be exploited by means of television and the period generally sought in respect of free television exploitation is 24 months from theatrical release although periods as short as six months are agreed to. The hold-back period for pay cable and satellite exploitation is more variable and will depend, in certain circumstances, on whether the owners of those rights have been involved in pre-sale arrangements.

When a videogram distributor is acquiring videogram rights alone without television rights, it is extremely important for the videogram distributor to negotiate a hold-back. Where the distributor is acquiring all rights, hold-back terms will not generally need to be agreed since the order of exploitation will be controlled by the distributor.

Where television rights have been acquired by a distributor in the United Kingdom, a television availability date may be agreed. This will be the earliest date at which the exploitation of free television or pay cable or satellite television rights in a film may be permitted. The Films on Television Committee of the British Screen Advisory Council recommends that there should be no television hold-back on films whose cost of production is less than £4 million, and in the case of films whose cost of production is in excess of £4 million, the hold-back* period should be two years from first theatrical release. There are additional provisions in the relevant union agreements between the PACT and Equity and the Musicians' Union relating to limited theatrical releases providing, in some cases, for an 18 month television hold-back on films receiving theatrical release in the United Kingdom.

31.11   Remuneration

The remuneration payable under a videogram licensing agreement is a combination of an advance or minimum guarantee and a royalty*. The royalty is generally based on the distributor's wholesale price exclusive of Value Added Tax and net of all customary discounts. Where rights in more than one film are acquired by a distributor, any advance or minimum guarantee will need to be apportioned between the relevant films (to enable the licensor granting the rights to the distributor to report back to the producers of the various films the amounts of income actually received in respect of each film).

Where a distributor acquires videogram rights, together with theatrical, non-theatrical and other rights, it is normal for the distributor to negotiate a provision permitting the distributor to off-set the amount of any shortfall incurred in theatrical distribution from profits derived from videogram distribution. This provision is referred to as a cross-collateralisation* provision, since it enables the distributor to cross-collateralise revenue received from one area or territory of exploitation and apply it towards deficits incurred in another area or territory of exploitation. In the case of acquisitions of 'packages' of films, a distributor will frequently wish to cross-collateralise, not only the various media in respect of each film, but also, the receipts in respect of one film against losses or unrecouped advance minimum guarantees in respect of other films. This provision may be acceptable to a licensor where the films have all been produced by one company, but is unlikely to be acceptable where the films have been produced by different producers.

The amount of the royalty payable by videogram distributors in the United Kingdom in respect of audio-visual product is a matter of commercial negotiation. It should be noted, however, that it is now usual to apply a different and lower rate in respect of sell-through videogram exploitation than it is in respect of videogram exploitation through rental outlets. This is because the sell-through unit price is considerably lower than the full price and the distributor's profit margin is considerably reduced. The distributor will hope that the increased volume of sales at the sell-through level by comparison with rental outlets will still generate substantial revenue, but without any reduction in the distributor's overheads (in the form of a reduction in the figure which the distributor has to pay to the licensor by means of royalty). The distributor's return would be likely to be marginal and might not provide sufficient incentive to the distributor to effect sell-through release, thereby causing the licensor or producer a loss of potential profit.

A further royalty variation is available in the method of treatment of rental income, which is again a matter of commercial negotiation and depends on industry practice.

31.12 Synchronisation Licence

In addition to the royalties payable to the licensor, certain additional sums may be payable to copyright owners and licensors controlling rights in music incorporated in the film. It is normal to expect a producer of a film to acquire a synchronisation licence* which will entitle the producer to incorporate music and/or lyrics in synchronisation with or in timed relation to a film. Frequently, however, music publishers and other rights owners will be prepared to allow the initial incorporation of music and grant a synchronisation licence on terms which permit the theatrical exhibition and broadcast (which still generate income to the publishers in the form of performance royalties) but require the producers or the distributors to pay further sums to the copyright owners in order to authorise the manufacture of videogram copies.

In the United Kingdom, it is frequent for licensors in films to require the distributors to pay any royalties which may be due to copyright owners in respect of the manufacture and distribution of videograms. Whether a distributor is prepared to pay such royalties is a matter for commercial negotiation and the amount of such synchronisation royalties is likely to be taken into account in determining the amount of royalty payable to the licensor by the distributor. If a distributor assumes an obligation to pay the royalty, it will normally wish to specify a maximum rate and frequently the rate card rates of the Mechanical Copyright Protection Society Limited will be accepted by the parties. The terms of the licence offered by the Mechanical Copyright Protection Society Limited should, of course, be inspected carefully before acceptance.

32 Distribution Agreements or Pre-Sale or Negative Pick-up Agreements

32.1 Description of a Distribution Agreement

The distribution agreement* is one of the key documents in the film and television industry. A distributor will not normally be involved directly in the production or financing of films, although, in many cases, it will have committed to distribute a film before production of the film commences. A film distributor will normally acquire the right to distribute a film in a number of media including theatrical distribution, videogram distribution, free television, pay television and non-theatrical media (see Chapter 31).

A film distribution agreement licenses rights in a film to a distributor who will then distribute the film by various means, including by means of having third parties manufacture and distribute physical copies of the film in the videogram format. A film distribution agreement is to be distinguished and differentiated from an agreement for the distribution of physical copies of the film sold as videograms. (For a comparative analysis see Chapter 5 which deals with the provisions of a pressing and distribution agreement for records. This type of agreement is very similar to the provisions found in agreement for the physical distribution of videograms.)

The parties to a distribution agreement are:

- the producer* or rights owner of the film (referred to in this Chapter as the "Producer"); and
- the company effecting the physical distribution of the film (referred to in this Chapter as the "Distributor").

32.2 Transaction Analysis

A typical film distribution agreement might be expected to contain the following clauses:

- Delivery (see Paragraph 32.3)
- Rights (see Paragraph 32.4)

- Remuneration (see Paragraph 32.5)
- Insurance (see Paragraph 32.6)
- Warranties* (see Paragraph 32.7)
- Accounting (see Paragraph 32.8)
- Sales policies (see Paragraph 32.9)
- Credit (see Paragraph 32.10)
- Censorship (see Paragraph 32.11)
- Boilerplate* (see Paragraph 32.12).

32.3   Delivery

The distribution agreement will invariably contain an obligation on the part of the Producer to deliver to the Distributor certain delivery materials in relation to the film on a prespecified delivery date.

Generally, the bulk of the advance* or minimum guarantee payable by the Distributor will be payable on delivery or within a specified time after delivery. It is normally a point of concern for the Producer to ensure that, if there is any defect discovered in the material on or soon after delivery, the Distributor will not reject the material out of hand, but will give the Producer notice of the defect and an opportunity to provide replacement materials within a specified number of days.

32.4   Rights

The distribution agreement will normally specify the precise extent of rights to be acquired by the Distributor, including the media, the territory and the term of the rights granted to the Distributor.

If the Distributor is acquiring all media in a territory, the Producer may wish to specify hold-backs* and windows* (see Chapter 31) in respect of certain media, in order to guarantee the orderly exploitation of the film.

The Distributor will normally obtain the grant by way of assignment or exclusive licence of the exclusive distribution rights, together with confirmation from the Producer in relation to performers' rights, moral rights and various other rights to the product of persons rendering services in connection with the film (see Chapter 21).

32.5   Remuneration

The remuneration payable pursuant to a distribution agreement will depend on the perceived market value of the film. This is determined, not only by the script, but also by the identity of the director, producer and principal cast. Normally, a producer will expect a distributor to pay an advance (sometimes referred to as a minimum guarantee) which is a fixed sum payable on instalments, as to a certain percentage on the signature of the distribution agreement, another percentage on delivery and, occasionally, a further sum a specified period after delivery.

From the Producer's point of view, if the final instalment of the minimum guarantee or advance is payable on or within a certain period of time from the first theatrical release and if the film is never released theatrically, the Distributor will not be liable to pay the Producer anything. For this reason, payments due on release of a film are often expressed to be due, in any event, no later than a pre-specified number of months from delivery.

Normally, a distribution agreement will provide that the Distributor may recover the amount of the advance or minimum guarantee from net receipts. Net receipts (see Paragraph 24) will normally defined as 100% of gross receipts received by the Distributor from the exploitation of the film after the deduction of distribution commission and distribution expenses.

32.6 Insurance

The distribution agreement will normally contain a number of insurance provisions which are analogous to those contained in a production financing and distribution agreement (see Paragraph 21.7).

32.7 Warranties

The distribution agreement will normally contain a number of warranty provisions which are analogous to those contained in a production financing and distribution agreement (see Paragraph 23.3).

32.8 Accounting

The distribution agreement will normally contain a number of accounting provisions which are analogous to those contained in a production financing and distribution agreement (see Paragraph 22.9).

32.9 Sales Policies

The distribution agreement will normally contain a number of distribution and sales policy provisions which are analogous to those contained in a production financing and distribution agreement (see Paragraph 22.10).

32.10 Credit

The distribution agreement will normally contain a number of credit provisions which are analogous to those contained in a production financing and distribution agreement (see Paragraph 21.8).

32.11 Censorship

The distribution agreement will normally contain a number of censorship provisions which are analogous to those contained in a production financing and distribution agreement (see Paragraph 21.9).

32.12 Boilerplate

The boilerplate section of a typical distribution agreement may contain the following provisions:

* No obligation (see Paragraph 52.6)
* Notices (see Paragraph 52.8)
* Severability (see Paragraph 52.10)
* Entire agreement (see Paragraph 52.3)
* Waiver (see Paragraph 52.11)
* No partnership (see Paragraph 52.7)
* Governing law (see Paragraph 52.5)
* Certificate of value (see Paragraph 52.2).

33 Sales Agency Agreement

33.1 Description of a Sales Agency Agreement

Where films are financed by a US major studio, that studio will normally control distribution of the film throughout the world. In some instances, US studios share domestic (US) and foreign (non-US) rights between them, such as in the case of James Cameron's "Titanic". Examples of these types of co-operation are, however, comparatively rare.

For films that have not been produced by US studios, the choice of potential video distributors, theatrical distributors and broadcasters on a territory-by-territory basis is very great. Normally, an independent producer* will lack the time and industry contacts required in order to sell rights in the films which they produce. For this reason, the role of an independent sales agent acting on behalf of producers and negotiating the best sale and distribution arrangements on a territory-by-territory basis (both in relation to advances*/minimum guarantees and in relation to co-ordination of distribution), has evolved.

The parties to this particular transaction are:
* the sales agent (the "Agent"); and
* the producer who has produced the relevant film (the "Producer").

33.2 Document Analysis

A typical sales agency agreement might be expected to contain the following clauses:

* Appointment of agent (see Paragraph 33.3)
* Delivery (see Paragraph 33.4)
* Agent's undertakings (see Paragraph 33.5)
* Producer's warranties* (see Paragraph 33.6)
* Remuneration (see Paragraph 33.7)
* Accounts (see Paragraph 33.8)
* Determination (see Paragraph 33.9)
* Effect of determination (see Paragraph 33.10)
* Boilerplate* (see Paragraph 33.11).

33.3 Appointment of Agent

The agreement* will normally contain an appointment by the Producer of the Agent as the Producer's sole or exclusive agent to negotiate licence agreements in respect of the film during a term*. Where an appointment is as sole agent, the Producer will have the right to sell the film at the same time as the Agent. Where the appointment is exclusive, the Producer will have no right to sell the film. Most appointments are on an exclusive or sole and exclusive basis.

The term of the agreement is variable. Generally, sales agents do not acquire rights for the full copyright period of the films. The services of sales agents are of a particularly personal nature so, in many cases, this would be inappropriate.

The average duration (or term) of sales agent's rights is around 15 years, but it is important from the sales agent's point of view, that it should have the flexibility to negotiate and agree licence agreements beyond this period. Normally, the Agent will be entitled to negotiate and enter into licence agreements for a variable length of time, which could be up to the full period of copyright in the film.

The legal effect of agency arrangements is interesting. The concept of agency is one of extremely long-standing, which has evolved over centuries of maritime trade on similar principles throughout the world. Where an Agent acts on behalf of a third party (such as a Producer) whose identity is disclosed to a purchaser, the Agent is immune from legal proceedings. If it subsequently emerges that the Producer did not own the film or has infringed someone's rights or is otherwise in breach of any warranty or obligation. For this reason, it is normal for Agents to disclose the fact they are contracting as agent on behalf of a Producer in order to give themselves immunity from being sued.

A number of duties are implied in the relationship between an Agent and its principal. These duties are implied "by operation of law" (ie automatically) even in the absence of a signed contract. They include a duty of good faith owed by the Agent to the principal, which includes an obligation not to make a secret profit and not to accept bribes or secret commissions. The principal is also obliged to indemnify the agent in relation to losses and expenses and the Agent has a right to be remunerated for its services.

Normally, the Agent's entitlement to commission will end when the contract* expires, unless express provision is incorporated entitling the Agent to post-termination remuneration. The United Kingdom has recently passed the Commercial Agents Regulations (Council Directive) of 1993 implementing an EU Directive which permits Agents for the sale of goods to receive compensation on the expiry of their agency rights. Although a film sales agent is normally responsible for the sale of intellectual property rights, its duties will also involve it supplying physical materials to third party distributors and for this reason, it is believed that the Commercial Agents Regulations will apply to films.

33.4 Delivery

In order to perform its function, the sales agent will require delivery of certain film and publicity materials (see Chapter 23) and will also require a laboratory access letter* (see Paragraph 51.3).

The Producer will normally undertake to provide these items to the Agent by a designated delivery date.

33.5   Agent's Undertakings

In addition to the obligations on the part of an Agent which are implied by law (see Paragraph 33.3) a sales agency agreement may contain the following warranties on the part of an Agent.

Delivery Material

The title to delivery material remains vested in the Producer.

Copyright Protection

The Agent will not impair or prejudice copyright protection in the film or delivery material.

Return of Material

The Agent will return all material to the Producer on the termination of the agreement.

Promotional Material

The Agent will obtain the consent and the approval of the Producer in relation to all promotional art work material.

Licence Agreements

The form of licence agreement to be used by the Agent is approved by the Producer.

No Alterations

The Agent will not dub or otherwise alter the film.

Supply of Material

The Agent will supply all licensees with material they require during the term.

Claims

The Agent will notify the Producer immediately of any claim in relation to the film.

No Assignment

The Agent will not assign or license any rights under the agreement, except as expressly permitted.

No Duplication

The Agent will not copy or duplicate any delivery materials, except for the purpose of providing them to licensees.

Freight

The Agent will wherever possible require licensees to pay all freight costs.

Control of Delivery Material

The Agent will retain control and possession of delivery materials at all times.

Exploitation

The Agent will use its best endeavours to exploit the rights.

No Undisclosed Agency

The Agent is not the undisclosed agent of another person.

Confidentiality

The Agent will keep all information relating to the agreement confidential.

Indemnity

See Paragraph 53.16.

33.6 Producer's Warranties

Some sales agency agreements contain express warranties on the part of Producers. Strictly speaking, many of these warranties may be inappropriate, since the Agent will not have any liability towards third parties for acts or omissions on the part of the Producer.

Where an agent does require warranties from a Producer, these may often take the form of the warranties required in a distribution agreement (see Paragraph 23.3).

33.7 Remuneration

The remuneration provisions of a sales agency agreement work in both directions. First, the Producer will normally require remuneration from the Agent in the form of an advance or minimum guarantee. Where a Producer has obtained funding from third parties, the territories and media granted to such third parties will normally be excluded from the scope of rights granted to the Agent and the Agent's advance or minimum guarantee will provide the balance of the budget required to enable the Producer to make the film.

Often, the advance or minimum guarantee is payable on delivery and the Agent's commitment to pay this sum will have to be 'discounted' (see Chapter 27) by the Producer in order to obtain cash-flow finance to make the film. Because the Producer will require some form of security to guarantee that the advance or minimum guarantee will actually be payable on delivery the agreement may provide that this has to be secured by an irrevocable letter of credit (see Paragraph 51.5) which the Producer will be entitled to draw upon subject to delivery of a signed laboratory access letter certifying that the laboratory is in possession of the delivery materials required to be delivered to the Agent under the agreement.

So far as concerns remuneration moving from the Producer to the Agent, the Agent will normally require payment of a commission (of between 15% to 25% of gross receipts). If the Agent is responsible for receiving the gross receipts under the distribution agreements, it will deduct all sums owed by way of commission from these and will also normally deduct distribution expenses actually incurred in selling the film. Frequently, a Producer will wish to place a 'cap' on the distribution expenses to be incurred by the Agent and these may be limited to 5% of gross receipts in the first year of the term.

33.8 Accounting

The procedure for the collection of receipts and the accounting procedure are issues which are of fundamental importance to the Producer. If the sales agent is to collect all gross receipts arising from the film and becomes insolvent, the sums held by the sales agent may end up being applied for the benefit of the sales agent's creditors and not the Producer. In cases where a reputable sales agent is involved which has provided a substantial advance to the Producer by way of a letter of credit, it will normally be acceptable for the sales agent to collect income derived from the film.

If any question exists in relation to the Agent's financial stability, two possibilities exist. First, it may be possible to have the licence agreements administered by a reputable third party agent, such as the National Film Trustee Company Limited, who will collect all revenue pursuant to distribution agreements and apply it for the benefit of the Agent and the Producer in accordance with their agreement. A second, less effective, alternative is to provide for the Agent to establish a trust account in the name of the Producer and to give irrevocable directions to all licensees to pay sums to this account.

The procedure for providing statements of account and payments will normally reflect film industry standard accounting practice. Normally, one would expect quarterly accounting from licensees, 45 or 60 days after each quarter date. It is important for the Producer not to impose standard accounting dates on the Agent, since that will defer by three months, possibly longer, the Producer's receipt of funds. Care needs to be given to the timing of the accounting periods. In addition, the Producer may wish to provide that the Agent will bring sums above a certain amount into account within 14 days of receipt.

33.9 Determination

The sales agency agreement will normally contain provisions entitling the Producer to terminate if:

* the Agent is in breach of any material term which is incapable of remedy or any remediable term which is not remedied within a certain number of days from notice;
* any of the Agent's representations proves to be incorrect;
* the Agent transfers or disposes of part of its assets which is material in opinion of the Company;
* the Agent becomes insolvent or suffers the appointment of the Receiver or similar officer;
* the Agent abandons or announces that it intends to abandon the business of distributing films.

On the occurrence of any of the above events, the Producer will normally have the right to terminate the agreement.

33.10 Effect of Determination

On termination by the Producer of its rights under the agreement, it is normal to provide that the Producer may retake possession of all delivery material and enter into the Agent's premises and that the Agent's right to receive commission or other income under licence and distribution agreements will end. Where the Agent has advanced a substantial sum to the Producer, the Producer may permit the Agent to recoup this sum, even after termination, but the question whether the Agent is to remain to recoup commissions is negotiable. Normally, however, this will be unacceptable to the Producer and its financiers because if the film is being sold by a third party, this will require two sets of commissions to be paid.

33.11   Boilerplate

The boilerplate section of a typical sales agency agreement will contain the following provisions:

- Assignment (see Paragraph 52.1)
- Notices (see Paragraph 52.8)
- Severability (see Paragraph 52.10)
- Entire agreement (see Paragraph 52.3)
- Waiver (see Paragraph 52.11)
- No partnership (see Paragraph 52.7)
- Governing law (see Paragraph 52.5).

34   Video Licence Agreement

34.1   Description of a Video Licence Agreement

The purpose of a video licence agreement* is to transfer the right to distribute a film or programme by means of videogram in a particular country to a video distributor in that country.

The parties to this particular transaction are:

- the company owning the videogram rights (the "Company") and
- the video distributor (the "Licensee").

34.2   Transactions Analysis

A typical video licence agreement might be expected to contain the following clauses:
- Grant of rights (see Paragraph 34.3)
- Company's warranties* (see Paragraph 34.4)
- Remuneration (see Paragraph 34.5)
- Distribution obligation (see Paragraph 34.6)
- Licensee's undertakings (see Paragraph 34.7)
- Payment (see Paragraph 34.8)
- Accounting (see Paragraph 34.9)
- Substitution (see Paragraph 34.10)
- Determination (see Paragraph 34.11)
- Effect of determination (see Paragraph 34.12)
- Boilerplate* (see Paragraph 34.13).

34.3   Grant of Rights

The video licence agreement will normally grant to a Licensee the right to manufacture videograms in the territory and the sole and exclusive right to sell and distribute videograms in a territory during a licence period or term*.

The right to manufacture may be granted on a non-exclusive basis because the Company may need to reserve the right to permit licensees from other countries to manufacture videograms in the territory. These might include licensees for other countries within the European Economic Area (within which the free circulation of goods is permitted), as well as licensees for media not granted to the Licensee, such as ship and airline rights.

The precise definition of what constitutes a videogram needs to be considered. In many agreements, the definition is limited to video cassette rights. In some cases, however, Licensees may require rights to be granted in digital video discs, laser discs, CD interactive, CD-Roms etc. Because there is an overlap between interactive and "on-line" video distribution with broadcast media including specifically cable transmission, it would be normal to exclude from a videogram licence the right to exploit a film or programme by on-line means such as video on demand.

The rights are normally licensed to a licensee for a particular territory and a particular term. Because the provisions of the European Union Treaty do not permit restrictions on the free movement of goods or services between member states of the European Union or the European Economic Area, the licence granted to the Licensee cannot contain protection against parallel imports (see Paragraph 53.11).

Additionally, in the United Kingdom, retail prices legislation prevents the Company specifying that the Licensee is obliged to sell videograms at a minimum price. If the Company wishes to obtain reassurance that it will receive a minimum sum for each videogram manufactured and sold, it is permissible, for the Company to insert a minimum royalty obligation in its agreement. It is also permissible for the Company to impose a general indication as to the general pricing policy in relation to the sale of videograms of the film or television programme by designating that the Licensee will treat these as "top-line" products and will not distribute them as budget items or as part of a promotion without the consent of the Company.

In addition to the right to manufacture videograms and the exclusive right to distribute them in the territory, the Licensee will normally require a non-exclusive licence to reproduce publicity material and to use names and biographies of persons contained in the film or programme. The Licensee may also require the right to use short excerpts from the film for the purposes of promotion or advertising in prespecified media.

34.4 Company's Warranties

A videogram licence agreement may contain the following warranties and undertakings on the part of the Company.

Right to Enter Agreement

The Company has the right to enter into the agreement and grant the Licensee the rights.

Non-Infringement

The film or programme licensed does not infringe or violate any right of copyright and is not obscene or blasphemous or defamatory.

Third Party Liabilities

The Company will pay all sums under any agreement with any person who rendered services or supplied goods in relation to the film, including sums payable by equitable remuneration in relation to the rental of videograms (see Paragraph 53.6). Whether or not the Company is obliged to pay mechanical royalties* in relation to the use of music is a question for discussion.

Music Liabilities

The Company may wish to exclude from the definition of third party liabilities any liability to pay mechanical/synchronisation licence* fees and require these to be paid by the Licensee. Whether or not this is commercially acceptable will depend on the type of programming and also the territory for which rights have been granted. In some cases, the Licensee may be prepared to pay standard mechanical royalties at the rate of the Mechanical Copyright Protection Society Limited* or its analogous overseas body. In some territories, notably the United States of America, the practice of paying mechanical royalties for videogram manufacture is not as developed as in Europe and many US licensees require video mechanical fees to be prepaid or "bought out".

Hold-back

The videogram market potential for some types of films or programmes is seriously damaged if they receive television exposure before their first video exploitation or shortly after the video release dates. For this reason, it is common for licensees to require that the Company holds back the exploitation of television rights (whether free, pay, cable or satellite) for a certain period after first videogram release. The issue of hold-backs* and availability periods in separate media is becoming increasingly complicated as the types of audio-visual delivery systems increase and the technology develops.

Sell-off Period

The video licence agreement should normally contain a sell-off* period. The sell-off period is frequently thought of as being for the benefit of the Licensee, but it is in fact, for the benefit of the Company. After the term or licence period expires, the Licensee may be left in possession of significant numbers of unsold videograms. If these items have previously been lawfully manufactured, they are not infringing copies and may be sold by the Licensee, even after the loss of its exclusive rights, unless a contractual restriction is placed on the Licensee limiting its rights to do so.

Normally, the Company will be prepared to permit the Licensee to sell-off stocks during a three- or six-month period following termination by effluxion of time (ie if the agreement is terminated for breach, the sell-off period will not apply). At the end of any sell-off period, the Licensee may be required either to destroy surplus stock or return it to the Company.

The sell-off provision, therefore, permits the Company to clean up the videogram market in a particular territory before relicensing rights to another licensee. The possibility will always exist that a Licensee may "schlock" product onto the market at a low price immediately before or during the sell-off period. This might prevent a new licensee selling videograms in the territory at normal rates. If this is a point of concern to the Company, the agreement should address it.

34.5 Remuneration

The remuneration provisions contained in a videogram licence agreement will normally require the Licensee to pay the Company an advance payment, which will be paid as to a certain percentage on signature and as to the remainder, on delivery of specified delivery material. The Company will wish the advance to be described as non-returnable, although the Licensee may wish to provide specifically that amounts paid are returned in the event of non-delivery. The Licensee will normally wish to describe the advance as recoupable in order to permit it to recoup the advance* from future royalties. In other words, until the level of royalties paid under the agreement exceeds the amount previously paid to the Company by way of advance, the Licensee will not be obliged to pay further sums.

The basis on which the royalty is calculated is one which the Company must consider carefully. In most agreements, the royalty base price (see Chapter 1) is the actual wholesale price of videograms, less bona fide arm's length discounts. It is important from the Company's point of view that the royalty base price is not defined as the Licensee's receipts from exploiting the videogram and that the Licensee is expressly prohibited from sub-licensing rights. If these provisions are not included in the licence agreement, the Company may find that, instead of receiving a royalty of 25% of the wholesale price, it is receiving a royalty of 25% of the Licensee's receipts from a sub-licensee (ie 25% of 25%).

34.6 Distribution Obligations

A videogram licence agreement may contain the following distribution obligations on the part of the Licensee.

No Alteration

The Licensee will not cut or permit the cutting or alteration of the videograms otherwise than for the purpose of censorship.

Copyright Protection

The Licensee shall take all steps as may be necessary to secure the copyright protection of the film and shall include in all videograms whatever anti-piracy warning the Company requires.

Promotional Material

The Licensee will not create any promotional material without the consent of the Company. All promotional material created will belong to the Company. This is to permit the Company to use the promotional materials created for one market place in another.

Statements

The Licensee will supply the Company with statements of shipments and sales of videograms on a monthly or another basis.

Sale or Return

The Licensee will not consign the videograms on a sale or return or stock-balancing basis without the consent of the Company.

Export

The Licensee will not sell or permit any videograms to be sold or exported outside the territory without the prior written consent of the Company.

Claim

The Licensee will give the Company full particulars immediately on becoming aware of any actual or threatened claim in relation to the videograms.

Damage or Defect

Following receipt of delivery material, the Licensee shall notify the Company, within three working days, of any damage or defect.

Collective Agreements

The Licensee will conform with all local industry trade union guild, collective bargaining or other agreements relating to the manufacture and distribution of videograms.

Release

The Licensee will release the videograms within six months from delivery and maintain them on release in the territory throughout the term.

Advertisement

The Licensee will advertise the videograms throughout the territory in the same manner as other videograms of major films distributed by the Licensee.

Exploitation

The Licensee will exploit the rights granted to the best of its skill and ability to ensure the highest possible royalties.

Fair Treatment

The Licensee will ensure that the videograms are given fair and equitable treatment and are not discriminated against in favour of any other videograms which the Licensee distributes.

Censorship

The Licensee will submit the videograms to every competent authority, to whom they are required to be submitted, for censorship, certification or other purposes.

Music Liabilities

Depending on the commercial terms agreed between the parties, the Licensee may be required to ensure the payment of all music liabilities.

34.7   Licensee's Undertakings

A videogram licence agreement will also contain a number of specific undertakings on the part of the Licensee, which may include the following.

Capacity to Contact

The Licensee is free to enter into the agreement and has not entered into any arrangement which might conflict with it.

Title

All rights and title in the delivery material are reserved to the Company.

Copyright Protection

The Licensee shall not impair or prejudice copyright in the videograms or deal with the delivery material in such a way that any third party may obtain any lien over it.

Return of Delivery Material

The Licensee will return the delivery material at the end of the term or on the prior termination of the agreement. In practice, this provision may be varied if delivery material is lent to the Licensee.

Prompt Payment

The Licensee will promptly pay to the Company all sums due.

Assignment and Licensing

The Licensee is expressly prohibited from assigning or licensing or otherwise parting with possession of the benefit or burden of the agreement without the prior consent of the Company.

Duplication

The Licensee will not copy or duplicate the delivery material otherwise than for the purpose of exploiting rights granted to it under the agreement.

Freight and Import Costs

The Licensee will pay all costs, fees, import, freight and customs and similar duties and expenses.

Possession of Delivery Material

The Licensee will retain control or possession of the delivery material and keep it in a safe and secure place.

Replacement of Delivery Material

If any part of the delivery material is lost or damaged, the Licensee shall pay the Company the cost of replacing it.

Insurance

The Licensee will maintain adequate insurance in relation to the replacement of all delivery material.

Stocks

The Licensee will at the end of the sell-off period permit the Company to purchase stocks of videograms at the manufacturing cost of the Licensee or shall destroy the same and provide the Company with an appropriate certificate of destruction.

Indemnity

See Paragraph 53.16.

34.8 Payment

Where a video licence agreement involves a foreign state, the Licensee may wish to insert a provision permitting it to withhold from sums payable to the Company any sums which it is required to deduct by way of withholding taxes*. From the Company's point of view, it is important that this provision should not extend to any sum payable by way of advance. It is also important to ensure that the Licensee provides the Company with actual documentary evidence of its liability to deduct any amount before making the deduction. In cases where a double taxation treaty exists between the Licensee's country of incorporation and the state in which the Company is resident, it may be necessary to provide evidence of incorporation in a particular form. If this is required, the documentation should contain an appropriate provision. In practice, withholding taxes do not generally present any problem in contractual arrangements between companies situated in the European Union or European Economic Area, but will always need to be considered.

The Company may wish to ensure that the Licensee remits funds by way of bank transfer. In this case, the agreement should contain details of the Company's bank account and account code. The agreement may also require the Licensee to ensure a specific message reference appears on the transfer to assist in bank reconciliations.

Where the Licensee is situated in a foreign jurisdiction, the question of currency conversion needs to be considered. The time when the Licensee is expected to convert royalties and the rate at which it is expected to convert them will need to be specified in the agreement. In some circumstances, the Company may wish the Licensee to remit unconverted funds in the Licensee's currency to the Company's account or give notice before any accounting period, requiring the Licensee not to convert the funds in order to minimise the effect on the Company of adverse currency fluctuations, or to fund future purchases which the Company may be intending to make in the Licensee's territory.

34.9 Accounting

The agreement will require the Licensee to provide the Company with a full statement showing all videograms manufactured, sold and returned in each accounting period. Accounting periods in the video industry are generally quarterly, ending on 31 March, 30 June, 30 September and 31 December in each year. The accounting date on which the statement for which the preceding period is required to be rendered is normally 45 or 60 days after the relevant quarter day.

The agreement should provide that all payments due to the Company by the Licensee will be exclusive of Value Added Tax, which will be payable on receipt of the Company's Value Added Tax invoice. In practice, where arrangements are in force between companies in the European Union, the obligation to pay VAT may not apply in circumstances where the invoice contains correct details of the other party's VAT Registration Number prefixed by their country code.

The Licensee will normally be required to keep full and proper books and records of account and permit the Company to inspect the same on reasonable prior notice during normal business hours. In the event any inspection reveals an underpayment to the Company in excess of a stated percentage of sums actually paid in any accounting period, the Licensee will normally be expected to pay to the Company the reasonable costs of any inspection and audit actually incurred by the Company. The percentage, subject to negotiation, is either 5% or 10%.

34.10 Substitution

In some circumstances, the Company may wish to provide in the agreement a substitution provision. This type of provision is not normally included in the agreement if it relates to simply one film or programme, but, where a number of films or programmes are included, the Company may well wish to provide for the possibility that one film or programme may not be completed or delivered or may suffer from distribution problems, either through censorship or certification difficulties or problems with its chain of title*. In such circumstances, the agreement will provide that the Company has the right to withdraw the affected film, subject to providing a substitute film or reimbursing the Licensee with such amount of the advance which has been apportioned to the affected film.

317

34.11 Determination

The licence agreement will normally contain provisions entitling the Company to terminate if:

- the Licensee is in breach of any material term which is incapable of remedy or any remediable term which is not remedied within a certain number of days from notice;
- any of the Licensee's representations proves to be incorrect;
- the Licensee transfers or disposes of part of its assets which is material in opinion of the Company;
- the Licensee becomes insolvent or suffers the appointment of the receiver or similar officer;
- the Licensee abandons or announces that it intends to abandon the business of distributing films.

On the occurrence of any of the above events, the Company will normally have the right to terminate the agreement.

34.12 Effect of Determination

On termination by the Company of its rights under the agreement, it is normal to provide that the Company may retake possession of all delivery material and enter into the Licensee's premises.

34.13 Boilerplate

The boilerplate section of a typical video licence agreement might be expected to contain the following clauses:

- Force majeure (see Paragraph 52.4)
- No assignment (see Paragraph 52.1)
- Notices (see Paragraph 52.8)
- Severability (see Paragraph 52.10)
- Entire agreement (see Paragraph 52.3)
- Waiver (see Paragraph 52.11)
- No partnership (see Paragraph 52.7)
- Governing law (see Paragraph 52.5).

35   Broadcast Licence Agreement

35.1   Description of a Broadcast Licence Agreement

The Broadcast licence agreement* is the document pursuant to which the owner or licensee of rights in a particular film or programme licenses to a broadcaster the right to broadcast the film or programme in a particular territory for a particular licence period.

The parties to this particular transaction are:

- the owner of the rights in the film (the "Company"); and
- the broadcaster acquiring a licence to broadcast the film (the "Licensee").

35.2   Transaction Analysis

A typical broadcast licence agreement might be expected to contain the following clauses:

- Grant of rights (see Paragraph 35.3)
- Remuneration (see Paragraph 35.4)
- Company's warranties* (see Paragraph 35.5)
- Licensee's undertakings (see Paragraph 35.6)
- Substitution (see Paragraph 35.7)
- Music (see Paragraph 35.8)
- Determination (see Paragraph 35.9)
- Effect of determination (see Paragraph 35.10)
- Boilerplate* (see Paragraph 35.11).

35.3   Grant of Rights

The agreement will specify precisely what rights are being granted to the Licensee over a prescribed territory and during a predefined licensed period. Normally, a broadcast licence will permit the Licensee to have the right to effect a number of transmissions of a film or programme over a period of years. Traditionally, where the only means of effecting television transmission has been by analogue transmission from terrestrial transmitters, a broadcast licence might refer to transmitters licensed to or operated by the Licensee. Because of the fact that the range of analogue television signals is limited, "overspill*" has never been much of a problem in television broadcasting.

In view of the fact, however, that most terrestrial broadcasters are scheduled to commence digital broadcasting of their scheduled transmissions in parallel with their standard analogue broadcasts in clear, unencrypted mode and, in view of the fact also that some transmissions from the United Kingdom (notably those of the BBC) are picked up and relayed by cable in parts of Belgium and the Netherlands, the impact of digital terrestrial broadcasting on the licensing and distribution pattern of films and other programmes will need time to be assessed, but it is certain that existing practices will change.

A Licensee will generally require the right to use material for advertising and publicity purposes and the right to use name, likenesses and biographies connected with the film or films licensed in much the same way as the videogram licensee (see Paragraph 34.3).

Where rights in films or programmes are licensed to broadcasters, they are normally licensed subject expressly to the rights of the Performing Right Society Limited*, Phonographic Performance Limited and Videogram Performance Limited (see Paragraph 2.5). These societies control the public performance right and broadcast right in musical works, sound recordings and videograms made by their members. These rights are normally acquired from these organisations by broadcasters, subject to payment of an annual blanket fee. They authorise the broadcasters to use works whose public performance/broadcasting rights are controlled by the relevant societies.

35.4 Remuneration

The remuneration payable under a broadcast licence agreement is normally a licence fee which is payable in instalments, usually a percentage on signature and a percentage on delivery of the delivery materials for each film.

35.5 Company's Warranties

The warranties given by the Company to the Licensee are similar to those which may be given by the Company to a videogram licensee (see Paragraph 34.4), except that no reference will be made to mechanical royalties which are payable only in relation to the manufacture of videogram copies of films or programmes and not their public performance and broadcasting.

35.6 Licensees' Undertakings

A broadcast licence agreement will normally contain a number of warranties and obligations on the part of the Licensee, which may include the following.

Capacity to Contract

The Licensee has the power to enter into the agreement.

PRS

The Licensee acknowledges it is required to obtain the necessary licenses from the PRS, PPL and VPL.

Copyright

The Licensee will not by any act or omission impair or prejudice the copyright in the film.

Delivery Material

The Licensee will not permit any third party to acquire a lien over the delivery material and will return it to the Company either at the end of the period on which it is made available on loan or the end of the licence period and will pay for the cost of repairing any damage to returned delivery material.

Publicity Material

The Licensee will not create any advertising or publicity material without the consent of the Company and all material so created will belong to the Company.

Subtitling and Dubbing

The Licensee will not impose sub-titles or dub the film without the consent of the Company.

Cutting

The Licensee will not cut the film otherwise than for the purposes of censorship or for the insertion of reasonable commercial breaks, provided that such breaks will not amount in any way to a derogatory treatment of the film.

Statement

The Licensee will supply the Company with statements of all transmissions of the film.

Third Party Claims

The Licensee will immediately advise the Company of any claims made against it by any third party in relation to the film.

Prompt Payment

The Licensee will promptly pay all sums due to the Company.

Copyright Notices

The Licensee will not cut or fail to transmit copyright notices, trade names and logos etc.

Import Fees and Expenses

The Licensee will be responsible for all import fees, freight charges, customs, duties and other expenses.

Delivery Material

The Licensee will retain control and possession of delivery material, notify the Company within a specified number of working days of any defect and insure the material against all risks.

Union Agreements

The Licensee will conform with the provisions of all union agreements relating to the exploitation of rights.

Indemnity

See Paragraph 53.16.

35.7 Substitution

See Paragraph 34.10.

35.8   Collecting Societies

The agreement will normally provide that, where any money is payable by collecting societies in relation to the transmission or secondary transmission of the film, the entitlement to such money will belong to the Company, not the Licensee.

35.9   Determination

See Paragraph 34.11.

35.10   Effect of Determination

See Paragraph 34.12.

35.11   Boilerplate

The boilerplate section of a typical broadcast licence agreement might contain the following provisions:

* Assignment (see Paragraph 52.1)
* Notices (see Paragraph 52.8)
* Severability (see Paragraph 52.10)
* Entire agreement (see Paragraph 52.3)
* Waiver (see Paragraph 52.11)
* No partnership (see Paragraph 52.7)
* Governing law (see Paragraph 52.5).

36 Cable/Satellite/Pay TV Licence Agreement

36.1 Description of Cable/Satellite/Pay TV Licence Agreement

The somewhat odd official distinction which used to exist in relation to distribution of a film by cable or satellite is beginning to be blurred, as a number of channels are available both by means of satellite and cable.

The distinction between basic services (which are given to a cable or satellite subscriber for part of their basic monthly subscription) and premium channels (for which an additional amount is charged) remains of significant commercial importance, but the practice of "bundling" (where channels are only made available to subscribers in clusters) is likely to come under review from regulatory authorities and competition authorities when digital terrestrial television services are available.

The rapid development of encryption technology and the recent experiments in video on demand and near video on demand services are clear pointers that the pay TV market will grow in commercial significance. The effect of the imminent arrival of digital multiplex services on the market is very difficult to predict.

The parties to a cable/satellite/pay TV licence agreement* are:

- the owner of the rights of the film being licensed (the "Company"); and
- the entity responsible for organising the cable/satellite/pay TV exploitation (the "Licensee").

36.2 Transaction Analysis

All media industry transactions are geared to specific sets of circumstances, and the combined effect of the factors mentioned above means that it is very difficult to create a document structure which might apply to all cable/satellite/pay TV agreements. A typical list of basic elements, before any transaction structure is tailored to meet the particular circumstances, might, however, be expected to contain the following provisions:

- Grant of rights (see Paragraph 36.3)
- Remuneration (see Paragraph 36.4)

- Company's warranties* (see Paragraph 36.5)
- Licensee's undertakings (see Paragraph 36.6)
- Substitution (see Paragraph 36.7)
- Music (see Paragraph 36.8)
- Overspill*, publicity and sponsorship (see Paragraph 36.9)
- Accounting (see Paragraph 36.10)
- Boilerplate* (see Paragraph 36.11).

36.3 Grant of Rights

From the Company's point of view, if the films are being licensed on the basis of the payment of a royalty* per subscriber, it is essential to specify that the films will be exploited otherwise than as part of the basic service. This is normally done by specifying the channel or service on which the film or films may be shown. The agreement will also specify the territory and the extent of the licence period during which the Licensee has rights.

Normally, rights to transmit films are limited to a prespecified number of transmissions. The period during which a film is available to be transmitted by cable or satellite or pay TV may also be restricted, since specific hold-backs (see Paragraph 31.10) may have been given in relation to other media.

The agreement will, therefore, provide for a restricted period during which the Licensee may transmit the film and the agreement may therefore specify a total maximum number of exhibition days or transmission days. It is likely that the Licensee will want to transmit the film more than once on each transmission/ exhibition day and the agreement will, therefore, specify the maximum number of times the film may be transmitted on each day.

The Licensee will acquire the right to use certain materials for the purposes of advertising and publicity (see Paragraph 35.3) and the licence will normally be subject to the rights of the PRS*, PPL and the VPL (see Paragraph 35.3).

36.4 Remuneration

The remuneration in licence agreements of this type is subject to wide variation. The remuneration may take the form of a basic fee, payable as a percentage on signature, a percentage on delivery and a percentage on the availability date of each film.

An additional fee may be payable and this might be calculated either with reference to the theatrical gross box office performance of each film or the amount expended on prints and advertising for the UK theatrical release of each film or on the total amount of subscribers of the service for which the film is being licensed. Because subscriber rates to cable and satellite services are liable to "churn", where a remuneration provision is linked to the number of subscribers, this is frequently calculated as the average figure at the beginning and end of each month on which an exhibition/transmission day in relation to any relevant film has occurred.

36.5 Company's Warranties

See Paragraph 35.5.

36.6 Licensee's Undertakings

See Paragraph 35.6.

36.7 Substitution

See Paragraph 34.10.

36.8 Music

See Paragraph 35.8.

36.9 Overspill, Publicity and Sponsorship

In those circumstances where a Licensee's signal "overspills" and is available outside the territory, the agreement will need to contain an acknowledgement on the part of the Company that such overspill does not infringe the Company's rights. Normally, the Company will wish to limit overspill as far as possible and may provide that the Licensee's signal is to be encrypted and that the decryption devices will not be made available outside the territory. In circumstances where overspill is permitted, the Company will need to ensure that licences granted to licensees in neighbouring territories are adjusted in an appropriate manner.

The Company will also wish to control the issue of publicity in relation to transmission of the film and ensure that it does not occur before the availability date since prior publicity may lead to the Company being in breach of a hold-back provision given to (for example) a video distributor in the territory.

The Company will also wish to limit the possibility of the Licensee entering into any sponsorship arrangement in relation to any film, unless the Company consents. The purpose of this restriction is to require the Licensee to account to the Company for any benefits received by the Licensee from any sponsor of a broadcast of the film.

36.10 Accounting

The agreement will normally require the Licensee to provide the Company with details of exhibition/transmission days and subscriber levels for each month during which transmissions have occurred.

If the payment obligations only require the Licensee to pay when an exhibition/transmission day occurs, there will be a possibility that the total number of exhibition days may not have been used at the end of the licence period and the agreement may contain a provision to the effect that any unused exhibition days will be paid for at the subscriber level prevailing at the end of the licence period.

36.11   Boilerplate

The boilerplate section of a typical cable/satellite/pay TV licence agreement might contain the following provisions:

- Assignment (see Paragraph 52.1)
- Notices (see Paragraph 52.8)
- Severability (see Paragraph 52.10)
- Entire agreement (see Paragraph 52.3)
- Waiver (see Paragraph 52.11)
- No partnership (see Paragraph 52.7)
- Governing law (see Paragraph 52.5).

37 All-Media Acquisition Agreement

37.1 Description of All-Media Acquisition Agreement

The all-media acquisition agreement* is an agreement drafted from the point of view of a company which is acquiring rights in a particular project and, in many ways, it resembles the documents referred to in Chapters 32–36 with two differences. First, if the company acquiring the rights has control of the documentation, it will generally require the owner of the rights to make a number of warranties in relation to them. Second, the Company itself will wish to give less warranties* than those it would seek to impose on a licensee.

The parties to this particular transaction are:

- the company acquiring the rights (the "Company"); and
- the rights owner granting the rights (the "Owner").

37.2 Transaction Analysis

A typical rights acquisition agreement might be expected to contain the following clauses:

- Grant of rights (see Paragraph 37.3)
- Owner's warranties (see Paragraph 37.4)
- Indemnity* (see Paragraph 37.5)
- Company's warranties (see Paragraph 37.6)
- Remuneration (see Paragraph 37.7)
- Reservation (see Paragraph 37.8)
- Accounts (see Paragraph 37.9)
- Boilerplate* (see Paragraph 37.10).

37.3 Grant of Rights

The form of the grant of rights clause will depend on what media rights are intended to be granted. These may include the rights to distribute a film by theatrical means, by non-theatrical means, by means of videogram, free broadcast television or satellite, cable or pay TV. For a description of the various rights in films see Chapter 31.

The terms and conditions of the grant of rights clause will generally be similar to the provisions referred to in Paragraphs 34.3, 35.3 and 36.3.

37.4   Owner's Warranties

A rights acquisition agreement may contain the following warranties on the part of the Owner.

Capacity

The Owner has the right to enter into the agreement and grant the necessary rights.

Ownership

The Owner is the sole, absolute, unincumbered legal and beneficial owner of all rights granted to the Company.

Copyright and Obscenity

Nothing contained in the film is obscene or blasphemous or defamatory or infringes any right of copyright, right of publicity, right of privacy, trademark or performer's right or any other right.

Moral Rights

All authors of copyright works have waived their moral rights*.

Defect

The Owner has no actual or constructive notice of any defect.

Non-Exploitation

The film has not been exploited in the territory by means of any of the media granted to the Company.

Third Party Liabilities

The Company shall not have any obligation to pay any sum to any person providing services or facilities in the film. Whether or not the Company is to assume the liability for paying synchronisation and mechanical royalties (see Paragraph 34.3) is a matter for commercial negotiation.

Credit Obligations

All material complies with all credit obligations.

Quality

The delivery material will be in first-class condition and of suitable technical quality.

Title

All material created by the Company will belong to the Company.

Copyright Registration

The Company will have the right to take all steps as it considers necessary to protect the film, including registering copyright.

Particulars of the Film

The particulars of the film as set out in the agreement are correct.

Sell-Off

The Company will have a sell-off* period following termination of the agreement by effluxion of time (see Paragraph 34.4).

Censorship

The film will achieve prespecified censorship ratings.

Errors and Omissions

The Owner has effected errors and omissions insurances and has noted the interest in the Company as named insured.

37.5 Indemnity

See Paragraph 53.16.

37.6 Company's Undertakings

An acquisition agreement may contain the following undertakings on the part of the Company.

Exploitation

To exploit the rights granted throughout the territory.

Advertisement

To advertise the rights in such a manner as determined by the Company in its commercial discretion.

Theatrical Release

To secure as effective a theatrical release for the film in the territory as the Company considers practicable.

37.7 Remuneration

The remuneration provisions for an acquisition agreement will normally contain an obligation to make payment of an advance*, which may be payable as to a certain percentage on signature and a certain percentage on delivery. The advance may be expressed to be non-returnable and will normally be expressed to be recoupable from additional sums payable by the Company to the Owner.

For an indication as to the remuneration terms which might apply, see Chapter 31 generally and also Paragraphs 34.5, 35.4 and 36.4.

37.8 Reservation

The agreement may contain an express acknowledgement, on the part of the parties, that all rights which are not expressly granted to the Company are reserved to the Owner.

37.9   Accounts

The agreement will normally provide that the Company is to provide the Owner with statements of account on industry-standard accounting dates (see Paragraph 34.9). The agreement will also permit the Company to deduct and retain withholding taxes* to the extent that they are required to be deducted and to make reserves against returns.

   The Company will also agree to keep full and proper books of account in relation to the exploitation of the rights and permit the Owner, or its representative, on reasonable prior notice to inspect, audit and take copies of the same, during business hours.

37.10   Boilerplate

The boilerplate section of a typical rights acquisition agreement may contain the following clauses:

*   Assignment (see Paragraph 52.1)
*   Notices (see Paragraph 52.8)
*   Severability (see Paragraph 52.10)
*   Entire agreement (see Paragraph 52.3)
*   Waiver (see Paragraph 52.11)
*   No partnership (see Paragraph 52.7)
*   Governing law (see Paragraph 52.5).

E: Multimedia

38 Multimedia Development Agreement

38.1 Description of a Multimedia Development Agreement

A multi media development agreement* is designed to enable the completion of all preliminary development work needed to evaluate the commercial possibilities of an intended multimedia work. In many ways, the provisions of a multimedia development agreement are very similar to those of a film or television development agreement.

The structures of the two types of agreements are almost identical. In practice, the only significant area of difference is in the definition of development material. A multimedia development agreement is likely to require the production of certain computer-generated material, which will not be required in film or television development agreements (other than those relating to animation).

The parties to this particular transaction are:

- the company commissioning the development of a multimedia work (the "Company"); and
- the entity producing the development material (the "Producer*").

38.2 Transaction Analysis

A typical development agreement might be expected to contain the following clauses:

- Development (see Paragraph 38.3)
- Grant of rights (see Paragraph 38.4)
- Producer's obligations (see Paragraph 38.5)
- Payment (see Paragraph 38.6)
- Producer's warranties* (see Paragraph 38.7)
- Production (see Paragraph 38.8)
- Boilerplate* (see Paragraph 38.9).

38.3   Development

See Paragraph 19.3.

38.4   Grant of Rights

See Paragraph 19.4.

38.5   Producer's Obligations

See Paragraph 19.5.

38.6   Payment

See Paragraph 19.6.

38.7   Producer's Warranties

See Paragraph 19.7.

38.8   Production

See Paragraph 19.8.

38.9   Boilerplate

A multimedia development agreement may be expected to contain the following boilerplate provisions:

• Notice (see Paragraph 52.8)
• Entire agreement (see Paragraph 52.3)
• Assignment (see Paragraph 52.1)
• Waiver (see Paragraph 52.11)
• No partnership (see Paragraph 52.7)
• Governing law (see Paragraph 52.5).

39 Multimedia Production Agreement

39.1 Description of a Multimedia Production Agreement

A multimedia production agreement* is designed to enable the creation of all preliminary production work needed to evaluate the commercial possibilities of an intended multimedia work. In many ways, the provisions of a multimedia production agreement are very similar to those of a film or television production agreement.

The structures of the two types of agreements are almost identical. In practice, the only significant area of difference is in the definition of production material. A multimedia production agreement is likely to require the production of certain computer-generated material, which will not be required in the film or television production agreements (other than those relating to animation).

The parties to this particular transaction are:

- the company commissioning the production of a multimedia work (the "Company"); and
- the entity producing the production material (the "Producer*").

39.2 Transaction Analysis

A typical multimedia production agreement might be expected to contain the following provisions:

- Production delivery and essential elements (see Paragraph 39.3)
- Copyright (see Paragraph 39.4)
- Production contracts* (see Paragraph 39.5)
- Producer warranties* (see Paragraph 39.6)
- Production representative and reports (see Paragraph 39.7)
- Insurance (see Paragraph 39.8)
- Credit censorship and contents (see Paragraph 39.9)
- Budget production fee and underspend (see Paragraph 39.10)
- Banking (see Paragraph 39.11)

- Books and records (see Paragraph 39.12)
- Royalties* (see Paragraph 39.13)
- Royalty accounting (see Paragraph 39.14)
- Determination (see Paragraph 39.15)
- Take-over (see Paragraph 39.16)
- Consequence of take-over (see Paragraph 39.17)
- Boilerplate* (see Paragraph 39.18).

39.3   Production, Delivery and Essential Elements

See Paragraph 21.3.

39.4   Copyright

See Paragraph 21.4.

39.5   Production Contracts

See Paragraph 21.5.

39.6   Producer Warranties

See Paragraph 23.3.

39.7   Production Representative

See Paragraph 21.11.

39.8   Insurance

See Paragraph 21.7.

39.9   Credit, Censorship and Contents

See Paragraphs 21.8 and 21.9.

39.10   Budget, Production Fee and Underspend

See Paragraphs 22.4 and 22.8.

39.11 Banking

See Paragraph 22.5.

39.12 Books and Records

See Paragraph 22.7.

39.13 Royalties

See Paragraph 1.10.

39.14 Royalty Accounting

See Paragraph 1.11.

39.15 Determination

See Paragraph 23.4.

39.16 Take-over

See Paragraph 23.5.

39.17 Consequence of Take-over

See Paragraph 23.6.

39.18 Boilerplate

The boilerplate section of a typical multimedia production contract might contain the following provisions:

- Notice (see Paragraph 52.8)
- Severability (see Paragraph 52.10)
- Force majeure (see Paragraph 52.4)
- Entire agreement (see Paragraph 52.3])
- Waiver (see Paragraph 52.11)
- No partnership (see Paragraph 52.7)
- Governing law (see Paragraph 52.5).

40 Multimedia Work Licence Agreement

40.1 Description of a Multimedia Licensing Agreement

The provisions of a licensing agreement* for a completed multimedia work in off-line format are very similar to the provisions for a licensing agreement for other work contained on physical media, such as records and videograms.

Since payment and delivery mechanisms in an on-line environment are at an early stage of development, there is no commercial distribution system for multimedia works in an on-line environment equivalent to the standard off-line distribution agreement for physical media.

Because of the current impossibility of preventing unauthorised digital copying of material made available on-line, it is advisable for companies licensing exploitation of multimedia works to withhold on-line exploitation rights. In some circumstances, however, works or extracts from works may be made available on-line, for example, in websites.

The parties to this particular transaction are:

• the company owning the rights in the multimedia work (the "Company"); and
• the third party distributing physical copies of the work (the "Licensee").

40.2 Analysis of a Multimedia Work Licence Agreement

A typical licence agreement for a multimedia work might be expected to contain the following clauses:

• Grant of rights (see Paragraph 40.3)
• Company's warranties* (see Paragraph 40.4)
• Remuneration (see Paragraph 40.5)
• Licensee's undertakings (see Paragraph 40.6)
• Royalty accounting (see Paragraph 40.7)
• Determination (see Paragraph 40.8)
• Boilerplate* (see Paragraph 40.9).

40.3   Grant of Rights

See Paragraph 34.3.

40.4   Company's Warranties

See Paragraph 34.4.

40.5   Remuneration

See Paragraph 34.5.

40.6   Licensee's Undertakings

See Paragraph 34.7.

40.7   Royalty Accounting

See Paragraph 34.9.

40.8   Determination

See Paragraph 34.11.

40.9   Boilerplate

The boilerplate section of a typical agreement for licensing a multimedia work might contain the following provisions:

- Notice (see Paragraph 52.8)
- No partnership (see Paragraph 52.7)
- Force majeure (see Paragraph 52.4)
- Entire agreement (see Paragraph 52.3])
- Governing law (see Paragraph 52.5).

41 Multimedia Rights Licence Agreement

41.1 Description of Multimedia Rights Licensing Agreement

The multimedia rights licensing agreement* is an agreement pursuant to which the right to develop and market a multimedia work is granted to a third party. The parties to the transaction are:

- the owner of the rights in the literary, dramatic, musical or artistic work which it is intended to turn into a multimedia product (the "Owner"); and
- the licensee who wishes to have the right to develop the multimedia work (the "Licensee").

41.2 Transaction Analysis

A typical licensing agreement for the licensing of a multimedia work to be created from a literary, dramatic or artistic work might be expected to contain the following provisions:

- Grant of Rights (see Paragraph 41.3)
- Owner's warranties* (see Paragraph 41.4)
- Remuneration (see Paragraph 41.5)
- Licensee's undertakings (see Paragraph 41.6)
- Royalty accounting (see Paragraph 41.7)
- Determination (see Paragraph 41.8)
- Boilerplate* (see Paragraph 41.9).

41.3 Grant of Rights

The Company will grant the Licensee the right, for a specified licence period, to develop a multimedia work of a prespecified nature based on the underlying work controlled by the Company. If the Licensee fails fully to develop the multimedia work, at the end of the period, its rights will terminate.

The Licensee will agree to consult with the Company at all times during the development of the work to ensure that the multimedia work will be faithful to the basic conceptualisation of the underlying work, reflect the same high standards of quality and adhere to the same portrayal of any characters portrayed in the underlying work.

The Company may have the right to approve certain basic qualities and characterisations, powers and accessories of characters. The Licensee will, however, normally, wish to have control of all creative and business matters relating to the development of the multimedia work. The Licensee may agree to consult with and give good faith consideration to the views of the Company in relation to the multimedia work.

41.4 Company's Warranties

The agreement may contain a number of warranties on the part of the Company:

Capacity to Contract

The Company is free to enter into the agreement and is the owner of the rights granted.

Copyright

The rights granted do not infringe any right of copyright or trademark or right of publicity or privacy or any other right.

Obscenity and Defamation

The underlying work is not obscene or defamatory.

41.5 Remuneration

The terms of the remuneration sections of agreements licensing multimedia rights vary widely, but may reflect those granted in option and purchase agreements (see Chapter 17). In view, however, of the fact that the primary medium for commercial distribution and exploitation of multimedia works remains off-line (ie in physical format) at the time of writing, it is possible the agreement may provide for remuneration by way of royalty on the sale of CD-Roms or CDs. These royalty provisions may incorporate "royalty breaks*" as used in typical recording industry contracts (see Chapter 1).

The Company will normally wish to limit the right of the Licensee to make deductions by way of withholding taxes*, if the Licensee is in another jurisdiction and require the Licensee to produce documentary evidence of its obligation to withhold sums. Additionally, the Company may require the Licensee to deposit any sums which cannot lawfully be transferred to the Company (so-called "blocked funds*") in an account in the name of the Company or its nominee in the Licensee's territory.

41.6 Licensee's Warranties

The agreement will contain a number of warranties on the part of the Licensee, which may include the following.

Reservation

All rights in the underlying work other than those specifically granted are reserved to the Company.

Marketing

The Licensee will complete the development of the work and commence its marketing by no later than a specified date. It will provide the Company with not less than a certain number of copies of the work in each format.

Copyright

The Licensee will not infringe or prejudice the copyright in the underlying work or violate any moral right and will ensure that all copies of the multimedia work and associated materials contain full and accurate copyright notices and credits.

Promotional Material

The Licensee will not create any promotional material or artwork without the consent of the Company.

Claims

The Licensee will give full particulars to the Company as soon as the Licensee becomes aware of any claim.

Prompt Payment

The Licensee will make prompt payment of all sums due.

No Assignment

The Licensee will not assign, license or sub-license any rights.

Commercial Release

The Licensee will release the multimedia work commercially by the date specified in the agreement and will maintain the multimedia work in distribution throughout the licence period.

Censorship

To the extent that the multimedia work is required to be submitted to any censorship authority in any territory the Licensee will submit the multimedia work and make all alterations required by law.

Liabilities

The Licensee will pay, in full, all sums required in relation to the production and or exploitation of the multimedia work, including any and all mechanical, synchronisation and other payments.

No Compilation

The Licensee will not permit the multimedia work to be coupled, compiled or issued as part of a package incorporating other multimedia works.

Promotion

The Licensee will promote and advertise the multimedia work throughout the territory in the same manner as other leading titles distributed by the Licensee.

Exploitation

The Licensee shall exploit the rights to the best of its skill and ability, with the view to ensuring the highest level possible of royalties.

No Discrimination

The Licensee will not discriminate against the multimedia work in favour of any other multimedia works.

Sell-Off

The Licensee will return to the Company, or destroy and provide an affidavit of destruction, any unsold multimedia works existing at the end of the licence period.

Indemnity

See Paragraph 53.16.

41.7   Royalty Accounting

See Paragraph 34.9.

41.8   Determination

See Paragraph 34.11.

41.9   Boilerplate

The boilerplate section of a typical agreement for the licensing of multimedia rights might contain the following provisions:

*   Notice (see Paragraph 52.8)
*   Force majeure (see Paragraph 52.4)
*   Entire agreement (see Paragraph 52.3)
*   No partnership (see Paragraph 52.7)
*   Governing law (see Paragraph 52.5).

F: Merchandising and Product Endorsement

42 Merchandising Agency Agreement

42.1 Description of a Merchandising Agency Agreement

A merchandising agency agreement* is a document pursuant to which the owner of the merchandising rights in a property appoints a third party to act as its agent in order to secure the best possible terms of exploiting the property throughout the world.

The parties to this particular transaction are:

- the owner of the rights which are to be exploited (the "Company"); and
- the party acting as agent to secure the exploitation of the rights (the "Agent").

42.2 Transaction Analysis

A typical merchandising agency agreement might be expected to contain the following clauses:

- Appointment of agent (see Paragraph 42.3)
- Agent's undertakings (see Paragraph 42.4)
- Company's warranty* (see Paragraph 42.5)
- Remuneration (see Paragraph 42.6)
- Determination (see Paragraph 42.7)
- Effect of determination (see Paragraph 42.8)
- Boilerplate* (see Paragraph 42.9).

42.3 Appointment of Agent

The legal concept of agency is one that has evolved over many centuries and imposes obligations on both parties to the relationship, even though these may not be specifically identified in a contract. Some of the relevant issues are referred to in Paragraph 33.3 and Paragraphs 54.26–54.29.

The appointment clause will appoint the Agent as the Company's sole or exclusive or sole and exclusive agent during the term* in order to negotiate, on behalf of the Company, licence agreements in respect of merchandising rights in a particular property throughout an identified territory.

In order to perform its function, the Agent will need to receive from the Company certain items in relation to the property (such as transparencies, style bible, approved sample merchandise etc) which the Company should agree to deliver.

The property may already be subject to existing licences, in which event, the Agent may undertake to liaise with existing licensees. Because the services of merchandising agents are often personal, the Company may make it a condition of the appointment that the Agent makes available the services of designated key personnel throughout the term.

42.4 Agent's Undertakings

A merchandising agency agreement will contain a number of undertakings on the part of the Agent, which might include the following.

Reservation of Rights

All rights in the property are reserved absolutely to the Company.

Copyright and Trademark

The Agent will not impair, prejudice or infringe the copyright or trademark or any right in the property.

Return of Material

The Agent will return all material provided at the end of the agreement.

Promotional Material

The Agent will not create any promotional or artwork material without the consent of the Company. All material created will belong to the Company.

License Agreements

The form of licence agreements will be approved by the Company and no other form will be used by the Agent.

Payment Direction

All licence agreements will contain irrevocable undertakings on the licensee to pay all sums to a designated collection account in the name of the Company. Whether or not this is appropriate will depend on what arrangements have been agreed between the Company and the Agent in relation to the collection of money. These will, in turn, depend on security factors in relation to the appointment of sales agents, which are referred to generally in Paragraph 33.8.

Notices

The Agent will not alter any of the credits, titles, copyright notices or trademarks in relation to the property.

Statements

The Agent will supply the Company with monthly or other statements of exploitation.

Claims

The Agent will give full particulars to the Company of any claims.

No Assignment

The Agent will not assign, license or sub-license any of its rights.

No Duplication

The Agent will not copy or duplicate any material otherwise than for the purpose of providing materials to licensees pursuant to license agreements.

Freight and Customs

The Agent will pay all freight and custom charges or ensure that they are paid by licensees under the licence agreements.

Control and Possession

The Agent will retain control and possession of all material delivered to it.

Replacement

The Agent will replace any material damaged.

Exploitation

The Agent will exploit the property to the best of the Agent's skill and ability in order to ensure the highest possible gross receipts.

No Discrimination

The Agent will ensure that the property is given fair and equitable treatment and is not discriminated against in favour of any other property.

Copyright and Trademark

The Agent will take all such steps as may be necessary or advisable to ensure that the copyright and trademark rights are protected throughout the territory.

Disrepute

The Agent will not harm or misuse the property, or bring it into disrepute

Prompt Payment

The Agent will, so far is practicable, procure the prompt payment by all licensees of all sums which they owe under licence agreements.

No Undisclosed Agency

The Agent is not itself the undisclosed agent of any third party.

No Credit

The Agent will not pledge the credit of the Company.

Confidentiality

The Agent will keep confidential all information relating to the agreement.

Indemnity

See Paragraph 53.16.

42.5 Company's Undertakings

Because the relationship of agent and principal already implies a number of undertakings and warranties on the part of the Company, the Agent may be sufficiently protected if the Company warrants that it has the right to enter into the agreement and has not entered into any arrangement which may conflict with it (see Paragraph 33.6 and Paragraphs 54.26–54.29).

42.6 Remuneration

The remuneration provisions under a merchandising agency agreement will normally entitle the Agent to commission for the Agent's labours, together with certain expenses.

The amount of the commission may vary between 15% and 20%. The Agent's ability to recover expenses will normally depend on it providing receipts or other vouchers as evidence that the expenditure has taken place. The amount of the expenditure may frequently be "capped" or fixed at a maximum limit.

42.7 Determination

The agreement will normally contain provisions entitling the Company to terminate if:

- the Agent is in breach of any material term which is incapable of remedy or any remediable term which is not remedied within a certain number of days from notice;
- any of the Agent's representations proves to be incorrect;
- the Agent transfers or disposes of part of its assets which is material in opinion of the Company;
- the Agent becomes insolvent or suffers the appointment of the receiver, liquidator, administrator or similar officer;
- the Agent abandons or announces that it intends to abandon the business of a merchandising agent.

On the occurrence of any of the above events, the Company will normally have the right to terminate the agreement.

42.8 Effect of Determination

On termination by the Company of its rights under the agreement, it is normal to provide that the Company may retake possession of all delivery material and enter into the Agent's premises and that the Agent's right to receive commission or other income under licence agreements will end. In circumstances where an Agent has paid substantial sums to the Company by way of advance*, in some cases, the Company may be prepared to accept that the Agent will have the right to recoup such sums—but not ongoing commissions.

42.9 Boilerplate

The boilerplate section of a typical merchandising agency agreement might contain the following provisions:

- Force majeure (see Paragraph 52.4)
- Assignment (see Paragraph 52.1)
- Notices (see Paragraph 52.8)
- Severability (see Paragraph 52.10)
- Entire agreement (see Paragraph 52.3)
- Waiver (see Paragraph 52.11)
- No partnership (see Paragraph 52.3)
- Governing law (see Paragraph 52.5).

43 Merchandising Licence Agreement

43.1 Description of a Merchandising Licence Agreement

The merchandising licence agreement* is an agreement under which the owner of a particular property (a literary or artistic work or film) licenses a manufacturer to make certain goods incorporating elements of the property.

The parties to the transaction are:

*   the owner of the property being merchandised (the "Company"); and
*   the party acquiring the merchandising rights (the "Licensee").

43.2 Transaction Analysis

A typical merchandising licence agreement might be expected to contain the following clauses:

*   Grant of rights (see Paragraph 43.3)
*   Company's warranties* (see Paragraph 43.4)
*   Remuneration (see Paragraph 43.5)
*   Distribution (see Paragraph 43.6)
*   Third party infringement (see Paragraph 43.7)
*   Quality and design of licensed product (see Paragraph 43.8)
*   Labelling (see Paragraph 43.9)
*   Promotional material (see Paragraph 43.10)
*   Enhancements (see Paragraph 43.11)
*   Payment (see Paragraph 43.12)
*   Accounting (see Paragraph 43.13)
*   Determination (see Paragraph 43.14)
*   Effect of determination (see Paragraph 43.15)
*   Boilerplate* (see Paragraph 43.16).

43.3 Grant of Rights

The rights acquired by the Licensee are the right to manufacture, the right to advertise and the right to sell product of a generic type (such as yoghurt) incorporating elements of a literary or artistic property (such as Roger

Hargreaves' "Mr Men") owned by the Company. The generic product incorporating the property manufactured by the Licensee (yoghurt pots featuring "Mr Men" characters) is generally referred to as the "licensed product".

The agreement will grant to the Licensee the non-exclusive right to manufacture licensed product in a defined territory during a specified term* or licence period, together with the exclusive right to package, market and sell the licensed product in the territory during the term. The reason why the manufacturing right may be non-exclusive is to permit the Company to allow other licensees to use factories in the territory to manufacture items of product. This may not always be appropriate.

In addition to granting the right to manufacture and sell licensed product, the Company will agree to enter into a licence with the Licensee in order to protect any trademarks relating to the property.

43.4 Company's Warranties

The warranties which might be given on the part of the Company in a merchandising licence agreement, might include the following.

Capacity to Contract

The Company has the right to enter into the agreement and grant the rights.

Ownership

The Company is the owner of the rights

Non-infringement

None of the rights in the property infringes any right of copyright, trademark or any other right.

43.5 Remuneration

The remuneration provisions will normally provide that the Company is to receive a non-returnable advance*, together with a royalty*, which will normally be a percentage of the wholesale or retail price of all items of licensed product manufactured by the Licensee. The advance will normally be recoupable from sums payable by way of royalty.

43.6 Distribution

The merchandising licence agreement will contain a number of warranties on the part of the Licensee, which may include the following.

356

Capacity to Contract

The Licensee is free to enter into the agreement.

Trademark and Copyright Infringement

The Licensee will not do, or permit there to be done, anything which might infringe or invalidate any trademark, right, copyright or other right.

Product Liability Insurance

The Licensee will maintain, at its own expense, product liability insurance and note the name of the Company as named insured.

Protection of Property

The Licensee will take all necessary or advisable steps to secure or protect the property and the trademark and any rights of copyright.

No Sale or Return

The Licensee will not sell any items of licensed product on a sale or return or stock-balancing basis.

Claims

The Licensee will advise the Company immediately of any third party claim.

Marketing

The Licensee will commence marketing of the licensed product within not less than a specified number of months after delivery of delivery materials.

Advertisement

The Licensee will advertise the licensed product throughout the territory during the term and, in each year, spend not less than a predesignated amount of advertising expenditure.

Exploitation

The Licensee will exploit the rights to the best of its skill and ability in accordance with the Company's pricing policies from time to time.

Manufacturing Costs

No manufacturing costs or distribution or other costs will be deducted from the royalty payable to the Company.

Minimum Levels

The Licensee will ensure that sales of the licensed product are in excess of certain minimum specified levels for specified periods.

No Premiums

The Licensee will not enter into any arrangement where any item of product is offered to the public in connection with sale or promotion of another product or services, so as to promote the other product or services or their manufacture.

Disrepute

The Licensee will not do anything to harm the property or bring it into disrepute.

Defects

The Licensee will not knowingly manufacture or distribute any defective or sub-standard item of product.

Prompt Payment

The Licensee will promptly pay all sums due to the Company.

No Assignment

The Licensee will not assign or license or sub-license any of the rights.

Indemnity

See Paragraph 53.16.

43.7 Third Party Infringement

The agreement will normally provide that, if the Licensee becomes aware of any infringement of the property or the licensed product, it will take all steps necessary to prevent such infringement. Whether or not the Licensee is to have the right to commence proceedings in its own name, how the costs of the proceedings are to be shared and how the compensation by way of damages is to be divided may also be specified in the agreement, depending on what is agreed between the parties.

43.8 Quality and Design of the Licensed Product

The Licensee will agree with the Company that the licensed product will be of a sufficient high standard, style, appearance and quality so as to be adequate and suited to the exploitation to the best advantage of the property and the protection and enhancement of the value of the property and the goodwill relating to it.

The Licensee will also normally provide that the licensed product will be fully compliant with all applicable laws and regulations and that its distribution policy will be consistent with earning the highest possible royalties and making available product of the highest possible standard, so as not to reflect in any adverse manner on the good name of the Company.

The Licensee will normally agree to provide the Company with a designated number of samples for approval before manufacture. The Company's approval right should extend to all cartons, containers, packaging and wrapping material, as well as any publicity and advertising material, all of which should be required to be of the same high quality as specified above.

Additionally, the Licensee should provide the Company with samples of the licensed product from time to time, in order to verify consistency and should also permit the Company, or its authorised representative, to inspect the method of manufacture of the licensed product, the materials used, and its packaging and storage.

43.9 Labelling

The agreement will normally specify what copyright notices and trademark notices are to be applied on items of licensed product and associated packaging.

The Licensee will also acknowledge that it has not obtained any interest in the property or the trademark, other than the licence to manufacture licensed property and it will confirm that all goodwill relating to the trademark and the property belongs to the Company.

43.10 Promotional Material

The Licensee will agree that all artwork and publicity material relating to the property is to be submitted to the Company for its approval before it is used and will confirm that the Company will acquire ownership of such material. This is required in order to permit the Company to make this material available to other licensees in other territories, where appropriate.

43.11   Enhancements

It is not unknown for licensees of rights to enhance, in some manner, the product for which they are initially licensed. For this reason, many agreements provide that, if the Licensee discovers some means of enhancing the property, then all rights in respect of such enhancement will belong to the Company, subject to the Licensee's licence for the territory and term granted to it in the agreement.

It is also not uncommon to find that a merchandising licence agreement may contain a provision restricting the Licensee from the manufacture or selling of any item or product which is similar to the licensed property, since this could cause confusion in the marketplace.

43.12   Payment

See Paragraph 34.8.

43.13   Accounting

See Paragraph 34.9.

43.14   Determination

See Paragraph 42.7.

43.15   Effect of Determination

See Paragraph 42.8.

43.16   Boilerplate

The boilerplate section of a typical merchandising licence agreement might contain the following provisions:

*   Force majeure (see Paragraph 52.4)
*   Notices (see Paragraph 52.8)
*   Severability (see Paragraph 52.10)
*   Entire agreement (see Paragraph 52.3)
*   Waiver (see Paragraph 52.11)
*   No partnership (see Paragraph 52.7)
*   Governing law (see Paragraph 52.5).

44 Product Endorsement Agreement

44.1 Description of Product Endorsement Agreement

In a product endorsement agreement*, a company which manufactures a product acquires the services of private individual to endorse or publicise and or promote the product.

The parties to this particular transaction are:

- the company which manufactures the product being endorsed (the "Company"); and
- the artist endorsing the product (the "Artist").

44.2 Transaction Analysis

A typical product endorsement agreement might be expected to contain the following clauses:

- Artist's services (see Paragraph 44.3)
- Grant of rights (see Paragraph 44.4)
- Remuneration (see Paragraph 44.5)
- Expenses (see Paragraph 44.6)
- Payment (see Paragraph 44.7)
- Artist's warranties* (see Paragraph 44.8)
- Conduct (see Paragraph 44.9)
- Restriction (see Paragraph 44.10)
- Insurance (see Paragraph 44.11)
- Suspension (see Paragraph 44.12)
- Effect of suspension (see Paragraph 44.13)
- Termination (see Paragraph 44.14)
- Effect of termination (see Paragraph 44.15)
- Boilerplate* (see Paragraph 44.16).

44.3 Artist's Services

The agreement will specify the precise services which the Artist is to render and the period or periods during which they are to be rendered. Obviously, the type of services required is capable of wide variation, but, if audio-visual recording services are required, the number of days of principal photography, wardrobe fittings and post-production will be specified. Additionally, the Company may require the services of the Artist to be available for a photo shoot for printed materials and the Company may require the services of the Artist for a product launch or for personal appearances.

Depending on the nature and the extent of the campaign, the Company may wish to have options to engage the services of the Artist for a second, third or fourth year of the campaign and, if options are required, the appropriate contractual provisions should be built in (see Chapter 1).

44.4 Grant of Rights

A product endorsement agreement will normally provide expressly that the Company is the owner of all audio and audio-visual material which it makes featuring the services of the Artist. Where the Artist is a well-known recording artist, it will probably be necessary to obtain the consent of the Artist's record company (see Chapter 1). Where the Artist contributes in any way to audio or audio-visual elements of the script, it may also be necessary to obtain the consent of the Artist's publishing company (see Chapter 2).

The agreement will also provide confirmation that the Artist has given all consents required in relation to the performances of the Artist incorporated in whatever commercials are produced in order to promote the product, as well as an irrevocable waiver of any moral rights* of the Artist in relation to any original work created by the Artist. These provisions are standard.

The agreement will provide that the Company and its successors and licensees has the right to use the name, likeness, photograph, voice, silhouette and all other elements of the Artist in connection with the endorsement of the relevant product.

44.5 Remuneration

The remuneration provisions for product endorsement agreements are obviously subject to a wide number of variations. The essential point, from the Company's point of view, is that the Artist should perform the services before being eligible to receive remuneration, since, if the services are not fully performed, the Company will not have the benefit of any end-product.

For this reason, most product endorsement agreements will make the Artist's entitlement to remuneration conditional on full and entire performance and observance by the Artist of all material obligations and warranties in the agreement.

44.6 Expenses

The expense provisions of product endorsement agreements for artists are often complicated. In some cases, they will be determined by the Artist's personal circumstances or family ties and transportation and accommodation arrangements may be required to be made in respect of the artist's entourage.

Normally, the expenses clause in a product endorsement agreement is the most heavily negotiated. Questions of whether round-trip airline fares should be first class or club class or should be return Los Angeles or return New York or for two people or 16 people and whether the Company should be obliged not only to pick up hotel accommodation, but also meals and drinks, or whether a US $150 per diem fee is adequate or not, or whether a 24-hour rest period to get over jet lag before principal photography is sufficient, seem to occupy a disproportionate degree of time in negotiating product endorsement arrangements.

The importance of arrangements relating to the Artist's personal welfare is, however, entirely understandable when the product endorsement agreement is considered from the point of view of the Artist. It is normally something which is not central to the Artist's career. Agreements of this type are one of the few opportunities that Artists have to demand and insist on what they really want.

44.7 Payment

See Paragraph 20.11.

44.8 Artist's Warranties and Obligations

A product endorsement agreement will normally contain a number of warranties and obligations on the part of the Artist, which may include the following.

Capacity to Contract

The Artist is free to enter into the agreement and grant the Company the rights granted in it. It should be noted that, where the Artist wishes to make their services available through a service company, an inducement letter (see Paragraph 51.2) will normally be required.

No Restriction

The Artist is not under any disability, restriction or prohibition which might prevent the Artist form rendering the services or observing any obligations.

Exclusivity

The services will not be made available to any other person during the term* of the agreement.

No Conflict

The Artist has not entered and will not enter into any arrangement which may conflict with the agreement.

Adaptation

The Company will have the right to alter, adapt, change, revise, delete from, add to and/or rearrange the whole or any part of the performances, recordings, photographs and other products of the services of the Artist and substitute or combine the same with any other material to the extent the Company requires. In the event the Company elects to do so, the Artist shall not have any claim for compensation for loss of opportunity to enhance professional reputation or for any other reason at all.

Professionalism

The Artist will render their services to the best of their skill and ability in a professional and workmanlike manner, in willing co-operation with others, in accordance with the requirements of the Company, will observe all call times and do everything within their capacity to ensure performance is of first-class quality.

Confidentiality

The Artist will not, without the consent in writing of the Company, reveal or make public any financial or other information relating to the agreement.

Health

The Artist is in a good state of health and will take all practical steps to maintain such state in order to ensure the full and proper performance of the services and in order to enable the Company to effect insurance on the Artist.

Hazardous Activities

The Artist will not, during the period of the agreement, participate in any hazardous or dangerous pursuits or voluntarily take any risks which might prevent the Artist from being ready to perform the services and, in particular, will not take part in any motor-racing, skiing, hang-gliding, climbing etc.

Fit Condition

The Artist will be present and in a condition fit to render services at such locations as are specified by the Company at the date and hour notified in advance.

Portrayal

The Company will have the exclusive right to decide on all aspects relating to the portrayal of the Artist on screen and in advertising material and in particular, in relation to the Artist's dress, make-up, hair, beard etc.

Third Parties

The Company will have the right to make the services of the Artist available to third parties. The Artist will co-operate fully and follow all lawful directions and instructions of such third parties.

Whereabouts

The Artist will, at all times throughout the engagement period, ensure that the Company is informed of the whereabouts and telephone number of the Artist.

Regulations

The Artist will, at all times, comply with all safety, fire prevention and union regulations and all other rules and regulations relating to the services and the locations at which they are provided.

Indemnity

See Paragraph 53.16.

44.9 Conduct

The conduct provision is of material importance to a product endorsement agreement. Normally, an agreement will provide that the Artist will not, during any term of the engagement, do any act which might bring the Artist, the

Company or the product into public disrepute or offend community or public morals or prejudice the Company or the exploitation of the product. Additionally, the agreement may provide that the Artist shall, at all times throughout the engagement, respect public conventions and morals.

In recent times, companies have also shown a desire to protect themselves from the Artist being placed in the public spotlight, not by reason of any act or omission of the Artist during the term of the engagement, but by reason of the Artist's prior history. It may be considered normal for the conduct clause to extend to past conduct of the Artist, as well as conduct during the engagement.

44.10   Restriction

The restriction provision clause is one of the most important clauses in a product endorsement agreement from the point of view of the Company. The basis of the entire arrangement is that the Company is acquiring the services of the Artist to endorse a specific item or items of the Company's product. It is therefore essential that the Artist will not provide any services in connection with any other item of competing product.

The period during which the Artist is prevented from providing such services extends before the commencement of the engagement (because advertising and publicity material sometimes takes a few months or years to be made available), will continue throughout the term of the Artist's services and may also continue for a number of months or years after the end of the campaign term, in order to allow any advertising and publicity material to be fully exploited by the Company.

The obligation on the part of the Artist is to ensure that the Artist's personality, name and likeness is not used in connection with any competing item of product. The question of what is and is not a competing item of product is one which needs to be considered very carefully and the restriction accepted by the Artist needs to be absolutely clear and unambiguous.

44.11   Insurance

See Paragraph 20.17.

44.12   Suspension

See Paragraph 20.18.

44.13   Effect of Suspension

See Paragraph 20.19.

44.14   Termination

See Paragraph 20.20.

44.15   Effect of Termination

See Paragraph 20.21.

44.16   Boilerplate

The boilerplate section of a typical product endorsement agreement might contain the following provisions:

* No obligation (see Paragraph 52.6)
* Notices (see Paragraph 52.8)
* Severability (see Paragraph 52.10)
* Assignability (see Paragraph 52.1)
* Entire agreement (see Paragraph 52.3)
* Waiver (see Paragraph 52.11)
* No partnership (see Paragraph 52.7)
* Governing law (see Paragraph 52.5).

45 Product Placement Agreement

45.1 Description of a Product Placement Agreement

The purpose of a product placement agreement* is to place a particular item of product in a particularly conspicuous manner within a designated scene or scenes in a film or television programme, so that the product is brought to the attention of the audience and associated with the characters in the film or programme.

The parties to this particular transaction are:

- the company which makes the particular product being placed (the "Company"); and
- the producer* producing the film or programme in which the product is to be placed (the "Producer").

45.2 Transaction Analysis

It is difficult to generalise on the contents of the "average product placement agreement, since each agreement tends to be drafted specifically with reference to the particular item of product and the particular film or programme in which it is to be placed, but some of the following clauses might be included:

- Grant of rights (see Paragraph 45.3)
- Product (see Paragraph 45.4)
- Remuneration (see Paragraph 45.5)
- Production expenses (see Paragraph 45.6)
- Advertisements (see Paragraph 45.7)
- Company's name (see Paragraph 45.8)
- Indemnity* (see Paragraph 45.9)
- Insurance (see Paragraph 45.10)
- Termination (see Paragraph 45.11)
- Boilerplate* (see Paragraph 45.12)

45.3 Grant of Rights

The Producer will normally grant the Company the right to place and promote the name of the Company and its product in the film, subject to the performance by the Company of its obligations.

45.4 Product

The Company will undertake to provide the Producer with a designated number of real items of product (which may bear the Company's name and logo in a position determined by the Company) which are intended to be used by the Producer for the filming of certain designated scenes which will be included within the film.

The Producer may require models for items of the product, in advance of principal photography, in order to meet the needs of production. The Company may require the Producer to ensure that the designated items of product will be featured in the film, as released for general theatrical release, in such a manner that the Company's name and logo shall be clearly and legible to a viewer of the film, not only in cinemas, but also on television and by means of video.

The Company may also require approval of storyboards of the particular scenes in the film in which the Company's product appears and will require the Producer to shoot the film and the items of product in accordance with the storyboards.

The Company will normally wish to receive a screen credit, in which the Producer gratefully acknowledges the support of the Company in the making of the film, and will wish to receive an absolute obligation from the Producer or its distributor to the effect that the film will receive a commercially viable theatrical release in the principal territories in which the Company's product is marketed.

As a final protection/precaution, the Company may wish to provide that all discarded shots of scenes incorporating the Company's products are delivered to the Company or destroyed, but whether this provision is acceptable or not is a matter for commercial negotiation.

45.5 Remuneration

The remuneration provisions of placement agreements vary very widely. They may consist simply of a straight cash payment made by the Company to the Producer. Alternatively, they may take the form of a commitment on the part of the Company to purchase television and newspaper advertisements featuring the film and the Company's product in it within a six-week period before first commercial release of the film.

Such advertisements will generate heightened consumer perception of the film in the marketplace and may maximise the gross receipts to be derived from the film, thus providing a more effective return to the Producer than if the Company had simply provided the Producer with the equivalent amount in cash.

45.6   Production Expenses

It would be normal to expect the Producer to agree that all costs and expenses incurred in relation to the filming of the Company's product will be the responsibility of the Producer, not the Company.

45.7   Competing Product and Advertisements

A specific point of concern for the Company is to ensure that no other competing product or advertisement for any competing product is included in the film. The Company may, additionally, require assurance that the Producer will not include or feature in any part of the film the name or logo or brand name of any competitor.

This will mean that the Producer, when shooting on location, will need to ensure that, for example, advertisements on the side of buses, trains etc do not feature a competing product.

45.8   Company Name

The agreement will also normally contain provisions in relation to the Company's name itself. The Producer may require an assurance that the Company name does not infringe any right of trademark or any other right.

The Company, for its part, will require an acknowledgement from the Producer that it has not obtained any right, title or interest in or to the Company's name or any logo of the Company or any item of the Company's product.

45.9   Indemnity

The agreement may contain a mutual indemnity from both parties. See Paragraph 53.16.

45.10   Insurance

The question of insurance in relation to items of the Company's product and the Producer's use of the product also needs to be addressed in the agreement.

45.11   Termination

The Company will normally have the right to terminate the agreement and be suspended from the obligation to make further payments to the Producer and be entitled to receive repayment of sums already paid, as well as remuneration for the provision of items of the Company's product if certain events occur.

The relevant events may include:

- failure of the Producer to release the film in key markets within a specified period from the date of the agreement;
- failure of the Producer to ensure that the Company's product is featured in accordance with the agreement;
- other material breach of the Producer of its obligations in the agreement;
- insolvency, winding-up or similar appointment of a receiver or administrator or other analogous officer;
- abandonment or cessation by the Producer of production of the film; or
- take-over by a completion guarantor.

45.12   Boilerplate

The boilerplate section of a typical product placement agreement may contain the following provisions:

- Assignment (see Paragraph 52.1)
- No partnership (see Paragraph 52.7)
- Governing law (see Paragraph 52.5).

G: Publishing

46 Author's Agreement

46.1 Description of an Author's Agreement

The author's agreement* is one of the three key agreements in the publishing world (the others are agreements for the acquisition and licensing of rights, examined in Chapters 47 and 48). It is the means by which a publishing company commissions and acquires rights in original literary works. In the United Kingdom, the Society of Authors and the Writer's Guild of Great Britain have negotiated with many book publishers a standard minimum terms agreement which provides that rights in works by members of the WGGB or Society of Authors are licensed to publishers, as opposed to being assigned (see Paragraph 53.2) for a specified period of years.

The minimum terms agreement also provides certain minimum basic royalty obligations, and many United Kingdom publishers now ensure that their commissioning agreements incorporate terms agreed to in the minimum terms agreement.

The parties to an author's agreement are:

- the publishing company acquiring the rights in the work being written (the "Publisher"); and
- the author of the work (the "Author").

46.2 Transaction Analysis

A typical author's agreement might be expected to contain the following clauses:

- Description of the work (see Paragraph 46.3)
- Editing, corrections and author's credits (see Paragraph 46.4)
- Publication (see Paragraph 46.5)
- Promotion (see Paragraph 46.6)
- Advance* (see Paragraph 46.7)
- Royalties* (see Paragraph 46.8)
- Specific royalty provisions (see Paragraph 46.9)

- Rights (see Paragraph 46.10)
- Subsidiary rights (see Paragraph 46.11)
- Author's warranties (see Paragraph 46.12)
- Accounts (see Paragraph 46.13)
- Acceptance and rejection (see Paragraph 46.14)
- Remainder sales and recapture (see Paragraph 46.15)
- Actions for infringement (see Paragraph 46.16)
- Alternative dispute resolution (see Paragraph 46.17)
- Termination (see Paragraph 46.18)
- Boilerplate* (see Paragraph 46.19).

46.3 Description of the Work

The agreement will normally describe the type of work involved, specify the length by number of words or pages of text , identify whether illustrations are required and whether these are to be original to the Author or selected by the Author in consultation with the Publisher.

The agreement will also specify the date by which the Author is to deliver the work and will specify exactly what material the Publisher is anticipating to receive. Normally, this will take the form of clearly typed typescripts that some authors may wish to deliver as manuscript material. The agreement will normally provide that the Author is required to keep a copy of any material submitted to the Publisher, as well as providing that in the event of loss of material, the Publisher will have no liability to the Author.

Where the Author is using third party material such as photographs or illustrations or quoting from published works, it is normally the responsibility of the Author to obtain releases or permissions in a form satisfactory to the Publisher. The cost of illustrations and third party material will normally be paid for by the Publisher up to a prespecified limit and costs in addition to that will be borne by the Author.

The agreement will also contain provisions relating to the preparation of an index (if this is appropriate) and will state how the costs of preparation are to be borne—whether they are to be shared between the Author and the Publisher or paid by the Publisher alone—and may also provide for an upper limit on the costs of creating an index.

46.4 Editing, Corrections and Author's Credit

The agreement will normally provide that the Publisher will have the right to notify the Author of the changes which the Publisher thinks should be made to the work. It will also frequently provide that the Publisher will consult with the Author in relation to copy editing the work, illustrations, jacket design, introduction and cover notes.

The Author is usually required to check and correct all proofs of the work and return them to the Publisher within 21 days from receipt. Agreements often provide that the Author is responsible for bearing the cost of corrections and alterations to proofs, other than printer's errors when this is in excess of 10% of the cost of compositional typesetting of the work. This provision is intended to discourage the Author from making extensive last-minute revisions and is not often invoked by Publishers.

The copyright notice, which will appear on the introductory pages of the work, will be determined by whether the copyright is assigned to the Publisher or licensed. If the copyright is the subject of an exclusive licence, the copyright notice will remain in the name of the Author. If the Author has decided to assert his or her right to be identified (see Paragraph 53.10), the introductory pages will contain a statement to this effect. The agreement will also normally provide that the Publisher will provide that the Author receives credit on the title page of the work in a certain form and will provide that no casual or inadvertent failure on the part of the Publisher will amount to a breach of this obligation.

Normally, the Publisher will acquire the right to make all alterations to the text of a work, to make corrections and, in some cases to make the text conform to the Publisher's house style and also for the purposes of authorising translations or removing any material which might be actionable at law. Many agreement contain provisions where the Author's consents to the Publisher doing such things.

Some agreements provide that the Publisher will not change the title of the work in the British or Commonwealth market. Some also provide that the Publisher will disclose to the Author the size of all print-runs of the work. If it is necessary to have the work read by a legal advisor, the agreement should determine how the costs are to be shared between the Author and the Publisher.

46.5 Publication

From a Publisher's point of view, undertaking to publish a work before it has been received may involve an element of risk. Therefore, in those agreements where publishers undertake to publish a work, this undertaking is frequently conditional on full performance by the Author of his or her obligations under the agreement and also conditional on the Publisher accepting the work. In such circumstances, if the Publisher decides to reject the work, it will follow that the Publisher will automatically be relieved of this obligation to publish it.

The agreement may state the number of copies which the Publisher intends to print in hardback and/or paperback format and indicate the anticipated retail price. In agreements where these indications are given, it is also normal for the Publisher to add that they do not constitute obligations on the part of the Publisher in relation to the print run, the pricing of the first run or any subsequent run of the work.

The agreement will normally provide that the Publisher will consult with and advise the Author of the proposed publication date. This is helpful in circumstances where the Author's services in relation to promotion of the work are required. Most agreements also provide that the Author is to be entitled to a certain number of free copies of the work.

46.6 Promotion

Depending on the type of work, it is appropriate in some agreements for the Publisher to require the Author to supply the Publisher with details of persons and periodicals who might be suitable recipients of review copies of the work and to provide other information which might assist the Publisher in publicising and advertising the work.

The Publisher will normally acquire the right to use the name, likeness and biography of the Author in advertising and publicity material for the purpose of promoting the work, but not for the purpose of product endorsement.

46.7 Advance

It is normal in publishing agreements to pay advances* to the Author.

Normally, advances are payable in two or three instalments: a certain percentage on signature of the agreement, a certain percentage on delivery and acceptance of the work and a certain percentage on first publication.

Whether the advance is returnable or non-returnable will depend on the circumstances. If the advance is not stated to be non-returnable, then, if the author fails to deliver material, the Publisher may be able to seek repayment of it. Normally, an advance is intended to be recoupable from royalty obligations.

46.8 Royalties

An analysis of the current minimum terms agreement reveals a number of common features which might be considered to be prevailing commercial practice in the publishing industry in the United Kingdom. These are set out below.

Advance

The advance normally equals 65% of the estimated Author's receipts, or 55% of estimated Author's receipts if the agreement is for both hardback and all paperback rights. In order to calculate the estimated Author's receipts, the total estimated sales or print-run of the work should be multiplied by the royalty percentage, royalty rate and estimated retail price.

Hardback Royalties

Hardback royalties are 10% of the published price of the first 2,500 copies, 12.5% of the next 2,500, and 15% after that. Some agreements provide for a variation on sales at discounts of 45% or 50%.

Hardback Licenses

There are two approaches for dealing with royalties on hardback licences. Either the Publisher's receipts are shared in the proportions 60/40, in the Author's favour, or the Author is paid a royalty of 10% for the first 1,500–2,000 copies, 12.5% on the next 2,000 copies and 15% after that.

Paperback Licences

Royalties on paperback licences are expressed as a percentage of the publisher's receipts. The applicable percentage is 60% to the Author and 40% to the Publisher, up to a point to be negotiated, and 70% to the Author and 30% to the Publisher after that.

Book Clubs

Three different bases and percentages exist, namely, 7% of the book club list priced on the first 10,000 copies and 10% after that; or 10% of publisher's receipts on bound copies or sheets sold to the book club; or 60% of the Publisher's receipts on copies of books printed by the book club.

46.9 Specific Royalty Provisions

Some agreements provide that, where the Publisher sub-licenses rights to a US publisher or sells sheets or bound copies, the Publisher retains a percentage commission and pays the balance to the Author.

Most agreements contain a small reprints exemption. This provides that where a reprint is ordered by the Publisher of 1,500 copies or another agreed figure, the royalty paid to the Author remains at the lowest rate and the number of books in the so-called small reprint are not taken into account for the purpose of calculating whether an increased royalty is payable.

Most publishing agreements also provide that the Publisher is not obliged to pay royalties to the Author on copies of the work sold or given to the Author or distributed for the purposes of publicity, advertising, distributed as review copies or on copies of the work which are lost or destroyed, for which the Publisher does not receive payment.

46.10 Rights

The publishing agreement will normally assign or licence to the Publisher (see Paragraph 53.2) the right to exploit the work in volume form throughout a specified territory for a designated period, which will either be the full copyright period or an agreed licence period.

In those cases where an Author is a member of the Authors' Licensing and Collecting Society Limited, it is permissible for the Author to reserve reprographic rights and also to reserve public lending rights. These reservations are normally acceptable to a Publisher since the ALCS licenses reprographic rights controlled by Authors to the Copyright Licensing Agency and the Publishers' Association similarly licenses reprographic rights controlled by Publishers to the Copyright Licensing Agency. When the CLA grants licenses for photocopying of works the money is divided 50-50 between Publishers and the ALCS.

46.11 Subsidiary Rights

Some publishing agreements make provision for Publishers to participate in what is referred to as subsidiary rights. There are a number of various types of subsidiary rights which are set out below. An analysis of the minimum terms agreements indicates the percentages of receipts derived from subsidiary rights which major Publishers are prepared to pay to authors and these are also set out below:

Anthology and quotation rights	60%
Digest rights	75%
First serial rights	90%
Merchandising rights	80%
Motion picture and television rights	90%
Paperback rights	60% rising to 70% at points to be negotiated
Reading rights	75%
Second and subsequent serial rights	75%
Single issue rights	75%
Transaction rights	80%
US rights	80%

46.12 Author's Warranties

An author's agreement will usually contain a number of warranties and undertakings on the part of an Author, which may include the following.

Sole Author and Owner

The Author is the sole author of the work and is the sole, absolute, unincumbered legal and beneficial owner of all rights of copyright in the work and was at all material times, when the work was written, a qualifying person for the purposes of United Kingdom copyright legislation.

No Incumbrances

The Author has not assigned, incumbered or otherwise licensed, transferred or disposed of any rights granted to the Publisher and has not entered into any conflicting agreement.

Originality and Non-infringement

The work is original to the Author and does not infringe any right of copyright, moral right, right of privacy, right of publicity or personality.

Obscenity, Secrecy, Blasphemy

The work is not obscene or blasphemous or offensive to religion or defamatory. It does not contain any material which has been obtained in violation of the Interception of Communications Act or the Official Secrets Act or any analogous foreign legislation. Nothing contained in the work would, if published, constitute a contempt of court.

Factually Correct

All statements purporting to be facts in the work are true and correct and no advice, formula or instruction would, if followed, cause loss, damage or injury.

No Claim

There is no present or prospective claim or litigation in relation to the work or its title or ownership.

Copyright

Copyright in the work is valid and subsisting for the full period of copyright provided under international conventions.

Confidentiality

The Author will not disclose, reveal or make public any information relating to the business of the Publisher or the agreement without the consent of the Publisher.

Indemnity

See Paragraph 53.16.

46.13 Accounts

Because many Authors are represented by agents, the author's agreement will normally contain an agency direction requiring all payments to be made to the Author's agent and confirming that receipt by the Agent shall be deemed to be receipt by the Author

In the publishing world, statements of account are rendered normally within 90 days from 30 June and 31 December in each year. In some instances, a publisher may wish to have the right to maintain a reserve against returned books where, for example, paperbacks have been supplied on a sale or return basis. If a reserve is maintained, the agreement should contain a provision stating when the balance of the reserve remaining after adjustments for returned books is to be liquidated and paid to the Author.

Many publishing agreements will contain a provision permitting the Publisher to deduct withholding taxes* and providing that, if the Publisher is in receipt of sums which foreign exchange control provisions prevent being remitted, the Publisher will, if requested by the Author, place their sums in such accounts as may be designated by the Author.

46.14 Acceptance and Rejection

The Author's agreement will normally provide an established procedure for acceptance or rejection of the typescript. The agreement may provide that the Publisher has the right to request the Author to make certain revisions. It will also probably provide that, if the work contains any material which, in the opinion of the Publisher, might be actionable or damage the Publisher's reputation or business interests, the Publisher will have the right to reject the work or give the Author notice requesting changes to be made.

If the Author fails to deliver a typescript of the work revised to incorporate such revisions and amendments as the Publisher requests, the Publisher will have the right to reject the work. If rejection occurs as a result of failure or an ability of the Author to make changes in the agreement may provide that sums previously paid to the Author by way of advance are repayable to the Publisher on demand.

46.15 Remainder Sales and Recapture

Some authors' agreements contain provisions entitling the Author to acquire copies of the work which are to be disposed of at a remainder price.

Additionally, some Publishers agree that if all editions of the work published by them, although licensees are out of print or, if over a two-year period, annual sales of the work are less than a pre-specified number that the Author is entitled to give the Publisher notice in writing requiring the Publisher to indicate whether or not it intends to reprint or reissue the work. If the Publisher fails to give notice that it intends to reprint or reissue the work, then the rights revert to the Author at the end of a pre-specified period.

46.16 Actions for Infringement

Although infringement actions in relation to books are relatively rare, there are good reasons for including in an author's agreement a provision dealing with what happens if a third party infringes the copyright in the Author's book. The agreement may provide that the Publisher is authorised to take proceedings and recover the costs of proceedings from any damages awarded and share a pre-agreed percentage of the balance with the Author.

46.17 Alternative Dispute Resolution

Alternative dispute resolution provisions are becoming increasingly common in contracts. Some authors' agreements will contain provisions which apply if any dispute arises between the parties, giving them the right to resolve the dispute through a resolution procedure carried out in accordance with the recommendations of the Centre for Dispute Resolution.

Most agreements containing alternative dispute resolution proceedings will provide that, if attempts to resolve fail within a certain number of days, then either party will have the right to exercise their rights at law.

46.18 Termination

The author's agreement will normally contain a right, on the part of the Author to terminate the agreement if the Publisher is in breach of any material obligation and has not remedied such a breach to the extent possible within 30 days of notice being given. Termination on the part of the Author may be expressed to be without prejudice to the continued existence of any licence or any sub-licence granted by the Publisher, as well as the right of the Author to receive remuneration from the Publisher and claims by the Author against the Publishers as of the date of termination.

46.19 Boilerplate

The boilerplate section of a typical author's agreement might be expected to contain the following provisions:

- Notices (see Paragraph 52.8)
- Force majeure (see Paragraph 52.4)
- Entire agreement (see Paragraph 52.3)
- No partnership (see Paragraph 52.7)
- Governing law (see Paragraph 52.5).

47 Rights Acquisition Agreement

47.1 Description of a Rights Acquisition Agreement

The rights acquisition agreement* is an agreement under which a publisher acquires, from the owner of rights in a copyright work, the right to print, publish and distribute the work (and possibly sell subsidiary rights in the work throughout the world or throughout designated territories) for a specific period of time.

The provisions of a rights acquisition agreement are almost identical to those of an author's agreement. The main difference is that the person contracting with the publisher will not itself be the author of the work, but will be a person who has acquired rights from the author. The person contracting with the publisher may, in fact, be another publisher who has acquired the works from an author under an authors agreement.

The parties to this particular transaction are:

- the owner of the work being assigned or licensed (referred to as the "Proprietor"); and
- the publisher acquiring the rights in the work (the "Publisher").

47.2 Transaction Analysis

A typical rights acquisition agreement might be expected to contain the following clauses:

- Grant of rights (see Paragraph 47.3)
- Notices and credits (see Paragraph 47.4)
- Publication and promotion (see Paragraph 47.5)
- Advances* and Royalties* (see Paragraph 47.6)
- Specific royalty provisions (see Paragraph 47.7)
- Reserved rights and subsidiary rights (see Paragraph 47.8)
- Proprietor's warranties* (see Paragraph 47.9)
- Accounts (see Paragraph 47.10)

- Actions for Infringement (see Paragraph 47.11)
- Alternative dispute resolution (see Paragraph 47.12)
- Termination (see Paragraph 47.13)
- Boilerplate* (see Paragraph 47.14).

47.3 Grant of Rights

See Paragraph 46.3.

47.4 Notices and Credits

See Paragraph 46.4.

47.5 Publication and Promotion

See Paragraphs 46.5 and 46.6.

47.6 Advance and Royalties

See Paragraphs 46.7 and 46.8.

47.7 Specific Royalty Provisions

See Paragraph 46.9.

47.8 Reserved Rights and Subsidiary Rights

See Paragraph 46.10.

47.9 Proprietor's Warranties

See Paragraph 46.12.

47.10 Accounts

See Paragraph 46.13.

47.11   Actions for Infringement

See Paragraph 46.16.

47.12   Alternative Dispute Resolution

See Paragraph 46.17.

47.13   Termination

See Paragraph 46.18.

47.14   Boilerplate

See Paragraph 46.19.

48 Rights Licensing Agreement

48.1 Description of a Rights Licensing Agreement

The rights licensing agreement* is the document which contains the terms pursuant to which rights in a particular work are licensed from a publisher to a licensee—who may well be a publisher in another territory.

The parties to this particular transaction are:

- the owner of the rights in the work being licensed (the "Publisher"); and
- the party to whom the rights are being licensed (the "Licensee").

48.2 Transaction Analysis

A typical rights licensing agreement might be expected to contain the following clauses:

- Grant of rights (see Paragraph 48.3)
- Publisher's warranties* (see Paragraph 48.4)
- Remuneration (see Paragraph 48.5)
- Licensee's undertakings (see Paragraph 48.6)
- Royalty* accounting (see Paragraph 48.7)
- Determination (see Paragraph 48.8)
- Boilerplate* (see Paragraph 48.9).

48.3 Grant of Rights

The agreement will grant the Licensee the right to exploit designated publication rights in a work in a designated territory for a specified licence period. The licence may be expressed to be conditional on a full and timely performance by the Licensee of its obligations under the agreement.

The Publisher will agree to deliver to the Licensee, within a specified number of days from the date of the agreement or receipt of remuneration, all delivery materials required in order to permit the Licensee to print and publish the work in the Licensee's territory.

48.4   Publisher's Warranties

The agreement will contain a number of warranties on the part of the Publisher, which may include the following.

Capacity

The Publisher is free to enter into the agreement and has not entered into any arrangement which might conflict with it.

Sell-off

Following the expiry of the licence, the Licensee will have a further three month non-exclusive period to sell-off* copies of the work already printed.

Non-infringement

So far as the Publisher is aware, the work is not obscene or defamatory and does not infringe any right of copyright or any other right.

48.5   Remuneration

The rights licensing agreement will normally provide for the Licensee to pay to the Publisher an advance and certain royalties (see Paragraphs 46.7, 46.8 and 46.11).

48.6   Licensee's Undertakings

A rights licensing agreement will normally contain a number of warranties and undertakings on the part of the Licensee, which may include the following.

Reservation of Rights

The Licensee acknowledges that all rights, other than those expressly granted, are reserved to the Publisher.

Publication

The Licensee will undertake to publish, by a specified date, not fewer than a specified number of copies of the work.

Copyright

The Licensee will not impair or prejudice the copyright in the work and will ensure that all copies published contain full and accurate copyright notices, credit provisions and acknowledgements.

Delivery Materials

The Licensee will return delivery materials at the end of the licence period or, if they are made available on loan to the Licensee, at the end of the loan period.

Promotional Material

The Licensee will not create any promotional material or artwork without the prior consent of the Publisher and, if the Licensee does so, the entire copyright in this material will belong to the Publisher.

Claims

The Licensee will give full particulars to the Publisher of any claim by any third party.

Prompt Payment

The Licensee will promptly pay to the Publisher all sums owed under the agreement.

No Assignment

The Licensee will not assign, sub-license or otherwise part with possession of any of the rights.

No Duplication

The Licensee will not copy or duplicate the delivery materials otherwise than for the purpose of printing the work.

Control of Delivery Materials

The Licensee will retain possession and control of the delivery materials at all times.

Catalogue

The Licensee will maintain the work in a prominent position in the Licensee's catalogue and ensure that the work does not go out of print at any time during the licence period.

Advertisement

The Licensee will advertise the work throughout the territory in the same manner as other books published by the Licensee.

Credits

The Licensee will not alter or adapt the work in any way or omit or remove any credits or acknowledgements or add any imprint or trademark.

Exploitation

The Licensee will exploit the rights granted to the best of its skill and ability, with a view to ensuring the highest possible royalties, will ensure that the work is given fair and equitable treatment and will not discriminate in favour of any other books the Licensee may publish.

Sell-off Period

At the end of the sell-off* period, the Licensee will permit the Publisher to purchase from the Licensee all copies of the work in the possession of the Licensee at the actual cost of manufacture.

Indemnity

See Paragraph 53.16.

48.7   Royalty Accounting

The rights licensing agreement will provide that the Licensee is required, on each accounting date, to provide the Publisher with a full and complete statement showing all money owed to the Publisher in respect of the preceding accounting period. The statement will be in such form as may be required by the Publisher and will be accompanied by payment of all sums owed without reserve.

The royalty accounting provisions will need to contain provisions relating to the exchange of currency if the Licensee is resident in a foreign jurisdiction, and will also need to specify the currency of account (whether this is to be pounds sterling or another currency).

The agreement will also need to contain a Value Added Tax provision in relation to all companies which are trading within the European Economic Area.

The Licensee will be required to keep full and proper books of account relating to the exploitation of its rights for the full period of the licence period plus six years, and permit the Publisher, or its representative, to inspect, audit and take copies of the books of account on reasonable prior notice during normal business hours. In the event that an inspection discovers an error which is to the detriment of the Publisher of more than 5%–10%, the Licensee will be required to pay the reasonable costs of audit and inspection incurred by the Publisher.

48.8 Determination

See Paragraph 34.11.

48.9 Boilerplate

The boilerplate section of a typical rights licensing agreement might be expected to contain the following provisions:

* Notice (see Paragraph 52.8)
* Entire agreement (see Paragraph 52.3)
* No partnership (see Paragraph 52.7)
* Governing law (see Paragraph 52.5).

H: Theatre

49 Theatrical Rights Licence Agreement

49.1 Description of a Theatrical Rights Licence Agreement

The theatrical rights licence agreement* grants to a licensee the right to produce and run a play in a designated territory for a set period.

The parties to the agreement are:

* the owner of the rights in the play (the "Owner"); and
* the party being granted the rights in the play (the "Licensee").

49.2 Transaction Analysis

A typical theatrical rights licence agreement might be expected to contain the following clauses:

* Owner's undertakings (see Paragraph 49.3)
* Grant of rights (see Paragraph 49.4)
* Royalties* (see Paragraph 49.5)
* Accounting (see Paragraph 49.6)
* Approvals (see Paragraph 49.7)
* Expenses (see Paragraph 49.8)
* Credits (see Paragraph 49.9)
* Reservation of rights (see Paragraph 49.10)
* Advertising right (see Paragraph 49.11)
* Termination (see Paragraph 49.12)
* Withholding tax* (see Paragraph 49.13)
* Boilerplate* (see Paragraph 49.14).

49.3 Owner's Undertakings

The Owner's warranties and undertakings in a theatrical rights licence agreement might be expected to contain the following.

Ownership

The Owner is the sole owner of the copyright in the play throughout the world.

Capacity to Contract

The Owner has the right to enter into the agreement and license the rights to the Licensee.

Originality

The play is an original work which does not infringe the copyright or any rights of any third party.

Obscenity/Defamation

The play is not obscene, defamatory, blasphemous or offensive to religion.

49.4 Grant of Rights

The Owner grants to the Licensee the exclusive licence to present the play in a designated territory, expiring 12 months from the date of the agreement.

Normally, the Licensee will be given the opportunity to extend the period within which it has to present the play for a further one-year or other period on payment of a sum to be negotiated. In addition, the Licensee may negotiate for the right to try out the play in the territory outside the main theatrical area for a period not exceeding eight or twelve weeks.

The licence of rights to the Licensee is normally conditional upon the Licensee ensuring that the play opens within the designated period and achieves a minimum of 21 consecutive performances and not less than 50 performances (or such other number as may be agreed) in each year of the licence period.

49.5 Remuneration

The Licensee will agree to pay the Owner an advance which shall be non-returnable and recoupable from the royalties payable to the Owner.

The royalties payable to the Owner are normally a designated percentage of gross box office receipts until the certified cost of production of the play have been recouped and after that, a higher percentage of gross box office receipts.

49.6 Accounting

The Owner will normally require daily returns and weekly statements showing the week's gross box office receipts from the play and will expect to receive payment of the royalty not later than the Friday following the end of the week in which performances have taken place.

The Licensee will normally give the Owner (or its authorised representative) access, at all reasonable times, to the box office accounts, will agree to provide the Owner with a certified copy of the cost of production statement, together with such documentation as may be necessary in order to identify the week in which the costs of production have been recouped and such other reasonable accounting information as may be required by the Owner.

49.7 Approvals

The Owner will have the right of to approve leading members of the cast, the director and the designer. The Licensee may require that the Owner's right of approval is not to be unreasonably withheld or delayed.

The Licensee will notify the Owner at least 14 days in advance of the rehearsal dates and the Owner or its representative will have the right to attend rehearsals of the play for all productions.

The Licensee will give the Owner, at the Licensee's expense, a designated number of seats in rows 4 to 10 of each theatre for each performance.

49.8 Credits

The licence agreement will normally provide the form of credit which the Owner is entitled to receive, in relation to front of house publicity, posters, signage on the outside of the theatre, radio and television advertising, and programmes.

49.9 Expenses

The Owner may be required by its agreement with the author of the play to require the Licensee to pay for travelling and subsistence expenses of the author of the play, including air travel expenses and a living allowance (or per diem fee) of a certain amount per day.

49.10 Reservation of Rights

The agreement will normally reserve to the Owner all rights which are not expressly licensed to the Licensee.

49.11 Advertising Right

The Licensee may require the right to advertise excerpts from the play. The Owner may grant the right to use certain excerpts from the first run of the play in each location, for the purpose of broadcast advertising, provided that the exploitation of advertising rights does not interfere with any sale of film or television rights.

49.12 Termination

The agreement will normally contain termination provisions which will be analogous to those in all rights licensing agreements (see Paragraph 48.8).

49.13 Withholding Tax

Depending on the circumstances and the states in which the Owner and the Licensee are resident, the agreement may need to contain a provision permitting the Licensee to deduct withholding tax* from all sums payable to the Owner.

49.14 Boilerplate

The boilerplate section of a typical theatrical rights licence agreement might contain the following provisions:

*   No partnership (see Paragraph 52.7)
*   Governing law (see Paragraph 52.5).

50 Theatrical Production Investment Agreement

50.1 Description of a Theatrical Production Investment Agreement

The theatrical production investment agreement* sets out the terms in which an individual investor is prepared to invest sums towards the financing of the production of a play.

The parties to this particular transaction are:

- the investor (the "Investor"); and
- the producer producing the play (the "Producer").

50.2 Transaction Analysis

A typical theatrical production investment agreement might be expected to contain the following clauses:

- Investment (see Paragraph 50.3)
- Overcall* (see Paragraph 50.4)
- Producer's entitlement (see Paragraph 50.5)
- Production account (see Paragraph 50.6)
- Repayment of investment and overcall (see Paragraph 50.7)
- Net Profits (see Paragraph 50.8)
- Reserve (see Paragraph 50.9)
- Accounts (see Paragraph 50.10)
- Production details (see Paragraph 50.11)
- Boilerplate* (see Paragraph 50.12).

50.3 Investment

The Investor agrees to make available to the Producer a precise sum to be applied solely by the Producer towards the production of the play.

50.4 Overcall

Because the costs and expenses of theatrical production are somewhat unpredictable, the Producer will wish most Investors to agree to be prepared to contribute to additional costs incurred if the costs of production exceed those originally anticipated. These costs are normally referred to as "overcall" costs and, normally, Investors will agree to pay overcall sums provided that they are limited to not more than a set percentage (sometimes 20% or 25 %) of the sums originally advanced by the Investor.

50.5 Producer's Entitlement

Normally an investment agreement will contain an acknowledgement, on the part of the Investor, that the Producer is entitled to raise production finance from such sources as the Producer considers may be appropriate.

50.6 Production Account

The Producer will normally agree to establish a production account into which all admission receipts and all other sums relating to the play will be paid.

50.7 Repayment of Investment and Overcall

The agreement will normally provide that, after the Producer has recouped the cost of production, the operating and running expenses and any reserve deducted by the Producer to meet contingencies*, the balance will be applied to all Investors pro rata, pari passu* until their investments have been repaid.

50.8 Net Profits

Following repayment of all investors, the Producer will agree to pay them the appropriate percentage of net profits of the play.

50.9 Reserve

There are circumstances where a production may suffer additional running costs after it has broken even. Because of this, it is normal in investment agreements for Producers to obtain an acknowledgement from their Investors that if the Producer's reserve against contingencies is applied after break even the Producer shall be entitled to recoup it out of the Investors' percentage of net profits. When the production closes, the unapplied benefit of the reserve is liquidated as an asset of the play and applied towards all the Investors in the percentage in which they are entitled to participate in net profits.

50.10 Accounts

Normally the Producer will designate a firm of reputable accountants to be responsible for maintaining the books of account of the production and the agreement will provide that, if any question is raised by any Investor, this will be dealt with by the accountants and their decision will be final and binding.

The Producer will normally agree to provide the Investors with details of gross weekly box office receipts and running expenses, production statements and various other financial details.

50.11 Production Details

The agreement will normally provide that the Producer has the right to decide how tangible assets used in the play are to be dealt with, whether and when they are to be sold and at what price.

The Investors will normally acknowledge that all matters relating to production of the play are at the entire and sole discretion of the Producer, whose decisions will be final and binding.

50.12 Boilerplate

The boilerplate section of a typical theatrical production investment agreement will contain the following provisions:

- No obligation (see Paragraph 52.6)
- Notice (see Paragraph 52.8)
- Severability (see Paragraph 52.10)
- Entire agreement (see Paragraph 52.3)
- Waiver (see Paragraph 52.11)
- No partnership (see Paragraph 52.7)
- Governing law (see Paragraph 52.5).

I: General

51 Miscellaneous Documents

51.1 List of Miscellaneous Documents

This chapter provides a short summary of a number of miscellaneous documents frequently encountered in media industry transactions:

- Inducement letter (see Paragraph 51.2)
- Laboratory access letter* (see Paragraph 51.3)
- Laboratory pledgeholder's letter* (see Paragraph 51.4)
- Letter of credit (see Paragraph 51.5)
- Performer's consent (see Paragraph 51.6)
- Personal guarantee (see Paragraph 51.7)
- Publisher's release (see Paragraph 51.8)
- Quitclaim* (see Paragraph 51.9)
- Trust letter* (see Paragraph 51.10).

51.2 Inducement Letter

An inducement letter is used when the services of an individual are made available to (say) a film producer* through the individual's loan-out* company. The function of the inducement letter is to create a binding contractual agreement between the individual and the producer.

For example, if Jo Bloggs Limited has a contract without an inducement letter to provide the services of Ms Jo Bloggs to Feature Film Limited and Ms Jo Bloggs decides not to turn up for the shooting of the film, although Feature Film Limited would be able to sue Jo Bloggs Limited it would be unable to do anything about Ms Jo Bloggs.

An inducement letter effectively "locks in" the individual to the commitments undertaken by their loan-out* company and will contain acknowledgements that their company is the owner of all rights of copyright in their services and has the right to grant moral rights* waivers and performers' rights consents on their behalf. It will also permit persons contracting with their loan-out company to sue the individual in certain circumstances if, for example, they do not turn up.

51.3 Laboratory Access Letter

The function of the laboratory access letter is to provide access to materials which are held by a laboratory. The laboratory access letter will not permit the person given access to remove any original materials from the laboratory, but it authorises the laboratory to accept orders for the creation of duplicate film materials at the cost and expense of the person given access.

Normally, the laboratory will acknowledge that, if the person granted access runs up any unpaid bills, the laboratory will not have any lien over the original materials deposited with it.

51.4 Laboratory Pledgeholder's Letter

The function of the laboratory pledgeholder's letter is to provide financiers of films with security over material deposited from time to time with the laboratory.

In the letter, the laboratory will agree to hold all material placed with it relating to a film by order of the financier. It will agree that it will not allow the material to be removed outside the laboratory or take any orders for the reproduction of the material without the consent of the person to whose order the materials are held.

51.5 Letter of Credit

A letter of credit is an irrevocable commitment from a bank to pay a fixed sum of money on the occurrence of a certain event. Letters of credit are used to guarantee payment obligations assumed by companies. In film financing transactions, they are frequently used to guarantee payment obligations which arise on delivery of a film. In these circumstances, the sums payable under the letter of credit can only be drawn upon by producing an original laboratory access letter, which will be delivered to the bank, enabling it to release funds. The bank will then transmit the original laboratory access letter to the company who placed funds with the bank in order to permit the bank to issue the letter of credit. When the company has received the access letter, it will then have access to the film and be able to obtain the materials which it was entitled to receive on payment of the letter of credit.

51.6 Performer's Consent

A performer's consent confirms that a musician or actor has consented to recordings of their performance being made and exploited. The consent is necessary because laws in the United Kingdom, the European Union states and certain other countries recognise that performers have rights in their performances and also property rights in their performances. Performers' property rights entitle performers to equitable remuneration (see Chapter 53.6) and although the ability to assign these rights is limited, the performers may permit collecting societies (see Chapter 53.3) to exercise the right to administer their rights to equitable remuneration*. Where a Company is obtaining a written consent from a performer, it will also be normal for the Company to obtain confirmation from the performer, that the amount paid to him or her constitutes equitable remuneration for the rental or lending of films or sound recordings incorporating their performance (see Paragraphs 53.3 and 53.6).

51.7 Personal Guarantees

Personal guarantees are often encountered in media industry transactions. Their function is to make an individual liable for the performance of certain obligations either of other individuals or, more usually, a company.

Personal guarantees should always be treated with caution, the individual giving them should always obtain legal advice, if possible from a different law firm from the one advising the company or persons whose obligations are to be guaranteed.

Companies have limited liability: their liability is limited to the amount of their share capital and other assets. An individual's liability, however, is without limit. From an individual's point of view, therefore, it is desirable to limit the amount of the guarantee and to limit the time period within which any claim may be brought against the individual.

Personal guarantees should only asked for in exceptional circumstances, and then only where the individual giving the guarantee has complete control over the company whose obligations are being guaranteed. It is not the norm for individuals to assume personal liability for companies which they do not have complete control over and any document requiring them to do so should be treated with great caution.

51.8 Publisher's Release

A publisher's release* is a letter of confirmation normally obtained from the first or main publisher of a book by the film or television producer which has acquired film and television rights in it.

The function of the release is two-fold. First, it provides confirmation that the publisher has never owned or controlled film or television rights in the work. Formerly, it used to be the practice of publishers to obtain these rights, and this confirmation is sometimes essential in relation to old works.

Second, it permits the film or television producer to exercise written synopsis rights and print short resumés of the work (normally limited to 7,500 or 10,000 words). Since the publisher will normally control the exclusive right to print and publish the work (see Chapter 46) their consent is necessary in order to authorise the production of summaries for press kits, TV listings etc.

51.9   Quitclaim

A quitclaim is a form of assignment under which a person or company will assign all rights which they own in relation to a work, but will make no warranty as to whether in fact they own any rights or whether the rights are encumbered. Frequently quitclaims are obtained from persons or companies who might technically have some residual interest in a particular work in order to eliminate any doubt.

Because a quitclaim does not contain warranties as to unincumbered ownership (which are normally required) or title guarantees (which are helpful but normally not enough to establish ownership—see Chapter 53.15), it will not normally provide adequate evidence of ownership of a work.

51.10   Trust Letter

The purpose of a trust letter is to deal with the situation where a film or television producer needs money urgently, either to stop rights in a project reverting or to fund liabilities incurred in production and the necessary documentation, whether a PFD agreement* or some other document has not been finalised in time.

The trust letter permits a financier to advance funds to the producer and provides that all rights acquired or material produced by the producer will be held by the producer on trust for the financier absolutely. In other words, the financier owns everything. The trust letter is often backed up by an assignment of copyright from the producer to the financier. Trust letters are frequently used as stop-gap measures and are usually superseded by some form of production finance documentation.

52 Boilerplate

This Chapter contains a brief description of the principal function of a number of general clauses.

52.1 Assignment

Normally, a party acquiring rights under an agreement will wish to have the ability to assign those rights to other third parties. Frequently, the assignment provision is qualified to state that the party assigning will not be relieved of liability under the contract if the person they assign to does not perform. There are some circumstances where it would be commercially unacceptable or undesirable for the party to be able to assign or license its rights under a contract* (such as appointment of a sales agent or appointment of a foreign licensee) and in these instances, assignment or sub-licensing may be expressly prohibited. See also Paragraphs 53.1 and 53.2.

52.2 Certificate of Value

Where rights of copyright in the United Kingdom are assigned, there is a technical liability for stamp duty to be paid on the value of the copyrights assigned if this is in excess of £100,000. The amount of the duty is:

£0– £60,000	Nil
£60,001–£250,000	1%
£250,001–£500,000	2%
£500,001+	3%.

Although it is not general practice in the media industry to insert stamp duty provisions in documentation, there is a technical requirement to do so and, in some transactions, such as sale and purchase of film libraries etc, it is essential to do so.

52.3 Entire Agreement

It is normal for contracts to state that they contain the entire agreement*
between the parties and also that they expressly supersede all previous
arrangements. They may also state that no variation or waiver of the agreement
will be valid or binding on the parties, unless it is in writing. The legal validity of
this is questionable, but its inclusion is not damaging.

52.4 Force Majeure

Many contracts contain force majeure provisions which are not what they
appear to be (see Chapter 53.8). A force majeure provision will generally relieve
one or both parties of their obligations to perform under the agreement if an
event occurs which is beyond their control. In some types of agreement (such
as agreements for personal services) it is desirable to specify the maximum
length of time by which an event of force majeure can suspend performance of
contractual obligations.

52.5 Law

Where agreements are between entities situated in the same jurisdiction it is
technically not necessary to state which country's law will govern the contract
since that will be the state in which the two entities are incorporated. When
dealing with entities in different jurisdictions, the choice of law to govern the
contract is very important.

Although parties to an agreement are, in many cases, free to choose which
law will apply, there are certain matters which should be borne in mind in order
to prevent an invalid choice of law. Some foreign jurisdictions expressly exclude
the laws of other states applying. For example, the sale of any property situated
in France must be governed by the laws of France.

A separate, but linked, issue is the issue of which state is to have jurisdiction
in the event of a dispute. The selection of one country to have exclusive
jurisdiction in the event of a dispute is inadvisable. It is perfectly acceptable to
state that the courts of England and Wales are to be courts of competent
jurisdiction. This would not prevent proceedings being brought to courts of the
USA or anywhere else. Some contracts provide that, if one party commences
proceedings against the other, then the country in which the proceedings are
commenced will have exclusive competence to deal with the dispute. Whether
this is acceptable or not is a matter for negotiation.

52.6 No Obligation

Where agreements relate to the financing of a film or the acquisition of rights
in a film project, it is normal to state that the company acquiring the rights will
have no obligation to make the film.

52.7   No Partnership

The law which governs partnerships in the United Kingdom (the Partnership Act) was passed in 1890 and is still in force. It states that, where two or more parties carry on business in common with a view to profit, a partnership is created. The partners are liable for each other's acts. There are also taxation implications for companies which enter into partnerships with each other. For these reasons, it is prudent to insert into agreements which share income between companies a provision which states that the parties are not trading in partnership.

52.8   Notice

Many agreements contain a provision which states that, if a letter is dispatched by first class pre-paid post and correctly addressed, it is deemed to have been received by the addressee a certain number of days after being posted. Notice provisions are designed to prevent persons from denying they have received important letters requiring them to remedy breaches of contract or letters exercising options etc.

52.9   Set-off

Some agreements contain provisions which state that a party, which is required to pay money to another party, may set-off against its liability any debt owed to it by the other party (or any party associated with the other party). Although set-off provisions are normal in loan agreements they are not generally acceptable in film financing agreements or film distribution agreements, particularly where companies are specifically incorporated to make one particular film.

52.10   Severability

A severability provision normally provides that, if any part of the contract is found to be void, that part will be severed and the remaining clauses will not be affected. The effectiveness of severability clauses depends almost entirely on the skill of drafting contracts and, in some cases, a severability clause has failed to save a particular provision from being rendered ineffective because it has been construed as being a dependent clause on an unenforceable clause which has been deleted.

52.11   Waiver

The waiver provision will normally state that no failure or delay to exercise a right will amount to a waiver and no waiver will be deemed to be a continuing waiver. This is a normal provision.

53   Specific Problem Areas

53.1   Assignability

The question of whether a company should be free to assign rights which it acquires is often problematic. An assignor may seek to restrict assignability of rights in order to guarantee future payment obligations. In some cases, such as film production and financing agreements, limitations on the right to assign are unacceptable. In other cases, the company's right to assign might be made conditional upon its assignee entering into a directly enforceable contractual undertaking to pay the assignor sums due under the contract*.

53.2   Assignment or Licence

There are some situations where an owner of copyright may be reluctant to assign rights to a company on the basis that, if the company fails to pay, the owner cannot terminate the assignment and all it can do is sue the company. In situations where the company has assigned rights on to a third party, if the owner obtains judgment against the company and the company has no other assets, the owner will be unable to recover amounts properly due to it. These reasons are often used to justify a transfer of rights being in the form of an exclusive licence rather than an assignment, on the basis that a licence can be terminated if payment is not made. Licence agreements frequently contain terms which permit sub-licensees to continue to exercise their rights even though the licence has been terminated.

Many assignments or licences purport to grant rights throughout the "universe" and are stated to exist in "perpetuity". Since the period of copyright in any work is a finite period, the term of any assignment or licence can only be for the period of protection provided by law. On the expiry of that period, the exclusive right of the assignee or licensee will terminate, but they will be entitled to a non-exclusive right in relation to the work, just as anyone else is when a work falls into the "public domain". For this reason assignments, and licences should not be expressed to be in "perpetuity".

So far as concerns the territorial ambit of assignments and licences, it is sufficient to refer to the "world". Any concern as to whether the known world includes the universe is quickly dispelled by a reference to the Shorter Oxford English Dictionary which presents the word "universe" as the first synonym for world and vice versa.

53.3 Collecting Societies

Collecting societies are playing a growing part in the media. There is a risk of overlap between some rights which are currently being claimed by collecting societies and rights which may be acquired by film production companies.

Currently, some confusion exists in relation to the role of collecting societies in collecting equitable remuneration (see Paragraph 53.6). Whether collecting societies can collect revenue in relation to cable re-transmission will depend on precisely what rights have been assigned to film production companies. All provisions in contracts referring to collecting societies or referring to equitable remuneration need to be vetted carefully.

53.4 Cross-Collateralisation

The principle of cross-collateralisation* is frequently encountered in media industry transactions. To illustrate the concept, let us assume that the owner of rights in a series of films, licenses a company the right to exploit the films and the company pays the owner an advance of £1,000,000, apportioned in varying amounts between the various films. It is to be anticipated that some films will be far more successful than others and it is, therefore, probable that the company will have recouped the amount of the advance apportioned to some particular films and not recovered the advance payable in relation to others.

In normal circumstances, as soon as an advance is recouped the company will be liable to pay royalties* or a participation of the net profits or net receipts. Where, however, income in relation to a batch of films (or books or anything else for that matter) is cross-collateralised, the company will have the right instead of paying to the owner the royalties due after recoupment on the successful films, to apply the amount of such royalties towards recouping the advances* on those films which have not been successful.

The same principle of cross-collateralisation may be applied, not just between different films, but also in relation to the exploitation of one film in different media or in different territories. Where, however, the owner of rights specifies that the advance is to be apportioned in certain amounts against specific territories and specific media, if it requires that the income is not cross-collateralised, this will prevent the company off-setting revenue derived from successful territories to support underperformance in other territories. This may generally be expected to produce a better result for the owner.

53.5 Credits

Failure to grant a person a screen or advertising credit is one of the few contractual breaches which are not adequately compensated for by damages, since it is very difficult to put a value on the loss of a person's opportunity to enhance their reputation. For this reason, it is common practice in most media industry contracts to include a provision which excuses a company exploiting rights in a property in the event of casual or inadvertent failure to accord the correct credit.

53.6   Equitable Remuneration

The concept of equitable remuneration* is a recent creation of the European Commission. Writers, composers, actors and musicians are all entitled to receive equitable remuneration in respect of the exploitation of their works or performances by way of rental. The Commission has not itself provided firm guidance on what constitutes equitable remuneration.

It could, in some or all circumstances, constitute a single payment made at the time the individual was engaged. Equally, it could in some circumstances impute an entitlement to royalty income. Currently, no one is able to state with certainty precisely what the right entitles individuals to and it should be appreciated that the entitlement will, in any case, be different in each of the 17 states comprising the European Economic Area. It is too early to predict whether the concept will translate into transactional difficulties, but it is likely that case law in this area will evolve over the next few years.

53.7   First Refusal/Matching Offer

Many media industry transactions contain "options*" which are merely agreements to agree and are therefore contractually unenforceable. Some contracts contain first refusal provisions, which take the form of an obligation to negotiate in good faith for a stated period. This type of provision is also unenforceable, since it is implicit that any party who is negotiating in good faith is free at any time to terminate the negotiations. Contractual provisions which create a "lock-out" situation, where, one party is prevented from negotiating with others for a stated finite period are, however, enforceable, but the wording of all option/first refusal provisions need to be examined with care.

Matching offer provisions (which state that, after the first refusal right is lost, the party has a right to match other offers made by third parties) are problematic on a practical level and are often resisted. Provisions which purport to limit a party's freedom to contract on terms which are no less favourable than an original offer often cause difficulties in practice because of the difficulty in creating exact comparables between different parties. Even though the financial terms of an offer may be identical, there may be other elements relating to the parties (such as the size and efficiency of their marketing and distribution network) which make ostensibly equal commercial terms extremely unequal.

53.8   Force Majeure

If the performance of a contract becomes frustrated (ie a contract is not capable of being performed in the way contemplated by the parties at the time it was entered into) under United Kingdom law, the parties are relieved from further performance provided they pay back what has been paid to them previously, unless the contract specifically provides otherwise. Force majeure provisions are intended to prevent the application of this general law. Many force majeure provisions do not do what, on first reading, they might appear to do and provisions of these type should always be examined very closely.

53.9 Insolvency

Insolvency is a valid reason to terminate a grant of rights, since it normally means that the party who has acquired the rights will be unable to exploit them to the maximum advantage. Some media industry contracts, however, provide that, if an owner or a licensor of rights becomes insolvent, the person being granted the rights is not obliged to make any payment. This type of provision is unfair and there is no reason why the receiver, administrator or liquidator of an insolvent rights owner should not recover payments due under existing contracts. The rights owner's creditors should be entitled to receive such sums.

53.10 Moral Rights

Many media industry transactions require owners of copyright to waive their moral rights*. The suggestion that writers should be required to waive their moral rights often meets with an unduly emotional response.

What many writers and agents do not appreciate is that the usual moral rights waiver clause applies only to an author's statutory rights (ie those created by statute, specifically, the Copyright, Designs and Patents Act 1988). These moral rights exist independently of any contractual rights* which an author may acquire.

It is perfectly possible (and not at all unfair) for an author to waive their statutory moral rights to be identified or to object to derogatory treatment if their contract gives them an express contractual right to be identified (by way of a credit), as well as total or initial control over the final form of the work. In view of the fact that most agreements for the publication of a book deal with the work in finished form, as produced by the author and, in the audio-visual industries, the director of a film is normally given the right to make the directors cut, this is a fair compromise.

53.11 Overspill/Parallel Imports

Although television broadcasts from terrestrial transmitters are automatically limited in their range because of curvature of the earth, the footprint of satellite broadcasts normally extends over national boundaries and it is impossible to prevent broadcast signal "overspill*". Although a satellite broadcaster can prevent the satellite broadcast from being retransmitted by cable in adjoining territories, the broadcaster will be unable to prevent its signals from being received outside the territory for which they are primarily designated.

Companies granting rights to satellite broadcasters will, for this reason, frequently require the broadcaster to encrypt their signal and to ensure that the means of decryption is not available outside the national market for which the rights are licensed. This will protect the value in adjoining territories. It is equally important to make express provision in licence agreements for adjoining territories to acknowledge the existence of overspill* in order to protect the owner from claims as to derogation from exclusivity in the adjoining territory.

In the European Economic Area it is not possible for the owner of rights to grant an exclusive licensee of a work in (say) France protection against imports of that work ordered from another licensee in the European Economic Area, located (say) in Belgium. Goods which are imported from a foreign territory onto a national licensee's marketplace are referred to as parallel imports. It is a basic principle of European Community law that the free circulation of goods and services in the European Economic Area must not be restricted and exclusive licences cannot, therefore, give licensees protection against parallel imports.

53.12 Payment Directions

Many media industry transactions contain directions to make payment to third parties. Although these are frequently expressed to be irrevocable, no contractual term in any agreement* between two parties is ever irrevocable, since the contract may always be varied by the parties in the future. In practice this means that the third party who receives the "benefit" of an "irrevocable" payment direction* has no security that it will continue to receive the directed payments in future.

There are two ways, however, of achieving security. First, a legal assignment might be created in relation to the amount being paid. This, however, will only be effective if an entire debt or payment obligation is being assigned and will not create a legal assignment of (say) an agent's commission of 10% of the sums payable to an author.

The second way to achieve security is to join the person wishing to have the benefit of the direction as a party to the contract for the purpose of obtaining a contractual commitment obligation from the person paying to the agent or other party which they can enforce direct.

53.13 Power of Attorney

Powers of attorney are frequently inserted in media industry transactions to guarantee execution of documents which may be required in future. Some contracts attempt to create general powers of attorney.

General powers of attorney should not be dispensed liberally. A person given a general power of attorney can do anything and everything in the name of the person giving it, eg sell their house, car, resign from their job and give away all their worldly goods etc. There can be no legitimate reason for anyone ever requiring another party to give it a general power of attorney. All powers of attorney in contracts should be limited powers of attorney which are expressly limited to the subject matter of the contract (say a record or a book or a film).

53.14 Termination and Rights Recapture

These two linked topics are areas where competent legal input will always be necessary.

The termination of a contract is like a duel with pistols. The person attempting to terminate gets only one shot. If the attempt at termination is ineffective, it will probably constitute an act of repudiation, entitling the other party to terminate, the results of which could be fatal.

When a contract is terminated, in many cases, rights will be recaptured or licences will terminate. This is not, however, always the case. The position will depend on the precise terms of the contract being terminated. This will normally need careful review.

53.15 Title Guarantee

Following a recent change in legislation, many British media industry contracts have started to contain references to "full-title guarantee*", which is intended to be a shorthand way of providing that the person granting the rights is the sole, absolute, unincumbered owner of such rights.

A warranty* as to full-title guarantee does not, however provide this assurance. References to title guarantee should be treated with caution.

53.16 Warranties and Indemnities

The difference between warranty and indemnity* provisions and the contractual effect of such provisions is not always appreciated.

Breach of a warranty will normally entitle the innocent party to claim damages for their loss. They will only be able to recover damages from the party in breach where they have established that this party is, in fact, responsible and produced evidence to a court substantiating the innocent party's loss—which they have a duty to use their best endeavours to mitigate.

An indemnity provision, however, amounts to a directly enforceable undertaking to ensure that no loss is occasioned by the innocent party. It entitles the innocent party to demand payment of any expenses that have been incurred as a result of the breach, without having first established the basis of the claim, without proving the amount of its loss and without imposing any obligation on the innocent party to ensure that the costs incurred by it are reasonable.

Indemnity provisions are capable of imposing hard financial obligations on individuals and, although there may be limited instances where it is reasonable to require indemnity protection from individuals, many media industry transaction documents seek to impose indemnity obligations on individuals in all circumstances. This is not reasonable and individuals need to be made clearly aware of the adverse consequences and serious financial risk involved in giving indemnities.

54 Law of Contract and Law of Agency

A INTRODUCTION

54.1 Purpose of this Chapter

The purpose of this Chapter is to examine the basic legal principles which apply to the creation and enforceability of contracts*.

An understanding of the basic principles of contract law will assist media industry personnel from inadvertently creating contractual relationships or entering into contracts which are voidable or unenforceable.

Appreciating the consequences of misrepresentation (even where it is innocent) and the complexities which result where the parties to a contract are mistaken in certain matters may assist in reinforcing the importance of clarity and accuracy—unattainable ideals towards which we all aspire.

The business dealings of media industry personnel bring them into contact with a wide circle of people, some of whom have interesting characteristics, when viewed in a legal context. That is why this Chapter also examines the capacity of agents, personal representatives and executors to enter into contracts on behalf of living or dead authors.

All of us are aware that contracts go wrong and the overriding concern of all prudent businessmen must be to eliminate risk and to limit liability in such situations. The law relating to agency provides companies with the means of excluding liability to third parties. The brief summary of the law relating to agency at the end of this chapter may assist media industry personnel to appreciate its significance.

B FORMATION AND ENFORCEABILITY OF CONTRACTS

54.2 What is a Contract?

A contract is a legally enforceable agreement. For most practical purposes, there is little distinction between the word "contract" and the word "agreement*".

There is no requirement for contracts to be in writing, unless the contract involves land. An oral contract (ie a verbal contract made between two people talking) is just as binding as a contract in writing, although it may be difficult to prove that the contract was made and as Samuel Goldwyn once famously remarked, "An oral contract isn't worth the paper it's written on".

A number of elements are, however, required to be satisfied before a contract can be brought into existence. These elements are set out in Paragraphs 54.3–54.8. The persons involved must also have the capacity to enter into a contract.

54.3   Capacity of Persons

A valid contract may be made by any person whom the law recognises as having legal personality, such as individuals, limited liability companies, partnerships, corporations and the Crown.

There must be at least two separate and definite parties to a contract, so, for example, an organisation cannot enter into a contract with itself. The parties to the contract must be definite persons which exist at the time the contract was made. It is not possible to contract on behalf of a proposed company which is not in existence. Any such attempt will result either in a void contract, which cannot be ratified by the company, even when it is formed or in a contract which will not bind the proposed company, but which will bind the unfortunate individual who attempted to enter into the arrangements on behalf of the proposed company.

A contract between two divisions of a company or two branch offices will also be void, since these are not two separate legal entities. A contract between a company and its main shareholder is, however, enforceable, since they are two separate legal entities.

It is important to be aware that a number of classes of person do not have the capacity to enter into contracts or are capable of contracting only to a limited extent. These classes of person include bankrupts (whose property, with effect from the declaration of bankruptcy, belongs to their trustee in bankruptcy), minors (who are persons under the age of 18, although in some cases, minors will be liable for contracts for goods suitable to the condition in life of the minor and the minor's actual requirements), persons of unsound mind, alien enemies and drunkards. There are additional circumstances in which corporations, companies, their receivers and partnerships, are not capable of entering into binding contracts, particularly in relation to insolvency.

54.4   Limited Liability Companies

Under United Kingdom law, limited liability companies may be either private companies or public companies. Private companies are prohibited from offering their shares or debentures to the public and their company names include the word "limited" which distinguishes them from public companies. Public companies are permitted to offer their shares or debentures to the public and to include in their company name the words "public limited company" or "plc".

Every public and private company is required by law to adopt and file at the Companies Registry a memorandum of association and articles of association which controls the future activities of the company in the same way as a constitution. The memorandum of association sets out the company's objects and powers. The articles of association contain the provisions which govern the relationship between the company's members (or shareholders).

A company has a totally separate and distinct legal identity from its members (or shareholders) and its directors. In principle, neither shareholders nor directors are liable for the acts or debts of the company, although there are exceptions, where individuals may be liable in the case of wrongful or fraudulent trading and misrepresentation (see Paragraph 54.17).

The liability of the company is generally limited to the value of the company's share capital, plus the sum of its assets—hence the term "limited liability company"—and the company's creditors do not have recourse to the assets of the directors or shareholders, except in the case of wrongful trading or misrepresentation. This contrasts greatly with the position where an individual enters into a contract. In such circumstances, his or her liability is unlimited. The protection which limited liability offers individuals from the uncertainties of unlimited liability (and the risk of bankruptcy) is one of the most persuasive factors in support of trading through a limited liability company, rather than in one's own name. This protection is, of course, surrendered where personal guarantees are provided by owners of companies. There are circumstances where entities who find themselves committed to significant expenditure in reliance on a contractual commitment with a company whose share capital (and therefore maximum liability) is £100, should seek the additional protection offered by personal guarantees.

Although a person cannot enter into a contract with himself or herself, a company can enter into a contract with a director or a shareholder. Where directors have interests in contracts which are entered into by their companies, they are required by law to declare their interests.

The relations of public or private limited liability companies, both between their members and within themselves, are governed by legislation—principally the Companies Acts 1985–1989 and the Insolvency Act 1986. The Companies Acts contain provisions which, amongst other things, specify the duties owed by directors, rights of shareholders (minority or otherwise), accounting and record keeping formalities, procedures for changing a company's memorandum of association or articles of association. They also outline the circumstances in which a company can be dissolved (or wound up) or put into liquidation (solvent or insolvent).

Any contract which is outside the scope of the powers of a company (as set out in its memorandum of association) is void, even if the contract is subsequently ratified by every member of the company. In the case, however, of a person dealing with the company in good faith, any transaction decided on by the directors of the company is deemed to be one which is within the capacity of the company to enter into and the power of the directors to bind the company is deemed to be free of any limitation under the memorandum or articles of association of the company. The provisions of the Companies Act 1989, which came into force from 1 March 1990, further protect third parties from any lack of capacity on the part of the directors of a company. They provide that the validity of any acts done by a company shall not be called into question by reason of anything in its memorandum of association.

54.5 Elements of a Contract

The parties must be in agreement. Normally, a consensus (or agreement) is reached by the process of offer and acceptance. The law requires that an offer on identifiable terms receives unqualified acceptance from the person to whom the offer was made.

Offer

The offer may come from the person who intends to buy (eg "I will buy your book for £500") or it may come from the person who intends to sell (eg "I will sell you my book for £500"). It is important, however, to distinguish between an offer and what is known as an invitation to treat. An invitation to treat consists of a statement or conduct which invites a party to make an offer, such as an author sending an unsolicited manuscript to a company. For example, the display of goods for sale in a shop window with their prices attached is not an offer made by the seller, but an invitation to treat. Other examples of invitations to treat include menus in restaurants (the offer is made only when the customer has selected what they wish to eat and, if the dish is off the menu, there will be no acceptance) and the display of goods in a shop (the offer arises when the prospective buyer asks for an item in the shop, or presents it at a till).
Normally, a business offer will be slightly more complicated than "I offer to buy your book for £500". It may, in practice, contain a number of detailed terms and provisions and may require acceptance within a certain time or in a certain manner.

Acceptance

Acceptance of an offer does not have to be in writing. In some cases, acceptance does not even have to be oral, since it can be implied by the conduct of the person to whom the offer was made. Silence cannot, however, constitute acceptance. Acceptance must, however, be unconditional and unqualified and must be in the same terms as the original offer.

If the purported acceptance seeks to introduce new terms or seeks to vary the terms of the original offer, a contract will not be created and the purported acceptance will be merely a counter-offer, which will not create a contract, unless it is accepted.

Difficulties may arise where two parties try and create a contract by using (say) their standard purchase orders or standard sales forms. Where a buyer issues a purchase order on its standard terms of trading and the seller, on receipt of the order, then issues the seller's own terms, it is sometimes difficult to establish what the contractual position is. Difficulties may also arise where only one party issues a standard form document, which the other party returns with amendments. The contractual position will depend on the circumstances in each case, but great care should be taken to avoid, if at all possible, the "battle of the forms" situation.

54.6 Withdrawal and Acceptance of Offers

Until it is accepted, an offer can be withdrawn at any time. Where valid acceptance has occurred, a binding contract will have been created. An offer may, however, stipulate a time within which acceptance must be made. If this is the case, there is, generally speaking, nothing to prevent the person who has made the offer from withdrawing the offer before the end of such time, provided withdrawal of the offer is communicated to the person to whom the offer was made.

If the withdrawal of the offer is not communicated, then the person to whom the offer is made will be free to accept the offer and a binding contract will be created. There are some exceptions to this rule, such as the situation where the person to whom the offer was made, has moved address without telling the person making the offer.

In order for the acceptance of an offer to complete the formation of a contract, the acceptance must be communicated to the person who made the offer. Where there is no requirement for notice of the acceptance to be in writing, acceptance may be communicated orally.

Where acceptance is made by post, the acceptance takes effect the moment the letter is posted. The court regards the letter as being posted when it is put in the control of the Post Office, or one of the employees of the Post Office who is authorised to receive letters. This rule applies only, however, where it was reasonable to expect the offer to be accepted by post.

54.7 Legal Relations and Consideration

An agreement will not be contractually enforceable unless it evinces an intention to create legal relations. Certain arrangements (such as arrangements between members of the same family) are never intended to be contracts and have been held by the courts to lack the necessary intention to create legally enforceable contractual arrangements. As a general rule, all a company's dealings are likely to be intended to create legal relations, so this requirement is unlikely to cause difficulties.

A contract must also be supported by consideration. The legal definition of consideration is some right, interest, profit, or benefit accrues to one party or some forbearance, detriment, loss or responsibility is given, suffered or undertaken by the other party.

In layman's terms, consideration normally means either the payment of money or an agreement to pay money. The payment of an advance by a company when a musician signs a contract is consideration. The agreement by a company to pay an advance on completion of recordings is consideration. A company's agreement to pay a royalty following release of an album is consideration. Even a company's agreement to release a record is capable of being consideration.

Money which has already been paid is not consideration and, if a contract contains an undertaking (ie agreement) from a company to pay a musician a sum of money which has already been paid, there will not be sufficient consideration, and (in the absence of other matters which might amount to consideration) a binding contract will not be created.

A further pitfall to avoid is the payment of the consideration to a person who is not a party to the contract. If, for example, a musician agrees to play in a concert in consideration of the company agreeing to pay the musician's friend £500, that will not constitute valid consideration, since the money is being paid to a third party. The rule relating to third party consideration may appear curious when account is taken of the fact that payment of the consideration cannot, in some circumstances, be made to a third party.

Payment to third parties happens frequently where actors, musicians and writers direct that payments are to be made to their agents. Such directions are perfectly acceptable and do not mean that the consideration of the contract is payable to the agent, since the agent is not a party to the contract. Although the actor/musician/writer may have directed that all payments are made to the agent, the actor/musician writer can in many cases revoke, at any time, the direction and receive payment direct. It is also possible for a person to assign his or her right to receive royalties from a particular contract to a third party.

The courts do not concern themselves, whether the bargain made by someone who enters into a contract is a fair one or not. The payment by one party of too much money or too little money may, however, be evidence of duress or mistake or may induce the court to imply a breach of warranty*. It may, therefore, give the court grounds for setting aside a bargain on the basis of fraud, undue influence or unconscionability (see Paragraph 54.23).

The consideration necessary to support a contract must be of some value, although it may be nominal. There is no legal requirement for consideration to be paid for an assignment or licence of copyright and it is theoretically possible for a company to obtain all its rights authorisations (by way of assignment or licence) with no payments to third parties. There would be practical disadvantages to a company conducting business in this manner, since there are certain obligations which companies need to be able to impose on media industry personnel and other parties (such as the obligation to perform certain services) and warranties which need to be contractually enforceable. For this reason, many documents, notably releases and permissions, contain a nominal consideration of £1.

A contractual relationship may, however, be created, even where no consideration is payable. Where a document is executed as a deed, it will create a contract, even if no consideration is payable. Individuals are sometimes nervous, however, when asked to sign deeds, although they may be perfectly happy to sign a letter which contains a reference to nominal consideration.

Where a contract is not supported by any consideration, it may still be enforceable if entered into by way of deed. Certain statutes require contractual documents to be under seal where they relate to conveyances of land or conveyances of any interest in land or where they relate to transfers of shares in certain companies and transfers of suretyships. Some contracts must, by law, be made by deed and some are required to be made or evidenced in writing.

54.8 Implied Terms and Custom and Practice

Although the courts will not make a contract where none exists, they will uphold bargains made between businessmen, wherever possible and will recognise that such agreements frequently record only the most important elements in a crude and summary fashion. If the courts can establish the meaning intended, a contract will not be defective simply because it is open to more than one construction.

If satisfied that there was an ascertainable and determinable intention to contract, the courts will try to give effect to the intention and will look at the substance of the agreement which was intended to be made between the parties. This approach is particularly important for parties who have acted in the belief that certain terms have created a contract between them.

As a general rule, the courts will not make or improve contracts if the express terms* are clear. The express terms will be applied even if the courts think some other term might have been more suitable. However, the courts will imply terms where the parties must have intended the term to form part of the contract ("something so obvious it goes without saying") or where the term is necessary in the business sense to give efficacy to the contract.

In the absence of any contrary intention, the courts may imply into a contract any local custom or usage which normally governs the particular type of contract in question, as representing the presumed intention of the parties. It may also be possible to import a term into a contract on the basis of a previous course of dealing between the parties.

C   PERFORMANCE OF CONTRACTUAL OBLIGATIONS

54.9 Performance

The general rule, in contract law, is that a party to a contract is required to perform exactly what that party undertook to do and is not entitled to substitute for the promised obligations other obligations which may be equally advantageous for the other party.

As a rule, a party to a contract cannot transfer its liability under the contract without the consent of the other party, although the benefit of a contract may, however, be assigned. There is no objection to the substitution of the performance by a third party of duties that are not connected with the skilled character or other qualifications of the original party of the contract. Liability under a contract may also be transferred with the consent of all parties, so as to discharge the original contract and to novate (or create a new contract).

Rights and liabilities of parties to a contract may, in some circumstances, be assigned by operation of law when, for example, a party dies or becomes bankrupt. No right or liability of a purely personal nature (ie one which is dependent on skill or qualification of the party) can be assigned by operation of law.

54.10 Time for Performance

Where a contract does not provide a time by which obligations are to be performed, the law implies an undertaking by each party to perform their part of the agreement within a reasonable time. Where a contract provides for a certain action to be performed by a certain date, failure to perform by that date will not be considered a breach of the contract, unless time is expressly stipulated by the parties to be "of the essence" or unless the subject matter of the contract or the surrounding circumstances, show that time should be considered to be of the essence. Failure by a person to perform an obligation by a stated date will not be a contractual breach unless the contract provided that time was of the essence.

Where time is not initially of the essence, a party who has been subjected to unreasonable delay may give notice to the party in default, fixing a reasonable time for performance and stating that in the event of non-performance within the fixed time, the contract will be treated as being broken.

54.11 Payment

Payment may be proved to have been made either by production of a receipt or by any other evidence from which the fact of payment may be inferred. In some circumstances, payment may even be presumed, from the length of time which has elapsed since the debt became due.

A receipt is not conclusive evidence of payment, merely an admission and evidence may be considered by a court to prove the intention with which the receipt was given and whether any payment was in fact made and, if so, on what terms and in respect of what matter.

The posting of a cheque which is lost will not constitute payment, unless the person making the payment was requested to make it in such manner. In this case, the person requesting this may have been taken to have run the risk of a cheque being lost.

D   EXCLUSION CLAUSES AND UNFAIR CONTRACTUAL TERMS

54.12 Exclusion Clauses Generally

An exclusion clause is a clause to exclude or limit one party's liability for breach of contract or misrepresentation. Exclusion clauses fall into two basic categories. One type seeks to exclude or cut down the primary obligation of the contract.

(A provision in a distribution agreement which states that the distributor will have no liability to a record company if the distributor fails to perform certain obligations would fall into this category.) The second type seeks to restrict the rights of the other party in the event of breach of some primary obligation by, for example, limiting The amount of damages which can be recovered.

An exclusion clause which excludes all liability in relation to the performance of the primary obligation, may have the effect of rendering the agreement unilateral and removing all contractual force from the agreement, making it unenforceable. For example, a provision in a record distribution agreement which stated that the distributor had no liability for any breach whatever would make performance of the agreement by the distributor optional and the court might find such a provision unenforceable.

54.13   Sale of Goods

Some obligations cannot be excluded. For example, in any contract for the sale of goods, there are certain implied undertakings as to the title (or ownership of the goods) being free from incumbrances (such as security interests or other rights of third parties). In some contracts there are also implied undertakings as to compliance with description, suitable quality, fitness for purpose and correspondence with samples. These undertakings cannot be excluded in the case of any person dealing as a consumer and may be excluded in other cases only so far as reasonable.

Any term which attempts to exclude any of the above implied undertakings and warranties is therefore void, if it is contained in a contract with a consumer (see Paragraph 54.14 for the definition) and in any other cases will be enforceable only to the extent that it is fair and reasonable (see Paragraph 54.15 for the test of reasonableness). The above restrictions on the validity of exclusions do not apply to international supply contracts or to agreements the proper law of which is the law of the United Kingdom, but which, apart from the choice of United Kingdom law, would be governed by the laws of another country.

54.14   Exclusion of Liability

Any provision of an agreement which would exclude or restrict liability of one party for any misrepresentation made before the contract was made is unenforceable, except to the extent that a court may allow reliance on the representation as being fair and reasonable in the circumstances.

A person deals as a consumer if they do not make the contract in the course of business or hold themselves out as doing so and the other party to the contract does make it in the course of the business and the goods passing under the contract are of a type ordinarily supplied for private use or consumption.

Liability for death or personal injury resulting from negligence cannot be excluded or restricted in any contract. In the case of other loss or damage, liability for negligence may be excluded or restricted only so far as may be reasonable.

54.15 Reasonableness

The test of reasonableness, applied to any contractual term is whether or not the term was a fair and reasonable one to be included in the contract, having regard to circumstances which were or ought reasonably to have been known to or in the contemplation of, the parties at the time the contract was made.

Where a person wishes to rely on an exclusion clause, the court will consider the resources which that person could expect to have available for the purpose of meeting the liability which is sought to be excluded and how far it was open to such person to obtain insurance cover in respect of the risk.

In determining whether or not a provision satisfies the test of reasonableness the courts will consider a number of provisions including the following:

* the relative strength of bargaining positions of the parties taking into account (amongst other things) alternative means by which the customer's requirements could have been met;
* whether the customer received an inducement to agree to the relevant term or whether the customer had an opportunity of entering into a similar contract with other persons without having to accept a similar term;
* whether the customer knew or ought reasonably to have known, of the existence and extent of the term, having regard, amongst other things, to the custom of the trade and any previous course of dealing of the parties;
* where the term excludes or restricts, any relevant liability if some condition is not complied with, whether it was reasonable at the time of the contract to expect that compliance with that condition would be practicable;
* whether the goods were manufactured, processed or adapted, to the special order of the customer.

54.16 Construction of Exclusion Clauses

Exclusion clauses are construed strictly by the courts and hidden meanings cannot, therefore, be read into them. Exclusion clauses require clear wording, since any ambiguity in them will be construed by the courts against the party which seeks to rely on them. General words of exclusion will not normally be construed so as to cover fundamental breaches, which go to the very root of the contract; they may also be construed as having no application to liability for negligence.

Exclusion clauses will be construed in such a way that they do not afford protection to a party who is acting outside the scope of the contract or to a party whose performance is different in kind from that contemplated by the contract they will not normally be interpreted in such a way as to deprive an agreement of contractual content and to turn it merely into a declaration of intent.

Where an exclusion clause appears in a printed standard form of contract and there is a conflict between that clause and another clause which is written or typed in or otherwise added to the printed form, then the latter will generally prevail, since the courts will give greater weight to what the parties have expressly agreed in detail, rather than to what appears in standard forms. The courts may also refuse to give effect to an exclusion clause which might wholly nullify another positive clause of the contract.

In those circumstances where companies wish to exclude liability, they should pay particular attention to the matters set out above, in order to ensure that the exclusion may be contractually enforceable.

E   MISREPRESENTATION AND MISTAKE

54.17   Misrepresentation Generally

There are many occasions where persons enter into contracts as a result of statements or representations which have been made to them. Where the representations are included in the contract they will very often take the form of warranties. Any untrue representation may be a breach of the warranty and may entitle the person to whom it was made to rescind or terminate the contract.

But what is the position where the representation is not incorporated in the contract? The person to whom it was made may be entitled to rescind the contract, recover any money they have paid and may also be entitled to recover damages in respect of any loss they have suffered.

What if the contract contains an exclusion clause (see Paragraph 54.12) which excludes or restricts liability in the event of misrepresentation? Any such clause will be of no force or effect unless it satisfies the test of reasonableness referred to in Paragraph 54.15.

What does a company have to prove to recover damages for misrepresentation? A company will have to show that the representation:

* was not only false, but fraudulent; or
* was negligent; or
* cannot be proved to have been believed to be true by the person who made it.

A statement will be fraudulent if the person making it did not know it to be true or knew or believed that it was false or did not actually and honestly believe it to be true. A statement which is made with indifference or recklessness will be fraudulent unless the person making it can show that they actually and honestly believed that it was true.

There are, however, occasions where a person makes a statement which in objective terms has a meaning different from the one intended, but this will not amount to misrepresentation if that person can show the statement was true in the sense the statement was intended and that this sense was one which might reasonably be attached to the statement.

It is not necessary for a person who makes a fraudulent misrepresentation to intend to defraud. Caprice, mischievousness or stupidity will be sufficient for a person to be liable, if they cannot demonstrate they actually and honestly believed the statement and there is no requirement to prove wickedness or intent to deceive or injure.

54.18 Mistake and Impossibility

If two parties reach an agreement that is based on a fundamental mistake, that mistake will negate their consensus (see Paragraph 54.5) and prevent a binding contract from coming into existence. Where the mistake is not fundamental to the formation of an agreement, it will not negate the contract.

A mistake is fundamental if the mistaken party would not have entered into the contract had they realised the mistake. Mistakes may be categorised into three types:

- mistake as to person;
- mistake as to subject matter; and
- mistake as to terms.

Where a promise is, at the time when it was made, manifestly incapable of performance, either by fact or by law, then a binding contract cannot exist, either because there can have been no intention to create legal relations or because there was no consideration.

For example, where, unknown to the parties, the buyer is already the owner of what the seller purports to sell, any intended transfer of ownership is clearly impossible and the sale is void. Alternatively, if both parties are mistaken in relation to the existence of some quality which the subject of the contract is thought to have and whose absence makes the subject matter essentially different from what it was believed to be, then the contract will be void. Mistake as to quality by one party alone will not render the contract void, whether or not the other party is aware of it, unless the mistake is fundamental and is actively caused by the other party.

F   FRUSTRATION AND FORCE MAJEURE

54.19 Impossibility and Frustration

A contract which is incapable of performance at the time when it is made, is, generally void from the very beginning. A perfectly valid contract may, however, be rendered incapable of performance by subsequent impossibility. This will normally bring the contract to an end from the moment of impossibility. In some cases, however, a contracting party may have made an absolute promise to perform certain obligations and will not be excused by non-performance even if this is subsequently rendered impossible.

Where an agreement has been entered into on the assumption that some fundamental state of affairs should continue to exist and an event occurs which renders performance of the contract impossible or only possible in a very different way from that originally contemplated by the parties, all further performance of their obligations may be excused as a result of the application of the doctrine of frustration.

In order for the doctrine to apply, the frustrating event must arise without fault of either party. Deliberate choice not to perform the contract or to put performance out of the power of the parties, will constitute default. An act of negligence will not necessarily, however, deprive a party of the possibility of using the doctrine of frustration, as a defence for any claim.

Frustration may be caused by a number of different types of event, including physical destruction of the subject matter of the contract, cancellation of an expected event, delay, subsequent legal changes, death or incapacity.

A contract will not be discharged by the doctrine of frustration simply because it becomes more difficult to perform or becomes more onerous. The doctrine cannot generally be used to excuse performance of a contract, on account of rises or falls in price, depreciation of currency or unexpected obstacles to the execution of the contract. These are the ordinary risks of business and will not excuse inability of performance by any party, unless otherwise agreed.

Companies should avoid entering into contractual arrangements which require them to perform obligations which are outside their control. The normal method chosen to limit liability in such circumstances is to agree upon provisions which apply in the event of force majeure*. Such provisions frequently provide for the return of sums paid under the contract.

54.20 Force Majeure and Acts of God

Many contracts contain provisions which provide that their performance may be excused, if they are rendered impossible by the occurrence of an act of God or an event of force majeure. These provisions are effective so long as they are not uncertain. They may even allow the courts to take account of a party's obligations under other contracts, despite the normal rule that it is generally no excuse that contracts with third parties prevent the fulfilment of the contract in question. Where, however, a contract excuses a party from delay due to unavoidable causes, they may not be able to rely on the law relating to force majeure if they fail, before making the contract, to enquire whether such unavoidable causes existed and to inform the other party.

An Act of God may be defined as being an extraordinary occurrence or circumstance, which could not have been foreseen and which could not have been guarded against. An alternative definition is that it is an accident, due to natural causes, directly and exclusively without human intervention, which could not by any amount of ability have been foreseen or, if foreseen, could not by any amount of human care and skill have been resisted. An Act of God need not be unique, nor need it have happened for the first time. It is enough for it to have been extraordinary and not reasonably capable of having been anticipated.

While there are circumstances where the inclusion of force majeure provisions in a contract will be in a company's interest, there will equally be occasions when it is not—where, for example, the company wishes to impose an absolute obligation on a third party.

When force majeure provisions are included in a contract, they are normally inserted towards the end, amongst the so-called "boilerplate*" and occasionally force majeure provisions may be found which, on a close reading, can be seen to excuse performance for less than compelling reasons.

G ILLEGAL, VOID AND VOIDABLE CONTRACTS

54.21 Illegal and Void Contracts

Even where a contract is not defective by reason of form or of lack of agreement or for want of consideration, the contract may still be illegal, void or voidable. This may be the case either where the contract involves the commission of an unlawful act (whether the act is unlawful by statute or by common law) or because the contract offends against the principles of order or morality.

Any contract entered into with the object of committing an illegal act is unenforceable and may not be enforced by any party to the contract or by the courts. The fact that one or both parties were ignorant that the contract involved a breach of law or that their purpose of entering into the contract was unlawful, is irrelevant.

Generally the courts will refuse to enforce a contract for the commission of an unlawful act. Various different categories of illegal or void contracts have been developed by the courts including agreements which tend to be injurious to the public or against the public good; contracts made with the enemy in time of war; agreements which oust the jurisdiction of the courts or interfere with the course of justice; agreements which are in unreasonable restraint of trade.

Other categories exist, such as contracts for the sale of public offices or titles, agreements which interfere with the free exercise of votes, contracts which are made upon consideration for a sexually immoral purpose and contracts which are prejudicial to family life.

Contracts of the last two categories are not illegal but are void because they offend public policy. Void contracts are unenforceable, but unlike illegal contracts, a method of giving effect to the contract may be found through the application of the doctrine of severance.

54.22 Severance

Severance is a process by which the void or illegal parts, are cut away from a contract which may otherwise be entirely lawful, leaving the valid parts of the contract to be enforced, without the void or illegal parts. Where the objects of a contract involve illegal, rather than simply void, provisions, severance is generally not possible.

In the instances where severance is permitted, it must be possible simply to strike out the offending parts of the contract, since the courts will not rewrite or rearrange the contract. A court may not be prepared to sever a provision if to do so would entirely alter the scope and intention of the agreement. Once the void (or in exceptional cases, illegal) provisions have been deleted from a contract, what is left must contain all the characteristics of a valid contract. It will follow that if the severed part contains the only consideration clause, the contract will be unenforceable (see Paragraph 54.7).

54.23 Voidable Contracts

A contract may be voidable by any party who has entered into it under duress or undue influence or whilst drunk or insane.

Duress means compulsion, under which a person acts through fear of personal suffering from actual or threatened, injury to the body or confinement. A threat of criminal prosecution or civil or bankruptcy proceedings will not, of itself, amount to duress, but may do so if it is intended and calculated, to cause terror. A contract obtained by duress is voidable or, in some cases, void. If, however, the party entitled to avoid such a contract acts on it, then it will become binding on that party.

Undue influence is the unconscionable use by one person of power possessed by that person over another, in order to induce the other to enter into a contract. If the parties were, at the time of a transaction or shortly before it, in a particular confidential relationship to each other (such as that of parent and child, trustee and beneficiary, adviser and client) undue influence will, in some cases, be presumed unless it can be shown that it did not exist. It can be proved that undue influence did not exist by showing that the transaction appeared fair and that the party who might have been subject to undue influence received competent independent advice.

The fact that a person was drunk when entering into an agreement may be a defence to an action brought to enforce the agreement, if the drunkenness was so extreme as to deprive that person of the ability to reason. The courts will not, however, avoid a contract if the extent of drunkenness merely deprived the person of business sense. Relief may, however, be granted by the courts to a drunken person, if it can be shown that the person's condition was known to the other party at the time the contract was made and that some unfair advantage was taken of it. The drunken person will, however, become liable under any contract made under the influence of drink if, after becoming sober, such person ratifies the contract or enters into a new contract. A contract for the reasonable price of necessities (ie goods suitable to a person's condition in life and to such person's actual requirements at the time of sale and delivery), which are sold and delivered to a drunk person, will be binding.

H AGENTS, PERSONAL REPRESENTATIVES AND EXECUTORS

Normally, the persons with whom a media company enters into contracts with, will be acting in their own capacity, but there are three common situations where media industry personnel will have dealings with persons who act in a special capacity as agent or personal representative or as an executor.

54.24 Agents

Many media industry personnel are represented by agents who negotiate the terms of contracts on their clients' behalf.

In the eyes of the law, the acts of the agent are considered to be the acts of the person whom the agent represents (or principal). The powers and duties of the agent, including the agent's powers to sign agreements on behalf of its principals will, however, depend on whatever agreement exists between the agent and their client. The general principles of the law of agency are considered in Paragraphs 54.26–54.29.

It would appear that very few agents require clients they represent to execute agency agreements and this might cause difficulties to a media company. If a contract is executed by an agent on behalf of a client it is possible that, unless the agent had express written authority, a client (or more likely the client's estate) could maintain that the contract was not binding on the client, either because the agent had no authority to sign or because the client had not consented or because the consent of the client had been given on grounds of mistake or had been induced by a misrepresentation.

Contracts with actors/musicians/authors form part of the tools of a media company's trade and are the source of all rights which the company exploits in its business. Any uncertainty which might affect them is, from the company's point of view, highly undesirable. Companies should, therefore, as a matter of routine, require all significant contracts to be executed by the relevant actor/musician/author and, if possible, witnessed. Where there is any doubt as to the mental capacity of the actor/musician/author, a company will need to seek specific legal advice, as failure to attend to this matter could invalidate any contract entered into.

From the point of view of an agent, any claim that the agent has exceeded his or her authority is similarly undesirable and should be eliminated. An agent will, however, wish to safeguard their right to receive remuneration and it would, therefore, be appropriate, in suitable cases, for the contract to contain an irrevocable payment direction in the agent's favour directing the company to pay to the agent all sums due to the actor/musician/author under the contract.

54.25   Personal Representatives and Executors

Death is an inevitable fact of life and all media companies will, from time to time, have to deal with the estates of deceased persons.

On the death of a person, their property passes by what is known as "operation of law" to the person's personal representatives. The time of transmission of the property is the moment of death. In order to prove that they have the legal right to deal with the deceased's property, the personal representatives have to obtain a grant of probate of the deceased's will or letters of administration from the court.

They will then be able to transfer any copyrights and rights in performances in accordance with the directions contained in the deceased person's will or, if the person died without a valid will (intestate), in accordance with the intestacy rules.

A company acquiring rights from a person's estate should therefore normally ask to see the following original (or certified copy) documents: the will, the grant of probate (or if no will, the grant of letters of administration of the estate, which takes the place of the grant of probate) together with any vesting assent executed by the personal representatives. A vesting assent is a document which will transfer the copyright in a work to the beneficiary named in the will or, where there was no will, the person entitled under the intestacy rules.

The company will need to check that the details of the above documents comply with the provisions of the will. Wills may contain provisions which deal with manuscripts (or typescripts) separately from their copyrights. Where a will bequeaths documents or other material things incorporating unpublished original literary, dramatic, musical or artistic works or films or sound recordings to a person, the copyright in those works will pass to the person entitled to those documents or other material things, unless the will (or any codicil to it) contains a contrary intention.

It is also possible for an author to appoint a literary executor by will and, once the will has been admitted to probate, the literary executor will be able to deal with the relevant copyrights on the terms stated in the will (or codicil).

I   GENERAL PRINCIPLES OF THE LAW OF AGENCY

54.26   Agency Generally

The concept of the agency relationship is that the acts of the agent are considered to be binding on the person whom the agent represents (the principal). Agency has been described as the relationship which arises whenever one person has authority to act on behalf of another and consents to act in such a way. The concept of agency is not limited to individuals. A company may act as agent on behalf of another company.

An agent may be a sole agent or an exclusive agent and be appointed for a particular purpose or for a particular territory. The appointment of the agent may be oral or in writing.

If the agreement between agent and principal is oral, the terms and scope of the agent's authority will be questions of fact and will depend on the circumstances of the particular case. The extent of an agent's authority, will, in such cases, be determined by inference from all the circumstances.

The primary duty of the commercial agent is to perform what the agent has undertaken to do and not to exceed its authority. In performing its obligations, the agent has a duty to show proper skill and care in accordance with the terms of the contract and the principal's instructions.

54.27   Agent's Fiduciary Duties

Fiduciary duties (or duties of good faith) are implied into all agency relationships, unless they are excluded by contract. They could, broadly speaking, be described as duties to act in the utmost good faith towards the principal.

The most important of the agent's fiduciary duties to the principal are:

- an agent has a duty not to place itself in a position where the agent's duties conflict with its own interests;
- an agent is usually not entitled, although there are exceptions, to delegate

its duties and generally is required to carry out its principal's instructions personally;
- an agent should not place itself in a position where it has to balance the agent's own interests against those of the principal. This duty is closely associated with the agent's duty not to take advantage of its principal or make a secret profit, by exploiting its position;
- an agent has a duty not to accept bribes or secret commissions;
- an agent has a duty to hand over money it is holding for the principal.

Sometimes an agent will be under a duty to keep the principal's money separate and will be treated as trustee of the principal. The agent also has a duty to keep accurate accounts and to produce them to the principal, if so required.

54.28 Rights of Agent against Principal

The agent is entitled to be indemnified by the principal for losses suffered and reimbursement for all expenses and liabilities reasonably incurred in the performance of the agent's duties.

An agent possesses the right against its principal to be remunerated for the agent's services if the contract so provides. The agent's entitlement to receive commission will normally end on the expiry of the agency relationship, unless the contract contains express provision to the contrary.

Where a person is acting as agent in relation to the sale of goods, they have the right to be compensated for termination of their agency and they also have the right to receive compensation for transactions introduced after the end of the agency agreement in certain circumstances.

54.29 Liability and Contractual Rights

In what circumstances can an agent become personally liable under a contract the agent made on behalf of its principal with a third party? The general rule is that an agent simply establishes contractual relations between the principal and third party and then "drops out of the transaction". The agent is not a separate party to the contract and does not therefore become personally liable under it. The agent may not sue a third party on the contracts. The only person who may sue is the principal and the only person who can be sued is the principal.

However, the general rule is always subject to the correct inference to be drawn from all the circumstances and there are a number of instances where the agent may be liable on the contract. The most obvious is where the agent makes some misrepresentation or where the agent acts on behalf of an undisclosed principal. Until the third party discovers the existence of the undisclosed principal, the third party's contract is with the agent, who is liable under the contract. Once the principal's existence is established, the third party will have the choice of whether to sue the agent or the principal.

Where an agent contracts with a third party on behalf of its principal, the agent is not a party to the contract and cannot sue the third party on it. However, where the parties intended that the agent should have rights, as well as liabilities, under the contract, the agent will be entitled to sue the third party. Furthermore, the agent's agreement with its principal may give the agent exclusive rights to collect income and may appoint the agent as the principal's attorney for the purpose of commencing legal proceedings and collecting income.

An agent's authority may expressly permit it to enforce contracts on behalf of the principal, authorising it under a power of attorney or other express provision, to enforce, sue upon and collect money arising under prespecified agreements.

Glossary

Above-the-Line Costs These include items relating to the acquisition of underlying rights and all fees payable to the producer*, director and principal cast of a film or other production.

Advance An advance is a payment normally made on signature of an agreement or on exercise of an Option*. Advances are normally expressed to be recoupable. If an advance is recoupable, the amount of the advance will be deducted from the amount or royalties payable. Occasionally an advance may be expressed to be non-recoupable in which event, royalty payments will be made in addition to the advance. Sometimes an advance may be described as being non-returnable.

AF of M American Federation of Musicians.

Agreement See Contract*.

ASCAP American Society of Composers, Authors and Publishers.

All-in Deal An all-inclusive deal with labour for the production of a film, under which, payments higher than the guild or union minima are made and treated as pre-payments of overtime at the minimum rate. The effect of this is that the producer need not use any Contingency* part of the budget on overtime.

Artwork Exception Many contracts* contain provisions relating to the screen or advertising credit which an artist is entitled to receive. These credit provisions normally also recite certain circumstances in which the artist will not be entitled to receive an advertising credit (for example printed advertising of less than a certain number of column inches). Where the credit provisions stipulate that the size of screen credit given to the artist will be not less than 100% of the size of the title of the film, the contract will usually also stipulate that this obligation will not apply where the title is used in an art-work format, and will be calculated with reference to the normal typographical use of the title.

BASCA	British Academy of Songwriters, Composers and Authors.
BMI	Broadcast Music Incorporated.
Barring	The practice where one cinema may prevent (bar) an adjoining cinema from playing a film until the first cinema has shown the film or until a specified number of weeks have elapsed from first showing.
Below-the-Line Costs	These costs in the budget of a film are: studio and equipment costs; design and wardrobe costs; fees of members of the cast other than principal cast; travelling and accommodation costs; film stock costs, laboratory costs; special effects and all post-production costs.
Black Box Income	Black box income is unidentifiable income. The concept is encountered in music publishing arrangements where it is not possible, on occasions, to identify works in relation to which income is received.
Blocked Funds	Sums of money which due to either exchange control restrictions or withholding taxes* are not freely remittable from the country or territory in which they are earned.
Boilerplate	The boilerplate section of a contract contains standard provisions. The expression "boilerplate" is of American origin and dates from the early days of newspaper syndication. The newspapers would send by railroad "hot metal" in the shape of pre-assembled, pre-cast boiler metal shaped shells ready to be fitted on to a printing press. This pre-fabricated material would contain national news and it would also have gaps on the front page and on other pages to permit the insertion of local news stories. The task of the local newspaper editor would be to produce the text to go in the spaces for the local stories. Once this had been achieved the rest was simply "trilerplate".
Break Figure	In theatrical exhibition, the figure at which the percentage fee to the distributor increases.
Buy-out	In many cases, contracts express the fees of writers and performers to be paid on a "buy-out" basis. The intention is to pre-pay future sums which would be payable by way of residual fees, repeat fees or reuse fees, in order to permit the film or television programme in question to be exploited on a worldwide all-media basis without any further payment liability.
Certificate of Value	This is a certificate which is required to be executed in any document transferring intellectual property rights executed in the United Kingdom. The transfer of intellectual property rights attracts stamp duty under UK legislation, and a certificate of value is required. This certificate sets out the total value of all property transferred under the relevant transaction or any linked transaction, in order to calculate the rate at which stamp duty is to be paid.

Chain of Title   The chain of title of a literary work, film, or sound recording is a set of documents which shows how "title" to or ownership of the work/film/sound recording was acquired by its original author/creator and has been transmitted to its current owner.

Condition Precedent   A condition precedent is a condition which is required to be satisfied before the liability to perform a contractual obligation is triggered. Conditions precedent are normally used in relation to financial obligations, and a financier will not be under any obligation to provide finance until all conditions precedent have been satisfied.

Contingency   The contingency element of a budget is normally 10 per cent of the direct cost of the film.

Contingent Fees   Contingent fees are fees payable only on the happening of specified events, such as when receipts from a film reach a certain level.

Contract   To all intents and purposes the word "contract" is freely interchangeable with the word "agreement*". Frequently, however, there is a nuance, in that the word "contract" may be intended to refer to a document. It will be appreciated that agreements or contracts may be created verbally, although in the immortal words of Sam Goldwyn: "An oral agreement isn't worth the paper its written on."

Contractual Rights   Contractual rights are rights which are created by a contract*.

Controlled Compositions   Controlled compositions are compositions which were written by and are owned and controlled by artists. They are normally the subject of special provisions in recording contracts.

Cover Version   A cover version is a recording of the song made by an artist other than the artist who made the original first recording of the song. Often, cover versions are in a language which is different from the language of the original recording. These cover versions are often referred to as foreign language covers.

Cross-collateralisation   The pooling of income from different films or from the exploitation of the same film in different territories enabling a distributor to off-set losses in areas or countries where the advance* or minimum guarantee has not been recouped by retaining overages payable in respect of films or territories where the advance or minimum guarantee has been recouped and applying these towards the losses.

Cross Default Provision   A provision where an event of default under one contract* will be an event of default under other contracts.

Cut-off   The expression cut-off is frequently encountered in the context of screenplay agreements. A screenplay agreement will normally provide for the writer to produce a first draft screenplay and will give the company commissioning the

439

screenplay the right to request a revised first draft screenplay, a second draft screenplay, a revised second draft screenplay, and perhaps also, a final polish. The company may not wish to assume the liability to pay the writer to produce all this material, since it may find, after delivery of the first draft, that it is unable to raise finance. Normally the writer's fee is payable in a number of instalments, each instalment being linked to the delivery of written material (first draft, revised first draft etc). If the writer's fees are payable on a "cut-off" basis, this will mean that if the company decides not to proceed to a revised first draft screenplay, it will not be liable to pay the writer for the additional fees which would have been payable had the company decided to proceed further.

Deferment
A deferred fee payable out of a producer's first receipts from a film before recoupment of the cost of production of the film.

Direct Cost
The aggregate of the above-the-line costs* and the below-the-line costs*.

Discounting
The re-financing of a distribution guarantee payable to a producer* at some point in the future (normally delivery of a film) by a person prepared to provide immediate finance to a producer before delivery so this finance can be used as production finance for a 'discount' (ie the producer receives a discounted amount which is less than the original distribution guarantee).

Double Deductions
Some draft contracts provide that commissions and on-line expenses are deducted more than once. Normally, a court will give effect to the clear ordinary meaning of words, even if this is commercially disadvantageous to one party and double deductions are, therefore, generally to be avoided if it all possible.

Equitable Remuneration
The concept of equitable remuneration is of recent origin, being a creation of the European Economic Community. It is designed to compensate writers and performers for the rental and lending of films and sound recordings containing their works or performances.

Exclusion of Set-off Letter
An exclusion of set-off letter is a letter which is required by film financiers to be given by the bank at which the producer maintains the production account of a film. The bank will confirm that it will not set-off any sums credited to the production account for the film against any other liabilities which the producer may owe towards the bank.

Favoured Nations
A favoured nations clause is a clause which guarantees that a party to the contract (normally the recipient of royalties) will receive "most favoured nations" treatment. This means that if the company paying the royalties* accords more favourable treatment to another artist, by paying them on a more favourable royalty rate basis, or

by paying them a higher fee, or by giving them a bigger dressing-room, the more favourable provisions contained in the other artists contract are automatically incorporated into the contract of the artist who has favoured nations protection.

Further Assurance

A further assurance provision pursuant to which a party to a contract* undertakes to do further facts and execute further documents in order to confirm the grant of rights under the contract.

Hold-back

A hold-back period is a period during which the exploitation of a film or television programme in a particular medium is "held back" or prohibited in order to protect the interests of one of the parties to a contract*. For example, the value of a film to a video distributor is likely to be substantially diminished if the film is exploited on television prior to its release on videogram. For this reason video distributors who acquire rights in films normally negotiate in the acquisition contract a provision where the person selling the rights will guarantee that the film will not be exploited by means of television in the video distributor's territory until the expiry of a specified number of months following the release of the film on video.

Holdover

The right of a distributor to require an exhibitor to continue to show (or holdover) a film. The right is normally exercisable if gross box office receipts are above a certain figure.

House Nut

An agreed allowance which an exhibitor may retain from gross box office receipts under certain forms of theatrical exhibition deals. The allowance is normally the exhibitor's cost of doing business plus a cushion.

Incumbrance

An incumbrance is a charge or a mortgage or other security interest which has been created over physical property, intellectual property or intangible property.

Indemnity

An indemnity obligation requires the person assuming it to protect the other party to a contract from all loss.

Indirect Costs

The indirect costs of a production include fees payable to the completion guarantor and any commitment fees or similar charges payable in respect of finance, legal fees and accountancy fees.

Joseph Grand

Lowly employee of the town hall of Oran—the setting of Albert Camus' *The Plague*. Joseph Grand's life is marked by his inability to find the right word, whether to claim the promotion he was promised 22 years ago, or to keep the woman he loves. Grand's derisory salary obliges him to live in reduced circumstances, but for years he has been dedicating his evenings and weekends to the pursuit of some private labour which he will not speak about.

As the plague takes hold of Oran, Grand confides in Dr Rieux that the private labour he is engaged in consists of writing a book which he intends will be a work of such

441

perfection that his publisher will, after reading it, say "Gentlemen—hats off!". Rieux, though little acquainted with the world of publishing, thinks that things might not happen quite like that and, also suspects that when publishers are in their offices they might be bare-headed, but says nothing.

Later, in his apartment, Grand tells Rieux of the great difficulty he has in bringing his work to perfection, how he spends evenings, or entire weeks on a word, sometimes merely a conjunction. His dining room table is covered with sheets of paper containing microscopic writing, the endless reworking of the first sentence of his novel which he reads to Rieux:

"One fine morning in the month of May, an elegant Amazon rode on a superb chestnut mare through the flowery lanes of the Bois de Boulogne."

As the plague rages around them, Grand continues his work, announces that he has definitely abandoned "elegant" for "svelte" and debates changing the colour of the mare, which is now "sumptuous" rather than "superb". Grand is the first person to contract the plague and recover, but he remains unable to find the right words for the first sentence of his book.

During the four years it took to find the right words for the three word title of this work and the further twelve months of private labour during the evenings and weekends which it took to write the text, Joseph Grand (to whom this book is dedicated) was often in the author's thoughts. Rieux's suspicions were well-founded: enquiries have established that nobody in Butterworths wears hats these days.

Key Person

Some contracts* contain what is referred to as a key person clause. A key person clause guarantees that the services of certain specified key personnel will be made available for the purposes of the contract.

Laboratory Access Letter

A laboratory access letter will permit the person to whom it is addressed to obtain access to film materials which are held in a laboratory, in order to obtain release prints. The letter normally stipulates that the person to whom access is granted is to pay the laboratory's charges for manufacturing materials, and the access letter will not permit its addressee to remove materials from the laboratory.

Laboratory Pledge-holder's Letter

A laboratory pledgeholder's letter is a letter issued by a laboratory at which film materials are to be developed, in which the laboratory will give an undertaking to the principal financier of a film to hold all film and sound materials which are deposited in the laboratory to the order of the financier and not to part with possession of such materials without the financier's prior written consent.

Loan-Out
An arrangement where the services of an individual are made available through that individual's service corporation which loan out his or her services to third parties.

MCPS
Mechanical Copyright Protection Society Limited.

Mechanical Rights
The rights to arise the mechanical reproduction of musical works is frequently referred to as the "mechanical right". The expression originates in the very early days of the 20th century when mechanical reproduction was effected by means of piano rolls. Nowadays mechanical reproduction generally refers to the manufacturer of records, tapes, videograms and CDS. This reproduction may not be effected without the consent of the copyright owner who will generally require the payment or a royalty to authorise the mechanical reproduction of that copyright owners musical works. This royalty is frequently refers to as a mechanical royalty or simply as a "mechanical".

Minimum Guarantee
A minimum guarantee is a fixed amount which is required to be paid under a contract*. The term "minimum guarantee" is often thought to be synonymous with the term "advance*", but whereas advances are normally payable in advance, minimum guarantees are normally payable in arrears and frequently, in instalments.

Moral Rights
There are four moral rights established under the laws of United Kingdom. These are: the right to be identified; the right to object to derogatory treatment; the right not to have a work falsely contributed; and the right to privacy in relation to certain films and photographs commissioned for private domestic purposes. All these rights can be waived. The laws of other countries also contain provisions relating to moral rights.

Net Sales
Net sales are frequently defined as 90 per cent or 85 per cent of sales of records less those records which are returned during any period. There are historical reasons for accounting for 90 per cent records sold (or 85 per cent in North America). The original 10/15 per cent of allowance was permitted in order to compensate the record companies for breakages back in the days when manufactured records were made of shellac and were highly fragile.

Negative Cost
The cost of production of a film—literally the cost of the negative.

Negative Pick-up
The acquisition of a film for a particular territory.

Off-the-Top
An off-the-top arrangement is sometimes an arrangement where costs and expenses are deducted from first receipts (or off-the-top) and the balance remaining is then split in agreed percentages between the parties to the contract*.

Option
The term is used in a number of different senses in the media industries. Sometimes it is used to refer to an option

443

	to acquire rights in a literary work. On other occasions it is used to refer to the right to extend the term of an agreement.
Outline	A short, one or two page, outline of a story suitable for forming the basis of a film.
Overage	Any element of overspend above the budgeted cost of production of a film.
Overages	Any sums payable after a distributor has recouped an advance or minimum guarantee.
Overcall	Additional costs which may be required to be paid by investors in live stage productions.
Overspill	Where a television signal originating in one territory is receivable in another territory this is known as overspill.
PFD Agreement	Production Finance and Distribution Agreement.
PRS	Performing Right Society Limited.
Packaging Deductions	Packaging deductions are deductions which are made from the Royalty Base Price* in order to calculate the amount of any royalty.
Pari Passu	This expression is usually applied when dealing with recoupment of investments to indicate that no individual financier will have priority of repayment.
Parallel Imports	A parallel import is an item of product manufactured in another country in the European Economic Area which has been imported into the United Kingdom. A company which has been granted the exclusive right to distribute videograms of a particular film in the UK does not have the right to prevent videograms of that film which have been lawfully manufactured in another member state of the European Economic Area from being imported into the UK.
Pay or Play	This expression is used solely in connection with the engagement of artists and indicates the requirement of a guaranteed fee to be paid over a specified period regardless of whether or not the film is made. Pay or play provisions are only rarely accepted and even then usually subject to force majeure suspension and termination provisions.
Payment Directions	A payment direction is a direction contained in a contract* requiring money payable under that contract to be paid to a third party which is normally the agent of an artist or a writer.
Per Diem	A per diem fee is a daily fee. Per diem fees are normally paid to artists in relation to their food and incidental expenses.
Performing Rights	Those rights which are assigned to performing societies often refer to as the performing rights. These rights include not only the right to perform works in public but also the right to transmit works by radio and television.

Post-Synchronisation Contracts* for the services of artists in films generally provide that, after principal photography has been completed the services of the artist will be required for up to three days of post-synchronisation services. The purpose of this provision is to permit the producer of the film to be able to re-dub any sections of dialogue which need re-recording for whatever reason.

Premium Premium goods are free or subsidised products (videos, records or books) which are given as an incentive to buy other goods.

Pre-sale An agreement* to distribute a film before completion or commencement of principal photography of a film.

Prints and Advertising Commitment A prints and advertising commitment is a commitment by a distributor of a film to expend not less than a certain amount of money on ordering release prints of the film and organising an advertising campaign around the time of the films first release.

Producer The term "producer" is used in a number of different contexts in the media industries. It may refer to the individual or company which is responsible for the making of a film or sound recording. In the audio-visual industries it may refer to an executive producer or a line producer or an associate producer.

Pull-out Where a distributor of a further has agreed a holdover figure with an exhibitor, it may at the same time agreed a "pull-out" arrangement where the exhibitor will have the right to extricate itself from a holdover by paying a pull-out fee.

Quitclaim A quitclaim is a document pursuant to which, a person who owns rights in a work, transfers their rights to another party, but without making any warranty as to ownership, incumbrances etc.

Recording Bar A provision contained in a recording contract which prevents artists from re-recording material which they have recorded during the term recording contract* for a number of years after the end of the contract.

Release A confirmation letter stating, for example, that a publisher does not have any interest in the film rights of a particular book, or that an individual consents to their portrayal in a film.

Remitted Receipts Remitted receipts are sums actually received by a person. They are distinguishable from source receipts.

Residual Repeat and Re-Run Fees Pursuant to guild and union regulations these fees fall due to be paid after completion of a film on its exploitation in certain media such as US network exploitation, videogram exploitation etc. Frequently residual payment obligations are "bought-out" ie paid in advance.

Glossary

Retention Period The concept of a retention period is encountered in music publishing agreements where copyright is assigned or licensed to a music publisher for a period beyond the term of the agreement. This period is referred to as the retention period.

Rollover A rollover advance is an advance payable pursuant to a publishing agreement* which is continually re-circulated or "rolled over" during the term of the agreement. As soon the advance has been recouped, it becomes payable again.

Royalty Royalties payable under contracts* are normally calculated on Net Sales* multiplied by the Royalty Base Price* after the deduction of packaging deductions.

Royalty Break A royalty break is a provision in a contract which reduces the amount of the royalty* payable under the contract*.

Royalty Base Price The royalty base price is the price on which the royalty* payable under a contract* is calculated.

SAG Screen Actors Guild.

SECAM Séquentiel à Mémoire.

SESAC Society of European Songwriters, Authors and Composers.

Sell-off The period following the end of an exclusive licence during which a licensee has the right to sell-off records or videograms previously manufactured by the licensee during the term.

Source Receipts Source receipts are sums arising at "source " (ie money paid to end-users). Remitted receipts will normally be less than source receipts, because they will suffer the deduction of commissions, fees, and expenses.

Statutory Rights Statutory rights are rights which are created by statute, such as moral rights created by the Copyright, Designs and Patents Act 1988.

Synchronisation Licence A synchronisation licence is a licensed to use music and/or words in synchronisation with or in timed relation to moving pictures. When music is used in a film, and videograms of the film are manufactured, mechanical/synchronisation royalty* will be payable for each videogram.

Syndication The sale of television programming in the USA to syndicates of independent television stations and affiliates of the networks who need to fill non-network time.

Synopsis Rights The right to prepare short summaries and synopses of works usually of not more than 7,500 or 10,000 words.

Term The term of a contract* is the period for which it will subsist.

Tie-in The right to exploit a product in association with another product.

446

Title Guarantee
Transfers of intellectual property rights may be expressed to contain title guarantees. The rights may be expressed to be transferred with "limited title guarantee" or "full title guarantee". Even transfers which are made with " full title guarantee" contain certain limitations.

Treatment
A 15 or 20-page summary of the basic plot elements and characteristics of the main characters on which it is intended to base a draft screenplay.

Trust Letter
A trust letter is normally a temporary arrangement where a company that is intending to sign documentation is advanced money which it needs on an urgent basis after signing a trust letter under which it confirms that all rights and materials acquired or produced by it with the money advanced to it will be held on trust by it for the person advancing the money.

Turnround
Agreements for the sale of screenplays often contain what is referred to a "turnround provision". This type of provision permits a writer or rights owner to put the literary work or screenplay which they have sold in "turnround", or in other words re-acquire the work or screenplay. The circumstances in which the turnround right becomes exercisable are normally if a film based on

the screenplay or literary work is not made with a certain period of years from the acquisition of the work or screenplay. The price payable in order to reacquire the work or screenplay is negotiable. The rights owner or price to be the total sum paid to the writer/rights owner in order to acquire the work or screenplay but the company acquiring the rights the work/screenplay may wish to be paid interest on the price it originally paid, and may also wish to recover other sums which it has spent on developing the work/screenplay into a film.

WG of A
Writers' Guild of America.

WGGB
Writers' Guild of Great Britain.

Warranty
A warranty is an undertaking or a guarantee from a person in a contract* that certain facts are correct, or that certain actions will be taken.

Window
A period during which exploitation of a film in one medium is held back to permit maximum exploitation of the film in another medium.

Withholding Taxes
Taxes which are required to be deducted from payments made to foreign countries. Where however, a double taxation treaty exists between the United Kingdom and another state, withholding taxes would generally not be required to be deducted from payments which are made to individuals or corporations which are residents in that other country.

Index

Master Acquisition Agreement—*contd*
right to commence proceedings, 3.4
rights, grant of, 3.4
royalties, 3.7
royalty accounting, 3.8
transaction analysis, 3.2
Master Licence Agreement
advance, 4.5
advertisements, 4.6
boilerplate provisions, 4.12
claims, 4.6
company's warranties, 4.4
delivery material, 4.6
description, 4.1
determination, 4.10
force majeure, 4.9
indemnity, 4.6
insurance, 4.6
licensee's warranties, 4.6
non-discrimination, 4.6
parties to, 4.1
promotional material and artwork, 4.6
release of records, 4.6
remuneration, 4.5
rights, grant of, 4.3
royalties—
accounting, 4.8
blocked funds, 4.7
currency conversion, 4.7
deductions, 4.5
mechanical, 4.5
payment, 4.7
rate breaks, 4.7
withholdings, 4.7
stock disposal, 4.6
termination, effect of, 4.11
transaction analysis, 4.2
Mechanical Collection Societies. *See also* COLLECTING SOCIETIES
function of, 2.5
registration with, 10.7
Merchandising
agency agreement—
agent—
appointment, 42.3
undertakings, 42.4
boilerplate provisions, 42.9
company's undertakings, 42.5
description of, 42.1
determination—
effect of, 42.8
grounds for, 42.7
parties to, 42.1
remuneration, 42.6
transaction analysis, 42.2

Merchandising—*contd*
licence agreement—
accounting, 43.13
boilerplate provisions, 43.16
company's warranties, 43.4
description of, 43.1
determination, 43.14, 43.15
enhancements, 43.11
labelling, 43.9
licensee's warranties, 43.6
parties to, 43.1
payment, 43.12
promotional material, 43.10
quality and design of product, 43.8
remuneration, 43.5
rights, grant of, 43.3
third party infringement, 43.7
transaction analysis, 43.2
rights, production, financing and
distribution agreement, 21.4
tour agreement, 13.11
Minor
contract with, 1.7, 2.7
Misrepresentation
exclusion of liability for, 54.14
fraudulent, 54.17
negligent, 54.17
proof of, 54.17
Moral Rights
master acquisition agreement, under, 3.4
publishing agreement, under, 2.5
recording contract, under, 1.5
waiver, 53.10
Mortgage
film. *See* FILM MORTGAGE
Multimedia
development agreement—
boilerplate provisions, 38.9
description of, 38.1
development, 38.3
parties to, 38.1
payment, 38.6
producer's obligations, 38.5
producer's warranties, 38.7
production, 38.8
rights, grant of, 38.4
transaction analysis, 38.2
licensing agreement—
analysis, 40.2
boilerplate provisions, 40.9
company's warranties, 40.4
description of, 40.1
determination, 40.8
licensee's undertakings, 40.6
parties to, 40.1
remuneration, 40.5